만능실용영어
회화사전

네이티브에 특히 강한
All New SMART

영어회화
필수표현
3000

CHRIS SUH

MENT⊙RS

네이티브에 특히 강한 All New SMART
영어회화필수표현 3000

2024년 08월 20일 인쇄
2024년 08월 27일 개정판 포함 15쇄 발행

지 은 이 Chris Suh
발 행 인 Chris Suh
발 행 처 **MENTORS**

경기도 성남시 분당구 분당로 53번길 12 313-1
TEL 031-604-0025 FAX 031-696-5221
mentors.co.kr
blog.naver.com/mentorsbook
* Play 스토어 및 App 스토어에서 '멘토스북' 검색해 어플다운받기!

등록일자 2005년 7월 27일
등록번호 제 2022-000130호
I S B N 979-11-988743-4-4
가   격 15,600원(MP3 무료다운로드)

PREFACE

최종목적은 영어로 말하고 듣기

TOEIC으로 대표되는 '수험영어시대'에서 이제는 실제 말하고 듣는 능력, 즉 「실제 영어회화력」으로 영어의 무게중심이 이미 이동했습니다. 시험성적과 실제 말하는 능력과 정비례하지 않은 답답한 현실에 기인된 것이기는 하지만 TOEIC이나 TOEFL 등도 궁극적으로 영어를 실제 말하고 들어야하는 '목적'으로 가기 위한 과정, 즉 '수단'이라는 점을 생각한다면 현재의 변화는 의미가 깊습니다. 결국 최근의 경향은 모든 영어학습의 종착점은 한마디로 말해서 「영어회화」라고 확인해주는 것에 다름 아닙니다.

영어회화에는 「이해」와 「응용」이 필요해

영어회화는 하지만 TOEIC이나 TOEFL 등 수험영어처럼 족집게 강의를 듣거나 기출문제를 풀어 단기간에 점수를 올리듯 그렇게 하루아침에 실력을 향상시킬 수가 없습니다. 무궁무진한 그리고 변화무쌍한 대화의 세계를 전부 수험서처럼 정리해놓을 수는 없기 때문이죠. 다시 말해 수험영어에는 「단순한 암기」와 「기억」이 필요하지만 영어회화에서는 「이해」와 「응용」이 필요합니다. 그때 그때에 맞춰 무슨 말을 해야 하는지 정답이 없기 때문에 가장 많은 표현을 가장 오래 기억되도록 「이해」하고 「암기」해야 하고 그리고 상황에 맞게 「응용」을 해야 합니다. 그렇다면 가장 빠르게 가장 많은 영어회화표현을 자기 것으로 만드는 방법은 무얼까요? 영어회화 표현은 일 이백 개가 아니기 때문에 모든 표현을 개별적으로 외우는 건 비효율적입니다. 기왕이면 비슷한 의미의 표현들끼리 모아서 한꺼번에 이해하고 외워야만 오래 기억도 되고 또한 그 차이도 구별할 수 있어 일상생활에서 정확한 영어를 쓰는데 큰 도움이 됩니다.

기왕이면 비슷한 표현들끼리 한꺼번에 외워야

이책 『All New 네이티브에 특히 강한 영어회화필수표현 3000』은 영어회화에 자주 사용되는 표현 3000여 개를 상황별로 모아 정리하였습니다. Section 1(Basic Conversation)에서는 만남/약속, 감사/격려, 충고/불만, 기쁨/슬픔, 부탁/제안, 의사소통, 나의생각, 동의/반대 등 기본적인 상황에서 쓰는 표현들을 각각의 세분화된 상황별로 모았습니다. 또한 Section 2(Situation English)에서는 교통/여행, 전화영어, 음식/식당, 건강/운동, 쇼핑, 비즈니스, 숫자영어, 연애영어 등으로 구분하여 특정한 상황에서 많이 쓰이는 표현들을 묶어봤습니다. 마지막으로 Section 3(Talking about Me & You)에서는 우리나라에서나 외국에서 Native와 이야기할 때 알고 있으면 유용한 표현들을 정리했습니다. '이런 상황'에서는 '이런 표현'들이 쓰이는구나라고 이해를 하면서 그리고 같은 상황에서 쓰이는 표현들이라고 하더라도 어떻게 의미와 용법이 다른 지 각 표현에 달린 dialog를 통해 느껴보도록 합니다.

암기는 초중고때만 하는게 아냐

이해나 암기한 표현의 절대량이 부족한 상태에서는 응용력도 발휘할 수 없게 돼 자연 Native와 영어로 말하기는 「아픈 경험」만 됩니다. 지금이라도 영어회화를 학습하는 사람으로서 최소한의 예라 생각하면서 적어도 3000개 기본 표현들의 의미와 용법을 이해하고 또한 머리 속에 차곡차곡 외워두도록 합니다. 암기는 초중고 때만 하는 건 아닙니다. 바닥에서 헤메이는 영어회화실력을 한 단계 업그레이드 시키기 위해 초중고 때처럼 달달 외워보도록 합니다. 유창한 영어는 못하더라도 그때 그때 적합한 표현을 머리 속에서 꺼내쓸 수 있도록 말입니다.

How to Use This Book

❶ 특징

영어회화를 하다보면 꼭 써야 되는 그래서 꼭 알아두어야 하는「네이티브에 특히 강한 영어회화필수표현 3,000여 개」를 집중정리하였다. 가능한 한 비슷한 표현들을 함께 모아 놓아 한꺼번에 많은 표현들을 암기할 수 있도록 그래서 언제 어디서나 내가 필요한 표현을 찾아 활용할 수 있도록 꾸며졌다.

❷ 전체적 구성

Section 1   Basic Conversation 기본영어회화

만남/약속, 감사/격려, 충고/불만, 기쁨/슬픔, 부탁/제안, 의사소통, 나의생각 및 동의/반대 등 총 8개의 Chapter로 기초회화를 하는데 꼭 필요한 표현들을 총정리하였다. 일목요연하게 정리된 표현들을 달달달 외워두면 기본에 강한 그래서 언제든지 영어회화실력이 일취월장할 가능성을 갖게 된다.

Section 2   Situation English 상황영어회화

교통/여행, 전화영어, 음식/식당, 건강/운동, 쇼핑, 비즈니스, 숫자영어 및 연애영어 등 역시 8개의 Chapter로 특정한 상황에서 꼭 쓰이는 특정한 표현들을 모아놓았다. 기본에만 충실할 뿐만 아니라 자주 경험하게 되는 상황에서의 표현들을 함께 외워두면 영어에 자신감이 붙는다. 특히 인스타그램, 페이스북 등 SNS를 쓸 때의 유용한 표현들도 새롭게 담았다.

Section 3   Talking About Me & You 너와 나의 이야기

국내에서건 외국에 나가서건 간에 외국인과 이야기를 하다 보면 나 자신에 대해서 혹은 우리의 문화 등에 이야기를 할 때가 있다. 혹은 반대로 상대방이나 다른 제 3자에 대해 자기 의견을 말할 경우가 있다. 이렇게 나를 말하고 남을 이야기할 수 있는 표현들을 정리하였다. 이제 서슴없이 나와 우리를 말하면서 영어에 재미를 붙여본다. 역시 2018년 남북정상회담 등도 새롭게 담았다.

❸ 학습효과

1. 다시 한번 총정리한다

카테고리별로 빈출하는 영어회화표현을 집중해서 모아놓음으로써 지금까지 공부해온 그러나 활용하지 못했던 금쪽 같은 회화표현들을 한꺼번에 이해하고 다시 외운다.

2. 네이티브의 목소리로 예문을 들으며 표현이 언제 어떻게 쓰는 지 실감한다

모든 표현에는 AB dialog가 수록되어 있고 또한 네이티브 녹음이 되어 있어 표현의 실제 쓰임새와 뉘앙스를 직접 체험하면서 다양한 표현들을 자기 것으로 만들 수 있다.

3. 항상 휴대하면서 24시간 영어회화에 빠진다

언제 어디서든지 갖고 다닐 수 있는 크기로 수시로 보면서 머리 속에 확실하게 각인시켜 어느 상황이던지 네이티브 앞에서도 당당하게 기죽지 않고 영어를 말하게 된다.

④ 페이지 구성

학습할 표현들을 하나로 묶어주는 카테
고리와 이 표현들이 구체적으로 어떤
상황에서 쓰이는지를 말해준다.

학습할 상황의 대표적인 표현의 우리
말로 한 눈에 어떤 상황의 표현을 배
우는지를 알게 해준다.

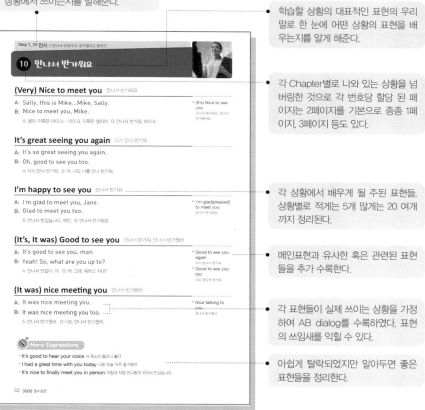

Step 1_10 인사 >>만나서 반갑다고, 반가웠다고 말하기

10 만나서 반가워요

(Very) Nice to meet you 만나서 반가워요

A: Sally, this is Mike...Mike, Sally.
B: Nice to meet you, Mike.

A 샐리, 이쪽은 마이크… 마이크, 이쪽은 샐리야. B 반가워요, 마이크.

* (It's) Nice to see you
  만나서 반가워요, 만나서 반가워요

It's great seeing you again 다시 만나 반가워

A: It's so great seeing you again.
B: Oh, good to see you.

A 다시 만나 반가워. B 어, 나도 너를 만나 반가워.

I'm happy to see you 만나서 반가워

A: I'm glad to meet you, Jane.
B: Glad to meet you too.

A 만나서 반갑습니다, 제인. B 만나서 반가워요.

* I'm glad[pleased] to meet you
  만나서 반가워요

(It's, It was) Good to see you 만나서 반가워, 만나서 반가웠어

A: It's good to see you, man.
B: Yeah! So, what are you up to?

A 만나서 반갑다. 야. B 어! 그래, 뭐하고 지내?

* Good to see you again
  다시 만나 반가워요
* Good to see you too
  나도 만나서 반가워

(It was) nice meeting you 만나서 반가웠어

A: It was nice meeting you.
B: It was nice meeting you too.

A 만나서 반가웠어. B 나도 만나서 반가웠어.

* Nice talking to you
  만나서 반가웠어

각 Chapter별로 나와 있는 상황을 넘
버링한 것으로 각 번호당 할당 된 페
이지는 2페이지를 기본으로 종종 1페
이지, 3페이지 등도 있다.

각 상황에서 배우게 될 주된 표현들.
상황별로 적게는 5개 많게는 20 여개
까지 정리된다.

메인표현과 유사한 혹은 관련된 표현
들을 추가 수록한다.

각 표현들이 실제 쓰이는 상황을 가정
하여 AB dialog를 수록하였다. 표현
의 쓰임새를 익힐 수 있다.

More Expressions

* It's good to hear your voice 네 목소리 들으니 좋다
* I had a great time with you today 너랑 오늘 아주 즐거웠어
* It's nice to finally meet you in person 마침내 직접 만나뵙게 되어서 반갑습니다

아쉽게 탈락되었지만 알아두면 좋은
표현들을 정리한다.

섹션 2 Chapter 7 비즈니스 중 '회의'와
섹션 3의 전부는 우리말을 먼저 읽어보고
이를 영어로 읽어보는 연습을 해보는 공간
으로 꾸몄다. 앞에서 배운 표현들을 기초로
스스로 영작해보는 훈련을 하는 공간이다.

Step 1_01 Talking About Me 자기의 이름, 그리고 어디에 사는지 말하기

01 대부분 지현이라고 불러

● 반가워. 민지현이라고 해. 대부분 지현이라고 부르지.
Hi. I'm Ji-hyun Min. Most people just call me Ji-hyun.

● 내 이름은 이민수이야. '이'는 성이고 '민수'는 이름이지.
My name is Lee Min-soo. Lee is my family name, and Min-soo is
my first name.

* My family name, 'Gil,' is pretty rare in Korea 성이 '길'인데 한국에선 드문 성이야

Contents

Section 1
Basic Conversation

Chapter 4 기쁨/슬픔

Chapter 5 부탁/제안

Chapter 6 의사소통

Section 2
Situation English

Section 3
Talking about Me & You

Start
Tray Hard
Keep Talking
Native Speaking

Section

기본영어회화

Chapter **01**

만남·약속

Step 1 인사

Step 2 초대 · 방문

Step 3 약속

01 잘지냈어?

How are you doing? 안녕?. 잘 지냈어?

A: How are you doing?

B: I'm great. How's everything with you these days?

A: 잘 지냈어? B: 좋아. 요즈음 너는 어때?

ㄴ are를 생략하기도 한다.

How are you? 잘 지내?(만났을 때). 괜찮어?(상대방에게 괜찮냐고 물어볼 때)

A: Hey, Suzie, how are you? Nice weather, huh?

B: Hi! Yeah, it's been great weather today.

A: 야, 수지, 안녕? 날씨 좋다, 그지? B: 안녕! 그래, 오늘 날씨 참 좋으네.

How's it going? 잘 지내?

A: How's it going today?

B: It's going pretty well.

A: 오늘 어때? B: 좋아.

▶ How's it going today?
오늘 어때?

How's everything going? 다 잘돼 가?

A: How's everything going with you these days?

B: Things couldn't be better.

A: 요즘 너 어때? B: 더할 나위없이 좋아.

What's new? 뭐 새로운 일 있어?

A: Hey, Joe, how great to see you! What's new?

B: Not much. I've just been really busy at work.

A: 야, 조, 반갑다! 뭐 새로운 일 좀 있어? B: 별로. 요즘 일 때문에 무지 바빠.

▶ What's new with you?
그러는 넌 별일 없어?
ㄴ What's new?라고 묻는
상대방의 인사에 답하는 전
형적인 인사.

What's up? 어때?

A: What's up, John?

B: Nothing much. How are you doing?

A: 존, 별 일 없어? B: 별로. 넌 잘 지내고?

ㄴ 상황에 따라 상대방에게
"무슨 일이야?"라고 구체적인
대답을 요구하는 표현으로도
쓰임.

What's happening? 어떻게 지내?, 잘 지내니?

A: What's happening?

B: Not a lot. How about you?

A: 어떻게 지내? B: 별로. 넌?

What's going on? 무슨 일이야?

A: What's going on?

B: Not much, We're just discussing today's schedule.

A: 뭐하고 있는 거야? B: 그냥 오늘 일정을 토의하고 있어.

▶ What's going on in there[here]?
거기[여기] 무슨 일 있어?
▶ What's going on with him?
그 사람 무슨 일 있어?

(You) Doing okay? 잘지내?, 괜찮어?

A: Doing Okay? You look a bit tired.

B: Well, I had a really rough day.

A: 괜찮아? 좀 피곤해보여. B: 어, 오늘 정말 힘들었어.

A: Is everything okay?

B: Not really.

A: 다 잘 되고 있지? B: 실은 그렇지 않아.

▶ (Is) Everything okay?
잘 지내지?, 일은 다 잘 되지?
▶ (Have) (you) Been okay?
그동안 잘 지냈어?

How're you getting along? 어떻게 지내?

A: How're you getting along?

B: I'm doing just fine.

A: 어떻게 지내? B: 그냥 잘 지내고 있어.

▶ get along (with)
…와 잘 지내다

How's the[your] family? 가족들은 다 잘 지내?

A: It's been a long time! How's the family?

B: Actually, I got divorced.

A: 오래간만야! 가족들은 잘 지내고? B: 실은, 나 이혼했어.

▶ How's the wife[your kid]?
부인[애들]은 잘 지내?

How's business? 일은 어때?

A: How's business?

B: It's a little slow this month.

A: 일은 어때? B: 이번 달은 좀 안좋아.

02 오랜만야?, 이게 누구야?

How (have) you been? 어떻게 지냈어?, 잘 지냈어?

A: How have you been?

B: I've been all right.

A: 그동안 잘 지냈어? B: 잘 지냈어.

What have you been up to? 뭐하고 지냈어?, 별일 없어?

A: What have you been up to?

B: Not too much.

A: 어떻게 지내고 있어? B: 별로.

ㄴ. 현재시제로 What are you up to?하게 되면 상대방이 지금 현재 뭘 하고 있는지 묻는 말.

What have you been doing? 뭐하고 지냈어?

A: What have you been doing?

B: Just working.

A: 뭐하고 지냈어? B: 그냥 일하고 있지.

Long time no see 오랜만이야

A: It's been a long time, hasn't it?

B: Yes, it has. How have you been?

A: 오랜만이다, 그렇지? B: 그래. 잘 지내. 너는 어떻게 지냈어?

▶ It's been a long time
오랜간만이야
▶ I haven't seen you for a long time[for ages]
오랜만이야

What're you doing here? 여긴 어쩐 일이야?

A: What're you doing here?

B: I'm waiting for my brother. What're you doing here?

A: 여기 웬일이야? B: 형 기다리고 있어. 넌?

Fancy meeting you here 이런 데서 다 만나다니

A: I haven't seen you in years.

B: Yeah, fancy meeting you here.

A: 오랜간 만에 보네. B: 그래, 이런데서 다 만나다니.

Look who's here! 아니 이게 누구야!

A: Hey Tom, look who's here! It's Kate!

B: Wow, she hasn't changed at all.

A: 야 탐, 이게 누구야! 케이트잖아! B: 야, 쟤 하나도 안 변했네.

└ 예상치 못한 장소, 혹은 뜻밖의 사람을 만났을 때 쓰는 표현.

I didn't expect to see you here 여기서 널 만날 줄 생각도 못했어

A: I didn't expect to see you here.

B: I decided I wanted to come to your party.

A: 여기서 널 볼 줄은 몰랐어. B: 네 파티에 오기로 결정했거든.

I never thought I'd see you here 여기서 널 만날 줄 생각도 못했어

A: Are you surprised I joined this club?

B: Sure, I never thought I'd see you here.

A: 내가 이 클럽에 가입해서 놀랐어? B: 물론, 널 여기서 보리라곤 생각못했거든.

Are you here on business? 여기 비즈니스로 온거야?

A: Are you here on business?

B: No, this is part of my vacation.

A: 비즈니스로 온거야? B: 아니, 휴가차 온거야.

What's the story? 어떻게 지내?

A: You look dressed up. What's the story?

B: I have a job interview today.

A: 잘 차려입었네. 무슨 일 있어? B: 오늘 면접이 있어.

▶ be dressed up
잘 차려입다

How's life[the world] treating you? 사는 건 어때?

A: How's the life treating you?

B: Same as usual.

A: 사는 게 어때? B: 늘상 그렇지 뭐.

Nice weather, huh? 날씨 좋으네 그지?

A: Nice weather, huh?

B: I guess. Do you have any plan?

A: 날씨 좋으네. 그지? B: 그래. 뭐 계획이라도 있어?

03 오늘 어땠어?

How was your day? 오늘 어땠어?

A: How was your day?

B: So far so good. And you?

A: 오늘 어때? B: 지금까진 괜찮아. 넌?

> └. How is your day?라고 쓰면 안된다.

How are you feeling? 기분 어때?

A: How are you feeling?

B: I'm feeling great.

A: 기분 어때? B: 아주 좋아.

Where're you headed? 어디 가?

A: Where are you going?

B: I'm going out to lunch with one of my co-workers.

A: 어디 가니? B: 동료와 점심하러 가는 길이야.

> ▶ Where're you going?
> 어디 가?
> ▶ Where're you off to?
> 어디 가?

What're you doing? 뭐해?

A: What are you doing?

B: Making chocolate milk. Do you want some?

A: 뭐해? B: 초콜렛 밀크 만들어. 좀 먹을래?

> └. What're you doing here?(여긴 웬일이야?)하면 예기치 못하게 누굴 만났을 때, What're you doing tonight 하게 되면 "오늘 밤에 뭐해?" 라는 뜻으로 약속 잡을 때 쓰이는 표현이다.

Where have you been? 어디 갔었어?

A: Hey, where have you been?

B: Oh, I went to have pizza, with Danny.

A: 야, 어디 갔다 오는 거야? B: 어, 피자먹으러 갔었어, 대니랑.

I ran into her 그 여자와 우연히 마주쳤어

A: I ran into Richard yesterday.

B: Oh yeah? Where?

A: 어제 리차드를 우연히 만났어. B: 어 그래? 어디서?

> ▶ I keep bumping into you
> 우리 자주 마주치네요

04 **생일 축하해!**

Happy birthday! 생일 축하해!

A: Happy birthday, honey!

B: Thanks. I'm 36 today. Can you believe it?

A: 자기야, 생일 축하해! B: 고마워, 이제 서른 여섯야. 믿겨져?

∟ honey는 줄여서 hon이라고도 한다.

Happy New Year! 새해 복많이 받아!

A: Happy New Year!

B: You too! Do you have any New Year's resolutions?

A: 새해 복많이 받아! B: 너도! 새해엔 뭐 결심한 거 있어?

▸ Happy New Year to you, too!
너도 새해 복많이 받아!

(You) Have a Merry Christmas! 메리 크리스마스!

A: You have a Merry Christmas!

B: Thank you, and the same to you.

A: 성탄절 즐겁게 보내! B: 고마워, 너도 즐겁게 보내.

▸ I wish you a Merry Christmas!
성탄절 즐겁게 보내!

Happy holidays! 휴일 잘 보내!

A: Happy holidays!

B: Thanks. Merry Christmas!

A: 휴일 잘 보내! B: 고마워, 메리 크리스마스!

Happy Valentine's Day! 발렌타인 잘 보내!

A: Be my valentine.

B: I'd love to.

A: 발렌타인 날에 내 애인이 되어줘. B: 좋아.

▸ Be my valentine
발렌타인 날에 내 애인이 되어줘

Happy Thanksgiving! 추석 잘 보내!

A: Happy Thanksgiving!

B: You too, sweetheart.

A: 추석 잘 보내! B: 너도 잘 지내, 자기야.

▸ Happy Chusok!
추석 잘 지내!

05 무슨 일이야?

What's wrong (with you)? 무슨 일이야?, 뭐 잘못됐어?

A: What's wrong with Paul?

B: He got into a car accident a few days ago.

A: 폴에게 무슨 일 있니? B: 며칠 전에 차사고를 당했어.

▸ get into a car accident
차사고나다

What's the problem? 무슨 일인데?

A: What's the problem?

B: The computers aren't working.

A: 뭐가 문제죠? B: 컴퓨터가 작동하지 않아요.

What's the matter with you? 무슨 일이야?, 도대체 왜그래?

A: What's the matter with you?

B: I'm feeling kind of sad today.

A: 무슨 일이야? B: 오늘 좀 기분이 울쩍해.

▸ kind of = sort of
약간, 좀

What happened? 무슨 일이야?, 어떻게 된 거야?

A: What happened?

B: Nothing. I'm going to take a shower.

A: 무슨 일이야? B: 아무 것도 아냐. 샤워할려고.

What happened to[with] you? 너 무슨 일이야?, 왜 그래?

A: Hey, what happened to you?

B: Nothing. I just felt like hanging out here and reading.

A: 야, 너 무슨 일이야? B: 아무것도. 여기서 그냥 책읽고 싶었어.

What's with you? 뭐 땜에 그래?

A: You look really depressed. What's with you?

B: Jim dumped me. He's such an asshole.

A: 너 굉장히 기운없어 보여. 왜 그래? B: 짐이 날 찼어. 나쁜 자식 같으니라고.

▸ What's with your hair? 머리가 왜 그래?
▸ What's with her [him, the guys]?
재(들) 왜 저래?

What's gotten into you? 뭣 때문에 이러는 거야?

A: Well, what's gotten into you?

B: Nothing, I guess I'm just tired of this dumb job.

A: 어, 너 왜 그래? B: 아냐, 그냥 이 바보같은 일에 지쳐 그런가봐.

▸ What's gotten into your head?
무슨 생각으로 그래?

What's cooking? 무슨 일이야?

A: What's cooking?

B: I thought I'd stop and say hello.

A: 무슨 일이야? B: 들려서 인사나 하려고.

What's eating you? 뭐가 문제야?, 무슨 걱정거리라도 있어?

A: What's eating you?

B: My husband has high blood pressure.

A: 무슨 일이야? B: 남편이 고혈압이야.

What gives? 무슨 일 있어?

A: Why the long face?

B: Someone stole my cellular phone.

A: 왜 그렇게 우울한 표정을 하고 있어? B: 누가 내 핸드폰을 훔쳐갔어.

▸ Why the long face?
왜 그래?, 무슨 기분 안좋
은 일 있어?

What's bothering you? 뭐가 잘못됐어?

A: What's bothering you?

B: I want to go on a holiday, but I don't have any money.

A: 뭐가 잘못됐어? B: 휴가가고 싶은데, 돈이 없어.

What's on your mind? 왜 그래?, 문제가 뭔대?

A: Can I talk to you for a minute?

B: Sure. What's on your mind?

A: 잠깐 얘기 좀 하자? B: 그래. 뭔대?

▸ Do you have something on your mind?
왜 그래?

What are you up to? 뭐해?, 뭘 할거야?

A: What are you up to today?

B: Not much... I'll probably just relax.

A: 오늘 뭐하려고 해? B: 별로…. 편하게 좀 쉴까 해.

▸ I know what you're up to
네 속셈 다 알아

06 너 좋아 보인다

Look at you! 얘 좀 봐라!, (어머) 얘 좀 봐!

A: Ah, look at you, you look great.

B: Do I? Thank you, so do you.

A: 야, 얘 좀 봐라, 너 멋져 보인다. B: 그래? 고마워, 너도 멋져.

└ 상대방이 멋진 차림을 하였거나 혹은 바람직한 행동을 했을 경우 혹은 어처구니 없는 행동을 한 상대방을 향해 비난하면서도 쓰인다.

You look great! 너 멋져 보인다!

A: You look great too. Did you get a haircut?

B: Yeah. I did this morning.

A: 너도 멋져 보인다. 머리깎었어? B: 어, 오늘 아침에 깎었어.

▶ You look good
  너 멋져 보인다

You haven't changed at all 너 하나도 안 변했네

A: I haven't seen you in ten years.

B: That's true. You haven't changed at all.

A: 10년 만에 보는거네. B: 맞아. 너 하나도 안 변했네.

▶ You haven't changed much
  너 별로 안 변했어
▶ You've really changed
  너 정말 많이 변했어

You've grown up 너 많이 컸다

A: You've grown up a lot.

B: I know. I'm not a little girl anymore.

A: 너 정말 많이 컸네. B: 그럼. 이제 어린 소녀가 아니라고.

Are you gaining weight? 살쪘어?

A: Are you gaining weight?

B: I'm afraid so.

A: 살쪘어? B: 그런 것 같아.

▶ Are you getting fatter? 뚱뚱해졌어?
▶ Are you losing weight? 살 빠졌어?

07 너 안좋아 보인다

You don't look good today 오늘 너 안 좋아 보여

A: You don't look good today.

B: Maybe I'm catching a cold.

A: 오늘 너 안 좋아 보여. B: 감기 걸린 것 같아.

▸ catch a cold = get a cold
감기걸리다

You look serious 너 심각해 보여

A: You seem so nervous. What's up?

B: I have to make a speech next week.

A: 너 초조해 보여. 무슨 일이야? B: 다음 주에 연설해야 돼.

▸ You seem nervous
너 초조해 보여

Something's wrong with you today 너 오늘 좀 이상해

A: Something's wrong with you today.

B: I had a fight with my husband this morning.

A: 너 오늘 좀 이상해. B: 오늘 아침 남편하고 싸웠어.

▸ have a fight with sb
…와 싸우다

You look depressed 너 매우 지쳐보여

A: You look so depressed.

B: I'm getting nowhere with this report.

A: 매우 지쳐 보이는데. B: 보고서를 작성하는 게 막막해서.

▸ You look sad, today
너 오늘 슬퍼보여
▸ get nowhere with~
…에 아무 진전이 없다

You look exhausted 너 지쳐보인다

A: You seem a little tired.

B: Yeah, I stayed up late and watched a movie.

A: 너 좀 피곤해 보여. B: 어, 늦게까지 안자고 영화봤거든.

▸ You look very tired
너 매우 피곤해 보여

You need a break 너 좀 쉬어야 돼

A: I've been feeling very stressed lately.

B: You need a break.

A: 요즘 스트레스를 넘 많이 받았어. B: 너 좀 쉬어야 돼.

08 잘 지내고 있어

I'm doing OK   잘 지내고 있어

A: David, how's it going?

B: I'm doing okay.

A: 데이빗. 어떻게 지내? B: 잘 지내고 있어.

I'm fine. How about you?   잘 지내. 넌 어때?

A: How are you today?

B: I'm fine. How about you?

A: 오늘 어때? B: 잘 지내. 넌 어때?

I'm cool   잘 지내

A: Are you okay?

B: Yeah, I'm cool.

A: 잘 지내고 있어? B: 어, 잘 지내.

Not bad   그리 나쁘지 않아

A: How's everything going?

B: Pretty good.

A: 어떻게 지내? B: 잘 지내.

▶ Pretty good
잘 지내

(It) Couldn't be better   최고야. 아주 좋아

A: So, how're you two getting along?

B: Oh, we couldn't be better.

A: 그래 너희 둘은 어떻게 지내? B: 어, 아주 좋아.

▶ Things have never been better
최고야

(Things) Could be better   별로야. 그냥 그래

A: How's it going with you?

B: Things could be better.

A: 어떻게 지내? B: 그냥 그래.

ㄴ Could be better는 '더 좋을 수도 있는데 그렇지 않다'라는 의미로 다소 부정적인 표현인 반면 다음의 Could be worse는 '더 나쁠 수도 있는데 그렇지 않다'라는 의미로 다소 긍정적인 표현임.

I couldn't ask for more 최고야. 더 이상 바랄 게 없어

A: How's your new job?

B: Everything's great. I couldn't ask for more.

   A: 새로운 일은 어때? B: 다 좋아. 더 이상 바랄게 없어.

(I) Can't complain 잘 지내

A: How have you been?

B: I can't complain.

   A: 어떻게 지냈어? B: 잘 지냈어.

▸ (I have) Nothing to complain about
잘 지내
▸ No complaints
잘 지내

Not (too) much 별일 없어. 그냥 그럭저럭

A: What's new?

B: Not much. I just finished my last exam yesterday.

   A: 별일없어? B: 별로. 어제 마지막 시험을 끝냈어.

▸ Nothing much
별로 특별한 건 없어, 별일 아냐
▸ So so
그저 그래

Nothing special 별일 아냐. 별일 없어

A: What's up, Pitt?

B: Nothing special.

   A: 피트, 어때? B: 별일 없어.

▸ Nothing in particular
별일 아냐

Same as always 맨날 똑같지 뭐

A: What's going on in your life these days?

B: The same old stuff.

   A: 요즘 사는 게 어때? B: 맨날 그렇지 뭐.

▸ Same as usual
늘 그렇지 뭐
▸ Same old story[stuff]
늘 그렇지 뭐

Not very well 안 좋아

A: How're you doing these days?

B: Not very well.

   A: 요즘 어떻게 지내? B: 잘 못지내.

▸ Not good
안 좋아
▸ Not so great
좋지 않아

09 데이빗이라고 합니다

Hello, my name is David 안녕하세요, 데이빗이라고 합니다

A: Hello, my name is David.

B: Nice to meet you. I'm Sally.

> A: 안녕하세요, 데이빗이라고 합니다. B: 만나서 반가워요. 전 샐리예요.

I'd like to introduce myself 제 소개를 하겠습니다

A: I'd like to introduce myself. My name is Peter.

B: I'm Mary. I work in the accounting department.

> A: 제 소개를 하죠. 피터라고 해요. B: 난 메리예요. 경리부에서 일하죠.

▶ work in~
  …에서 일하다

I'd like you to meet a friend of mine 내 친구 한 명 소개할게

A: I want you to meet Shaun.

B: Hi, Shaun. My name's John.

> A: 숀하고 인사해. B: 안녕, 숀. 내 이름은 존이야.

▶ I want you to
  meet Shaun
  숀하고 인사해

Paul, meet Jane 폴, 제인이야

A: Paul, meet Jane.

B: Hello, Jane. How are you?

> A: 폴, 제인이야. B: 안녕, 제인. 어떠세요?

Mina, this is Peter...Peter, Mina 미나, 이쪽이 피터야… 피터, 이쪽은 미나야

A: Mina, this is Peter...Peter, Mina.

B: Why don't you two take a bit of time to get acquainted?

> A: 미나, 이쪽이 피터야… 피터, 이쪽은 미나야. B: 너희 둘 시간 좀 내서 친해봐.

▶ Mr.Kim, this is
  Mr.Johnson, my
  boss
  미스터 김, 이분은 내 사장
  님인 존슨 씨야
▶ get acquainted
  친해지다

Mary, have you met Dan? 메리야, 댄 만나본 적 있니?

A: Mary, have you met Dan?

B: No, I haven't.

> A: 메리야, 댄 만나본 적 있니? B: 아니, 못만나봤어.

Tom, Laura is the girl I was telling you about
탐, 내가 말하던 로라가 바로 얘야

A: Tom, Laura is the girl I was telling you about.

B: Hi, Laura. I've been dying to meet you.

A: 탐, 내가 말하던 로라가 바로 얘야. B: 안녕, 로라. 굉장히 만나 보고 싶었어.

▸ be dying to =
can't wait to
몹시 …하고 싶어하다

I've heard so much[a lot] about you 네 얘기 많이 들었어

A: It's so good to finally meet you in person!

B: Yes, it is. I've heard so much about you.

A: 마침내 이렇게 직접 만나게 되니 반가워! B: 응, 그래. 네 얘기 많이 들었어.

Just call me John 그냥 존이라고 불러

A: Nice to meet you Mr. Smith.

B: Just call me John.

A: 스미스 씨 만나서 반가워요. B: 그냥 존이라고 해요.

▸ You can call me
by my first name
이름으로 불러

Who's this? 이 사람 누구야?

A: Who is this?

B: I'm sorry, this is Tom Gordon. He's a colleague.

A: 이 사람 누구야? B: 미안, 동료인 탐 고든이야.

Do you know each other? 둘이 아는 사이니?

A: Do you two know each other?

B: Actually, we've never formally been introduced.

A: 둘이 아는 사이니? B: 실은 정식으로 통성명한 적은 없어.

▸ Have you two met
before?
너희 둘 전에 만난 적 있
어?
▸ Don't I know you
from somewhere?
어디서 만난 적 있지 않나
요?

We've never met before 우린 초면야

A: I don't think we've met before. My name is Paul.

B: Hi, Paul. I'm Jennifer.

A: 초면인 것 같은데. 전 폴이라고 해요. B: 안녕하세요, 폴. 전 제니퍼라고 해요.

▸ I don't think we've
met before
초면인 것 같은데요

May I have your name, please? 이름 좀 알려줄래요?

A: May I have your name, please?

B: Let me give you my business card. Here you are.

A: 이름 좀 알려줄래요? B: 명함을 드릴게요. 여기요.

10 만나서 반가워요

(Very) Nice to meet you 만나서 반가워요

A: Sally, this is Mike...Mike, Sally.

B: Nice to meet you, Mike.

A: 샐리, 이쪽은 마이크… 마이크, 이쪽은 샐리야. B: 만나서 반가워, 마이크.

▸ (It's) Nice to see you
만나서 반가워요, 만나서 반가웠어요

It's great seeing you again 다시 만나 반가워

A: It's so great seeing you again.

B: Oh, good to see you too.

A: 다시 만나 반가워. B: 어, 나도 너를 만나 반가워.

I'm happy to see you 만나서 반가워

A: I'm glad to meet you, Jane.

B: Glad to meet you too.

A: 만나서 반갑습니다, 제인. B: 만나서 반가워요.

▸ I'm glad[pleased] to meet you
만나서 반가워요

(It's, It was) Good to see you 만나서 반가워, 만나서 반가웠어

A: It's good to see you, man.

B: Yeah! So, what are you up to?

A: 만나서 반갑다, 야. B: 어! 그래, 뭐하고 지내?

▸ Good to see you again
다시 만나니 반가워
▸ Good to see you too
나도 만나서 반가워

(It was) nice meeting you 만나서 반가웠어

A: It was nice meeting you.

B: It was nice meeting you too.

A: 만나서 반가웠어. B: 나도 만나서 반가웠어.

▸ Nice talking to you
만나서 반가웠어

More Expressions

- It's good to hear your voice 네 목소리 들으니 좋다
- I had a great time with you today 너랑 오늘 아주 즐거웠어
- It's nice to finally meet you in person 마침내 직접 만나뵙게 되어서 반갑습니다

11 금방 돌아올게

I'll be back 다녀 올게. 금방 올게

A: Excuse me. I'll be right back.

B: Don't be too long.

　　A: 미안, 바로 올게. B: 너무 오래 있다 오면 안돼.

▸ (I'll) Be right back
　바로 올게

Be back soon 금방 돌아올게

A: I'll be back in a little while! You stay here!

B: Why? Where are you going?

　　A: 잠시 후에 돌아올게! 넌 여기 있어. B: 왜? 어딜 가는데?

▸ (I'll) Be back in a
　sec
　곧 돌아올게
▸ (I'll) Be back in
　just a minute
　금세 돌아올게

She'll be back any minute 그 여자는 곧 돌아올거예요

A: Where's your mom?

B: She'll be back any minute.

　　A: 네 엄마 어디 계셔? B: 곧 돌아오실거야.

I'll be right with you 잠시만. 곧 돌아올게

A: Jimmy, can you help me?

B: I'll be right with you.

　　A: 지미, 나 좀 도와줄래? B: 곧 돌아올게.

▸ I'll be with you in
　a sec[minute]
　곧 돌아올게

Can[Could] you excuse us? 실례 좀 해도 될까요?, 자리 좀 비켜주시겠어요?

A: Could you excuse us? I need to talk to your wife.

B: What's the matter?

　　A: 실례해도 될까요? 당신 부인과 얘기 좀 해야 돼요. B: 무슨 문제인데요?

▸ Could[May] I be
　excused?
　이만 일어나도 될까요?, 실
　례 좀 해도 되겠어요?

12 이제 그만 가봐야겠어

I have (got) to go 이제 가봐야겠어, 이제 (전화를) 끊어야겠어

A: Well, I've got to go now.

B: Okay, thanks for all your help.

> A: 저기, 지금 가봐야겠는데. B: 그래요. 여러모로 도와줘서 고마워.

I'd better go now 이젠 가야겠어

A: Yeah. All right, I'd better go.

B: I think that would be best.

> A: 어. 그래. 이젠 가야겠어. B: 그래야 될 것 같아.

I have to go to + 장소 …에 가야 해

A: I'm really sorry but I have to go to work.

B: What kind of work do you do?

> A: 미안하지만 일하러가야 돼요. B: 무슨 일 하는데요?

┗ I have to go to 다음에 동사가 오면 「…하러 가야 돼」라는 의미가 된다.

I have to leave 출발해야겠어

A: I have to leave.

B: You have to leave now? How come?

> A: 가야 돼. B: 지금 가야 된다고? 왜?

▸ Let's leave
가자, 출발하자

I must be going 그만 가봐야 될 것 같아

A: Do you have time to have dinner?

B: Not really, I think I must be going now.

> A: 저녁 먹을 시간 있어? B: 아니. 지금 가봐야 될 것 같아.

I think I'd better be going 그만 가봐야 될 것 같아

A: Well, I think I'd better be going now.

B: Okay, then I'll see you tomorrow at the office.

> A: 그만 가봐야 될 것 같아요. B: 좋아요. 그럼 내일 사무실에서 봐요.

It's getting late and I'd better be going 늦어서 가봐야 돼

A: It's getting late and I'd better be going.

B: Okay, take care!

A: 늦어서 가봐야 돼. B: 그래, 잘가!

It's time we should be going 그만 일어납시다

A: It's time we should be going.

B: Oh no! You can stay longer with me!

A: 그만 일어나자. B: 안돼! 나하고 더 있자!

▸ It's time (that) S+V
  …해야 할 때이다

I should get going 서둘러 가봐야겠어

A: Actually, I gotta get going. Give me a call sometime.

B: Oh, but y'know, you didn't give me your phone number.

A: 실은 가야돼. 전화 한번 해. B: 어, 근데말야 전화번호를 줘야지.

▸ I'd better get going
  가보는 게 좋겠어
▸ I've got to get going
  가야겠어
▸ Let's get going
  이젠 어서 가자

I('ve) got to get moving 가봐야겠어

A: See you later. I've got to get moving.

B: OK, I'll see you tomorrow.

A: 나중에 봐. 가야 돼. B: 그래. 내일 보자.

▸ You'd better get moving
  너 그만 가봐야지

(It's) Time for me to go 갈 시간이야, 일어서야겠어

A: Time for me to go. It's very late.

B: OK. Do you want me to give you a ride to your house?

A: 갈 시간이야. 넘 늦었어. B: 그래. 집까지 데려다줄까?

▸ Time to move
  갈 시간이야

Let's hit the road 출발하자고

A: We're already 20 minutes behind schedule.

B: Okay, let's hit the road.

A: 벌써 예정보다 20분 늦었어. B: 맞아, 우리 출발하자.

▸ behind schedule
  예정보다 늦게

13 그만 일어서야겠어

I'm going to take off 그만 일어서야겠어

A: You know, I'm going to take off.

B: So soon?

A: 저기 말야, 일어서야겠어. B: 이렇게 일찍?

▸ take off
이륙하다. 출발하다. 가다
(leave)

I must be off 이제 가봐야겠어

A: Well, I must be off. Got to make dinner for the kids.

B: What are you making tonight?

A: 가봐야 돼. 애들 저녁 해줘야 하거든. B: 오늘 밤엔 뭘 만들어 줄거야?

▸ (I'd) Better be off
가봐야겠어

I am off (now) 나 간다

A: Well, this is it. I'm off to Chicago.

B: Have fun!

A: 그래, 드디어 올 것이 왔어. 나 시카고로 간다. B: 재밌게 보내!

▸ I'm off to bed
자러 갈래
▸ I'm off to Jeff's
제프네 집에 가려구
▸ I'm off to see your dad
너희 아빠 만나러 갈래 (be off to + 동사)

I've got to run 서둘러 가봐야겠어

A: I've got to run.

B: See you soon.

A: 빨리 가야 되겠어. B: 또 봐.

▸ (I've) Got to fly
난 이만 사라져야겠어

I'm out of here 나 갈게

A: All right, well. I'm out of here. Wish me luck.

B: Good luck!

A: 그래, 나 갈게. 행운을 빌어줘. B: 행운을 빈다!

▸ I'm not here
나 여기 없는 거야
▸ I'm gone
나 간다

I'm getting out of here 나 간다. 지금 나 갈건데

A: I'm getting out of here. This place is pretty scary.

B: I'm with you... let's go.

A: 나 간다. 여기 꽤 으시시해. B: 나도 갈래… 어서 나가자.

Let's get out of here 나가자, 여기서 빠져 나가자

A: Good enough! Pick up the tools and let's get out of here.
B: Sounds good to me!

A: 이 정도면 됐어! 연장챙겨서 가자. B: 좋아!

I'm leaving. Bye! 나 간다. 안녕!

A: I'm leaving. Bye!
B: Bye! Thanks for helping me today.

A: 나 간다. 안녕! B: 안녕! 오늘 도와줘서 고마워.

Are you leaving so soon? 벌써 가려구?, 왜 이렇게 빨리 가?

A: Are you leaving so soon?
B: Yeah. I've got a lot of work to do.

A: 벌써 가려구? B: 그래. 할 일이 많아.

▸ have got a lot of work to do
할 일이 많다

I don't want to wear out my welcome
너무 번거롭게 만드는 건 아닌지 모르겠네

A: Stay longer and have fun with me.
B: I don't want to wear out my welcome.

A: 여기 더 남아서 나랑 놀자. B: 넘 번거롭게 하는거 아닌지 모르겠어.

▸ How about~?
…해봐

A: How about asking Tony to lend you some money?
B: He lost his job. I don't want to wear out my welcome.

A: 토니에게 돈 빌려달라고 해봐? B: 실직했잖아. 폐 끼치고 싶지 않아.

I wish I could stay longer 더 남아 있으면 좋을텐데

A: Do you really have to leave?
B: Yes, but I wish I could stay longer.

A: 정말 가야 돼? B: 어, 근데 더 남아있으면 좋을텐데 말야.

▸ I wish I could+V
…하면 좋을텐데

You're excused 그러세요. 괜찮다. 그만 나가 보거라

A: I have a doctor's appointment this afternoon.
B: Alright, you're excused from class.

A: 오후에 병원예약 되어 있어요. B: 알았다. 조퇴하고 가봐라.

▸ You're dismissed
가도 좋아. 해산(解散)
▸ Class dismissed
수업 끝났습니다

14 나중에 보자

See you later 나중에 봐

A: I'll see you later!

B: Okay, bye!

A: 나중에 보자! B: 그래, 안녕!

▸ (I'll) See you guys later
애들아 나중에 봐
▸ I'll try to see you later
나중에 봐

(I'll) Be seeing you 또 보자

A: I'll be seeing you. Take care!

B: You too!

A: 또 보자. 잘 개! B: 너도!

See you soon 또 보자

A: Okay, I'll see you soon buddy. Be back in an hour.

B: Bye, Dad.

A: 그래, 다시 보자 야. 한시간 후에 올게. B: 가요, 아빠.

▸ See you around
또 보자

See you in the morning[tomorrow] 아침에[내일] 보자

A: See you in the morning.

B: Yes, bright and early, and don't forget your jogging shoes.

A: 내일 아침에 봐. B: 어, 아침 일찍. 조깅화 잊지마.

I'll see you then 그럼 그때 보자

A: Cool! I'll see you then.

B: All right.

A: 좋아! 그럼 그때 보자. B: 그래.

Catch you later 나중에 보자

A: Catch you later!

B: Hopefully before the next family reunion.

A: 나중에 봐! B: 다음 가족 모임 전에 보자고.

I'll catch up with you in the gym 체육관에서 보자

A: Sorry, but I gotta go now.

B: Okay then. I'll catch up with you later.

A: 미안하지만 가야 돼. B: 알았어 그럼. 나중에 보자.

▸ I'll catch up with you later
나중에 보자
▸ I'll try to catch you some other time
언제 한번 보자구

Goodbye for now 그만 여기서 작별하죠

A: I'll see you in the spring.

B: Sure thing. Goodbye for now.

A: 봄에 보자. B: 물론. 지금은 그만 헤어지자.

▸ Bye for now
그만 여기서 헤어지자
▸ Goodbye until next time
다시 만날 때까지 잘 있어

Bye Kash! 캐쉬야 잘가!

A: We're leaving. Bye Kash!

B: Bye!

A: 우리 간다. 캐쉬야 안녕! B: 안녕!

▸ Bye-bye!
안녕!

Don't work too hard 너무 무리하지 말구

A: Don't work too hard.

B: I won't. Have a good evening!

A: 너무 과로하지마. B: 안 그럴께. 저녁 잘 보내!

Take care! 조심하고!

A: Take care!

B: Okay... see you next week!

A: 잘지내! B: 그래… 다음 주에 보자고.

▸ Take care of yourself
몸조심해
▸ Be careful
조심해

Ciao! 잘 가!

A: See you later.

B: Hasta la vista.

A: 나중에 봐. B: 나중에 보자!

▸ Sayonara!
잘 가!
▸ Hasta la vista!
잘 가!, 또 보자!

15 오늘 잘 지내

Have a nice day 오늘 잘 지내

A: Have a nice day!

B: Same to you.

A: 오늘 잘 보내! B: 너도 그래.

Have a nice weekend 주말 잘 보내

A: Have a nice weekend!

B: Okay, I'll see you on Monday.

A: 주말 잘 보내! B: 응, 월요일에 보자.

Have a nice trip! 여행 멋지게 보내고!

A: I'm going to Japan during my vacation.

B: Have a nice trip!

A: 휴가때 일본에 갈려고. B: 여행 잘하고!

Have fun! 재미있게 보내!

A: We're going to Guam.

B: Have fun!

A: 우린 괌 간다. B: 재미있게 보내!

▶ have a date with sb
…와 데이트가 있다

A: I have a date with Susan tonight.

B: Have fun!

A: 오늘밤 수잔과 데이트가 있어. B: 재미있게 보내!

Enjoy yourself! 즐겁게 지내!

A: I'm planning to lay on the beach today.

B: Enjoy yourself!

A: 오늘 해변에 가서 누워있으려고. B: 즐겁게 보내!

A: I'm going to Guam next month.

B: Enjoy yourself! It'll be fun. A: 다음 달에 괌에 가. B: 즐겁게 보내! 재미있을거야.

Good luck 행운을 빌어

A: Good luck on your date.

B: Oh thanks!

A: 데이트 잘 되기를 바랄게. B: 어 고마워!

A: I've got a job interview next Monday.

B: Good luck, you'll need it.

A: 다음 주 월요일에 취업면접이 있어. B: 행운을 빌어. 행운이 필요할거야.

▸ Good luck with that!
행운이 있기를!
▸ (The) Best of luck (to someone)!
잘 되기를 빌게!
▸ I wish you success!
성공하길 빌어!

Good luck, go get'em 행운을 빌어 힘내라고, 행운을 빌어 (걔네들을) 가서 잡으라고

A: Okay guys, wish me luck!

B: Good luck, go get'em!

A: 그래 얘들아, 행운을 빌어줘! B: 행운을 빌어! 힘내라고!

└ go get'em의 형태로는 가서 걔네들을 잡아라 혹은 힘내라, 이겨라는 응원의 의미로도 쓰인다.

Good luck (to you), you'll need it 행운을 빌어, 행운이 필요할거야

A: Okay, I'm all ready to go now.

B: Good luck, you'll need it!

A: 좋았어, 이제 갈 준비가 다 됐어. B: 진심으로 행운을 빈다!

▸ be ready to+V [for+N]
…할 준비가 되다

My fingers are crossed 행운을 빌어요

A: Well, I have a job interview at City Bank tomorrow!

B: My fingers are crossed. I know you really want that job.

A: 내일 시티은행 면접있어. B: 행운을 빌게. 네가 원하는 직장이잖아.

▸ I'll keep my fingers crossed (for you)!
행운을 빌어줄게!

Lucky me 나한테 다행이구만

A: You've won the top prize.

B: Lucky me. I'm so excited!

A: 네가 1등상을 받았어. B: 내게 잘된 일이지. 정말 신난다!

▸ Lucky bastard!
그놈의 자식 운도 좋구만!

Wish me luck! 행운을 빌어줘

A: Wish me luck.

B: Good luck!

A: 행운을 빌어줘. B: 행운을 빌어!

16 너 보고 싶을거야

I'm going to miss you 보고 싶을 거야

A: Well, I guess this is goodbye.

B: I'm going to miss you so much.

    A: 자, 이제 헤어져야겠군요. B: 정말 보고 싶을 거예요.

▸ I will (really) miss you
네가 그리울 거야
▸ We're all going to miss you
우리 모두 널 보고 싶을 거야

I'm already missing you 벌써 그리워지려고 해

A: I've got to leave right away.

B: Don't go. I'm already missing you.

    A: 바로 떠나야 돼. B: 가지마. 벌써 그리워지려고 해.

I hope I can come back again 다시 오기를 바래

A: I had fun here. I hope I can come back again.

B: You're welcome any time.

    A: 재미있었어. 다시 오길 바래. B: 언제든지 환영야.

I hope to see you again (sometime)

(조만간에) 다시 한번 보자, 나중에 얼굴 한번 봐요

A: I hope to see you again sometime.

B: Okay, let me call you when I'm in the neighborhood.

    A: 다시 한번 너를 만나고 싶어. B: 그래, 이 근처에 오면 전화할게.

▸ Could I see you again?
다시 한번 볼 수 있어?

Don't stay away so long 자주 좀 와

A: Don't stay away so long.

B: I'll try to come visit you soon.

    A: 자주 좀 와. B: 조만간 가도록 할게.

▸ come+V = come and[to]+V
…하러 오다

Give me a call sometime 한번 전화해

A: If you have any questions, give me a call.

B: I'll do that. A: 질문이 있으면 나한테 전화해. B: 그렇게.

▸ Call me later
나중에 전화해

I wish I could go with you 너랑 같이 가면 좋을텐데

A: My trip to Paris begins tomorrow.

B: I wish I could go with you.

   A: 내일 파리로 여행가. B: 너랑 같이 가면 좋을텐데.

Let's get[keep] in touch! 연락하고 지내자!

A: Have you heard from Susan or Jim lately?

B: No. Let's get in touch with them.

   A: 최근 수잔이나 짐에게서 소식들었어? B: 아니. 걔들에게 연락해보자.

└ keep[be]을 쓰면 연락을 하고 지내다, get을 쓰면 연락을 취하다.

Don't forget to e-mail me 잊지말고 메일 보내

A: Bye for now!

B: See you later. Don't forget to e-mail me.

   A: 이제 안녕! B: 나중에 봐. 잊지말고 메일 보내고.

▸ Don't forget to write
잊지말고 편지 써
▸ Drop me a line
나한테 편지 좀 써

Give my best to your folks 가족들에게 안부 전해줘

A: Give my best to your folks.

B: I'll tell them you said hi.

   A: 가족들에게 안부 전해줘. B: 네 안부 전해줄게.

▸ All the best to everyone
모두에게 안부 전해줘

Please give my regards to your family 가족에게 안부 전해줘

A: I'm visiting my parents this weekend.

B: Give my regards to your family.

   A: 이번 주말에 부모님 댁에 갈거야. B: 내 안부 좀 전해드려.

Say hello to your wife 부인에게 안부 전해 주거나

A: It was nice to see you again, Sandra.

B: Say hello to your wife for me.

   A: 다시 만나 반가웠어, 샌드라. B: 내 대신 와이프에게 안부 전해줘.

Say hi to Mona 모나에게 안부 전해줘

A: Be sure to say hi to everyone in the office for me.

B: Don't worry. I will.

   A: 사무실 사람 모두에게 안부전해줘. B: 걱정마. 그렇게 할게.

▸ Be sure to+V
반드시 …해라

17 우리 집에 들러

Come over to my place[house] 우리 집에 들려

A: Come over to my house on Saturday night.

B: Why? What's going on?

> A: 토요일 밤에 우리 집에 와 B: 왜? 무슨 일인데?

▸ go on = happen

Please come to John's farewell party this Friday

금주 금요일 존 송별회에 와

A: Please come to John's farewell party this Friday.

B: I'd love to come, but I have an engagement.

> A: 금주 금요일 존 송별회에 와. B: 가고 싶지만 약속이 있어.

Please attend our office party 회사 회식에 참석해요

A: Please attend our office party.

B: When is it? A: 회사 회식에 참석해요. B: 언제인데요?

Drop by for a drink 언제 한번 놀러 와 한잔 하자고

A: Goodbye, Tammy. Drop by sometime.

B: Thanks. I will.

> A: 태미야 잘 가. 한번 들려. B: 고마워. 그럴게.

▸ If you're ever in Seoul, do drop by
서울에 오게 되면 들리라고
▸ drop by = stop by = come by = swing by

Drop by sometime 언제 한번 들려

A: We never get together these days.

B: You should drop by sometime.

> A: 요즘 통 만나질 못하네. B: 언제 한번 들려라.

▸ get together
만나다
▸ get-together
캐주얼한 만남

You're invited to Bob's bachelor party 밥의 총각파티에 참석했으면 해

A: You're invited to Bob's bachelor party.

B: I hope I can come. It sounds like fun!

> A: 밥의 총각파티에 참석했으면 해서. B: 나도 가고 싶어. 재미있겠다!

▸ We cordially invite you to attend the wedding
결혼식에 참석해주셨으면 합니다

Hope you can make it 너도 올 수 있으면 좋겠어

A: We're having a party for Sam. Hope you can make it.

B: Is it his birthday this month?

A: 샘에게 파티 열어주려고. 너도 올 수 있으면 좋겠어. B: 걔 생일이 이번 달이야?

▶ make it
(약속 장소 등에) 제시간에
도착하다, 가다

Hope you can come 네가 올 수 있기를 바래

A: The party is Friday. Hope you can come.

B: I'll try to make it.

A: 금요일 파티야. 너도 왔으면 해. B: 가보도록 할게.

I'm sorry I can't make it 미안하지만 못가

A: I'm going shopping today. Want to come along?

B: Sorry, I can't make it.

A: 오늘 쇼핑갈거야. 같이 갈래? B: 미안, 난 안돼.

A: Can you meet for lunch today?

B: I'm sorry, I can't make it.

A: 오늘 만나서 점심 먹을래? B: 미안, 난 안돼.

▶ come along
함께 가다

When can I come over? 내가 언제 갈까?

A: When can I come over?

B: Stop by any time after Friday.

A: 내가 언제 갈까? B: 금요일 이후엔 아무때나 와.

▶ come over
들르다

When can I stop by? 내가 언제 들를까?

A: I have your books in my office.

B: When can I stop by to pick them up?

A: 내 사무실에 네 책이 있어. B: 언제 가지러 들를까?

When can you come over? 언제 올 수 있어?

A: I'll give you a hand with your homework.

B: Great. When can you come over?

A: 너 숙제 도와줄게. B: 좋아. 언제 올 수 있어?

▶ give sb a hand
with~
…가 …하는 것을 도와주다

18 아무도 안계세요?

Hello, is anyone there? 여보세요?, 아무도 안계세요?

A: Is anyone here?

B: What do you want?

A: 누구 안 계세요? B: 왜 그러는데요?

▸ Is anyone here?
누구 안 계세요?

(Hello) Anybody home? 누구 집에 없어요?, 안 계세요?

A: Hello? Anybody home?

B: Come in! I'm in the kitchen.

A: 여보세요? 안 계세요? B: 들어와요! 부엌에 있어요.

I'd like to see Mr. James 제임스 씨를 만나뵈려고요

A: I came here to see Mr. James.

B: He's not in right now, but he should be back any time.

A: 제임스 씨를 만나러 왔습니다. B: 지금 안계시지만 금세 돌아와요.

▸ I came[am] here
to see Mr. Smith
스미스 씨를 만나뵈려 왔어
요

Who is it? 누구세요?, 누구야?

A: Who is it?

B: (outside the door) It's Jill, open up!

A: 누구세요? B: 질야, 문열어!

▸ Who's there?
누구세요?
▸ Who was it?
누군데? 누구였어?

Would you get that? 문 좀 열어줄래?, 전화 좀 받아줄래?

A: Would you get that? I'm in the shower.

B: Sure.

A: 문 좀 대신 열어줄래? 나 샤워중야. B: 그래.

▸ Could you answer
it for me?
대신 좀 열어[받아]줄래?

I'll get it 내가 받을게

A: Don't touch the phone! I'll get it.

B: Okay.

A: 전화받지마! 내가 받을거야. B: 알았어.

▸ Let me
내가 받을게

I'm home 나 왔어

A: Hi honey, I'm home!

B: Hi, how was your flight?

A: 자기야, 나 왔어! B: 안녕, 비행 어땠어?

Come on in 어서 들어와

A: Come on in. How are you?

B: I'm good!

A: 어서 들어와. 어떻게 지내? B: 좋아!

▶ Please come in
어서 들어와

Welcome home 어서 와

A: Well, I've finally finished my military service.

B: Welcome home. We've really missed you.

A: 어, 마침내 군복무를 끝냈어. B: 어서 와, 정말 보고 싶었다고.

▶ Welcome!
어서 와!

Welcome to our Christmas party 크리스마스 파티에 오신 걸 환영합니다

A: Welcome to our Christmas party. May I take your coat?

B: Thanks.

A: 크리스마스 파티에 온걸 환영해. 코트받아줄까? B: 고마워.

Welcome aboard 함께 일하게 된 걸 환영해, 귀국[귀향]을 축하해

A: Welcome aboard. I'm sure you'll like working here.

B: I think it'll be great.

A: 환영해. 여기 일 맘에 들거야. B: 아주 좋을 것 같아.

Won't you come in? 들어오지 않을래?

A: Is your son at home?

B: Yes, he is. Won't you come in?

A: 집에 아들 있어? B: 어, 있어. 들어오지 않을래?

└. won't의 발음은 [wount]

It's nice to be here 저도 여기 오게 돼서 기뻐요

A: Hi, Ms. Jones. Welcome to our headquarters.

B: Thank you. It's nice to be here.

A: 안녕하세요, 존스씨. 본사오신 걸 환영해요. B: 고마워요, 저도 여기 오게 돼서 기뻐요.

▶ It's great to be here
여기 오게 돼 무척 기뻐요

19 와줘서 고마워

I'm glad you could come 네가 와줘서 기뻐

A: I'm glad you could come.

B: It's my pleasure.

A: 네가 와줘서 기뻐. B: 내가 더 좋은 걸.

▸ How nice of you to come
와줘서 고마워

Thank you for coming 와줘서 고마워

A: Thank you so much for coming on such short notice.

B: Oh, not at all.

A: 일찍 연락 못했는데 와줘서 고마워. B: 괜찮어.

▸ on such short notice
급하게 연락에도, 촉박하게 연락했는데도

Thank you[Thanks] for inviting me 초대해줘서 고마워

A: Thank you for inviting me. I really enjoyed it.

B: Glad to hear that. I hope to see you again.

A: 초대해줘 고마워. 정말 즐거웠어. B: 그렇게 말해줘 고마워. 다시 보길 바래.

▸ attend the party
파티에 참석하다

A: Thank you for inviting me.

B: I'm glad you could attend the party.

A: 초대해줘 고마워. B: 파티에 참석해줘서 기뻐.

I like your house 너희 집 마음에 들어

A: I like your house.

B: I'm glad to hear that.

A: 니네 집 맘에 들어. B: 그렇게 말해줘 고마워.

▸ I really like your apartment
너희 아파트 정말 좋다

Can I park my car here? 여기 주차해도 돼?

A: Can I park my car here?

B: No, you'd better use my driveway.

A: 여기 주차해도 돼? B: 아니. 내 드라이브웨이에다 주차해.

▸ Is parking okay here?
여기 주차해도 괜찮어?
▸ Is it all right to park my car here?
차 여기다 주차해도 돼?

Have a seat 앉아

A: Have a seat right over here.

B: OK, Thanks.

A: 여기 이쪽에 앉아. B: 어, 고마워.

▸ Take a seat
앉아
▸ Please sit down
앉으세요

Make yourself at home 편히계세요

A: Please make yourself at home.

B: OK. I will.

A: 편히 해. B: 그래 그럴게.

▸ Please feel free to make yourself at home
집처럼 편히하세요

Please make yourself comfortable 편히하세요

A: Please make yourself comfortable.

B: Alright. Do you have any snacks?

A: 편히하세요. B: 그래요. 과자 좀 있어요?

Make yourself a drink and relax 술 한 잔 따라 마시며 편히 쉬어

A: Make yourself a drink and relax.

B: Where do you keep your scotch?

A: 술 한잔 마시며 편히 쉬고 있어. B: 스카치 어디 있어?

May I use your rest room? 화장실 좀 써도 될까요?

A: May I use your bathroom?

B: Sure, go ahead.

A: 화장실 좀 써도 될까요? B: 예, 그러세요.

▸ May I use your bathroom[toilet]?
화장실 좀 써도 될까요?

Where's the bathroom? 화장실이 어디예요?

A: Excuse me, where's the bathroom?

B: It's just down the hall to your left.

A: 죄송하지만 화장실이 어디 있나요? B: 복도를 내려가다 보면 왼편에 있어요.

▸ How can I get to the bathroom?
화장실 어떻게 가죠?

20 시간있어?

(You) Got a minute? 시간돼?

A: You got a minute?

B: Sure, what's up?

A: 시간돼? B: 그럼, 뭔대?

▸ Do you have
(some) time?
시간 있어요?

Are you available on Thursday morning? 목요일 오전에 시간 돼?

A: Are you available on Thursday morning?

B: I think so. I'll call to confirm.

A: 목요일 오전에는 시간이 되세요? B: 될 것 같은데요. 전화해서 확실히 알려드릴게요.

▸ Are you available
after the meeting
for lunch?
회의 후에 점심 가능해?
▸ Are you available?
시간돼?

Will you be free to go to the movies on the weekend?
주말에 영화보러 갈 수 있어?

A: Are you free in the afternoon?

B: Yes. How about one-thirty?

A: 오후에 시간 있으세요? B: 예. 1시 반이 어떨까요?

▸ Will you be free to
+ 동사 ?
…할 시간이 돼?
▸ Are you free in the
afternoon?
오후에 시간 있어?

Do you have time to talk for a bit? 잠깐 얘기할 시간이 있나요?

A: Do you have time to talk about the meeting?

B: Not this morning, but I'm free after lunch.

A: 회의에 대해 얘기할 시간 있어요? B: 아침에는 안 되지만 점심 후에는 괜찮아요.

▸ Do you have time
to + 동사 ?
…할 시간이 있어요?
▸ Do you have time
to see me on the
weekend?
주말에 만날 수 있을까?

Let's get together (sometime) (조만간) 한번 보자

A: Well, it was nice talking to you.

B: Yes. Let's get together again soon.

A: 저기, 말씀 나누게 되서 반가웠어요. B: 그래요, 곧 다시 만납시다.

Why don't we get together on Wednesday? 수요일에 만날까요?

A: Why don't we get together on Saturday?

B: Sure. Call me in the morning. A: 토요일에 좀 만나. B: 그래, 아침에 전화해.

▸ Why don't we+V?
= Let's+V
▸ Why don't I+V? =
Let me+V

Let's meet to talk about it 만나서 그 얘기해보자

A: Let's meet to talk about the new project.

B: All right.

A: 만나서 새로운 프로젝트건 얘기하자. B: 좋아.

▶ I'd like to meet
with you after
work if you're not
too busy
안 바쁘면 퇴근후 봤으면 해

I wonder if we could get together on the 15th 15일에 만날 수 있을까

A: I wonder if we could get together on the 15th.

B: First of all, let me check my schedule.

A: 15일에 만날 수 있을까. B: 먼저, 일정 좀 보고.

▶ get together
가볍게 만나다 혹은 그런
만남

Shall we get together on Thursday after five?

목요일 5시 이후에 만날래요?

A: Shall we get together on Thursday after five?

B: Sounds good to me.

A: 목요일 5시 이후에 만날래요? B: 저는 괜찮아요.

Are you doing anything this afternoon? 오후에 뭐 계획있어?

A: Are you doing anything this afternoon?

B: Nothing. Why?

A: 오후에 뭐 계획있어? B: 할 일 없는데. 왜?

Okay, let me check my schedule 일정을 한번 확인해 보죠

A: Can I help you, sir?

B: I'd like to set up an appointment for next week.

A: 무슨 일이시죠, 선생님? B: 담주로 약속 정하고 싶은데요.

▶ I'd like to set up
an appointment
for Thursday
목요일로 약속을 정하고 싶
군요

Can you make time to discuss our purchases?

시간내서 구매품의논할 수 있어?

A: Can you make time to discuss our purchases?

B: Well, actually, I'm really busy right now.

A: 시간내서 구매품의논할 수 있어? B: 글쎄요, 실은, 지금 너무 바빠서요.

▶ make time to+V
시간을 내서 …을 하다

21 내일 오전 어때?

How about tomorrow morning? 내일 오전 어때?

A: When and where can I meet you?

B: How about after work, at the bar on the corner?

    A: 언제 어디서 만날까? B: 퇴근 후 길모퉁이 바가 어때?

▸ How about + 구체
적인 장소/시간 ?
…가 어때?
▸ How about Friday
in my office?
금요일날 내 사무실에서 어
때?

About what time? 몇시에?

A: The birthday party is on Tuesday.

B: I see. About what time will it start?

    A: 생일파티가 화요일에 있어. B: 알았어. 몇시에 시작해?

Would this afternoon be all right with you? 오늘 오후 괜찮겠어요?

A: Would this afternoon be all right with you?

B: Sorry, I'm in a meeting all afternoon.

    A: 오늘 오후가 괜찮겠어요? B: 안돼요. 오후 내내 회의가 있어서.

▸ Is + 시간 + all
right?
…가 괜찮아?

When can you make it? 몇시에 도착할 수 있겠니?

A: I'll be late. I had a fender-bender.

B: Really? Then when can you make it?

    A: 늦을거야. 가벼운 접촉사고가 났어. B: 정말? 그럼 몇시에 올 수 있어?

∟ make it은 'to arrive in
time'이란 의미로 「약속 시간
에 닿다」라는 의미.

Can you make it? 올 수 있어?

A: Hey, so can you make it on Friday?

B: Oh yeah, I think so.

    A: 야, 그럼 금요일에 올 수 있는거야? B: 어 그래, 그럴 걸.

▸ Can you make it
at 7?
7시에 올 수 있겠니?

When and where can I meet you? 언제 어디서 만날까?

A: When and where can I meet you?

B: Let's meet at Burger King on Sunday.

    A: 언제 어디서 만날까? B: 일요일에 버거킹에서 만나자.

What time is[would be] good for you? 몇시가 좋겠어?

A: What time would be good for you?

B: Well, I have an hour free at four o'clock.

A: 몇시가 좋겠어요? B: 글쎄요. 4시에 한 시간쯤 비네요.

▸ When is good for you?
언제가 좋아?

What time would you like to meet? 몇시에 만날래?

A: What time would you like to meet tomorrow?

B: Let's see, how about four o'clock?

A: 내일 몇시쯤 만나면 좋을까요? B: 글쎄요. 4시는 어때요?

▸ When is the most convenient time for you?
언제가 가장 편리한 시간이야?

Does this afternoon work for you? 오후에 괜찮으세요?

A: Does this afternoon work for you?

B: Yes. How about three o'clock?

A: 오후에 괜찮으세요? B: 네. 3시 어때요?

A: How about getting together next Monday?

B: That works for me.

A: 담주 월요일에 만나는게 어때? B: 나도 그때가 괜찮아.

▸ That works for me
나도 그때가 괜찮아요.

You decide when 언제 만날지 네가 결정해

A: What time is okay for you?

B: Any time is good for me. You decide when.

A: 너는 언제가 좋아? B: 아무때나 좋아. 언제만날지 네가 결정해.

▸ You decide where
어디서 만날지 네가 결정해

That'll be fine. See you then 그게 좋겠군요. 그때 봐요

A: Let's get together at 9 o'clock in my office.

B: That'll be fine. See you then.

A: 그럼 9시에 내 사무실에서 만납시다. B: 그게 좋겠군요. 그때 봐요.

Whenever you're free 네가 시간나면 아무때나

A: When can I see you again?

B: Whenever you're free. Call me anytime.

A: 언제 다시 볼 수 있어? B: 네가 시간 되면 아무때나. 언제든 전화해.

▸ Whenever 아무 때나
▸ When you have time 네가 시간될 때
▸ Anytime is fine
아무 때나 좋아

22 다음으로 미루자

I'll take a rain check 이번에는 다음으로 미룰게

A: We're having a party tonight! Would you like to come?

B: Sorry, I can't. I'll take a rain check this time.

A: 오늘 파티있어! 올래? B: 미안, 안돼. 이번은 다음으로 미룰게.

▸ Do you mind if I take a rain check?
다음으로 미뤄도 될까?

Maybe some other time 다음을 기약하지

A: Would you like a drink?

B: No, maybe some other time.

A: 한잔할래? B: 아니, 다음에 하자.

▸ We'll try again some other time
나중을 기약하자

I have no time available this week 이번 주엔 시간낼 수가 없어

A: I have no time available this week.

B: That's all right. How about next Sunday?

A: 이번 주엔 시간을 낼 수가 없어. B: 괜찮아. 다음주 일요일은 어때?

▸ I have no time to see you in the afternoon
오후에 만날 시간이 없어

I'm afraid I have another appointment 미안하지만 선약이 있어

A: Are you available to meet on Monday afternoon?

B: I'm afraid I have another appointment.

A: 월요일 오후에 만날 수 있어요? B: 미안하지만 선약이 있어요.

▸ I'm afraid S+V
미안하지만 …해

I have another appointment at that time 그 시간에는 선약이 있는데요

A: Would you like to meet tomorrow morning?

B: I have another appointment at that time.

A: 내일 아침 만날래? B: 그 시간에 선약이 있어.

That's a bad day for me 그날은 안되는데

A: Can you make time for me on Friday?

B: That's a bad day for me.

A: 금요일에 내게 시간낼 수 있어? B: 그날은 안되는데.

Sorry, I won't be able to make it this weekend
미안, 주말 약속 못 지킬 것 같아

A: I won't be able to make it to the presentation.

B: That's okay. I'll take notes for you.

A: 발표회에 가지 못할 것 같아. B: 걱정 마. 내가 대신 노트해 줄게.

▸ I won't be able to make it to the presentation
발표회에 못가
▸ I won't be able to make it
못갈 것 같아

Could we change it to Monday? 월요일로 바꿀 수 있어?

A: How about meeting me on Friday?

B: That's bad day for me. Can we change it to Monday?

A: 금요일날 만나는 게 어때? B: 그날은 안돼. 월요일로 바꿀 수 있어?

▸ I'd rather make it later if that's okay
괜찮다면 약속 날짜를 더 미루는 게 낫겠어요

I'm afraid I have to cancel tomorrow's appointment
내일 약속 취소해야겠어요

A: Why are you calling, Mr. Park?

B: I'm afraid I have to cancel tomorrow's appointment.

A: 박 선생님, 왜 전화하셨어요? B: 내일 약속을 취소해야 돼서요.

I'll be there 갈게

A: Are you coming camping with us again this year?

B: Of course, I will be there!

A: 올해도 캠프 같이 가는 거지? B: 물론, 꼭 갈게!

▸ I'll be right there
곧 갈게, 지금 가
▸ I'm going to be there
갈게, 갈거야
▸ You bet I'll be there
꼭 갈게

She's going to be here 걔는 여기 올거야

A: Is your girlfriend coming over here tonight?

B: Sure. She is going to be here any second.

A: 너 애인도 오늘 밤에 여기 오니? B: 그럼. 올 때가 됐어.

I'm going to make it to the wedding 결혼식에 갈 예정이야

A: I don't think I'm going to make it to the wedding.

B: What? Something's come up?

A: 결혼식에 못가게 될 것 같아. B: 뭐야? 무슨 일이 있는거야?

▸ I'm going
나 가
▸ I'm not going
나 안가

23 좀 늦을 것 같아

I'm sorry but I'm going to be a little late 미안하지만 좀 늦을 것 같아

A: I'm going to be a bit late. I got caught in traffic.

B: Alright, how long do you think you'll be?

A: 좀 늦어. 길이 막혀 꼼짝도 못해. B: 괜찮아, 얼마나 늦을 것 같아?

I'm running a bit late 예상보다 좀 늦겠어요

A: Why are you so stressed out today?

B: I'm running a bit late and my boss is upset.

A: 오늘 왜 그리 열받아있어? B: 좀 늦었는데 사장이 화내더라고.

I might be about thirty minutes late 한 30분 정도 늦을 것 같아

A: Are you going to be on time?

B: I don't think so. I might be 30 minutes late.

A: 제 때에 올 수 있어? B: 아니. 30분 늦을 것 같아.

I'm sorry I'm late 늦어서 미안해

A: Sorry I'm late, I was stuck at work.

B: It's okay.

A: 늦어서 미안해, 일이 많아서 말야. B: 괜찮아.

Something's come up 일이 좀 생겼어

A: So we can't go on a date tonight?

B: I'm sorry. Something's come up.

A: 그래 우리 오늘 밤 데이트 못하는 거야? B: 미안해. 일이 좀 생겨서.

▶ Something
unexpected came
up
갑자기 일이 생겨서요

A: I can't go out tonight. Something's come up.

B: Let's do it tomorrow instead.

A: 오늘 밤 못가. 일이 좀 생겨서. B: 대신 내일 하자.

What time do you think you will show up? 몇시에 올 수 있을 것 같아?

A: I'll come after I finish working.

B: What time do you think you will show up?

A: 일 마치고 갈게. B: 몇시에 올 수 있을 것 같아?

▸ show up = turn up

I'll be there soon 곧 갈게

A: We're still waiting for you to come home.

B: I'll be there soon.

A: 네가 집에 오길 아직 기다리고 있어. B: 곧 갈게.

▸ be there
가다
▸ be here
오다

I'll try and get there as soon as I can 가능한 한 빨리 가도록 할게

A: I'll try and get there as soon as possible.

B: You have a lot of angry people waiting.

A: 가능한 한 빨리 도착하도록 할게. B: 많은 사람들이 화가 나 기다리고 있어.

I'm sorry I kept you waiting so long 너무 오래 기다리게 해서 미안해요

A: I have been here for twenty minutes.

B: I'm sorry I kept you waiting so long. I lost track of time.

A: 여기서 20분이나 기다렸다구. B: 넘 오래 기다리게 해서 미안. 시간이 이렇게 된 줄 몰랐어.

▸ I'm sorry to have kept you waiting for so long
너무 오래 기다리게 해서 미안해

How long have you been waiting? 얼마동안 기다린거야?

A: You are really late.

B: Oh, dear. How long have you been waiting?

A: 정말 늦게 오는 구만. B: 어, 자기야. 얼마나 기다린거야?

Please excuse me for being late 늦어서 미안해

A: Please excuse me for being late.

B: You'd better have a good reason for this.

A: 늦어서 미안해요. B: 왜 늦었는지 합당한 이유가 있겠지.

▸ I apologize for being so late
늦어서 죄송해요

What took you so long? 뭣 때문에 이렇게 오래 걸렸어?

A: What took you so long?

B: I ran into my ex-wife on my way here.

A: 뭣 때문에 이렇게 오래 걸렸어? B: 여기 오늘 길에 예전 아내를 우연히 만났어.

A: I finally finished my report.

B: What took you so long? I've been done for hours.

A: 보고서를 마침내 끝냈어. B: 왜 그리 오래 걸렸어? 난 몇시간만에 했는데.

I don't know what's keeping her   걔가 뭐 때문에 늦는지 모르겠어

A: I don't know what's keeping her.

B: Why don't you call her cell phone and find out?

A: 걔가 뭐 때문에 늦는지 모르겠어. B: 핸드폰으로 전화해서 알아봐.

I lost track of time   시간이 어떻게 되는지 몰랐어

A: Why weren't you here at six?

B: I lost track of the time.

A: 왜 6시에 여기 안 온거야? B: 시간이 어떻게 되는지 몰랐어.

I got held up at work   일에 잡혀서 말야

A: You should have been here hours ago.

B: Sorry. I got held up at work.

A: 몇시간 전에 도착했어야 하잖아. B: 미안. 일에 잡혀서 말야.

▸ I got held up in traffic

교통이 막혀서 꼼짝 못했어

Everyone's waiting for us   다들 우리를 기다리고 있어

A: Everyone's waiting for us.

B: We'd better hurry then.

A: 다들 우리를 기다리고 있어. B: 그럼 서둘러야겠네.

You kept me waiting for an hour   한 시간 동안 널 기다렸어

A: You kept me waiting for an hour.

B: I promise I'll never do that again.

A: 한 시간이나 널 기다렸어. B: 다신 그러지 않도록 약속할게.

You're always late for everything   매사에 항상 늦는구만

A: You're always late for everything.

B: I guess that's my nature.

A: 매사에 항상 늦는구만. B: 타고난 것 같아.

Chapter 02

감사·격려

01 고마워

Thank you very[so] much   고마워

A: Here are the papers you asked for.

B: Thank you very much. That was quick!

A: 부탁했던 서류 여기 있어요.   B: 고마워요. 빠르네요!

▸ Thanks a lot
고마워

Thank you for the lovely present   선물 고마워

A: Thanks a lot for the lovely present!

B: I'm glad you enjoyed it.

A: 근사한 정말 정말 잘 받았어요!   B: 그러셨다니 저도 기뻐요.

▸ Thank you for + 명사
…에 대해 고마워
▸ Thanks a lot for the great meal!
맛있는 식사 고마워

Thank you very much for your help   도와줘서 정말 고마워

A: Thank you very much for your help.

B: My pleasure.

A: 도와줘서 정말 고마워.   B: 뭘요.

▸ Thank you for the help
도와줘서 고마워

Thank you for giving me another chance   기회를 한 번 더 줘서 고마워

A: Thank you for giving me another chance.

B: You deserve it. I believe you can succeed.

A: 기회를 한 번 더 줘서 고마워.   B: 그럴 자격있지. 네가 해낼 수 있다고 믿어.

▸ Thank you for ~ ing
…해줘서 고마워

Thank you for telling me   말해줘서 고마워

A: Hey, Tony! Come over here. Your fly's open.

B: Thanks for telling me. That's so embarrassing.

A: 토니! 이리와봐. 지퍼가 열렸어.   B: 말해줘 고마워. 무척 창피하네.

▸ Thank you for letting me know
알려줘서 고마워

Thanks for saying so   그렇게 말해줘서 고마워

A: I really like your office.

B: Thanks for saying so.

A: 네 사무실 정말 맘에 든다.   B: 그렇게 말해줘서 고마워.

Thank you anyway 어쨌든 고마워

A: Sorry, I don't know.

B: Thank you anyway.

    A: 미안, 모르겠는데. B: 하여간 고마워.

▶ Thanks anyway,
  though
  어쨌든 고마워

Thank you in advance 고맙구만

A: I'm sure I can fix your car.

B: Thank you in advance.

    A: 네 차 고칠 수 있어. B: 고마워.

I really appreciate this 정말 고마워

A: I'll help you finish washing the dishes if you like.

B: I appreciate it. I'm so exhausted.

    A: 괜찮으면 설거지 도와줄게. B: 고마워. 정말 피곤해.

▶ I appreciate it
  고마워

I appreciate your help 도와줘서 감사해요

A: I can't express how much I appreciate all your help.

B: Don't mention it... it was nothing.

    A: 도와줘 얼마나 고마운지 몰라요. B: 천만에… 별거 아닌데.

A: I appreciate all of your help on the new project.

B: It has been a good experience for me as well.

    A: 새로운 프로젝트에 주신 도움 감사드려요. B: 저에게도 좋은 경험이었는걸요 뭘.

▶ I appreciate the
  support
  도와줘서 감사해요
▶ I appreciate your
  kindness
  친절을 베푸셔서 감사해요

 More Expressions

- Thank you for your time 시간내줘서 고마워
- Thank you for the compliment 칭찬해줘서 고마워
- Thank you for your concern 걱정해줘서 고마워
- Thank you for all you've done 여러모로 고마워

02 정말 친절하시군요

That's very kind of you 정말 친절하군요

A: Let me help you with your grocery bags.

B: Thank you, that's very kind of you.

  A: 식료품 가방 들어줄게요. B: 고마워요. 정말 친절하군요.

▸ How kind of you to say so
그렇게 말씀해주시니 정말 친절하네요

It's[That's] very nice of you 정말 친절하네요

A: It was very nice of you to call!

B: I'm glad that we finally had a chance to talk.

  A: 이렇게 전화를 다 해주고! B: 마침내 얘기 할 기회가 생겨 기뻐요.

That's so sweet 고맙기도 해라

A: I want you to move in with me.

B: That is so sweet.

  A: 나랑 함께 살자. B: 고맙기도 해라.

ㄴ. 주로 여성들이 쓰는 말로 주어를 바꿔 This is so sweet, It's so sweet라고 해도 된다.

You're so sweet 정말 고마워

A: Let me pay for your airline ticket.

B: That's wonderful. You're so sweet.

  A: 비행기값은 내가 낼게. B: 아이고 좋아라. 정말 고마워.

▸ You're so generous
맘씨가 참 좋으네

You're such a kind person 정말 친절하네요

A: You're such a kind man. Thank you for all you've done.

B: Not another word, my dear.

  A: 참 친절하네. 도와줘 고마워. B: 자기야, 그런 말 하지마.

▸ You've got such a good heart
넌 무척 자상한 애야

I'm really grateful to you 정말 감사드려요

A: I'm really grateful to you.

B: Don't worry about it.

  A: 정말 고마워요. B: 뭘 그런걸.

▸ I'm grateful to sb for ~ing
…가 …해줘서 고마워

I don't know how to thank you 고마워서 어쩌죠

A: I don't know how to thank you!

B: Don't worry about it.

> A: 이거 고마워서 어쩌죠! B: 걱정 말아요.

▸ I have no words
  to thank you
  뭐라고 감사해야 할지 모르
  겠어

I can't thank you enough 뭐라 감사하다고 해야 할지

A: I can't thank you enough.

B: You quite welcome.

> A: 뭐라고 감사하다고 해야 할지 모르겠어요. B: 별 말씀을 요.

I don't know what to say 뭐라고 말해야 할지

A: Here is a diamond ring for our anniversary.

B: My God! I don't know what to say.

> A: 우리 기념일 축하하는 다이아몬드야. B: 어머니! 뭐라 해야 할지 모르겠어.

You shouldn't have done this 이러지 않아도 되는데

A: I cleaned your house while you were gone.

B: Thanks. You shouldn't have done this.

> A: 외출했을 때 집청소를 해놨어. B: 고마워. 이러지 않아도 되는데.

▸ should have+pp
  …했어야 했는데 그러지 않
  았다
▸ shouldn't have+pp
  …하지 말았어야 했는데 그
  랬다

I'm flattered 그렇게 말해주면 고맙지, 과찬의 말씀을

A: You're my best friend.

B: I'm flattered.

> A: 넌 가장 소중한 친구야. B: 그렇게 말해주니 기분좋은데.

▸ I'm honored
  영광인데요

It was a great help 큰 도움이 됐습니다

A: Did you read that business report?

B: Yes, it was a great help.

> A: 그 사업보고서 읽었어? B: 어, 큰 도움이 되었어.

▸ You were a great
  help
  정말 많은 도움이 되었어요

You've been very helpful 넌 참 도움이 많이 됐어

A: You've been very helpful.

B: It's my job to offer advice.

> A: 넌 정말 도움이 많이 되었어. B: 조언을 하는 게 내 일인걸.

▸ You've been a
  big[great] help
  넌 큰 도움이 되었어

I owe it to my colleagues 제 동료 덕이에요

A: How did you become so successful?

B: Teamwork. I owe it all to my colleagues.

A: 이렇게 성공하게 된 요인은 요? B: 팀웍이죠. 다 제 동료 덕이에요.

I owe you a favor 신세를 졌구만

A: Here is the DVD you wanted to borrow.

B: Thanks Jeff. I owe you a favor.

A: 네가 빌리고 싶어하던 DVD야. B: 고마워, 제프. 신세를 졌구만.

I owe you one 신세가 많구나

A: I finished your homework for you.

B: Thanks! I owe you one.

A: 네 숙제 다했어. B: 고마워! 신세가 많어.

You saved my life 네 덕택에 살았네

A: I told the boss you were sick today.

B: Thanks! You saved my life.

A: 사장한테 너 오늘 아프다고 했어. B: 고마워! 네 덕에 살았어.

How nice! 고마워라!

A: It's my treat.

B: How nice!

A: 내가 낼게. B: 고마워라!

She's very supportive 그 여자는 도움이 많이 되고 있어

A: Your wife seems like a nice woman.

B: Yes, she is. And she's very supportive.

A: 네 와이프 좋은 여자 같더라. B: 어, 그래. 그리고 많은 도움이 되고 있어.

▶ He's been incredibly supportive of me
그 남자는 날 정말 많이 도와주고 있어

God bless you! 이렇게 고마울 수가!

A: Take the rest of the day off and go home.

B: God bless you!

A: 오늘은 그만 하고 집에 가지 그래. B: 이런 고마울 데가!

ㄴ God bless you!는 고맙다는 인사 뿐만 아니라 상대방이 재채기를 할 때 "신의 가호가 있기를"이라는 의미. 이는 재채기를 할 때 혼이 달아난다는 미신 때문에 생긴 표현.

03 뭘요, 별 말씀을요

You're welcome 천만에요

A: Thank you for the ride.

B: You're welcome. I was going this way anyway.

A: 태워다줘서 고마워요. B: 뭘요. 어차피 이 길로 가는 걸요.

ㄴ 강조하려면 You're very welcome, You're quite welcome이라고 하면 된다.

▸ Not at all
뭘요

▸ Don't mention it
신경쓰지 마요

(It's) My pleasure 도움이 됐다니 내가 기쁘네요

A: Thank you for the gift you sent on my birthday.

B: Oh, it was my pleasure. I hope you like it.

A: 내 생일에 보내준 선물 고마워. B: 뭘 그런 걸 갖고.네 맘에 들었으면 좋겠다.

▸ The pleasure is mine
제가 좋아서 한 일인데요

No problem 뭘 그런걸

A: Well, thanks for the books.

B: No problem.

A: 책 빌려줘 고마워. B: 뭘 그런걸.

▸ No sweat
뭘 별것도 아닌데

Never mind 마음쓰지마

A: I want to thank you for letting me use the car.

B: It was nothing.

A: 차 빌려줘서 고마워요. B: 별 것도 아닌데요 뭘.

▸ (Please) Think nothing of it
마음쓰지 마

▸ It was nothing
별거 아닌데

▸ Don't worry about it
별거 아닌데

I'm glad you think so 그렇게 생각한다니 고마워

A: You are always so generous!

B: I'm glad you think so.

A: 어쩜 그렇게 항상 마음이 넓으실까! B: 그렇게 생각해주니 기분 좋은데요.

▸ I'm glad I could help
내가 도움이 되서 기뻐

▸ I'm sure you would have done the same (in my position)
너도 (내입장이면) 나처럼 했을거야

04 아주 잘했어

(That's) Great! 잘됐다!

A: She and I are friends now.

B: That's great.

　A: 지금부터 걔하고 나하고 친구하기로 했어.　B: 잘됐다.

Excellent! 아주 좋아!

A: I'm ready to sign my contract.

B: Excellent. We couldn't be more pleased.

　A: 계약서에 서명하기로 했어요.　B: 아주 잘 됐군요. 기분이 아주 좋군요.

▸ Fantastic!
  끝내주네!
▸ Wonderful!
  멋져!

You did a good[nice] job! 아주 잘했어!

A: You did a good job! I was very impressed.

B: Thank you.

　A: 정말 잘 했어! 매우 인상적이었어.　B: 고마워.

Good for you 잘됐네, 잘했어

A: I won the speech contest at school today.

B: Good for you!

　A: 나 오늘 학교 웅변대회에서 우승했어.　B: 잘 됐네!

A: I found $100 on the ground yesterday.

B: Lucky for you!

　A: 어제 100달러 주웠어.　B: 잘 됐네!

▸ Good for me
  나한테 잘된 일야
▸ Lucky for you
  잘됐어

You deserve it 넌 충분히 그럴만해

A: I finally got the raise I asked for.

B: Good. You deserve it.

　A: 드디어 내가 요청한대로 임금을 인상받았어.　B: 잘됐어. 넌 받을만 해.

▸ You more than
  deserve it
  너 정도면 충분히 그럴 자
  격이 되고도 남아

Nice going! 참 잘했어!

A: I completed my first marathon.

B: Nice going. Was it difficult?

A: 첫번째 마라톤을 완주했어. B: 잘했어. 어려웠어?

ㄴ 말투에 따라 비아냥 거리는 표현

Well done 잘했어

A: This is an excellent report. Well done!

B: Thank you, professor.

A: 아주 훌륭한 보고서야. 아주 잘했어! B: 감사해요, 교수님.

▶ Top notch!
최고야!, 훌륭해!

Nice move 좋았어, 잘했어

A: Nice move.

B: I think I can win this chess game.

A: 좋았어. B: 이번 체스경기를 이길 것 같아.

Nice try (하지만) 잘했어

A: It's too bad you lost the contest. Nice try.

B: Maybe I'll win next year.

A: 네가 지다니 안됐네. 하지만 잘했어. B: 내년엔 이기겠지.

ㄴ 목적을 달성하지 못했지만 그래도 잘했다고 상대방이 한 시도를 칭찬할 때 쓰는 표현.

You can't beat that 짱이야, 완벽해

A: I'm going on a free trip to Hawaii this winter.

B: Wow! You can't beat that.

A: 이번 겨울에 하와이로 무료여행 갈거야. B: 야! 끝내준다!

▶ Can't top that
끝내준다

There is nothing like that! 저 만한 게 없지!

A: I spent five days relaxing on a private beach.

B: That's great. There's nothing like that.

A: 개인용 해변에서 며칠 쉬었어. B: 잘됐네. 그 만한게 없지.

A: Do you sell any sexy clothing in your store?

B: No, there is nothing like that here.

A: 야한 옷 파세요? B: 아뇨, 그런거 여기 없어요.

ㄴ 문맥에 따라서는 단순히 "그와 같은 건 없다"라는 의미로도 쓰인다.

Congratulations on your marriage! 결혼 축하해!

A: It was my first date since the divorce.

B: Well, congratulations! How did it go?

A: 이혼 후 첫번째 데이트였어. B: 그래, 축하해! 어땠는데?

▶ Congratulations on your promotion!
승진축하해!

▶ Congratulations!
축하해!

MEMO

05 잘하고 있어

You're doing fine! 잘하고 있어!

A: I just started driving this month.

B: Really? You're doing fine.

　　A: 이번달에 운전을 시작했어. B: 정말? 잘하는데.

Way to go! 잘한다 잘해!

A: I won the spelling contest.

B: Way to go! You're pretty smart.

　　A: 철자맞추기 대회에서 일등했어. B: 잘했어! 넌 아주 똑똑하잖아.

I am happy for you 네가 잘돼서 나도 기쁘다

A: Tammy and I are going to get married.

B: Oh my God! That's so great! I'm so happy for you guys!

　　A: 태미하고 나하고 결혼할거야. B: 정말! 잘됐다! 너희들 잘돼 기뻐.

That's the spirit! 바로 그거야

A: My dad taught me never to give up.

B: That's the spirit. He was right.

　　A: 아버지가 나보고 절대 포기말라고 가르치셨어. B: 바로 그거야. 아버지가 옳아.

▶ That's the stuff
　바로 그거야, 잘했어
▶ That's the ticket
　바로 그거야, 안성맞춤이
　야, 진심이야

It's not that bad 괜찮은데

A: How is the food at the cafeteria?

B: It's not that bad.

　　A: 카페테리아 식사가 어때? B: 괜찮은데.

└ not bad는 꽤 괜찮다는 의
미

Good boy 잘했어

A: I cleaned up my room.

B: Good boy.

　　A: 방청소했어요. B: 잘했어.

▶ Be a good boy
　착하게 굴어

That was very smart 아주 현명했네

A: I decided to buy real estate a few years ago.

B: That was very smart.

A: 몇 년전에 부동산을 사기로 했어. B: 아주 현명했네.

I envy you 부럽네

A: I'm getting married.

B: I envy you.

A: 나 결혼해 . B: 부러워라.

I knew I could count on you 넌 믿음직해

A: I'll come over and help you out.

B: I knew I could count on you.

A: 가서 너 도와줄게. B: 넌 믿음직해.

▸ I have confidence in you
난 널 신뢰해

▸ I'm depending on you
난 널 의지하고 있어

You were great! 너 대단했어!

A: You were great!

B: It was nothing.

A: 너 대단했어! B: 별거 아닌데.

I'm impressed 인상적이야

A: I'm so impressed. You're so good at math.

B: Thank you.

A: 정말 인상적이야. 너 수학 정말 잘하네. B: 고마워.

▸ Everyone was really impressed
사람들이 모두 정말 감동했어

Give me five 손바닥 부딪히자

A: Our team won the soccer game.

B: Awesome. Give me five!

A: 우리 축구팀이 이겼어. B: 멋져라. 손바닥 부딪히자!

▸ It gets two thumbs up
최고야

Attaboy! 야 잘했다!

A: I've been admitted to Harvard.

B: Attaboy! I knew you could get in!

A: 하버드에 입학됐어. B: 야 잘했다! 네가 들어갈 줄 알았어!

ㄴ 여성에게는 Attagirl!

06 한번 해봐

Give it a try! 한번 해봐!

A: Give it a try right now!

B: Okay, let's do it.

  A: 지금 당장 한번 해봐! B: 알았어, 한번 해 보자.

▸ Just try it!
  한번 해봐!
▸ Try it!
  해봐!
▸ Give it a whirl!
  해보라구!
▸ Try again! 다시 해봐!

Let's give it a try 한번 해보자

A: Do you think they'll agree to my plan?

B: Let's give it a try.

  A: 걔네들이 내 계획에 동의할 것 같아? B: 한번 해보자고.

Why don't you try it? 해보지 그래?, 한번 해봐

A: I'm not sure if this computer program will work.

B: Why don't you try it?

  A: 컴퓨터 프로그램이 작동될지 모르겠어. B: 한번 해보지 그래?

▸ Why don't
  you+V?
  …해봐

Go for it 한번 시도해봐

A: Should I ask her out?

B: Yes, go for it.

  A: 걔한테 데이트 신청해야 될까? B: 그래, 한번 해봐.

▸ Let's go for it
  한번 시도해보자

Give it a shot 한번 해봐

A: I don't think I can finish this tonight.

B: Give it a shot. Maybe you can.

  A: 오늘 밤까지 이걸 못 끝낼 것 같아. B: 한번 해봐. 아마 할 수 있을 거야.

▸ Let's give it a shot
  한번 해보자
▸ Let me have a
  shot at it
  내가 한번 해볼게

It can't[won't] hurt to try 한번 해본다고 해서 나쁠 건 없지

A: Should I go up to her and ask her out?

B: Go ahead! It won't hurt to try.

  A: 걔한테가서 데이트신청할까? B: 해봐! 손해볼 것 없잖아.

▸ It wouldn't hurt
  해본다고 나쁠 건 없어

It doesn't hurt to ask 물어본다고 손해볼 것 없어, 그냥 한번 물어본 거예요

A: The teacher might not know the answer.

B: It doesn't hurt to ask.

A: 선생님도 그 해답을 모를 수 있어. B: 물어봐야 손해볼 것 없잖아.

You've got nothing to lose 밑져야 본전인데 뭐

A: Should I apply to Harvard University?

B: Sure. You've got nothing to lose.

A: 하버드대에 지원해야 할까? B: 그럼. 밑져야 본전인데 뭐.

▶ Nothing to lose
밑질 거 없지

I will try my luck (되든 안되든) 한번 해봐야겠어

A: I don't think Donna will go on a date with you.

B: Don't worry. I'll try my luck.

A: 도나는 너하고 데이트 안할걸. B: 걱정마. 한번 해볼 테니까.

Get started 시작해봐

A: Mom said I have to clean my room.

B: Get started. That way you will finish faster.

A: 엄마가 내 방을 치우래. B: 시작해. 그래야 빨리 끝내지.

You can do it 넌 할 수 있어

A: I'm so nervous about the race next week.

B: Hey, don't worry about it. You can do it!

A: 담주에 열리는 경주 때문에 너무 긴장돼. B: 이봐, 걱정하지 말라구. 넌 잘 할 수 있어!

▶ If you try, you can do it
노력하면 넌 할 수 있어

You can do anything if you really want to
네가 진정 원한다면 뭐든 다 할 수 있어

A: Do you think you can become a doctor?

B: Yes. You can do anything if you really want to.

A: 네가 의사가 될 수 있을거라고 생각해? B: 그럼. 진정 원하면 뭐든 다 할 수 있어.

Get it together! 잘해봐!

A: I can't do it, I can't!

B: Get it together Jim! A: 난 못해, 못한다고! B: 잘해봐 짐!

↳ get it together의 의미는 'to be organized and successful in your life, job etc.'이다.

07 계속 해

Keep going! 계속 해!

A: I don't think I can finish this race.

B: Keep going! It's just one more kilometer.

A: 이 경주를 마칠 수 있을 지 모르겠어. B: 계속 해! 1킬로만 더 가면 돼.

▶ Keep going like this
지금처럼 계속해
▶ Get going
계속해

Let's keep going 자 계속하자

A: Shall we take a break now?

B: No, let's keep going.

A: 지금 잠시 좀 쉴까? B: 아니, 계속하자.

Keep talking 계속 이야기해봐

A: Are you interested in the deal I just offered?

B: Maybe. Keep talking.

A: 내가 방금 제시한 건에 관심있어? B: 그럴 수도 있어. 계속 이야기해봐.

Keep (on) trying 계속 정진해, 멈추지 말고 계속 노력해

A: These math problems are too difficult.

B: Keep on trying. You'll learn them.

A: 이 수학 문제들은 넘 어려워. B: 계속 노력해봐. 배우게 될거야.

Carry on 계속해

A: We need a few more hours to finish this work, sir.

B: Well, carry on.

A: 이 일을 끝내려면 몇시간 더 있어야 돼요. B: 그래, 계속하라고.

Go on (어서) 계속해

A: Can I have permission to go to the store?

B: Yes, but hurry back. Go on!

A: 가게에 가도 되나요? B: 그래, 하지만 빨리 돌아와. 자 어서 가!

Get on with it 제대로 계속해봐

A: I'm not feeling well today.
B: You've still got to work. Get on with it!

A: 오늘 몸이 좋지 않아. B: 아직 일해야 돼. 계속하라고!

Keep it up 계속 열심히 해

A: You're doing great. Keep it up!
B: Thanks a lot for noticing all my hard work.

A: 아주 잘 하고 있어. 계속 열심히 해! B: 열심히 하고 있는 걸 알아주니 아주 고마운데.

▸ Keep at it
열심히 해

Keep up the good work 계속 열심히 해, 계속 잘 하렴

A: Our department won an award for excellence.
B: Great! Keep up the good work.

A: 우리 부서가 우수상을 받았어. B: 잘됐네! 계속 잘하라고.

Do your best! 최선을 다해!

A: I don't think I can get this job done by tomorrow.
B: Cut the crap! Do your best!

A: 내일까지 이 일을 못 끝낼 것 같아요. B: 잡소리치워! 최선을 다하라고!

There's a chance 기회가 있어

A: Do you think she'd go out with me?
B: There's a chance. Ask her.

A: 걔가 나하고 데이트할 것 같아? B: 그럴 수 있지. 시도해봐.

▸ There's a
possibility
가능성이 있어

A: Is it supposed to snow tonight?
B: There's a possibility it will.

A: 오늘 밤에 눈이 온대? B: 그럴 수도 있대.

Try harder next time! 다음 번엔 더 열심히 해!

A: I can't believe my team lost the baseball game.
B: You've got to try harder next time.

A: 우리 야구팀이 지다니 말도 안돼. B: 다음 번에 더 열심히 하라고.

08 아직 포기하지마!

Don't give up (yet)! (아직) 포기하지마!

A: I'm afraid that I can't solve the problem.

B: Don't give up. There has to be a solution to it.

A: 그 문제를 해결할 수 없을 것 같아. B: 포기마. 분명 답이 있을거야.

▸ Never give up!
절대 포기하지 마
▸ Don't quit trying
포기하지 마

Don't give up too easily 너무 쉽게 포기하지마

A: I can't find a good job.

B: Don't give up too easily.

A: 괜찮은 직장을 못 찾겠어. B: 너무 쉽게 포기하지마.

▸ You (always) give
up too easily
넌 (늘) 너무 쉽게 포기하더라

Cheer up! 기운 내!, 힘내!

A: Cheer up! You look so sad.

B: I just lost my job.

A: 힘 좀 내봐! 너 정말 슬퍼보여. B: 방금 직장을 잃었어.

Get your act together 기운 차려

A: These grades are terrible. Get your act together.

B: I'm doing the best I can.

A: 성적이 엉망이야. 힘 좀 내라고. B: 최선을 다하고 있어요.

Pull yourself together 기운 내, 똑바로 잘해

A: Without him in my life, I don't want to live.

B: Pull yourself together. There are other men.

A: 그이가 없인 살고 싶지 않아. B: 기운 내. 다른 남자들도 있잖아.

Hang in there 끝까지 버텨

A: I don't think I can run around the track another time.

B: Hang in there! Just one more lap.

A: 한 바퀴도 더는 못 뛰겠어. B: 끝까지 해봐! 딱 한 바퀴만 더 뛰면 돼.

Stick with it 포기하지마, 계속해

A: I don't really like dental school.

B: Stick with it. It's a good career.

A: 치대는 정말 싫어. B: 포기하지마. 좋은 직업인데.

Never say die! 기운내!, 약한 소리하지마!

A: We'll beat this team. Never say die!

B: You're a big fan of the Korean soccer team.

A: 우린 이 팀을 물리칠거야. 약한 소리 하지마! B: 한국 축구팀을 무척 좋아하는구나.

Keep your chin up 힘 좀 내

A: I had a terrible day today.

B: Keep your chin up. Tomorrow will be better.

A: 오늘은 악몽과 같은 날이야. B: 기운 내. 내일은 좋아질거야.

Be positive 긍정적으로 생각해

A: You'll have a good job interview. Be positive.

B: Thanks. I'll do my best.

A: 면접을 잘 볼거야. 긍정적으로 생각해. B: 고마워. 최선을 다할게.

▸ Look on(at) the bright side
밝은 면을 보라고

You go back out there 다시 뛰어야지

A: I think I hurt my ankle.

B: You go back out there and finish the soccer game.

A: 발목이 다친 것 같아요. B: 다시 나가서 축구경기를 마쳐라.

▸ You gotta get back in the game
다시 뛰어야지, 다시 한번 싸워야지

It's not impossible 불가능한 일은 아니지

A: Do you think I can get rich by the time I'm forty?

B: Maybe. It's not impossible.

A: 내가 40에 부자가 될 수 있을까? B: 아마도. 불가능한 일은 아니지.

Don't lose your nerve 자신없어 하지마

A: I feel like giving up.

B: Don't lose your nerve. You can do it.

A: 포기하고 싶어. B: 기운차려. 넌 할 수 있어.

▸ Don't chicken out
겁먹고 물러서지 마
▸ Don't be a chicken[coward]
겁먹지 말라고

09 미안해

I'm (terribly) sorry (정말) 미안해

A: I am so sorry.

B: That's all right. I forgive you.

> A: 정말 죄송해요. B: 괜찮아요. 용서해드리죠.

▶ I'm so sorry!
정말 미안해!
▶ Oh, sorry
어, 미안
▶ Oops, so sorry
아이구, 미안해라

I'm sorry about that 미안해

A: I'm so upset that you forgot our anniversary.

B: Sorry about that. I won't let it happen again.

> A: 네가 기념일을 잊어버려 너무 속상해. B: 미안해. 다신 그런 일 없을거야.

▶ I'm sorry about
the other day
요전날 미안했어.

(I'm) Sorry for the inconvenience 불편하게 해서 미안해

A: Sorry for the confusion. I won't let it happen again.

B: Let's hope not.

> A: 혼란끼쳐서 미안. 다신 안그럴게. B: 안그러길 바래.

ㄴ 미안하게 된 원인을 말하
려면 I'm sorry for 다음에 명
사 혹은 동사의 ing를 붙이면
된다.

I'm sorry to trouble you 귀찮게 해서 미안해

A: I'm sorry to trouble you, but can I have a little time to talk?

B: Sorry. I'm so tied up right now.

> A: 귀찮게 해서 미안하지만 얘기할 시간 좀 있어? B: 미안. 지금 너무 바빠서 꼼짝달싹 못해.

I'm sorry if I caused any trouble 말썽피웠다면 미안해

A: I'm sorry if I caused any trouble.

B: Don't worry. You were a little drunk.

> A: 말썽피웠다면 미안해. B: 걱정마. 너 좀 취했었어.

ㄴ I'm sorry 다음에 (that) 절
혹은 if 절 등을 붙여 미안한
내용을 말해도 된다.
▶ I'm sorry it slipped
my mind
깜박해서 미안해

You can't believe how sorry I am 내가 얼마나 미안한지 모를거야

A: You can't believe how sorry I am.

B: That's okay. Your brother is the one I'm mad at.

> A: 내가 얼마나 미안한지 모를거야. B: 괜찮아. 네 형때문에 화낸건데.

I can't tell you how sorry I am 얼마나 미안한지 말로 할 수도 없어

A: I can't tell you how sorry I am.

B: That's all right. It's a common mistake.

A: 얼마나 미안한지 모르겠어. B: 괜찮아. 다들 하는 실수인데.

Excuse me 미안해

A: Excuse me for interrupting, but are you Jim Black?

B: As a matter of fact, I am.

A: 실례지만, 짐 블랙 씨인가요? B: 그렇죠, 나예요.

ㄴ. 역시 미안해하는 내용은 Excuse me for~ 이하에 말하면 된다.

I just want to apologize for that 내 사과할게요

A: What're you doing here?

B: I came to apologize for what I said yesterday.

A: 너 여기 무슨 일이야? B: 어제 한 말을 사과하려고 왔어.

I don't know how to apologize to you 뭐라 사과해야 할지 모르겠네요

A: It's all my fault. I don't know how to apologize to you.

B: Just get out of my face right now!

A: 다 내 실수예요. 뭐라 사과해야 할지. B: 지금 당장 꺼지라고!

▸ I have no words to apologize to you
뭐라 사과해야 할지 모르겠어요

Please accept my sincere apologies 진심어린 사과를 드립니다

A: Please accept my sincere apologies.

B: Your apology is accepted.

A: 제발 내 진심어린 사과를 받아줘요. B: 다 용서했어요.

▸ I accept your apology
용서했어요

Please forgive me 용서해줘

A: Please forgive me.

B: Why should I?

A: 제발 날 용서해줘요. B: 왜 그래야 하죠?

Chapter 02

10 내 잘못이야

It was my mistake   내 잘못이야

A: Who forgot to turn on the alarm?

B: Oops. My mistake.

  A: 누가 자명종 켜놓는 걸 잊어버린 거야? B: 아이고. 내 잘못이야.

▸ My mistake
  내 잘못이야
▸ Oops. My mistake
  아이고. 내 실수

I made a mistake   내가 실수했어

A: You shouldn't have hit him.

B: Right. I made a mistake.

  A: 걔를 때리지 말았어야지. B: 맞어. 내가 실수했어

It was a simple mistake   단순한 실수였어

A: You ate my sandwich?

B: It was a simple mistake. It could happen to anyone.

  A: 내 샌드위치를 먹었다고요? B: 단순한 실수였어. 누구나 그럴 수 있는.

▸ It was a big[huge] mistake
  크나큰 실수였어

It is my fault   내 잘못이야

A: Sorry. It's my fault.

B: No, it isn't... it's mine.

  A: 미안해요. 내 탓이에요. B: 아녜요… 내 잘못인 걸요.

▸ That's my fault
  내 잘못이야
▸ (That's) My bad
  내가 잘못했어

This is all[totally] my fault   모두 내 잘못야

A: Why is this party so boring?

B: This is totally my fault. I should've planned better activities.

  A: 왜 이렇게 파티가 지루해? B: 모두가 내 잘못야. 더 신나게 놀도록 계획했어야 하는데.

I did it wrong   내가 잘못했어

A: Why isn't the computer working?

B: I tried to connect to the Internet, but I did it wrong.

  A: 컴퓨터가 왜 작동이 안되는거야? B: 인터넷 연결하다 잘못했어.

It was careless of me to do so 내가 그렇게 한 건 부주의한 거였어

A: You really hurt Susan's feelings.

B: I'm sorry. It was careless of me to do so.

   A: 수잔의 감정을 망쳐놨어. B: 미안. 내가 부주의해서 그랬네.

I went too far 너무 지나쳤어

A: You shouldn't have done that.

B: I know, I went too far.

   A: 그렇게 하면 안되는 거지. B: 알어, 내가 넘 지나쳤어.

I screwed up! 완전히 망했네!

A: Don't be sorry.

B: But I screwed up big time.

   A: 미안해 하지 말라구. B: 하지만 제가 큰 실수를 했는 걸요.

▶ sb screw up (sth)
  망치다, 실수하다

I blew it (기회 등을) 망쳤다, 날려버렸다

A: How did your job interview go?

B: I blew it. I did the stupidest thing.

   A: 면접 어떻게 됐어? B: 망쳤어. 아주 멍청한 짓을 저질렀다고.

A: How was your interview?

B: Terrible. I blew it.

   A: 면접 어떻게 됐어? B: 끔찍해. 망쳤어.

I guess I dropped the ball 큰 실수를 한 것 같아

A: Your boss is angry because you missed the sales meeting.

B: Oh no! I guess I dropped the ball.

   A: 네가 영업회의에 불참해서 사장이 화났어. B: 아이고 저런! 내가 큰 실수를 했구만.

I was way off (base) 내가 완전히 잘못 짚었네, 내 생각[행동]이 틀렸네

A: I'm sorry I called you lazy. I was way off base.

B: I accept your apology.

   A: 게으르다고 해서 미안. 내가 틀렸어. B: 사과를 받아줄게.

11 그러지 말았어야 했는데

I shouldn't have done that 그러지 말았어야 했는데

A: Why did you hide that information from me?

B: I shouldn't have done it.

    A: 나한테 왜 그 정보를 숨겼죠? B: 그러지 말았어야 했는데.

I shouldn't have said that 그렇게 말하는 게 아니었는데

A: And then you told Jerry he was ugly.

B: I shouldn't have said that.

    A: 그럼 네가 제리한테 못생겼다고 말했지. B: 그렇게 말하는 게 아니었는데.

A: Do you really hate my new hairstyle?

B: No. I shouldn't have said that.

    A: 내 머리 스타일이 정말 싫어? B: 아니. 그렇게 말하는 게 아니었는데.

I should have asked him 걔한테 물어봤어야 하는데

A: Tom would have given you a ride home yesterday.

B: I should have asked him.

    A: 어제 탐이 널 태워줄 수도 있었을텐데. B: 걔한테 물어봤어야 하는데.

I feel so guilty 정말 미안해 죽겠어

A: I forgot our anniversary. I feel so guilty.

B: Buy your wife some nice jewelry.

    A: 기념일을 잊었어. 미안해 죽을 지경야. B: 아내에게 멋진 보석 좀 사줘.

▶ How silly[clumsy;
stupid] of me!
내가 참 명청하기도 하지!

▶ I regret doing that
그렇게 안하는 건데

I wish I was dead (잘못을 저지르고 미안해서) 미안해 죽겠어

A: I wish I was dead.

B: Why are you so upset?

    A: 죽었으면 좋겠어. B: 왜 그렇게 어쩔줄 몰라하는거야?

A: I shouldn't have hurt her. I wish I was dead.

B: You need to apologize for the pain you caused.

    A: 걔를 아프게 하는게 아닌데. 미안해 죽겠어. B: 네가 입힌 상처에 대해 사과하라고.

Chapter 02

I wish it had never happened 그러지 않았더라면 좋았을텐데

A: Did you have a good wedding ceremony?

B: No, I wish it had never happened.

A: 결혼식 멋지게 했어? B: 아니. 안했더라면 좋았을텐데.

A: Do you still have pain from your car accident?

B: Every day. I wish it had never happened.

A: 차사고로 아직도 통증이 있어? B: 매일. 안일어났더라면 좋았을 텐데.

Please don't be offended 기분 상하지마

A: Do you like my shirt?

B: No, I don't. Please don't be offended.

A: 내 셔츠 맘에 들어? B: 아니, 맘에 안들어. 기분상하진 말고.

A: Why didn't you eat the food I gave you?

B: Please don't be offended, but I didn't like it much.

A: 내가 준 음식 왜 안먹었어? B: 기분상하지만, 별로 안 좋아해서.

I was too nervous 내가 너무 긴장했었어

A: Did you ask her to marry you?

B: I couldn't. I was too nervous.

A:걔한테 결혼하자고 했어? B: 그렇게 할 수가 없었어. 넘 긴장해서 말야.

I didn't mean any harm 해를 끼칠려고 한 건 아니야

A: You've made everyone in the office upset.

B: Sorry. I didn't mean any harm.

A: 네가 사무실 사람 모두를 당황케했어. B: 미안. 해를 끼칠려고 한 건 아닌데.

I didn't mean to cause you any trouble 너를 곤란케 하려는 건 아니었어

A: I didn't mean to cause you any trouble.

B: Don't worry. I'll take care of it.

A: 너를 곤란케 하려는 건 아닌데. B: 걱정마. 내가 알아서 처리할게.

▸ I didn't mean to+V
…할 생각은 아니었다

I was only trying to be funny 난 단지 웃자고 한 거였는데

A: That was a stupid thing to say!

B: I was only trying to be funny.

> A: 한심하게 그런 말을 하나! B: 그냥 웃자고 한 말인데.

I didn't do it on purpose 일부러 그런 건 아니야

A: Your mistake cost me a lot of money.

B: I didn't do it on purpose.

> A: 네 실수 때문에 돈많이 까먹었어. B: 일부러 그런 건 아닌데.

▸ on purpose
일부러

I did it just for kicks 그냥 재미삼아 해본 건데

A: I heard you tried some illegal drugs.

B: Yeah, I did it just for kicks.

> A: 너 불법류의 약을 먹었다며. B: 어, 그냥 재미삼아 해본 거야.

▸ for kicks
재미삼아

No damage 손해본 건 없어

A: I'm sorry about the accident.

B: That's OK. No damage.

> A: 그 사고 안됐어. B: 괜찮어. 손핸본건 없어.

A: Excuse me. I didn't mean to bump you.

B: That's OK. No damage.

> A: 미안해요. 부딪힐려고 한게 아닌데요. B: 괜찮아요. 아무렇지도 않은데요.

No harm (done) 잘못된 거 없어

A: Did you hurt yourself when you fell?

B: No harm done.

> A: 넘어질 때 다쳤어? B: 다친데 없어요.

What's the harm? 손해볼 게 뭐야?

A: I'm just going to borrow her necklace. What's the harm?

B: You might lose it.

> A: 걔목걸이 빌릴려고. 손해볼 게 뭐야? B: 잃어버릴 수도 있잖아.

A: I don't think you should drink alcohol tonight.

B: Why not? What's the harm? A: 오늘 밤 술 마시지마라. B: 왜 안돼? 뭐 나쁘게 될 게 있어?

12 다신 그런 일 없을거야

I won't let it happen again 다신 그런 일 없을 거야

A: How could you do something like that?

B: I promise I won't let it happen again.

A: 어떻게 그럴 수가 있죠? B: 다신 그런 일 없을 거예요. 약속해요.

▸ I'll see it doesn't
happen again
다신 그러지 않도록 조심할
게요

▸ I'll try to be more
careful
더 조심하도록 노력할게

It won't happen again 이런 일 다시는 없을거야

A: How can I be sure?

B: Because I promise you it won't happen again.

A: 그걸 어떻게 믿죠? B: 다신 안 그러겠다고 약속했으니까요.

▸ It'll never happen
again
다시는 이런 일 없을 거야

▸ (I swear) I won't
do it again, I
promise
다시는 안 그러겠다고 맹세
할게, 믿어줘.

I take the blame 내가 책임질게

A: Who scratched my new car?

B: It was my fault. I take the blame.

A: 내 새차를 누가 긁은거야? B: 내 실수야. 내가 책임질게.

I have no excuses 변명의 여지가 없어

A: Why did you fail your exam?

B: I should have studied harder. I have no excuses.

A: 시험에 왜 떨어졌어? B: 더 열심히 했어야 했는데. 변명의 여지가 없어.

▸ That's no excuse
그건 변명이 안돼

I want to try to make it up to you 내가 다 보상해줄게

A: What can I do to make it up to you?

B: Nothing, just don't do it again.

A: 어떻게 하면 이 실수를 만회할 수 있을까요? B: 아무것도 필요없어요. 다시 그러지 않기만
하면 돼요.

▸ I[We] will make it
up to you
내[우리]가 다 보상할게

▸ I'll try to make it
up to you
보상하도록 할게

13 다 그런거지 뭐

That's (just) the way it is[goes] 다 그런 거지 뭐. 어쩔 수 없는 일이야

A: I'm always short of money. I've had it!

B: Take it easy! That's the way it goes.

   A: 항상 돈이 부족하단 말야. 지겨워라! B: 진정해! 다 그런거지 뭐.

That's the way the cookie crumbles 사는 게 다 그런거지

A: I can't believe my husband's cheating on me again!

B: Get real. That's the way the cookies crumbles.

   A: 남편이 다시 바람필 줄이야! B: 현실을 직시해. 다 그런거야.

▶ That's the way the ball bounces
  사는 게 다 그런거야

That's life 사는 게 그렇지

A: I'm sorry to hear that you got fired.

B: It's so frustrating, but that's life.

   A: 너 잘렸다며 안됐다. B: 죽을 맛이지만 사는 게 그런거잖아.

▶ Such is life!
  그런 게 인생이야

That happens[happened] 그럴 수도 있지. 그런 일도 있기 마련이지

A: Don't worry about that. That happens.

B: It's happened to you?

   A: 걱정마. 그럴 수도 있지 뭐. B: 너도 그런 적 있어?

▶ It happens
  그럴 수도 있지 뭐
▶ It happens to everybody[lots of people]
  누구에게나 그럴 수 있어

Those[These] things happen 그런 일도 생기기 마련이야

A: Sorry. I forgot to tell you that your manager called you.

B: It's okay, these things happen.

   미안. 부장이 전화한 걸 깜박했네. 괜찮어, 그럴 수도 있지.

▶ Shit happens
  (살다보면) 재수없는 일도 생기는 법이야

It could happen 그럴 수도 있겠지

A: I feel like an idiot.

B: It could happen to anyone.

   A: 바보가 된 기분이야. B: 누구한테나 다 그럴 수 있어.

▶ It could happen to anyone
  누구나 그럴 수 있어

I don't blame you   그럴 만도 해. 네가 어쩔 수 없었잖아

A: I'm so sorry that I hit your car.

B: I don't blame you. It was just an accident.

　A: 당신 차를 박아서 정말 미안합니다.　B: 어쩔 수 없죠. 그냥 사고였는걸요.

Don't blame yourself   너무 자책하지마

A: It's all my fault.

B: Don't blame yourself.

　A: 모든 게 다 내 잘못이야.　B: 너무 자책하지마.

It's not your fault   네 잘못이 아니야

A: You don't have to say sorry. It's not your fault.

B: It's very nice of you to say so.

　A: 미안해하지마. 네 잘못이 아냐.　B: 그렇게 말해줘서 정말 고마워.

Everyone makes mistakes now and then   누구나 때때로 실수하는거야

A: I shouldn't have talked about your ex-wife.

B: It's okay. Everyone makes mistakes now and then.

　A: 네 전 부인에 대한 말하지 말 걸.　B: 괜찮아. 다 때때로 실수하잖아.

▶ It's a common mistake
그건 누구나 하는 실수인데

▶ You have to expect a lot of ups and downs
좋을 때도 있고 안 좋을 때도 있는거야

It could[might] have been worse   그나마 다행이야

A: Was your house damaged by the storm?

B: A little. It could have been worse.

　A: 폭풍으로 집피해를 입었어?　B: 조금. 그나마 다행이야.

Win a few, lose a few   얻는 게 있으면 잃는 것도 있어

A: You don't seem upset about your divorce.

B: Oh well. Win a few, lose a few.

　A: 너 이혼하고도 괜찮은 것 같아.　B: 어, 그래. 얻는 게 있으면 잃는 것도 있는 셈이잖아.

That was a close call   하마터면 큰일날 뻔했네. 위험천만이었어

A: My wife almost caught me cheating.

B: That was a close call. Why don't you stop that!

　A: 바람피다 들킬뻔했어.　B: 아슬아슬했구만! 그만 좀 해라!

14 걱정마

Don't worry 걱정마. 미안해할 것 없어

A: I have to admit that it's pretty tough.

B: Don't worry. Things'll get easier.

  A: 정말이지 쉽지 않네요. B: 걱정하지마요. 점점 쉬워질거예요.

Don't worry about it 걱정마. 잘 될 거야

A: Oh my God! How could I have done that?

B: Don't worry about it.

  A: 어머나, 세상에! 내가 왜 그랬을까? B: 걱정하지마.

Not to worry 걱정 안해도 돼

A: Don't forget to wear a suit.

B: Not to worry, I won't.

  A: 정장 입고 오는 거 잊지 마세요. B: 걱정마세요. 잊지 않을테니까요.

▸ You don't have to worry
  걱정하지 마

There's nothing to worry about 걱정할 것 하나도 없어

A: Is everything taken care of?

B: It is. There's nothing to worry about.

  A: 다 잘 처리된거야? B: 어. 걱정 안 해도 돼.

▸ There's no need to worry about it
  걱정할 필요없어

That's all right 괜찮아

A: I'm sorry, I'm late again.

B: That's all right.

  A: 미안해, 또 늦었네. B: 괜찮아.

▸ It's all right
  괜찮아

It's[That's] okay 괜찮아

A: Hey! Sorry I kept you waiting so long.

B: That's okay. So, where do you want to go?

  A: 야, 오래 기다리게 해서 미안해. B: 괜찮아. 그래 어디 갈래?

No problem 문제 없어

A: I'm terribly sorry.

B: Hey, no problem.

   A: 정말이지 미안해. B: 야, 괜찮아.

▸ have no problem ~ing
…하는데 문제없어

Never mind 신경쓰지 마. 맘에 두지마

A: How can I make it up to you?

B: Never mind... just pay for the damages.

   A: 어떻게 보상해드리면 될까요? B: 걱정마시고… 손해배상만 하세요.

▸ Never mind that S+V
…을 신경쓰지마

That's[It's] no big deal 별거 아냐

A: Sorry about that.

B: Don't worry! It's no big deal.

   A: 그거 정말 유감이야. B: 걱정 매 별거 아냐.

▸ No biggie (= No big deal)
별거 아냐

What's the big deal? 별거 아니네?. 무슨 큰 일이라도 있는 거야?

A: You should be ashamed of cheating on your exam.

B: What's the big deal? A lot of students do it.

   A: 컨닝한 걸 수치스러워 해야지. B: 뭘 그런걸 갖고? 학생들 많이 그래.

It was nothing 별거 아닌데

A: Thank you so much for saving my son's life.

B: It was nothing. I was just doing my job.

   A: 아들 생명을 구해줘 정말 감사해요. B: 뭘요. 그저 제 할 일을 한거죠.

▸ This is nothing
별거 아니야
▸ Don't take it too seriously
너무 심각하게 받아들이지마

Don't be sorry 미안해 하지마

A: You don't have to say you're sorry.

B: Sure I do. It was all my fault.

   A: 미안하단 말은 할 필요 없어요. B: 어떻게 그래요. 이게 다 제 잘못인데.

▸ You don't have to say you're sorry
미안해 할 필요없어

Don't sweat it! (별일 아니니) 걱정하지 마라

A: I don't know what to do about it.

B: Okay, don't sweat it.

   A: 어떻게 해야 할지 모르겠어. B: 괜찮아, 별거 아냐.

15 그냥 잊어버려

Let it go 그냥 잊어버려, 그냥 놔둬

A: Would you let it go? It's not that big a deal.

B: Not that big a deal? You lied to me!

A: 그냥 잊어버려. 별일 아니야. B: 별일 아니라고? 너 나한테 거짓말했지!

▶ Would you let it go?
잊어버려요

Forget (about) it! 잊어버려, 됐어

A: I'm really sorry I stood you up on Friday.

B: Never mind, forget it.

A: 금요일날 바람 맞혀서 정말 미안해. B: 신경쓰지 마, 잊어버리라구.

Don't give it a second thought 걱정하지마

A: I'm sorry I've taken so much of your time.

B: Don't give it a second thought. Glad we sorted out the problem.

A: 시간을 너무 많이 뺏어서 미안해. B: 걱정마. 문제해결해서 기쁜걸.

Don't give it another thought 잊어버려

A: How can I ever repay you?

B: Don't give it another thought.

A: 어떻게 다 보답을 해야할지? B: 잊어버리세요.

Don't think about it anymore 더 이상 그것에 대해 생각하지마

A: I shouldn't have told that dirty joke to her.

B: Don't think about it anymore. She seemed to like it.

A: 걔한데 그런 야한 농담을 하지 않는건데. B: 그만 생각해. 걔도 좋아하는 것 같던데.

Don't be so hard on yourself 너무 자책하지마

A: I'll always be a failure!

B: Don't be so hard on yourself.

A: 난 항상 실패자가 될거야! B: 너무 자학하지마.

▶ be hard on sb
…을 심하게 대하다

Don't let it bother you 너무 신경 쓰지마!

A: Don't let it bother you.

B: It's easier said than done.

  A: 그딴 일로 신경쓸 필요없어. B: 말이야 쉽지.

Don't let sb[sth] get you down 그것[그 사람] 때문에 괴로워하지마

A: I heard you got divorced. Don't let it get you down.

B: That's easy for you to say. I've been divorced three times.

  A: 이혼했다며. 넘 상심마. B: 말하긴쉽지. 나 세번째 이혼야.

▸ let sb down
실망시키다

Don't feel so bad about it 너무 속상해하지마

A: I can't believe she slapped me in the face.

B: Don't feel so bad about it. You asked for it.

  A: 걔가 내 뺨을 때리다니 말도 안돼. B: 넘 기분나빠하지마. 네가 자초했잖아.

A: I wasn't able to get into Seoul National University.

B: Don't feel so bad about it. You can get into Korea University or Yonsei.

  A: 서울대에 못들어갔어. B: 넘 기분나빠하지마. 고려대나 연세대 들어가면 되잖아.

You must be very upset (about~) (…에 대해서) 정말 화나겠어

A: I didn't get the promotion.

B: You must be very upset about that.

  A: 승진을 하지 못했어. B: 그렇다니 정말 화나겠구만.

▸ You must be so
upset
정말 화나겠구만

Stop torturing yourself 자학하지마

A: I should have never broken up with her.

B: Stop torturing yourself.

  A: 걔하고 헤어지지 말았어야 하는건데. B: 그만 자책해.

▸ Stop beating
yourself up!
그만 자책해라!

Let's let bygones be bygones 지나간 일은 잊자고

A: Let's let bygones be bygones.

B: OK, we should try to be friends.

  A: 지나간 일을 다 잊자고. B: 그래, 친구가 되도록 노력하자고.

▸ It's no use crying
over split milk
엎지른 물을 다시 담을 수
없어

16 안됐구나

I'm sorry to hear that 안됐네

A: I'm very sorry to hear that you lost your job.

B: Maybe it's for the best anyway.

> A: 실직소식을 듣게 돼 매우 유감이야. B: 차라리 잘된 일인지도 몰라.

I'm sorry about that 안됐어

A: I'm getting a divorce again!

B: I'm sorry about that.

> A: 나 또 이혼해! B: 안됐네.

A: I lost my grandfather last week.

B: I'm sorry about that.

> A: 지난주에 할아버지가 돌아가셨어. B: 안됐네.

That's too bad 저런, 안됐네, 이를 어쩌나

A: We missed winning the lottery by one number.

B: That's too bad.

> A: 숫자 하나 차이로 복권에 안됐어. B: 참 안됐네.

What a pity! 그것 참 안됐구나!

A: I just missed him.

B: What a pity!

> A: 방금 그 남자를 놓쳤어요. B: 저런!

▸ That's a pity!
참 안됐네!

What a shame! 안됐구나!

A: Sara crashed her car and is in the hospital.

B: What a shame.

> A: 새러가 차사고나서 병원에 입원했어. B: 안됐네.

▸ What a shame if S+V!
…하다니 안됐구나!

Chapter 02

I know just how you feel 어떤 심정인지 알겠어

A: I know how you feel. My dog died last month.

B: I didn't think I'd be so upset.

A: 네 심정 이해해. 우리 개도 지난달에 죽었거든. B: 내가 그렇게까지 마음 아플 줄이라고는 생각 못했어.

I know the feeling 그 심정 내 알지

A: I'm pretty busy with school.

B: I know the feeling!

A: 학교 다니느라 무척 바빠. B: 알만 해!

That hurts 그거 안됐네, 마음이 아프겠구나

A: You're getting fat, my friend.

B: Hey, that hurts. You should be nicer.

A: 너 살쪘구나, 친구야. B: 야, 그 말 들으니 맘이 아파. 좀 더 착해져라.

You poor thing 안됐구나

A: Mona got fired this morning.

B: Oh, poor thing.

A: 오늘 아침에 모나가 잘렸어. B: 아, 가엾어라.

▶ Oh, poor thing!
가엾은 거!
▶ Ah, poor Jim!
아, 가엾은 짐!

It must be tough for you 참 어려웠겠구나

A: My husband and I decided to separate.

B: It must be tough for you.

A: 남편하고 별거하기로 했어. B: 힘들겠구만.

▶ Tough luck
참 운도 없네
▶ That's unfortunate
운이 없구만

How awful 참 안됐다

A: I can't afford to pay my rent this month.

B: How awful. What will you do?

A: 이번 달 월세를 낼 돈이 없어. B: 안됐구만. 어떻게 할 건대?

My heart goes out to you 진심으로 위로의 마음을 전합니다

A: My heart goes out to you.

B: I was really hoping that I'd get that promotion.

A: 진심으로 위로의 말을 전하겠습니다. B: 정말이지 승진 기대했었거든요.

You have all my sympathy 진심으로 유감의 말씀을 드립니다

A: You have all my sympathy.

B: I can't believe they fired me for something I didn't do.

진심으로 유감의 말씀을 드립니다. 내가 하지도 않은 일로 해고하다니!

▸ I really sympathize with you

진심으로 위로의 말을 전합니다

MEMO

17 다 잘 될거야

Everything's going to be all right 다 잘 될거야

A: How can this be happening? What're we going to do?

B: It's all right! Everything's going to be all right.

　A: 어떻게 이런 일이? 어쩌지? B: 괜찮아! 다 잘 될거야.

ㄴ 단독으로 All right은 그래, 알았어, 좋아

Everything will be fine 모든게 잘 될거야

A: Do you think I'll get a job this year?

B: Sure. Everything will be fine.

　A: 금년엔 내가 취직될 것 같아? B: 그럼. 다 잘 될거야.

She's going to be all right 걘 괜찮을거야

A: Is she gonna be all right?

B: I don't think so. Her mother's suffering from diabetes.

　A: 걔가 괜찮을까? B: 안 그럴걸. 걔 엄마가 당뇨병이잖아.

It's going to be all right 그건 괜찮을거야

A: I'm so worried about my wedding ceremony.

B: You're just nervous. It's going to be alright.

　A: 내 결혼식이 걱정 많이 돼. B: 단지 긴장되는거지. 괜찮을거야.

A: I'm really nervous about this test.

B: Don't worry. It's going to be alright.

　A: 이번 시험이 정말 걱정돼. B: 걱정마. 괜찮을거야.

It's going to be okay 잘 될거야, 괜찮을거야

A: I don't know if I can do it.

B: It's going to be okay.

　A: 내가 그걸 할 수 있을지 모르겠어. B: 잘 될거야.

A: Do you think we can pay for everything?

B: Sure. It's going to be okay. A: 돈을 다 지불할 수 있을까? B: 그럼. 잘 될거야.

Things will work out all right 잘 해결될거야

A: I don't know what to do.
B: I'm sure it'll work out.

> A: 뭘 어떻게 해야 할지 모르겠어. B: 잘 해결될거라고 확신해.

A: Jack and Cindy are always fighting.
B: Some couples do that. Things will work out all right.

> A: 잭하고 신디는 늘상 싸워. B: 그런 커플들이 있지. 잘 될거야.

It's going to get better 더 잘 될거야

A: I'm not sure I can keep working here.
B: Relax. It's going to get better.

> A: 내가 여기서 일을 계속 할지 잘 모르겠어. B: 진정해. 점점 더 나아질거야.

▸ get better
나아지다

You're going to be great 넌 잘 될거다

A: I'm really worried about my performance tonight.
B: Relax. You're going to be great.

> A: 오늘밤 공연이 많이 걱정돼. B: 진정해. 넌 잘할거야.

A: I don't know why I haven't been preparing for this.
B: Don't worry. You're going to be great.

> A: 내가 왜 이걸 준비못했는지 모르겠어. B: 걱정마. 넌 잘 될거야.

It's all for the best 앞으로 나아질거야

A: I just got fired today and I'm really pissed off.
B: It's all for the best. You can get a better job.

> A: 오늘 잘렸어. 왕짜증난다. B: 더 나아지려는 거야. 더 좋은 직장 갖게 될거야.

▸ I'm hoping for the best
잘 되길 빌고 있어

You never know 그야 모르잖아, 그야 알 수 없지

A: Do you think it will snow in October?
B: You never know. The weather has been odd lately.

> A: 10월에 눈이 올 것 같아? B: 모르지. 요즘 날씨 이상하잖아.

A: I think I won't be able to get a new job at Macy's.
B: You never know. Don't give up too easily.

> A: 메이시 백화점에 취직못할 것 같아. B: 그야 모르는 일이지. 넌 쉽게 포기하지마.

▸ You never know 주어+동사
···일지 누가 알아

You can never tell! 단정할 순 없지!

A: You're late again. You'll never get promoted.

B: You can never tell!

A: 또 지각야. 넌 승진못할거야. B: 그야 알 수 없는 일이지!

A: Is it possible for me to become rich by the time I'm thirty?

B: It would be difficult, but you can never tell.

A: 30살에 부자될 수 있을까? B: 어렵겠지만, 그야 알 수 없는 일이지.

Your time will come 좋은 때가 올거야

A: My boss never notices the hard work I do.

B: You'll be rewarded. Your time will come.

A: 사장은 내가 열심히 일하는 걸 몰라. B: 보상받을거야. 좋은 때가 올거야.

Tomorrow is another day 앞으로 나아질거야

A: I had a horrible fight with my mom.

B: Well, tomorrow is another day.

A: 엄마랑 대판 싸웠어. B: 그래, 앞으로 좋아지겠지.

Chapter 03

충고·불만

Step 1 충고
Step 2 불만
Step 3 싸움

01 진정해

Take it easy 좀 쉬어가면서 해, 진정해, 잘 지내

A: I don't think I can get through the night.
B: Just take it easy and try to relax.

A: 밤을 무사히 보낼 수 없을 것 같아. B: 걱정하지 말고 긴장을 풀어봐.

Calm down 진정해

A: I need you to pay attention. Do you hear me?
B: Yes! Calm down. I hear you.

A: 주목해봐. 내말 듣고 있니? B: 응! 진정해. 듣고 있어.

▸ Calm down and think carefully
진정하고 잘 생각해봐

Cool down[off] 진정해

A: Whoa! You saw my teacher's breasts?
B: I'll tell you about it later. Be cool.

A: 왜! 우리 선생님 가슴을 봤다고? B: 나중에 이야기해줄게. 진정하라고.

▸ Be[Keep] cool
진정해라
▸ Cool it
진정해, 침착해

Don't get[be] mad! 열받지 말라고!

A: I can't believe he humiliated me in front of everyone.
B: Don't get mad. He's just an asshole.

A: 걔가 다들 있는데서 날 모욕하다니. B: 화내지마. 못되먹은 놈이잖아.

▸ Don't get worked up
흥분하지마
▸ Don't get so uptight
그렇게 화내지말고

Don't be upset! 화내지 말고!

A: You got a problem with me?
B: Don't be upset. I didn't mean that.

A: 나한데 뭐 불만있어? B: 화내지마. 그럴려고 그런 게 아니야.

▸ Go get some rest
가서 좀 쉬어
▸ Just relax!
긴장풀고 천천히 해!

02 조심해

Watch out 조심해

A: Watch out! There's ice on the ground.

B: I'll be careful.

A: 조심해! 바닥에 얼음있어. B: 조심할게.

A: Watch it! This is dangerous place to cross the road.

B: Thanks. I don't want to be injured.

A: 조심해! 여긴 길을 건너기 위험한 곳이야. B: 고마워. 다치기 싫거든.

▸ Watch out for
him!
걔 조심해!
▸ Watch it!
조심해

Watch your step! 조심해!

A: Is it dangerous here?

B: Yes it is. Watch your step!

A: 여기 위험해? B: 어, 조심하라고!

ㄴ Watch your step은 넘어지지 않도록 조심하라는 의미뿐만 아니라 상대방에게 말이나 행동거지를 조심하라고 할 때도 쓰인다. 또한 Watch your back은 뒤(배신 등)를 조심하라는 표현.

Look out! 조심해!, 정신 차리라고!

A: Look out! The car almost hit you!

B: Wow! That was close!

A: 조심해! 차에 칠 뻔했잖아! B: 와! 아슬아슬했어!

(You) Be careful! 조심해!

A: Be careful! You almost crushed my hat!

B: Sorry.

A: 조심해! 내 모자를 밟을 뻔했어! B: 미안.

▸ Be careful of him
걔를 조심해

Heads up! 위험하니까 잘 보라구!

A: Here comes a baseball. Heads up!

B: That almost hit me!

A: 볼 날라온다. 잘 봐! B: 거의 맞을 뻔 했네!

▸ Behind you!
조심해!

Chapter 03

03 천천히해라 혹은 서둘러라

Easy does it 천천히 해, 조심조심, 진정해

A: Easy does it, don't drop the computer.

B: Don't worry. I won't.

A: 조심해. 컴퓨터 떨어트리지마. B: 걱정마. 안 그럴게.

▶ Easy, easy, easy!
천천히 조심조심!

Take your time 천천히 해

A: I'm sorry, I'm going to be a little late.

B: That's okay. Take your time.

A: 미안, 좀 늦을거야. B: 괜찮아. 천천히 와.

Hold your horses 서두르지마, 진정해

A: Where're you now? The kids are driving me nuts.

B: Hold your horses, honey. I'll be home in 30 minutes.

A: 어디야? 애들 땜에 미치겠어. B: 진정해. 30분 후에 도착해.

What's the[your] rush? 왜 이리 급해?

A: Hi, Joe! What's the rush?

B: I'm late for my doctor's appointment. I've gotta go now.

A: 안녕, 조! 왜 이리 급해? B: 병원예약시간에 늦었어. 가야돼.

▶ What's the hurry?
왜 그렇게 서둘러?
▶ Where's the fire?
왜 그렇게 서둘러?

There's[I'm] no hurry 서두를 것 없어, 급할 것 없어

A: When do you want it delivered?

B: There's no hurry.

A: 그걸 언제쯤 배달해 드리면 될까요? B: 급할 거 없어요.

▶ There's no need
to rush
서두를 필요없어

You don't need to hurry 서두르지 않아도 돼

A: You don't need to hurry.

B: I hate being late to work.

A: 서두르지 마. B: 지각하는 걸 싫어해.

▶ No rush[hurry]
급할 거 없어

Slow down 천천히 해

A: I've got to get this work done quickly.

B: Slow down. You're going to make mistakes.

A: 이 일을 빨리 끝내야 돼. B: 천천히 해. 실수하겠다.

▸ Haste makes
waste
서두르면 일을 망친다
▸ We still have a
long way to go
아직 가야할 길이 많아

Hurry up! 서둘러!

A: Just give me a few minutes to get ready.

B: Come on! Hurry up!

A: 준비할 동안 조금만 기다려 줘. B: 이봐! 서두르라구!

Step on it! 빨리 해. (자동차 엑셀레에터를) 더 밟아!

A: I haven't got all day. Step on it!

B: I'm trying my best.

A: 시간없어. 서둘러! B: 최선을 다하고 있다고.

I haven't got all day 여기서 이럴 시간 없어. 빨리 서둘러

A: The doctor can see you in an hour.

B: That's too long. I haven't got all day.

A: 한 시간 후에 의사선생님을 뵐 수 있어요. B: 너무 길어요. 나도 시간이 없는데.

Don't push (me)! 몰아 붙이지마!, 독촉하지마!

A: Stop being lazy. You need to study harder.

B: Don't push me. I'm doing my best.

A: 게으름피지마. 공부 더 열심히 해. B: 재촉마요. 최선을 다하고 있다고요.

Get a move on it! 서둘러!

A: Get a move on it!

B: I'm going as fast as I can.

A: 서둘러! B: 최대한 서두르고 있다고.

▸ I'd better get a
move on it
빨리 서둘러야겠어

Come on! 어서!, 그러지마!, 제발!, 자 덤벼!

A: Come on, or we're going to be late.

B: I'm coming as quickly as I can.

A: 서둘러, 안그러면 우린 늦는다구. B: 최대한 빨리 갈게.

04 정신차려라

Get a life! 정신차례!

A: Why don't you get a life?

B: Hey, I'm going to keep asking her until she says yes.

A: 정신 좀 차리지 그래? B: 걔가 좋다 할 때까지 계속 조를거야.

Get real! 정신 좀 차리라구!

A: I'm curious whether I'll get a raise next year.

B: Get real! You're an awful worker. I should fire you.

A: 내년엔 임금인상이 되는지 궁금하네요. B: 꿈깨! 넌 으악야. 널 해고해야 된다고.

Don't even think about it 꿈도 꾸지마, 절대 안되니까 헛된 생각하지마

A: I'm considering quitting my job.

B: Don't even think about it. We need the money.

A: 회사를 그만 둘까 생각중야. B: 꿈도 꾸지마. 돈있어야 살지.

▶ Don't you dare do that!
  그럴 꿈도 꾸지마!

A: Can I get a day off tomorrow?

B: Don't even think about it. We must get this job done.

A: 내일 쉬어도 될까요? B: 이 일을 끝낼 때까진 꿈도 꾸지마.

Act your age! 나이값 좀 해!

A: I want to eat some candy.

B: Act your age. Candy is for kids.

A: 캔디 좀 먹고 싶어. B: 철 좀 들어라. 애들이나 먹는 캔디를.

You have to grow up 철 좀 들어라

A: Why should I get a full-time job?

B: You have to grow up and act like an adult.

A: 왜 정규직에 들어가야 돼요? B: 철 좀 들어서 어른처럼 행동해라.

You can't have everything 너무 욕심내지마

A: I'd like to be rich, with a beautiful wife.

B: You can't have everything.

A: 부자고 되고 싶어 이쁜 아내도 얻고 싶어. B: 너무 욕심내지마.

Real life isn't that easy 사는 게 그렇게 쉽지는 않아

A: If only I could win the lottery.

B: Real life isn't that easy.

A: 로또에 당첨만 된다면 얼마나 좋을까. B: 사는 게 그렇게 쉬운건가.

You wish! 행여나!

A: I think you're in love with me.

B: You wish! I don't even like you.

A: 너 나 사랑하는 것 같아. B: 행여나! 난 널 싫어하는 걸.

A: I'm going to meet a rich guy tonight.

B: You wish!

A: 오늘 밤 돈많은 애를 만날거야. B: 행여나!

In your dreams! 꿈 깨셔!

A: I'm going to buy a BMW next year.

B: In your dreams!

A: 내년엔 BMW를 살거야. B: 꿈깨!

Dream on! 꿈 한번 야무지네!

A: Pamela is going to marry me someday.

B: No way. Dream on!

A: 파멜라가 언젠가 나랑 결혼할거래. B: 말도 안돼. 꿈 한번 야무지네!

Stop goofing off! 그만 좀 빈둥거려라!

A: Stop goofing off!

B: We were only taking a break.

A: 그만 좀 농땡이쳐! B: 좀 쉬고 있었을 뿐인데.

A: Stop goofing off!

B: Why? Is the boss coming? A: 그만 좀 농땡이쳐! B: 왜? 사장이 와?

▸ goof off
일할 시간에 농땡이치다
▸ goof around
빈둥거리다

05 한 번 더 생각해봐

Think twice before you do it 실행하기에 앞서 한번 더 생각해봐

A: I may quit this job.

B: Think twice before you do it.

> A: 회사 그만둘거야. B: 그러기 전에 한번 더 생각해봐.

▸ Think it over
carefully before
you decide
결정에 앞서 신중히 생각해
봐

You shouldn't be so quick to judge! 그렇게 섣불리 판단해선 안돼!

A: You shouldn't be so quick to judge!

B: I know, but she gave me a bad impression.

> A: 그렇게 섣불리 판단해선 안돼! B: 알아, 하지만 걔가 내게 나쁜 인상을 줬어.

You can't be too careful 아무리 조심해도 지나치지 않아

A: You can't be too careful.

B: That's true.

> A: 아무리 조심해도 지나치지 않아. B: 사실야.

(It's) Better safe than sorry 뒤늦게 후회하느니 조심해야지

A: You bought a lot of insurance.

B: It's better to be safe than sorry.

> A: 너 보험 많이 들었지. B: 나중에 후회하기 보다는 안전한 게 낫지.

Don't jump to conclusions! 섣부르게 판단하지마!

A: You're always late. You're dating other women!

B: Wait, don't jump to conclusions!

> A: 항상 늦네. 딴 애랑 데이트하지! B: 잠깐, 속단하지 말라고!

▸ Let's not jump the
gun
경솔하게 속단하지마

Don't count your chickens before they're hatched 김치국부터 마시지마

A: When I finish this book, I'll be famous worldwide.

B: Don't count your chickens before they're hatched.

  A: 이 책을 끝내면 세계적으로 유명해질거야. B: 김치국부터 마시지마.

Don't judge a book by its cover 겉만 보고 속을 판단하지마

A: Our new employee looks dishonest.

B: Don't judge a book by its cover.

  A: 신입사원이 부정직하게 보여. B: 겉만 보고 판단하지마.

▸ Never judge
something by its
looks
뭐든 외양만 갖고 판단하면
안돼

Don't fall for it (속아) 넘어가지마, 사랑에 빠지면 안돼

A: He promised to make me rich.

B: He's a liar. Don't fall for it.

  A: 걔가 나를 부자로 만들어준다고 했어. B: 걔 거짓말쟁이야. 속지마.

▸ fall for sb
사랑에 빠지다
▸ fall for sth
…에 넘어가다, 속다

Don't trust it 믿지마

A: The thermometer says it's cool outside.

B: Don't trust it. It's broken.

  A: 온도계를 보니 밖이 추운데. B: 그거 믿지마. 망가졌어.

▸ Don't be so
impatient
너무 조급해하지마
▸ He's better than
you think
걔는 네가 생각하는 거 이
상야

You'll be sorry 넌 후회하게 될거야

A: I'm going to loan Angel some money.

B: She won't pay it back. You'll be sorry.

  A: 엔젤에게 돈 좀 빌려줄거야. B: 걘 안 갚을거야. 후회할 걸.

▸ You'll regret it
넌 후회하게 될거야

You (just) wait and see 두고보라고

A: I'll bet you $10 you won't get an A.

B: You're on. I'll get an A, just wait and see.

  A: 난 네가 A를 못 받는 데 10달러 걸겠어. B: 좋아. 난 A를 받고 말거야. 두고 보라구.

We'll see 좀 보자고, 두고 봐야지

A: What do you want to do about it?

B: Let's just wait and see what happens.

  A: 그 일에 대해 어떻게 하고 싶니? B: 어떻게 되는지 일단 두고보자.

▸ You'll see
곧 알게 될 거야, 두고 보면
알아

06 말 조심해

Watch your tongue! 말 조심해!

A: Your mom is a bitch.

B: Watch your tongue, or I'll hit you.

　　A: 네 엄마 정말 못됐어. B: 말 조심해 아님 널 칠거야.

▶ Watch your
language[mouth]
말 조심해

Hold your tongue! 제발 그 입 좀 다물어!

A: I can't stand the boss. She sucks!

B: Hold your tongue! The walls have ears!

　　A: 더 이상 사장을 못참겠어. 아주 재주없어! B: 말 조심해! 낮말은 새가 듣고 밤말은 쥐가 듣는대잖아!

Bite your tongue 입 조심해

A: I don't like our boss.

B: Bite your tongue.

　　A: 우리 사장 싫더라. B: 입 조심해.

You've got a big mouth 너 참 입이 싸구나

A: I want to tell you some gossip.

B: You've got a big mouth.

　　A: 소문 좀 얘기해줄게. B: 너 참 입이 싸구나.

▶ He has got a big
mouth
입이 엄청 싸구만
▶ Big mouth!
입 한번 엄청 싸네!

Shut up! 닥쳐!

A: Tony! What're you doing?! You're smoking again?

B: Hey, shut up! You're not my real mom!

　　A: 토니! 뭐해?! 또 담배 펴? B: 야, 닥쳐! 네가 내 엄마라도 되는거야!!

▶ Shut your face!
입다물어

You talk too much 말이 너무 많네

A: You talk too much.

B: That's a very unkind thing to say.

　　A: 너 말 너무 많어. B: 그렇게 말해줘서 참 기분나쁘구만.

07 시간 낭비하지마

Don't waste your time 시간 낭비하지마, 시간낭비야

A: I want to meet you everyday.

B: Don't waste your time. I'm married!

A: 매일 널 보고 싶어. B: 시간 낭비하지마. 난 결혼했다고!

▶ waste one's time
…의 시간을 낭비하다

Don't waste my time 남의 귀한 시간 축내지마, 괜히 시간낭비 시키지 말라고

A: I'd like to sell you a suit today.

B: Don't waste my time.

A: 오늘 너한테 옷한벌 팔고 싶어. B: 귀한 내 시간 축내지마.

You're (just) wasting my time 시간낭비야, 내 시간 낭비마

A: This information is very important.

B: No, you're just wasting my time.

A: 이 정보는 매우 중요한거야. B: 아냐, 넌 내 시간만 축내고 있는거야.

It's a waste of time 시간낭비야

A: Have you seen that movie?

B: Yeah, it's a waste of time.

A: 그 영화 봤어? B: 어, 시간낭비야.

▶ What a waste of time and money!
시간과 돈 낭비야!

I don't like wasting my time 시간낭비하고 싶지 않아

A: Is that a yes or no? I don't like wasting my time.

B: Hold on, let me think it over.

A: 예스야 노야? 시간낭비하기 싫어. B: 잠깐, 생각할 시간 좀 줘.

It isn't worth it 그럴만한 가치가 없어, 그렇게 중요한 것도 아닌데

A: Why don't you and Adam start dating again?

B: He's too unkind. It isn't worth it.

A: 왜 아담하고 다시 사귀지 않는거야? B: 너무 무뚝뚝해. 사귈 필요없어.

▶ It isn't worth the trouble
괜히 번거롭기만 할거야

08 제대로 해라

Do it right 제대로 해

A: It's going to be difficult to build this house.

B: Take your time and do it right.

A: 이 집을 짓는 건 어려울거야. B: 시간을 갖고 제대로 해.

▶ Let's just do it right
제대로나 하자
▶ We can do it right!
우린 제대로 잘 할 수 있어!

Use your head! 머리를 좀 쓰라구! 생각이라는 걸 좀 해라!

A: I don't know how to do it.

B: Use your head. You can do it.

A: 어떻게 해야 할지 모르겠어. B: 머리를 쓰라고. 넌 할 수 있어.

Where's your head at? 머리는 어디다 둔거야?

A: I didn't study at all last night.

B: Where's your head at? You're going to fail this test.

A: 지난 밤에 공부 하나도 안했어. 머리는 어디다 둔거야? B: 이번 시험에 떨어지겠다.

You heard me 명심해, 내 말 알겠어?

A: Did you say you're leaving?

B: You heard me. I'm never coming back.

A: 네가 떠난다고 말한거야? B: 내가 말했잖아. 다시 안 돌아올거야.

└, 내 얘기를 들었으니 들은 대로 하라는 말

You'll get the hang of it 금방 손에 익을거야, 요령이 금방 붙을거야

A: really don't know how to use this program.

B: Don't worry. You'll get the hang of it.

A: 이 프로그램을 어떻게 쓰는지 몰라. B: 걱정마. 곧 익숙해질거야.

▶ get the hang of~
…에 익숙해지다

You'll get the knack of it 장차 요령이 붙을거야

A: I haven't learned to cook Korean food.

B: You'll get the knack of it.

A: 한국 음식 요리하는 법을 못배웠어. B: 앞으로 손에 익을거야.

▶ get the knack of~
…에 요령이 붙다

(There's) Nothing to it 아주 쉬워, 해보면 아무것도 아냐

A: Can you show me how to operate this computer?

B: Sure. There's nothing to it.

A: 이 컴퓨터 작동법을 알려줄테야? B: 물론. 해보면 아무것도 아냐.

A: You're such a great cook.

B: Thanks. There's nothing to it.

A: 너 참 훌륭한 요리사야. B: 고마워. 별것도 아닌데.

You have to get used to it 적응해야지

▸ I'm getting used to it
난 적응하고 있어

A: I can't stand this cold, wet weather.

B: I'm sorry, but you'd better get used to it.

A: 이렇게 춥고 습한 날씨는 견딜 수가 없어. B: 미안하지만 적응하라고.

A: How is your new apartment?

B: It's alright. I'm getting used to it.

A: 새 아파트 어때? B: 괜찮아. 적응해가고 있어.

Don't leave things half done 일을 하다 말면 안돼

A: Don't leave things half done.

B: I'll try to finish everything before I leave.

A: 일을 중간에 포기하면 안돼. B: 내가 가기 전에 다 끝낼거야.

You should finish what you start 시작한 건 끝내야지

A: Do I have to complete this report?

B: You should finish what you start.

A: 이 보고서 끝내야 돼요? B: 시작한 건 끝내야지.

Things change, roll with the punches 변화에 순응해라

A: I'm going to have to find a new apartment.

B: Things change. Roll with the punches.

A: 새 아파트를 찾아야 될거야. B: 상황이 바꼈으니 적응해야지.

09 다신 그러지마

Don't let it happen again 다신 그러지 마

A: I'm sorry, I totally forgot to call you last night.

B: Well, just don't let it happen again, okay? I was worried.

A: 미안, 어젯밤 전화하는 걸 깜박했어. B: 다신 그러지마, 알았지? 걱정했잖아.

Please be sure it doesn't happen again 다신 그러지 않도록 해

A: I'm sorry I'm late.

B: Please be sure it doesn't happen again.

A: 늦어서 미안해. B: 다신 그러지 않도록 해.

Not again! 어휴 또야!, 어떻게 또 그럴 수 있어!, 다시는 안그래

A: Your nose is bleeding!

B: Oh, not again!

A: 너 코피난다! B: 어휴 또야!

▶ I'm going through this alone. Not again.
나 혼자 이걸 겪지는 않을 거야. 다시는 안그래.

Please don't do that 제발 그러지마

A: I'm gonna teach that guy a lesson.

B: Jimmy, please don't do that.

A: 내가 그녀석에게 본때를 보여줄거야. B: 지미야, 제발 그러지마.

A: I'm going to tell him that I can't stand him.

B: Calm down. Don't do that.

A: 걔한테 너 못참겠다고 말할거야. B: 진정해. 그러지마.

▶ teach sb a lesson
혼내다, 본때를 보여주다
▶ can't stand sb
…을 참지 못하다

Don't do that anymore 더는 그러지마

A: Should I continue to meet Mrs. Johnson?

B: Oh, don't do that anymore.

A: 존슨 부인을 계속 만나야 하나요? B: 아니, 더는 그러지마.

Don't ever do that again 두번 다시 그러지마

A: I'm sorry I lied.

B: Don't ever do that again.

A: 거짓말해서 미안해. B: 절대로 다신 그러지마.

You can't do that! 그러면 안되지!

A: Maybe I should quit. Things've been getting too stressful.

B: You can't do that! Things will improve.

A: 그만둘까봐. 넘 힘들어. B: 그럼 안되지! 앞으로 좋아질거야.

We can't do that 우리가 그러면 안되지

A: Let's skip math class.

B: We can't do that.

A: 수학시간 빼먹자. B: 그럼 안되지.

Here we go again 또 시작이군

A: Guys, I'm in love with the most beautiful woman!

B: Oh no! Here we go again!

A: 얘들아, 최고의 미인과 사랑에 빠졌어! B: 맙소사! 또 시작이군!

There you go again 또 시작이군

A: I wish I was prettier.

B: There you go again. Don't be critical of yourself.

A: 내가 좀 더 이뻤으면. B: 또 시작이군. 그만 네 얼굴 타령해라.

Haven't you learned your lesson yet? 아직 따끔한 맛을 못봤어?

A: I'm going to the casino again tonight.

B: You'll lose money. Haven't you learned your lesson yet?

A: 오늘 밤 카지노에 다시 갈거야. B: 돈 까먹을거야. 아직 따끔한 맛을 못봤어?

▶ learn one's lesson
교훈을 얻다

Don't make such stupid mistakes again! 다신 그런 어리석은 실수하지마라!

A: I'm not going to study for the exam.

B: Don't make that stupid mistake again.

A: 시험공부 안 할거야. B: 그런 말도 안되는 실수는 하지마라.

10 그렇게 하면 안되지

You shouldn't + 동사 …해서는 안돼

A: I don't want to live with my parents.

B: You shouldn't say things like that

A: 부모랑 같이 살기 싫어 B: 그렇게 말하면 안되지.

You must not + 동사 …해서는 안돼

A: Do you think I'm too strict?

B: Sometimes. You must not hit your children.

A: 내가 너무 엄격한 것 같아? B: 때론. 애들을 치면 안돼지.

You'd better not + 동사 …하지 않는 게 좋아

A: You'd better not go outside. It's too cold.

B: You're right, but I want to see the game.

A: 나가지마. 밖은 너무 추워. B: 그렇지만, 그 경기를 보고 싶단 말야.

You're not supposed to do that 그러면 안되는데

A: You're not supposed to eat that!

B: Don't worry, Mom won't miss one cookie!

A: 너, 그 과자, 먹으면 안돼! B: 걱정 마, 하나쯤 없어져도 엄마는 모르실거야!

▶ You're not supposed to + 동사~
너는 …해서는 안돼
▶ I'm not supposed to be here
난 여기 있으면 안되는데

You don't want to + 동사 …하지 마라

A: You don't want to use that computer.

B: What's wrong with it?

A: 그 컴퓨터는 사용하지 않는게 좋아. B: 컴퓨터에 문제라도 있어?

▶ You're not using the Internet here.
넌 여기서 인터넷을 사용하지마.

You don't have to + 동사 …안해도 돼

A: You don't have to walk me home.

B: I know, but I want to.

A: 집까지 안 데려다 줘도 되는데. B: 알아, 하지만 내가 그러고 싶어.

▶ You don't have to~ = You don't need to~

You should know better than~ ···하지 않을 정도는 돼야지

A: You should know better than to tell him a secret.

B: I thought that I could trust him.

A: 너 그 사람한테 비밀을 말하면 안되는 줄 알았을 것 아냐. B: 믿을 수 있는 사람인 줄 알았는데.

Don't + 동사 ···하지 마라

A: Don't cut in line!

B: Sorry about that.

A: 끼어들지마! B: 미안해요.

▸ Don't touch me
만지지마
▸ Don't cut in line
끼어들지마

Don't be + 형용사 ···하지 마라

A: Don't be so anxious about the test. It'll be easy.

B: That's easy for you to say... you're a genius.

A: 너무 시험걱정하지마. 쉬울거야. B: 말은 쉽지··· 너는 천재니까.

▸ Don't be selfish
이기적이지 마라

Don't be jealous 질투하지 마라

A: That is a beautiful diamond necklace.

B: Don't be jealous. Ask your husband to buy one for you.

A: 저 다이아몬드 목걸이 정말 예쁘다. B: 샘내지마. 남편한테 하나 사달라고 해.

If I were you, I wouldn't + 동사 너라면 난 ···하지 않을 텐데

A: If I were you, I wouldn't let him know until tomorrow.

B: What's wrong with telling him now?

A: 내가 너라면, 내일이나 걔한테 말할텐데. B: 지금 말하면 문제될 게 있을까?

▸ I wouldn't if I were you
내가 너라면 그렇게 하지 않겠어

11 스스로 해라

Do it yourself 스스로 해라

A: Can you fix my computer?

B: Do it yourself.

A: 내 컴퓨터 고쳐줄 수 있어? B: 네가 해봐.

Do as[what] I said! 내가 말한대로 해!

A: Do as I said!

B: But I can't get this report done by 8 o'clock.

A: 내가 말한대로 해! B: 하지만 8시까지 이 보고서 못끝내는데요.

Do what I told you to do! 내가 지시한 대로 하라고!

A: Do what I told you to do.

B: But I don't want to sweep the floor.

A: 내가 시킨대로 해. B: 하지만 바닥청소를 하기 싫은데요.

Be + 형용사 …해라

A: Some days I just feel like giving up.

B: Be strong. Things will get better soon.

A: 언젠가 그냥 내가 포기하고 싶어. B: 강해져야지. 곧 더 나아질거야.

▶ Be good to others
다른 사람들에게 잘 대해
▶ Be strong!
건강하라고!

Be + 명사 …가 돼라

A: You shouldn't ever quit! Be a man!

B: Okay, I will.

A: 그만두면 안돼! 남자답게 굴어! B: 알았어, 그렇게 할게.

▶ Be a good boy
착한 애가 돼라. 나쁜 짓 하
지마라
▶ Be a man!
남자답게 행동해라!

You should do it this way 넌 이런 식으로 그걸 해야 돼

A: You should do it this way.

B: Show me again.

A: 넌 이런 식으로 그걸 해야 돼. B: 다시 한번 보여줘.

▶ This is the way
you should do it
이런 방식으로 그걸 해야
돼

This is the first thing to do 가장 먼저 해야 되는 건 이거야

A: I don't know the first thing about accounting.

B: This is the first thing to do.

A: 회계의 회자도 몰라. B: 네가 제일 먼저 해야 되는 건데.

▶ You should do
this first
이걸 먼저 해야 돼

Let me give you a piece of advice 내가 네게 충고 좀 할게

A: Honey, let me give you a piece of advice.

B: I don't need it! I know what I'm doing!

A: 자기야, 내가 충고 좀 할게. B: 집어쳐! 나도 다 안다고!

▶ I'm telling you this
from experience
내 경험상으로 말하는 건데

What you need is a little more effort 조금만 더 노력하면 돼

A: I think it's far beyond my ability.

B: Don't give me that. What you need is a little more effort.

A: 내 능력밖인 것 같아. B: 그런 말 마. 노력 좀만 더하면 돼.

Better than nothing 아무 것도 안 하는 것보단 낫지

A: I won a small prize in the contest.

B: It's better than nothing.

A: 시합에서 조그만 상을 탔어. B: 아무 것도 못타는 것보단 낫지.

It's your responsibility 너의 책임야

A: I'm done with my part. It's your responsibility now.

B: Don't worry about it. I'll do my best.

A: 내가 맡은 건 다했어. 이제 네 책임야. B: 걱정마. 최선을 다할 게.

▶ It's your duty
너의 의무야

That's the name of the game 그게 가장 중요한거야

A: Everyone wants to make money these days.

B: That's the name of the game.

A: 요즘은 다들 돈을 벌려고 해. B: 그게 가장 중요한 거잖아.

▶ That's the most
important thing
그게 가장 중요한 거야

Chapter 03

12 잠깐, 그만둬!

Wait a minute, please! 잠깐만요!

A: Wait a minute, I can't give this to her.

B: Why not?

　　A: 잠깐만. 이걸 걔한테는 못줘. B: 왜 못주는 거야?

▶ Just[wait] a
moment
잠깐만

Hold on (a second)! 잠깬!

A: I mean, we're having a baby together.

B: Hold on! You got my daughter pregnant?

　　A: 제 말은 우리가 함께 애를 가졌다는거죠. B: 잠깬! 내 딸을 임신시켰다는 거야?

∟. 전화 혹은 일반 상황에서.

Hold it! 잠깬, 그대로 있어!

A: Hold it! It's time for lunch.

B: It's about time.

　　A: 잠깬! 점심식사 시간야. B: 벌써 그렇게 되었네.

Stop that[it]! 그만해!

A: She turns me on all the time.

B: Stop that! You're not supposed to hit on your teacher.

　　A: 선생님을 보면 항상 흥분돼. B: 그만둬! 선생을 유혹하면 안돼지.

▶ Just drop it!
당장 그만둬!

Don't move! 움직이지마!

A: Don't move. Don't look at her.

B: Why? Did she catch us following her?

　　A: 움직이지마. 걔를 쳐다보지마. B: 왜? 걔가 우리가 미행하는 걸 눈치챘어?

▶ Don't make a
move!
움직이지마!
▶ Freeze!
꼼짝마!

Stop saying that! 닥치라고!. 그만 좀 얘기해!

A: And stop saying that! I hate it!

B: Okay!

　　A: 그만 좀 닥쳐라! 싫다고! B: 알았어!

Cut it out! 그만뒈, 닥쳐!

A: Cut it out!

B: Am I making too much noise?

A: 그만뒈! B: 내가 너무 시끄럽게 해?

Knock it off 조용히 해

A: I'm going to stare at you all night.

B: Knock it off.

A: 밤새 당신을 뚫어져라 쳐다볼거야. B: 그만 좀 해라.

Come off it! 집어쳐, 건방떨지마!

A: I'm the best looking guy here.

B: Oh, come off it.

A: 어, 집어쳐. 여기서 내가 최고 얼짱야. B: 어, 집어쳐.

Cut the crap 바보 같은 소리마, 쓸데 없는 이야기 좀 그만뒈

A: You're my best friend.

B: Cut the crap. We don't know each other well.

A: 넌 내 최고의 친구야. B: 집어쳐. 우린 서로 잘 알지도 못하잖아.

Listen to yourself 멍청한 소리 그만해

A: I'm a total failure in life.

B: Listen to yourself. You're not a failure.

A: 난 인생의 완벽한 패자야. B: 멍청한 소리 그만해. 넌 패자가 아냐.

 More Expressions

- Move on! 계속 움직여!
- Stay where you are! 그 자리에 멈춰!
- Time! 잠깐만!
- Give it up! 당장 때려 치워!
- Stop complaining[nagging]! 그만 징징대!
- Could you lay off, please? 그만 좀 할래?
- Let's just leave it at that! 그냥 그만 두재!

13 실망시키지마

Don't disappoint me 실망시키지마

A: I'll be a good boy tonight.

B: Please don't disappoint me.

A: 오늘 밤 얌전히 굴게. B: 날 실망시키지마.

▸ This is disappointing
실망스럽구만
▸ What a disappointment!
참 실망스럽네!

Don't let me down 기대를 저버리지마

A: I'll fix this by tomorrow.

B: Don't let me down.

A: 내일 아침까지 이거 고칠게요. B: 실망시키지마.

▸ let sb down
···을 실망시키다

You let me down 너한테 실망했어

A: Why are you so angry?

B: You let me down. I thought I could trust you.

A: 왜 내게 화나 있는거야? B: 실망했어. 널 믿을 수 있다고 생각했는데.

I'm ashamed of you 부끄러운 일이야, 부끄러워 혼났어

A: You got drunk and went to a strip club? I'm ashamed of you!

B: I don't know what to say. Please forgive me.

A: 취해서 스트립바에 갔다고? 창피한 줄 알어! B: 할 말이 없어. 용서해줘.

▸ It's nothing to be ashamed of.
전혀 부끄러울게 없어.

You should be ashamed 창피한 줄 알아

A: I can't believe they fired me for being late!

B: You should be ashamed. You should've been on time.

A: 늦었다고 해고하다니 말도 안돼! B: 창피해라. 늦지말았어야지.

▸ You should be ashamed of yourself
스스로 창피한 줄 알아

Aren't you ashamed of yourself? 창피한 줄도 몰라?

A: You were really drunk last night. Aren't you ashamed of yourself?

B: Honestly, I can't remember anything.

A: 간밤에 정말 취했더라. 창피한 줄도 몰라? B: 정말이지, 아무 것도 기억안나.

Shame on you 부끄러운 줄 알아야지, 챙피한 일이야

A: I got arrested for drinking and driving last night.

B: Shame on you.

A: 나 어젯밤에 음주 운전으로 체포됐었어. B: 부끄러운 줄 알아야지.

▸ For shame
챙피한 일이야

I was frustrated with you 너 때문에 맥이 풀렸어

A: Why did you yell at me?

B: I was frustrated with you.

A: 왜 내게 소리친거야? B: 너 때문에 맥이 풀려서 말야.

I'm bummed out 실망이야

A: You look unhappy today.

B: Yeah, I'm bummed out.

A: 너 오늘 기분나빠 보여. B: 응, 살맛이 안나서 말야.

▸ be bummed out
실망하다

I don't like it 마음에 안들어

A: I don't like it. Do it over again.

B: Can you tell me what part you don't like?

A: 맘에 안들어. 다시 해봐. B: 어느 부분이 맘에 안드는 지 말해줄래?

▸ I'm not happy
with it
만족못해, 마음에 안들어

Do you have a problem with me? 나한테 뭐 불만있는거야?

A: What's the matter? Do you have a problem with me?

B: Yes, I think you're hopeless.

A: 무슨 문제야? 내게 불만있어? B: 어, 너 구제불능야.

▸ Does anybody
have a problem
with that?
누구 문제 있는 사람 있어?

Do you have a problem with that? 그게 뭐 문제있어?

A: I plan to divorce you. Do you have a problem with that?

B: I think it will make us both happier.

A: 너하고 이혼하려고. 뭐 문제있어? B: 그게 우리가 더 행복해지는 길일거야.

14 정말 너무 하는 구만

That's (just) too much! 해도 해도 너무해!, 그럴 필요는 없는데!

A: My boss keeps asking me to go to a hotel.

B: That's just too much!

A: 사장이 호텔가자고 계속 졸라. B: 진짜 너무 하는 구만.

▶ take axking too much
너무 많이 요구하는 구만

You're going too far 너무하는군

A: I want revenge. I'll burn his house down.

B: You're going too far.

A: 복수해야 돼. 그놈 집을 태워버릴거야. B: 넌 지나친 거 아니야.

▶ You go too far
너 오바야

▶ You have gone too far
네가 너무했어, 심했다

A: I bought a Mercedes with company's credit card.

B: You've gone too far. Your boss is going to be furious.

A: 회사카드로 메르세데스 샀어. B: 넘하네. 사장이 격노할텐데.

What do you want from me? 나보고 어쩌라는 거야?

A: What do you want from me?

B: I really need your help.

A: 나보고 어쩌라는 거야? B: 정말이지 네 도움이 필요해.

He went overboard 그 사람이 좀 너무했어

A: This is an expensive apartment.

B: John went overboard when he bought it.

A: 아주 고가 아파트야. B: 걔가 이 아파트를 산 건 좀 무리한거지.

▶ Don't go overboard
과식[과음]하지마

How can you say that? 어떻게 그렇게 말할 수 있냐?

A: I hate all of my teachers.

B: How can you say that? A: 선생님들은 모두 다 싫어해. B: 어떻게 그렇게 말할 수 있어?

A: Honestly, I've never liked your cooking.

B: How can you say that? You've always eaten it.

A: 솔직히 말해서, 네 요리 좋아한 적이 없어. B: 어떻게 그런 말을? 항상 먹어놓고선.

How could you say such a thing? 네가 어떻게 그런 말을 할 수 있니?

A: You called me fat! How could you say such a thing?

B: Did I? When?

A: 내가 뚱뚱하다고! 어떻게 내게 그럴 수 있어? B: 내가 그랬어? 언제?

How could you not tell us? 어떻게 우리에게 말하지 않을 수 있지?

A: How could you not tell me you got married again?

B: I don't have to tell you everything!

A: 재혼했다고 어떻게 내게 말 안할 수 있어? B: 뭐든지 내가 너한테 다 말해야 돼!

▶ How could you not+V?
어떻게 …하지 않을 수 있어?

Chapter 03

How could you do that? 어쩌면 그럴 수가 있어?

A: I sold my mother's wedding ring.

B: How could you do that? She loves that ring.

A: 엄마 결혼반지를 팔았어. B: 어떻게 그래? 엄만 그 반지 좋아하는데.

How could you do this to me[us]? 내[우리]한테 어떻게 이럴 수 있니?

A: You are fired.

B: How could you do this to me?

A: 넌 해고야. B: 어쩜 내게 이럴 수가 있어요?

How dare you + 동사 ? 어떻게 …할 수가 있어?

A: You son of bitch! I'm gonna kill you!

B: How dare you insult me!

A: 이 개자식! 너 죽일거야! B: 감히 날 모욕하다니!

▶ You wouldn't dare
(to do something)!
어쩜 감히 이럴 수가!

You're pushing your luck 운을 과신하는 구만, 화를 부르는 구만

A: I'm leaving work early today.

B: You're pushing your luck.

A: 오늘 좀 일찍 나갈게. B: 운을 과신하는 구만.

A: I'm planning to ask my boss for a raise.

B: You're pushing your luck.

A: 사장한테 급여올려달라고 할거야. B: 화를 재촉하는 구만.

15 네 맘대로 해라

Have it your way 네 맘대로 해, 좋을 대로 해

A: You always get your way.

B: I don't know what you're talking about.

A: 넌 늘 네 멋대로야.　B: 무슨 말인지 모르겠는데.

▶ Do it your way!
너 좋을 대로 해!
▶ He gets his way
걘 제멋대로야

Suit yourself! 네 멋대로 해!, 맘대로 해!

A: I have to call in sick today.

B: Suit yourself! You've already done it five times this month.

A: 오늘 아파 결근한다고 전화해야 되겠어.　B: 맘대로 해! 이번달만 벌써 5번째야.

Do what you want 원하는 대로 해

A: Do you think I should move to Europe?

B: Do what you want. It's your life.

내가 유럽으로 이주해야 된다고 생각해?　원하는 대로 해. 네 인생이잖아.

Do whatever you want 뭐든 원하는 대로 해

A: I don't know if we should continue dating.

B: Do whatever you want. I don't care.

A: 우리가 계속 데이트해야 되는지 모르겠어.　B: 맘대로 해. 난 상관없어.

Do as you please 맘대로 해

A: Do you mind if I smoke?

B: Do as you please.

A: 담배펴도 돼요?　B: 맘대로 해.

Do as you like 좋을 대로 해

A: I'm going to go out with my friends tonight.

B: Do as you like. I still think it's a bad idea.

A: 오늘밤 친구들과 나가 놀거야.　B: 좋을 대로 해. 난 아직도 별로 좋은 생각같지 않아.

▸ Can you say this word for me? 이 단어 어떻게 말해요?

▸ I'm not sure how to say this word 이 단어 어떻게 말하는 지 모르겠어요

▸ How do you pronounce this word? 이 단어 어떻게 발음해요?

▸ What's the pronunciation of this word? 이 단어 발음이 어떻게 돼요?

▸ Please spell that word for me 이 단어 철자 좀 말해줘요

▸ What does 'tofu'mean? 'tofu'가 무슨 의미예요?

▸ Can I say it like this? 이거 이렇게 말해도 되나요?

▸ I wonder if this is the correct expression 이게 올바른 표현인 지 모르겠어요

▸ I wrote "to say the least of."Is this correct? "to say the least of"라고 썼는데 맞나요?

▸ Is it okay to say "As I said before~"? "As I said before"라고 말해도 되나요?

▸ Can I use this expression in a situation like this? 이런 상황에서 이 표현을 써도 돼요?

▸ Would it be rude to say "Never mind"to the teacher? 선생님께 "Never mind"라고 해도 무례가 아닌가요?

A: Leave a message that Mr. Horowitz called. 호로비츠가 전화했다고 전해줘요.
B: OK. Please spell your name for me. 예. 성함 철자 좀 알려주세요.

A: Is it okay to say "I wish you good luck?" I wish you good luck이라고 말해도 돼요?
B: No, that sounds odd. Just say "good luck." 아니, 좀 이상해. 그냥 good luck이라고 해.

▸ Here we are _ 자 (드디어) 도착했다, 여기 있다

▸ Here you are _ 여기 있습니다

▸ There you are _ 여기 있어, 그것봐, 내가 뭐랬어

▸ Here it is _ 여기 있습니다

▸ There it is _ 저것봐라, 저기 있네

▸ Here we go _ 자 간다, 여기 있다

▸ Here you go _ 자 여기 있어요

▸ There he goes _ 그 사람 저기 온다

▸ There you go _ 그래 그렇게 하는거야, 그것 봐 내 말이 맞지, 자 이거 받아

▸ Here goes _ 한번 해봐야지

▸ Here he comes _ 저기 오는구만

▸ Here it comes _ 자 여기 있어, 또 시작이군, 올 것이 오는구만

A: Can I have a Coke? 콜라하나 줄래?
B: Sure. There you are. 응. 여기 있어.

A: The train is arriving now. 기차가 지금 오고 있어.
B: Here it comes. 여기 들어오네.

16 날 뭘로 보는거야?

What do you take me for? 날 뭘로 보는 거야?

A: What do you take me for? I'm not a whistleblower.

B: Then how did they know about that?

A: 날 뭘로 보는 거야? 난 고자질쟁이가 아냐. B: 그럼, 그 사람들이 그걸 어떻게 알아낸거야?

Who do you think you're talking to? 너 나한테 그렇게 말하면 재미없어

A: You are such a dumb ass!

B: Who do you think you're talking to? I'm your boss.

A: 넌 정말 바보 멍청구리야. B: 내게 그렇게 말하면 안되지. 난 네 사장야.

▸ Who do you think
you're kidding?
설마 나더러 그 말을 믿으
라는 건 아니지

You're pulling my leg 나 놀리는 거지, 농담이지

A: I'm going to give you a lot of money.

B: You're pulling my leg.

A: 너한테 돈 많이 줄게. B: 날 놀리지마.

▸ Are you pulling
my leg?
나 놀리는 거니?
▸ Don't pull my leg
놀리지 마

Do I look like I was born yesterday? 내가 그렇게 어리숙해보여?

A: Can you loan me $10,000?

B: Do I look like I was born yesterday?

A: 만 달러만 빌려줄래? B: 내가 그렇게 바보로 보여?

▸ I wasn't born
yesterday!
누굴 햇병아리로 보나!

How dumb do you think I am? 내가 바본 줄 아니?, 누굴 바보로 아는 거니?

A: The boss wants you in his office.

B: How dumb do you think I am? He's gone for the day.

A: 사장이 사무실로 오래. B: 내가 바본 줄 알어? 사장님 퇴근했잖아.

Why are you picking on me? 왜 날 괴롭히는 거야?

A: Boy, you have an odd personality.

B: Why are you picking on me?

참, 너 성격 정말 이상하다. 왜 날 괴롭히는거야?

▸ pick on sb
…을 괴롭히다

I'm not stupid 난 바보가 아냐

A: Do you understand what I mean?

B: Yes, I'm not stupid.

A: 내 말 이해하겠어? B: 그럼, 나 바보 아냐.

Are you trying to make a fool of me? 나를 놀리려고 하는 거야?

A: Are you trying to make a fool of me?

B: No. Why do you say that?

A: 날 놀리려고 하는 거야? B: 아니. 왜 그런 말을 하는 거야?

▸ make a fool of sb
놀리다

You're telling me that 주어+동사? …라고 말하는 거야?

A: You're telling me that you can't finish it?

B: I think I can't handle all this work on my own.

A: 그걸 끝내지 못한다는 거야? B: 나 혼자 그일 모두를 처리못할 것 같아.

ㄴ. 말투나 상황에 따라 상대
방의 말을 확인하거나 혹은
시비를 걸 때 사용한다.

Stop kidding[joking] 농담하지마

A: I think he really likes you.

B: Stop kidding me!

A: 걔 널 정말 좋아하는 것 같아. B: 농담하지마!

Don't make fun of me! 나 놀리지 매

A: Those glasses make you look like a pig.

B: Don't make fun of me.

A: 그 안경쓰니까 너 꼭 돼지같아. B: 놀리지마.

▸ You're making fun
of me?
너 지금 나 놀리냐?

Don't tease me! 놀리지 매

A: Wow, you look cute tonight.

B: Don't tease me.

A: 야, 너 오늘 이쁘다. B: 놀리지마.

▸ You're teasing me
나 놀리는 거지

17 꺼지라고!

Get out of here! 꺼져. 웃기지 마!

A: Get out of here!

B: I'm sorry, but let me explain why I did it.

A: 그만 나가봐! B: 미안해, 하지만 내가 왜 그랬는지 설명할게.

A: Get out of here!

B: Why? What did I do to make you angry?

A: 꺼져! B: 왜? 내가 뭘 널 화나게 했는데?

ㄴ. 특히 상대방이 말도 안되는 얘기를 했을 때는 정말 꺼지라는 말이 아니다.

Get out of my face! 내 눈 앞에서 안보이게 사라져!

A: Get out of my face!

B: What did I do wrong?

A: 꺼져! B: 내가 뭘 잘못했는데?

Get out of my way! 비켜라! 방해하지마라!

A: I'm not going to let you drive drunk.

B: Get out of my way.

A: 너 음주운전 못하게 할거야. B: 비켜.

Go away! 꺼져!

A: Dude, it's Bob. Let me in.

B: Go away! I don't want to see anybody.

A: 어이 친구, 밥야. 문열어. B: 꺼져! 아무도 보고 싶지 않어.

Get lost! (그만 좀 괴롭히고) 꺼져!

A: Hey cutie!!

B: Get lost!

A: 안녕, 귀염둥이!!! B: 꺼져버려!

▶ get lost
길을 잃다

(You) Back off! 비키시지!

A: She doesn't want to see you right now.

B: Back off! She's my wife!

A: 부인은 지금 당신을 안보겠대요. B: 비켜! 걔는 내 마누라라고!

You stay out of it! 좀 비켜라!

A: You shouldn't hit him.

B: You stay out of it!

A: 걔를 때리면 안돼. B: 좀 비키라고!

▸ You stay out of trouble.
말썽일으키지마.

Keep[Stay] out of my way 가로 막지 좀 마

A: Keep out of my way!

B: You're the rudest man I ever met.

A: 가로 막지 좀 매! B: 너 같이 무례한 놈은 처음봤다.

Stay away from me! 꺼져!

A: Just come here and calm down.

B: Stay away from me!

A: 이리와서 진정하라고. B: 꺼져!

(You) Just watch! 넌 보고만 있어!

A: Do you really think she'll become your girlfriend?

B: Absolutely. You just watch!

A: 쟤가 네 여친이 될 거라고 정말 생각하는 거야? B: 물론이지. 넌 보고 만 있어!

Don't mess with me 나 건드리지마

A: You look mad.

B: I am. Don't mess with me!

A: 너 화나보여. B: 그래. 나 건드리지마!

▸ mess with
건드리다, 속이다

I don't want to get in the way 방해되고 싶지 않아

A: Come on, you can come on my date.

B: No thanks. I don't want to get in the way.

A: 야아, 데이트할 때 너 와도 돼. B: 됐네. 방해하고 싶지 않아.

18 점잖게 행동해

Behave yourself 버릇없이 굴면 안돼(아이들에게). 점잖게 행동해

A: You children behave yourselves.

B: We'll be good, Dad.

　　A: 너희들 예의 바르게 굴어.　B: 착하게 굴게요, 아빠.

Where are your manners? 매너가 그게 뭐야. 매너가 없구나

A: I have to eat this food with my fingers.

B: Oh no! Where are your manners?

　　A: 손가락으로 음식을 먹어야겠어.　B: 어 안돼! 매너가 그게 뭐냐?

Remember your manners 버릇없이 굴지 말구. 예의를 지켜야지

A: Remember your manners at the party.

B: I will.

　　A: 파티에서 매너를 지키라고.　B: 알았어.

Mind your manners! 방정맞게 굴지마!

A: How about giving me a kiss?

B: Mind your manners!

　　A: 내게 키스해주라?　B: 점잖게 굴어!

▶ Be sure to mind your manners!
예의바르게 굴도록 해!

Mind your P's and Q's! 품행[말]을 조심해라!

A: Mind your P's and Q's.

B: Do you think I'm being impolite?

　　A: 예의를 갖추라고.　B: 내가 예의가 없는 것 같아?

Don't be rude! 무례하게 굴지마!

A: I'm going to tell him he's an idiot.

B: Don't be rude!

　　A: 걔한테 걔가 바보라고 말할거야.　B: 무례하게 굴지마!

A: I really hate your friends.

B: Don't be rude. Some of my friends are very nice.

A: 네 친구들 정말 싫어. B: 너무 그러지마. 걔중엔 정말 좋은 친구들도 있어.

Watch your step 말(혹은 행동거지) 조심해

A: I've never liked you.

B: Watch your step. You're being rude.

A: 널 좋아한 적이 없어. B: 말조심해. 너무 무례하잖아.

Your behavior is out of place 네 행동은 무례한 짓이야

A: Your behavior is out of place.

B: That's because I'm really drunk!

A: 너 행동은 무례한 짓이야. B: 술 취해서 그래!

▶ be out of place
어색하다, 상식에 어긋나다

Be on your best behavior 점잖게 행동해라

A: Be on your best behavior at your grandparent's house.

B: I promise I will.

A: 할아버지 댁에 가서는 행동 바르게 해라. B: 그렇게 할게요.

You have a bad attitude 너 태도가 안 좋구나

A: I don't care about my work.

B: You have a bad attitude.

A: 일은 신경 안 써. B: 자세가 안 좋구만.

I don't like your attitude 너 태도가 맘에 안 들어

A: Why did you decide to fire me?

B: I don't like your attitude.

A: 나를 왜 해고하기로 한거죠? B: 당신 태도가 맘에 안들어서요.

Manners count, even between close friends 친할수록 예의를 지켜야지

A: Why are you angry with me?

B: Manners count, even between close friends.

A: 왜 내게 화내는 거야? B: 친할수록 예의를 지켜야지.

Chapter 03

Use good etiquette 예의바르게 행동해

A: I've been invited to meet the president.

B: Use good etiquette when you see him.

A: 초대받아서 사장님 뵐거야. B: 뵙거든 예의바르게 행동하고.

MEMO

19 너 미쳤어?

You crazy? 너 미쳤어?

A: What are you doing?! Are you crazy?

B: Don't worry, I know what I'm doing.

A: 뭐하는 거야?! 미쳤어? B: 걱정마, 내일은 내가 알아서 하니까.

▶ Are you insane[nuts]?
너 돌았니?

You're driving me crazy 너 때문에 미치겠다

A: You're driving me crazy with that!

B: Okay, I'll stop.

A: 너 때문에 미치겠어. B: 알았어, 그만할게.

▶ You've driving me up the wall
너 때문에 미치겠다

What do you think you're doing? 이게 무슨 짓이야, 너 정신 나갔어?

A: What do you think you're doing?

B: I was tired, so I fell asleep on my desk.

A: 당신 지금 뭐하는 거야? B: 피곤해서 책상에서 잠들었어요.

Are you out of your mind? 너 제 정신이야?

A: Are you crazy?

B: Are you out of your mind?

A: 너 미쳤어? B: 너 제정신이야?

▶ You're out of your mind!
너 미쳤구만!

He's out to lunch 걔 요즘 얼이 빠져있어

A: What's wrong with the manager?

B: He's too old. He's out to lunch.

A: 부장님 왜 그래? B: 나이가 너무 들었어. 정신없는 것 같아.

You are not yourself 제정신이 아니네

A: You're not yourself. Why don't you take a few days off?

B: I wish I could but I can't. I have a lot of work to do.

A: 너 이상해. 몇일 좀 쉬지. B: 그러고 싶지만 안돼. 할 일이 너무 많아.

▶ I'm not myself
나 지금 제 정신이 아냐

Chapter 03

Is he all there? 걔 미쳤어?

A: Walter is a pretty odd guy.

B: Is he all there?

    A: 월터는 정말 이상한 놈야. B: 걔 미친 거 아냐?

▸ He's not all there
걘 정신나갔나봐

There's nobody home! 정신 어디다 두고 있는거야!

A: That old guy is senile?

B: It's like there's nobody home.

    A: 저 나이든 양반 망령인가봐? B: 정신이 없는 것 같으셔.

The lights are on but nobody's home 어쩜 그렇게 맹하고 느려터졌니

A: Your grandma doesn't say much.

B: Yeah, the lights are on but nobody's home.

    A: 너희 할머니 말씀이 별로 없더라. B: 어, 정신이 별로 없으셔.

Anybody home? 집에 아무도 없어요?, 정신있니 없니?

A: Hello! Is anybody home? You told me you would call.

B: I'm sorry, but I've just been so busy!

    A: 너 정신없구나? 전화한다고 했잖아? B: 미안해, 너무 바빴어!

A: Anybody home?

B: Sorry, I was just thinking.

    A: 너 정신있니, 없니? B: 미안, 그냥 생각중이었어.

I'm losing my mind 내가 제 정신이 아니야

A: I've got too much stress. I'm losing my mind.

B: You need to relax.

    A: 스트레스를 너무 받아. 내 정신이 아냐. B: 좀 쉬어야 되겠군.

You seem spaced out 너 정신이 나간 것 같구나

A: You seem spaced out today.

B: I had a lot to drink last night.

    A: 너 오늘 정신이 없어 보여. B: 어젯밤에 술을 너무 많이 마셨어.

20 이건 말도 안돼

It doesn't make any sense 무슨 소리야. 말도 안돼

A: I think Jin Ho quit Seoul National University.

B: Really? It doesn't make any sense.

    A: 진호가 서울대를 그만둔 것 같아. B: 정말? 말도 안돼.

▸ make sense
말이 되다

It makes no sense 그건 말도 안돼

A: Can you understand what the professor is saying?

B: No. It makes no sense.

    A: 교수가 무슨 말하는지 이해돼?   B: 아니. 말도 안되는 이야기야.

Does that make any sense? 그게 말이 돼?

A: Abe is planning to give his money away.

B: Does that make any sense?

    A: 에이브가 돈을 나누어 줄거야. B: 그게 말이 되는 것 같아?

Don't be ridiculous 바보같이 굴지마

A: Is that an Armani suit?

B: Don't be ridiculous.

    A: 아르마니 옷이야? B: 말도 안되는 말 하지마.

Don't be silly[foolish] 바보같이 굴지마

A: Are you going to marry him?

B: Don't be silly. We just met last week.

    A: 그 남자랑 결혼할거야? B: 웃기지마. 지난 주에 처음 만난 걸.

This is ridiculous 이건 말도 안돼

A: Can you pay for dinner? I can't afford it.

B: This is ridiculous.

    A: 저녁값 낼래? 내가 돈이 없어서. B: 웃기는 구만.

Chapter 03

This is crazy[nuts] 이건 말도 안되는 짓이야. 말도 안돼

A: We're going to ask those guys for a date.

B: This is crazy.

A: 쟤네들한테 데이트 신청할거야. B: 말도 안돼.

Don't make me laugh! 웃기지 좀 매. 웃음 밖에 안 나온다!

A: I'm the richest man in America.

B: Don't make me laugh!

A: 미국에서 내가 가장 부자야. B: 웃기지 좀 매!

Don't lie to me 거짓말하지마

A: Don't lie to me. I'm not that stupid.

B: I'm not kidding. I'm dead serious.

A: 거짓말하지마. 내가 그렇게 바보는 아니라고. B: 농담아냐. 진심야.

▶ Don't tell me lies
거짓말하지마

Don't tell me lies 거짓말하지마

A: My uncle is a gangster in L.A.

B: Don't tell me lies. That's not true.

A: 삼촌이 LA에서 갱하고 있어. B: 거짓말 마. 사실이 아니잖아.

That's a lie! 거짓말야!

A: You told my girlfriend that I'm impotent!

B: No, I didn't say that! That's a lie.

A: 내 애인한테 내가 발기불능이라고 했지? B: 아니, 그런 말 안 했에 그건 거짓말야.

Liar! 거짓말쟁이!

A: I wasn't on a date with Cheryl.

B: Liar! She said you were!

A: 셰릴하고 데이트 안했어. B: 거짓말쟁이! 너랑 했다고 하던데!

Don't say stupid things 바보 같은 말 하지마

A: I'm going to beat Eddie up.

B: Just relax. Don't say stupid things.

A: 에디를 때려줄거야. B: 진정하라고. 바보 같은 말 하지말고.

Don't play dumb! 순진한 척하지마!

A: What is a room salon?

B: Don't play dumb. You've been to one.

A: 룸살롱이 뭐야? B: 순진한 척하지마. 가본적 있잖아.

▸ play dumb
순진한 척하다

MEMO

21 그런말 하지마

Don't give me that! 그런 말 마. 정말 시치미떼기야!

A: I can't work with that guy.

B: Don't give me that shit.

> A: 그 사람이랑 같이 일 못하겠어. B: 그 따위 소리 하지 말라구.

▶ I'll give you that.
네 말이 맞아.

That's no excuse 그건 변명거리가 안돼

A: My son got sick and I had to take him to the doctor.

B: Well, as far as the company is concerned, that's no excuse.

> A: 애가 아파 병원에 가야 했어. B: 회사입장에서는 이유가 안돼.

No more excuses! 변명은 그만해!

A: I lost my job last week.

B: No more excuses! Pay the money you owe me.

> A: 지난 주에 실직했어. B: 그만 변명해! 빚진 돈이나 갚아.

Don't make any excuses! 변명 좀 그만해!

A: My homework is late because I was sick.

B: Don't make any excuses!

> A: 아파서 숙제가 늦었어요. B: 변명 좀 그만해!

I've heard enough of your excuses 네 변명은 이젠 지겨워

A: I've heard enough of your excuses.

B: I'm telling the truth.

> A: 네 변명은 이제 지겨워. B: 진실을 말하는거야.

▶ That's not a good excuse
그럴 듯한 변명도 아니네

I don't want to hear any excuses 어떤 변명도 듣고 싶지 않아

A: Finish this by tomorrow. I don't want to hear any excuses.

B: Well, I'll do my best to complete it.

> A: 내일까지 이거 끝내. 아무런 변명도 듣고 싶지 않아. B: 어, 최선을 다해 끝내도록 할게요.

That doesn't excuse your behavior 그렇다고 너의 행동을 용인할 수가 없어

A: I've had a lot of pressure at work lately.

B: That doesn't excuse your behavior.

A: 최근에 일에 대한 압박이 너무 심했어. B: 그렇다고 너의 행동이 용인되지 않아.

That hardly explains your actions 그건 너의 행동에 대한 변명이 안돼

A: I dated her because my marriage was unhappy.

B: That hardly explains your actions.

A: 결혼생활이 불행해 걔랑 데이트했어. B: 그게 너의 행동에 대한 변명이 결코 될 수 없어.

Tell me another 거짓말마, 말이 되는 소리를 해라

A: I lost my job because other workers were jealous.

B: Sure. Tell me another lie.

A: 다른 직원들의 질투로 실직했어. B: 그렇게지. 말 되는 소리를 해라.

Spare me! 집어치워!, 그만둬!

A: He's going to be really angry because you're not done.

B: Spare me!

A: 네가 일 못끝내서 엄청 화낼거야. B: 설마 그럴라구!

▸ spare me the
details
요점만 말하다

No ifs, ands or buts! 군말 말고 시키는 대로 해!

A: Do I have to mow the lawn?

B: Yes. No ifs, ands, or buts.

A: 잔디를 깍아야 돼요? B: 그래. 군말 말고 시키는 대로 해.

Now what? 그래서 뭐?

A: Well, we finished cleaning the house.

B: Yep. Now what?

A: 저기, 집청소 끝났어요. B: 어, 그래서 뭐?

A: You have a telephone call.

B: Now what? People are always bothering me.

A: 전화왔어. B: 그래서 뭐 어쨌다고? 사람들은 항상 날 가만히 두지를 않아.

22 남의 일에 신경쓰지마

It's none of your business 남의 일에 신경쓰지마, 참견마

A: Are you dating Michael nowadays?

B: It's none of your business.

A: 요즘 마이클과 사귀니? B: 네가 알바 아니잖아.

Mind your own business! 상관 말라구!

A: I'm going to ask them what they're talking about.

B: Why don't you mind your own business?

A: 걔네들이 무슨 얘기하고 있는지 물어볼거야. B: 네 일이나 잘하지 그래?

▶ I'll thank you to mind your own business
신경꺼주면 고맙겠어

That's really my business 그건 내 일이니 신경꺼

A: How is your relationship with your parents?

B: That's really my business.

A: 부모님과의 관계는 어때? B: 그건 내 일이니 신경꺼.

Keep[Get] your nose out of my business 내 일에 참견마

A: I can give a message to your boyfriend.

B: Keep your nose out of my business.

A: 네 남자친구에게 메시지를 보내줄 수 있어. B: 내 일에 참견마.

Stay out of this! 상관마!, 참견마!

A: I think you are acting badly.

B: Stay out of this!

A: 너 좀 행동이 무례한 것 같아. B: 상관마!

└. Stay out of this!는 개인적인 문제이니까 "참견하지 마라"라는 의미이며 Stay away (from me)는 "내 면전에서 꺼지라"라고 말하는 경고성 문구이다.

Don't get involved 상관마

A: Sally and her husband are always fighting.

B: It's a private matter. Don't get involved.

A: 샐리부부는 늘상 싸워. B: 사생활이잖아. 간섭마.

▶ get involved (in)
상관하다, 관여하다

Who asked you? 누가 너한테 물었어?

A: I think you're wrong.
B: Who asked you?

A: 네가 틀린 것 같아. B: 누가 너한테 물었어?

Who cares what you think? 누가 너한테 물어봤어?, 맘대로 생각해라

A: I'd say you should apologize to her.
B: Who cares what you think?

A: 네가 걔한테 사과해야 될 것 같아. B: 맘대로 생각해라.

Butt out! 참견말고 꺼져!, 가서 네 일이나 잘해!

A: I don't think you should go to law school.
B: Butt out! It's my choice.

A: 로스쿨에 가지 않는 게 좋다고 생각 돼. B: 참견마! 내가 선택하는 거라고.

It's not your concern 상관마

A: Why do you look so upset?
B: It's not your concern.

A: 왜 그리 화나보여? B: 상관마.

A: You can always tell me about your problems.
B: Don't worry. It's not your concern.

A: 언제든지 문제 있으면 내게 말하도록 해. B: 걱정마, 네가 상관할 바가 아냐.

It's personal 개인적인거야

A: You were absent from work again.
B: I can't tell you why. It's personal.

A: 너 또 결근했어. B: 이유는 말 못해요. 개인적인 일이어서요.

A: Why were you absent all of last week?
B: It's personal. I can't talk about it.

A: 지난주 내내 왜 빠졌어? B: 개인적인 일이야. 말 못해.

23 들켰다

You caught me 들켰다

A: You've been eating my food.

B: Yeah, you caught me.

  A: 너 내 음식 먹고있는 거지? B: 응, 걸렸네.

▶ He caught me
smoking
담배피우다 그 사람한테 들
켰어

You screwed me! 날 속였군!

A: You stole my money! You screwed me!

B: I'm really sorry.

  A: 내 돈을 훔쳐갔어! 날 속인거야! B: 정말 미안해.

▶ You did a number
on me
내가 당했구만

I'm so busted 딱 걸렸어

A: My girlfriend saw me with you. I'm so busted.

B: Is she going to be angry?

  A: 여친이 너와 있는 걸 봤어. 딱 걸렸어. B: 걔가 화를 낼까?

Gotcha! 잡았다!, 속았지!, 당했지!, 알았어!

A: Are you sure that the boss wants me to see him right now?

B: I was just kidding. Gotcha!

  A: 정말 사장이 지금 당장 보자고 한거야? B: 장난친거야. 당했지!

I'm fucking with you 널 놀리는 거야

A: You want a divorce, because you're gay?!

B: Honey, I'm fucking with you.

  A: 이혼하자고, 당신이 게이이기 때문에?! B: 자기야, 장난이야.

She gave it to me 나 걔한테 혼쭐이 났어, 나 걔하고 섹스했어

A: They really gave it to me at the meeting!

B: I guess they were still upset about last month's sales.

  A: 회의에서 정말 호되게 질책하더라구! B: 전월 판매실적 땜에 골나 있었겠구만.

24 당해싸다

You asked for it 자업자득이지. 네가 자초한 일이잖아. 그런 일을 당해도 싸다

A: Why did you hit me?

B: You asked for it. You started the fight.

A: 내 나를 친거야? B: 네가 자초한거야. 네가 싸움걸었잖아.

▶ You'll pay for that!
당해도 싸다!, 꼴 좋군!

You had it coming! 네가 자초한거야!

A: My parents are angry at me.

B: You had it coming. You treated them badly.

A: 부모님이 나 때문에 화나셨어. B: 네가 자초한거야. 함부로 막 대했잖아.

(It) Serves you right! 넌 그런 일 당해도 싸. 꼴 좋다!

A: I got a speeding ticket.

B: Serves you right.

A: 속도위반 딱지 끊겼어. B: 당해 싸다.

That'll teach her! 그래도 싸지!, 당연한 대가야!

A: Jen got fat because she ate too much.

B: That'll teach her!

A: 젠은 너무 먹어대더니 뚱뚱해졌어. B: 당연한 대가지!

▶ Well, that'll teach you a lesson
그래, 이제 좀 정신차리겠지

You'll never get away with it 넌 그걸 피할 수 없어

A: You'll never get away with it.

B: Just watch me!

A: 넌 그걸 피할 수 없어. B: 두고 보라구!

▶ get away with it
죄를 짓고도 무사하다, 벌받지 않다

Well, you got what you deserved 당해 싸다

A: The police put me in jail for stealing.

B: Well, you got what you deserved.

A: 경찰이 절도죄로 나를 잡아 넣었어. B: 당해 싸다.

▶ You've brought this on yourself
네가 초래한거야

▶ There's no reason to complaint
당연한 결과지

25 나한테 왜 이래

You can't do this to me 나한테 이러면 안되지, 이러지마

A: I'm expelling you from our school.

B: You can't do this to me!

A: 널 퇴학시키겠어. B: 나한테 이러시면 안되죠!

Why are you doing this to me? 내게 왜 이러는 거야?

A: Why are you doing this to me?

B: Because I don't like you.

A: 내게 왜 이러는 거야? B: 널 싫어하니까.

▶ What have you done to me?
내게 무슨 짓을 한거야?

Don't tell me what to do! 나에게 이래라 저래라 하지마!

A: Move out of the way.

B: Don't tell me what to do!

A: 길 좀 비켜. B: 내게 이래라 저래라 하지마!

Don't call me names! 욕하지 마!

A: Come over here, dummy.

B: Don't call me names!

A: 바보야, 이리와봐. B: 내게 욕하지마!

▶ call sb names
욕하다
▶ call sb's name
…의 이름을 부르다

Don't blame me 나한테 뭐라고 하지마

A: How did this computer break?

B: Don't blame me!

A: 어쩌다 컴퓨터가 망가진거야? B: 나한테 뭐라고 하지마!

▶ Don't insult me
날 모욕하지마
▶ Don't say it's my fault
내 잘못이라고 하지마

I didn't do anything wrong! 난 잘못한 것 하나도 없어!

A: I think you caused this accident.

B: I didn't do anything wrong!

A: 너 때문에 이 사고가 난 것 같아. B: 난 잘못한 게 하나도 없는걸!

You're to blame 네가 잘못이다

A: I was smoking, and then the building started burning.

B: So you're to blame for the fire.

A: 담배피고 있는데 빌딩에서 불이나기 시작했어. B: 그럼 네가 화재에 책임있네.

▶ be to blame
…의 책임이다

You can't talk to me like that 내게 그렇게 말하면 안돼

A: You're the dumbest woman I ever met.

B: You can't talk to me like that!

A: 너같이 멍청한 여자는 처음야. B: 내게 그런 식으로 말하지마!

▶ Don't look at me like that
그런 식을 날 보지마

Don't talk back to me! 내게 말대꾸하지마!

A: I won't obey you!

B: Don't talk back to me!

A: 네 말 안 들을거야! B: 내게 말대꾸하지마!

▶ talk back to sb
…에게 말대꾸하다

Take it back 취소해

A: You are too ugly.

B: That's not true. Take it back!

A: 너 너무 못생겼어. B: 말도 안돼. 취소해!

I don't want to cause problems 문제 일으키고 싶지 않아

A: You can sleep here.

B: Is it OK? I don't want to cause problems.

A: 여기서 자도 돼. B: 그래도 돼? 문제일으키고 싶지 않은데.

Why are you trying to make me feel bad? 왜 날 기분 나쁘게 만드는 거야?

A: I regret the day I met you.

B: Why are you trying to make me feel bad?

A: 널 만난 날이 후회된다. B: 왜 날 기분나쁘게 만드는 거야?

26 넌 몰라

You don't know the first thing about it 아무것도 모르면서, 쥐뿔도 모르면서

A: The U.S. has a terrible foreign policy.

B: You don't know the first thing about it.

> A: 미국의 외교정책은 으악야. B: 쥐뿔도 모르면서.

▸ You don't know
  the half of it
  별로 알지도 못하면서

You have no idea 넌 모를거야

A: She is so amazing! You have no idea.

B: No idea? Who do you think brought her here?

> A: 걔 대단하다! 넌 잘 모를거야. B: 몰라? 누가 걜 데려왔는데?

You have no idea what this means to me!

이게 내게 얼마나 중요한 건지 넌 몰라!

A: Here's a diamond ring for you.

B: Thank you! You have no idea what this means to me.

> A: 여기 다이아몬드 당신꺼야. B: 고마워! 얼마나 고마운지 모를거야.

You have no idea how much I need this

이게 나한테 얼마나 필요한지 넌 몰라

A: Are you on vacation?

B: Yes. You have no idea how much I need this.

> A: 휴가중야? B: 어, 내가 얼마나 가고 싶어했는지 모를거야.

▸ You have no idea
  how much this
  hurts
  이게 얼마나 아픈지 넌 모
  를 거야

What do you know about + 명사? …에 대해 네가 뭘 알아?

A: You don't love him!

B: What do you know about love?

> A: 너 걔를 사랑하지 않아! B: 네가 사랑이 뭔지 알기나 해?

You never learn 넌 구제불능이야

A: I got dumped by another girlfriend.

B: You never learn.

A: 다른 여친한테 또 차였어. B: 못말리겠구만.

MEMO

27 잘난 척 마라

Who do you think you are? 네가 도대체 뭐가 그리도 잘났는데?

A: I'll buy drinks for everyone!

B: Who do you think you are? A millionaire?

　　A: 여러분 모두에게 술을 살게요! B: 뭐 그렇게 잘났어? 백만장자라도 돼?

Don't be a smart-ass 건방지게 굴지마

A: Where did you buy this old car? It's beautiful!

B: Don't be a smartass.

　　A: 이 중고차 어디서 샀어? 멋지다! B: 좀 아는 척하지마.

▶ Don't be smart
with me!
잘난 체 하지마!

You think you're so smart[big] 네가 그렇게 똑똑한 줄 알아

A: I got a new BMW for my beautiful wife.

B: You think you're so big.

　　A: 와이프줄려고 새로 BMW 뽑았어. B: 네가 그렇게 잘난 줄 아는구만.

▶ You are nothing
special
당신 대단한 거 없어

Look who's talking 사돈 남말하네

A: You'll never become successful.

B: Look who's talking. Neither will you.

　　A: 넌 결코 성공 못할거야. B: 사돈 남말하네. 너도 못할거야.

You're one to talk 사돈 남 말하시네

A: Your cooking is terrible.

B: You're one to talk. So is yours!

　　A: 네 요리솜씨 끔찍하다. B: 사돈 남말하네. 너도 그래!

▶ You're the one to
talk
이야기할 수 있는 사람

Very funny! 그래 우습기도 하겠다!

A: Here is your birthday gift.

B: One sock? Very funny!

　　A: 여기 생일선물. B: 양말 한짝? 장난하냐!

▶ Take your own
advice
너나 잘해
▶ Don't be bossy
빼기지 마

28 어디 한번 해보자고!

Bring it on! 한번 덤벼봐! 어디 한번 해보자구!

A: I'm going to kick your ass!

B: You think so? Bring it on!

    A: 너 내가 혼내 줄거야! B: 그럴까? 한번 덤벼봐!

▸ Gang up on me!
다 덤벼봐!

Bite me 배 째라! 어쩌라구!

A: That's the ugliest shirt I've ever seen.

B: Oh yeah? Bite me!

    A: 이런 흉측한 셔츠는 첨 본다. B: 그래, 그래서 어쩔래?

A: I don't like the way you designed this.

B: Bite me. I don't care what you think.

    A: 너 디자인한 게 맘에 안들어. B: 배째. 네 생각은 알바아냐.

ㄴ. 주로 10대들이 쓰는 무례한 표현으로 성인들 사이에서는 농담조로 쓰인다.

Make my day! 할테면 해봐라!

A: I'm giving you a ticket for speeding.

B: Great! Make my day!

    A: 교통딱지 끊겠습니다. B: 잘났어! 할테면 해보쇼!

▸ Go ahead, make my day!
덤벼봐, 한번 해보자구!

He's a dead man 쟨 이제 죽었다

A: Brian has been saying that you're a liar.

B: I'll kill him! He's a dead man!

    A: 브라이언이 네가 거짓말쟁이라고 하고 다녀. B: 죽여버릴거야! 걘 죽음 목숨야!

It's your funeral 그 날로 넌 끝이야

A: After I quit my job, I just plan to play computer games.

B: What a crazy idea. It's your funeral.

    A: 회사그만두고 컴퓨터게임할려고. B: 정신나갔구만. 넌 끝장야.

So sue me 그럼 고소해 봐

A: Your children are bothering me.

B: So sue me.

A: 너희 얘들이 날 괴롭혀. B: 그럼 고소해 봐.

A: You can't park your car there.

B: So sue me.

A: 거기에 주차하면 안됩니다. B: 그럼 고소해 봐.

We've got to get even 되갚아 줘야 돼

A: They've been spreading rumors about us.

B: We've got to get even.

A: 걔들이 우리에 관한 소문을 퍼트리고 있어. B: 우리도 갚아 줘야지.

▶ I want to get even with him
앙갚음 하겠어

I lost my temper 내가 열받았어

A: Why did you start yelling at Carly?

B: I'm sorry. I lost my temper.

A: 칼리에게 왜 소리치기 시작한거야? B: 미안, 내가 열이 받아서.

▶ I've run out of patience
더 이상 못참아

Stop fighting! 그만 싸워!

A: Stop fighting!

B: But she hit me first.

A: 그만들 싸워! B: 쟤가 먼저 날 쳤어.

Did you make up? 화해했니?

A: We had a fight today.

B: Did you make up?

A: 오늘 우리 싸웠어. B: 화해했어?

A: I can't stay angry at you.

B: Me either. Let's make up.

A: 계속 네게 화내지 못하겠어. B: 나도 그래. 화해하자.

▶ Let's make up
화해하자

Can't you patch things up? 화해가 안돼?

A: My husband and I are divorcing.

B: Can't you patch things up?

A: 남편과 이혼중야. B: 화해가 안돼?

 싸울 때 필요한 육지거리들

▸ Up yours! 그만, 젠장할

▸ Go to hell! 꺼져!, 그만 좀 놔둬!

▸ (You) Coward! Chicken shit! 겁장이!

▸ You beast! 짐승같은 놈!

▸ You animal! 짐승같은 놈!

▸ You loser! 멍충이!

▸ You're hopeless 넌 구제불능이야!

▸ You scum! 쓰레기 같은 놈!

▸ You asshole! 바보 같은 놈!

▸ You jerk! 얼간이 같은 놈!

▸ Blow me! 제기랄!, 엿먹어!

▸ Shoot! 이런!, 저런!

▸ Christ! 제기랄!

▸ You shit! 염병할!

▸ You're stupid! 멍충이!

▸ Son of a bitch 개자식!

A: You scum! I know you've been with other women! 버러지 같은 놈! 딴 여자하고 있었지!
B: So you want a divorce? 그래 이혼을 원해?

A: I'm sorry. I didn't mean to cheat on you. 미안해. 바람필려고 한 것 아닌데.
B: You animal. Why couldn't you control yourself? 짐승같은 놈. 왜 통제를 못하는거야?

Chapter **04**

기쁨·슬픔

01 정말 신난다

I'm so excited 정말 신나

A: We're moving in together! Isn't it great!

B: I know, I'm so excited!

　A: 우리 동거하는 거야! 멋지지 않아?　B: 알아, 정말 신난다!

▶ I'm so happy
　정말 기뻐
▶ I'm thrilled
　정말 짜릿해

I'm glad to hear that 그것 참 잘됐다, 좋은 소식이라 기쁘다

A: I'm going to marry a millionaire!!!

B: I'm glad to hear that!

　A: 백만장자랑 결혼할거야!!!　B: 그것 참 잘됐다!

▶ That's great to
　hear
　참 잘됐어

I'm glad that the exams are over 시험이 끝나 너무 좋아

A: I'm so glad that you could come over tonight.

B: Oh no, it's my pleasure.

　A: 네가 오늘밤 들려줘서 너무 기뻐.　B: 어 아냐, 내가 재밌었어.

▶ I'm glad that 주어+
　동사
　…해서 너무 기뻐

I'm glad you like it 네가 좋다니 기뻐

A: That new software package is great.

B: I'm glad you like it.

　A: 저 새로운 소프트웨어 대단해.　B: 네가 좋다니 나도 기뻐.

I feel great[good] 기분 아주 좋아

A: You're feeling all right?

B: Yeah, I feel great. It's because we're moving in together.

　A: 기분 괜찮아?　B: 아주 좋아. 우리 함께 살기로 했잖아.

▶ I feel terrific
　기분 끝내줘
▶ I feel a lot better
　now
　기분이 좀 나아져

You made me happy 너 때문에 행복해

A: Living with you would make me happy.

B: Mona, you don't have to say that.

　A: 너랑 함께 살면 내가 행복해질거야.　B: 모나, 그렇게 말할 필요없어.

I'm so embarrassed 당황했어

A: I heard a rumor that you're pregnant.

B: That's not true. I'm so embarrassed.

A: 너 임신했다는 소문들었어. B: 사실이 아냐. 정말 당황스러워.

I got screwed 망신 당했어, 수모를 당했어

A: How is the car you just bought?

B: It's broken again. I got screwed.

A: 방금 산 차 어때? B: 또 고장났어. 엿 먹은거지.

We're in trouble 곤란한 상황야, 우리 큰일 났어

A: How is business at your shop?

B: Not good. We're in trouble.

A: 가게 장사 어때? B: 안 좋아. 어려운 상황야.

I'm ashamed of myself 창피해

A: I failed the exam. I'm ashamed of myself.

B: You should have studied.

A: 시험에 떨어졌어. 창피하네. B: 공부를 했어야지.

▶ I'm ashamed that
I did that
내가 한 일로 챙피해

It's a big problem 문제가 커

A: Every year the air gets more polluted.

B: I know. It's a big problem.

A: 매년 공기가 점점 오염되고 있어. B: 알아. 큰 문제야.

▶ It's a really serious
problem
정말 곤란한 문제야

It's a pain in the neck[ass] 골칫거리야

A: Can you find a place to park your car?

B: Sometimes. Mostly it's a pain in the neck.

A: 주차할 자리 찾을 수 있어? B: 가끔. 대개는 골칫거리야.

That's the hard part 그게 어려운 부분야

A: We have to decide what to do.

B: That's the hard part.

A: 무엇을 해야 할 지 결정해야 돼. B: 그게 어려운 부분야.

04 정말 오늘 일진 안좋네

This is not my day 정말 일진 안좋네

A: I heard that you failed the entrance exam.

B: Yeah, this is not my day.

   A: 입학시험에 떨어졌다며. B: 그래, 오늘 일진이 안좋아.

▶ Today wasn't my day
   오늘 정말 일진 안좋았어

This is not your[his] day 오늘은 네가[걔가] 되는 게 없는 날이다

A: Did you hear she got into a car accident today?

B: Really? I guess this is not her day.

   A: 걔 오늘 차사고 난 거 알아? B: 정말? 오늘 걔 일진이 안좋구만.

Today is my lucky day 오늘 일진 좋네

A: Today is my lucky day.

B: Why do you say that?

   A: 오늘은 내가 일진이 좋은 날야. B: 왜 그러는 데?

▶ What a lucky day!
   정말 운 좋은 날이네!
▶ This must be my lucky day!
   오늘은 내가 운이 좋을거야!

It's your lucky day 너 재수 좋은 날이야

A: I found some money on the ground outside.

B: It's your lucky day.

   A: 길바닥에서 돈 좀 주었어. B: 재수 좋은 날이구만.

I had a bad day 진짜 재수없는 날이야

A: I had a really bad day at work.

B: Did your boss give you a hard time again?

   A: 오늘 정말 직장에서 왕재수였어. B: 사장이 또 괴롭히든?

I'm having a really bad day 정말 오늘 안좋네

A: Why are you frowning?

B: I'm having a really bad day.

   A: 왜 인상을 찌푸리고 있는 거야? B: 정말이지 오늘 안좋아서.

I had a rough day 힘든 하루였어

A: I had a rough day.

B: Yeah, I understand. Go get some rest.

A: 힘든 하루였어. B: 그래, 이해해. 가서 좀 쉬어.

Rough day for you? 힘든 하루였지?

A: Rough day for you? Go and get some rest.

B: Good idea.

A: 힘든 하루였지? 가서 좀 쉬어라. B: 그렇게 말해줘 고마워.

It has been a long day 힘든 하루였어

A: It's been a long day. How about for you?

B: Me too. Let's finish up and get some beer.

A: 힘든 하루였어. 넌 어때? B: 나도. 그만하고 맥주 좀 먹자.

I'm not feeling up to par today 오늘은 좀 평소와 달라. 컨디션이 좀 안좋아

A: I'm not feeling up to par today.

B: Do you want to go home early?

A: 오늘 컨디션이 안좋아. B: 집에 일찍 가고 싶어?

It hasn't been your day 되는 일이 아무 것도 없는 날이야

A: I had a fight with my husband and I fell while riding the subway.

B: That's too bad. It hasn't been your day.

A: 남편과 싸웠고 또 전철타다가 넘어졌어. B: 안됐네. 되는 일이 없는 날이구나.

Boy, what a day! 야, 정말 짜증나는 날이야!

A: Boy, what a day!

B: What happened at work?

A: 야, 지긋지긋한 날이네! B: 직장에서 무슨 일 있었어?

A: What a day! I'm really tired.

B: Do you want to take a nap before dinner?

A: 정말 짜증나는 날이네! 정말 피곤해. B: 저녁먹기 전에 낮잠 잘래?

05 이제 그만!

That's enough! 이제 그만, 됐어 그만해!

A: How could you say such a thing?

B: That's enough! I had no choice.

    A: 어떻게 그런 말을 하는 거야? B: 이제 그만해! 나도 어쩔 수 없었다고.

▶ That's enough for now
이젠 됐어

I've had enough of you 이제 너한테 질렸어

A: You cheated on me again! I've had enough of you.

B: I promise I'll never do that again. Please forgive me.

    A: 또 바람폈! 지긋지긋해. B: 다신 안 그럴게. 용서해줘.

▶ I've had enough of it!
이제 지겨워 죽겠다!

Enough is enough! 이젠 충분해!

A: I haven't finished the report.

B: Enough is enough! You're fired!

    A: 보고서 아직 못끝냈는데요. B: 이젠 충분해! 넌 해고야!

▶ I'm fed up with it!
진절머리나!
▶ It's boring
지루해, 따분해

I'm sick of this 진절머리가 나

A: I'm so bored with my life these days.

B: I know exactly what you need.

    A: 요즘 내 생활이 너무 따분해. B: 네가 원하는 게 뭔지 알겠다.

▶ I'm bored with~
…에 따분해, 지겨워

I've had it[enough]! 지겹다!, 넌더리나!

A: It's too hot this summer.

B: I've had it. Let's buy an air conditioner.

    A: 이번 여름은 넘 더워. B: 지겨워 죽겠어. 에어컨 사자.

I've had it with you guys 너희들한테 질려버렸다

A: I've had it with you guys.

B: Why are you so angry?

    A: 너희들한테 아주 질렸다. B: 왜 그렇게 성을 내는 거야?

↳ have it with sb[sth]
「…라면 질렸다」라는 숙어.

I've had it up to here with you 너라면 이제 치가 떨려, 너한테 질려버렸어

A: I've had it up to here with you!

B: Hey, calm down!

A: 너 질린다! B: 이봐, 진정하라고!

▸ I've had it up to here
아주 지긋지긋해

That does it 이젠 못참아

A: We're supposed to work late again.

B: That does it. I'm quitting.

A: 또 야근해야 돼. B: 이젠 못참아. 그만 둘래.

└ 주로 장난 삼아 화난 척할
때

I can't take it anymore 더 이상 못 견디겠어요

A: Please stop doing that! I can't take it anymore.

B: You don't love me anymore, is that it?

A: 제발 그만해! 더 이상 못 견디겠어. B: 날 사랑하지 않는구나, 그거지?

A: Turn down that music. I can't take it anymore.

B: Is it too bad?

A: 저 음악 좀 꺼. 더는 못참겠어. B: 그렇게 안좋아?

I can't stand this 이건 못참겠어

A: I hate waiting. I can't stand this.

B: Be patient.

A: 기다리는 건 짜증나. 못참겠어. B: 진정하라고.

A: Why were you angry after the game?

B: I can't stand losing.

A: 게임 후에 왜 그렇게 화난거야? B: 지는 걸 참지 못하겠어.

▸ I can't stand your
friends
네 친구들은 정말 지겨워
▸ I can't stand
losing
지고는 못살아

That's the last straw 해도해도 너무 하는군, 더 이상 못참겠어

A: He wants one more chance.

B: No! That was the last straw.

A: 걔가 한번 더 기회를 달래. B: 안돼! 더 이상은 안돼.

Chapter 04

06 나 좀 내버려둬

Leave me alone 나 좀 내버려둬, 귀찮게 좀 하지마

A: Is there anything I can do? Anything?

B: Yeah, just leave me alone for a while.

    A: 내가 뭐 도와줄 것 있어? 뭐 있어? B: 어, 잠시동안 날 좀 내버려 둬.

▸ Leave me in peace
나 좀 가만히 내버려둬

Give me a break 좀 봐줘요, 그만 좀 해라

A: I need to see your license.

B: Please give me a break. I'm late for my audition.

    A: 면허증 좀 보여주세요. B: 한번만 봐줘요. 오디션에 늦는단 말예요.

Give it a rest! 그만 좀 하지 그래!

A: I need to practice on the piano some more.

B: Don't! Give it a rest.

    A: 피아노 연습 좀 더 해야 돼. B: 제발! 그만 좀 하지 그래.

Stop bothering me 나 좀 가만히 놔둬

A: Would you like to buy some flowers?

B: No! Stop bothering me.

    A: 꽃 좀 살테야? B: 아니! 나 좀 가만히 놔둬.

▸ Don't bother me
귀찮게 하지 좀 마

Stop picking on me 못살게 굴지 좀 마

A: It looks like you never wash yourself.

B: Stop picking on me.

    A: 너 전혀 안씻는 것 같아. B: 못살게 좀 굴지마.

▸ Please stop bugging me
나 좀 귀찮게 하지마
▸ Stop pestering me
그만 좀 괴롭혀

Get your hands off of me! 내 몸에서 손떼!

A: I'm going to beat you up!

B: Get your hands off of me!

    A: 널 때려 눕힐거야! B: 내 몸에서 손떼라고!

Get off my back 귀찮게 굴지 말고 나 좀 내버려둬

A: Tom, get yourself a haircut. You look terrible.

B: Get off my back!

A: 탐, 머리잘라. 정신없어 보이잖니. B: 귀찮게 굴지말고 나 좀 내버려둬!

▶ Get off my case
  귀찮게 하지 좀 마
▶ Get off my tail
  날 좀 내버려둬

Go easy on me 좀 봐줘

A: I'm going to teach you how to fight.

B: Go easy on me.

A: 싸우는 법을 알려줄게. B: 살살해줘.

└ go easy on sth하게 되면
「…을 적당히 하다」라는 의미
의 표현으로 예로 Go easy
on the whisky하면 "위스키
좀 적당히 마셔"라는 뜻.

Have a heart 한번만 봐줘, 온정을 베풀라구

A: I don't care about poor people.

B: Come on, have a heart.

A: 가난한 사람들 알봐아냐. B: 그러지말고, 온정을 베풀라고.

Chapter 04

Don't be so hard on me 나한테 그렇게 심하게 하지마라, 그렇게 빡빡하게 굴지마

A: This is the worst painting I've ever seen.

B: Don't be so hard on me.

A: 이처럼 으악인 그림은 처음 본다. B: 넘 그렇게 내게 심하게 하지 마요.

A: You're doing a terrible job.

B: Don't be so hard on me.

A: 너 정말 일 엉망으로 한다. B: 그렇게 빡빡하게 굴지 마요.

Don't give me a hard time 나 힘들게 하지마

A: That is the ugliest tie I've ever seen.

B: Don't give me a hard time.

A: 이런 이상하게 생긴 넥타이는 처음 봐. B: 나 힘들게 하지마.

Cut me some slack 좀 봐줘요, 여유를 좀 줘, 너무 몰아세우지 마

A: You need to be a better employee.

B: Cut me some slack.

A: 넌 좀 나은 직장인이 되도록 해. B: 너무 몰아세우지 마세요.

▶ I can cut him
  some slack
  걔를 좀 봐줄 수도 있지

07 열받아!

I'm pissed off! 열받아. 진절머리나!

A: I'm really pissed off at you.

B: What for? I didn't do anything to you.

　　A: 정말이지 너한테 짜증나. B: 왜? 너에게 아무 짓도 안했는데.

▸ be pissed off
열받다

She made me mad 걔 때문에 화나

A: Why are you so mad at me?

B: Because you lied to me.

　　A: 왜 나한테 화가 난 거니? B: 거짓말 했잖아.

▸ I'm mad[angry; upset]
화나, 열받아

He got worked up 걔 열 받았어, 걔 대단했어

A: What did John do when his girlfriend yelled at him?

B: He got really worked up.

　　A: 존은 자기 여친이 자기한테 소리지를 때 어땠어? B: 정말 열 받았지.

You're a pain in the neck[ass] 너 참 성가시네

A: Lend me some more money.

B: No way. You're a pain in the neck.

　　A: 돈 좀 더 빌려줘. B: 안돼. 너 진짜 성가신 놈이네.

You're getting on my nerves 신경거슬리게 하네

A: What do you think about Henry?

B: I don't like him. He's getting on my nerves.

　　A: 헨리에 대해 어떻게 생각하니? B: 싫어. 날 짜증나게 해.

▸ get on one's nerves
신경거슬리게 하다, 귀찮게 하다

You're bothering me 너 때문에 귀찮아

A: Why do you want me to leave?

B: Because you're bothering me.

　　A: 왜 내가 가기를 원하는 거야? B: 네가 날 괴롭히고 있잖아.

That burns me (up)! 정말 열받네!

A: She's been saying you are lazy.

B: It's not true. That really burns me up.

A: 걔가 그러던데 너 게으르다며. B: 사실이 아냐. 정말 열받치네.

It's really getting to me 진짜 짜증나게 하네

A: I heard your job is stressful.

B: It is. It's really getting to me.

A: 너 일이 스트레스를 많이 받는다며. B: 맞아. 진짜 짜증나.

▸ She really gets to me
개때문에 열받아(= She really makes me mad)
▸ What gets me is~
내가 열받는 건 …

This makes me sick 역겨워

A: People waste a lot of food here.

B: Yes they do. It makes me sick.

A: 사람들이 여기에 많은 음식을 낭비해. B: 맞아 그래. 역겨워.

Chapter 04

That's disgusting 정떨어진다

A: I wanted to keep his underwear as a souvenir.

B: My God, Mona. That's so disgusting.

A: 걔 속옷을 기념으로 갖고 싶었어. B: 맙소사. 모나. 정말 역겹다.

▸ That's gross
역겨워

It sucks! 밥맛이야. 젠장할!

A: How's your job?

B: It sucks, but I need the money.

A: 일이 어때? B: 밥맛야. 하지만 돈을 벌어야지.

▸ That[This] sucks!
빌어먹을!
▸ You suck!
재수없어!
▸ This vacation sucks
이번 휴가는 엉망진창이야

It stinks 젠장. 영 아니야

A: As of today, we no longer have a travel allowance.

B: That stinks!

A: 오늘부터 출장비 없대. B: 거. 열받네!

▸ That marriage stinks
저 결혼은 영 아니야
▸ This party stinks
이 파티는 역겹구만

08 설마!

I can't believe it! 설마!, 말도 안돼!, 그럴 리가!,이럴 수가!

A: I can't believe it! I did it! I rode a bike!

B: See? I told you it was possible.

A: 말도 안돼! 내가 해냈어! 내가 자전거를 탔다고! B: 거봐? 할 수 있다고 했잖아.

▸ I can't believe you did that
네가 그랬다는 게 믿기지 않아

I don't believe this! 이건 말도 안돼!

A: It's going to cost $200 to repair your TV.

B: I don't believe this!

A: TV 수리하는데 200 달러 듭니다. B: 말도 안돼!

▸ I don't believe it!
그럴 리가!

Unbelievable! 믿을 수가 없어!

A: How did it go with Erin?

B: Oh, unbelievable! We had the best time!

A: 에린과는 어땠어? B: 믿을 수 없을 정도야! 최고의 시간을 보냈어.

▸ Incredible!
믿기지 않아!
▸ Awesome!
끝내주네!, 대단하네!

I'm surprised[shocked] 놀랐어[충격야]

A: Hello, Drake. I'm surprised to see you here.

B: I can't believe you married him.

A: 야 드레이크, 여기서 널 보다니 놀랍다. B: 네가 걔와 결혼하다니 믿기지 않아.

▸ What a surprise[shock]!
놀라워라!

You surprised[scared] me 너 때문에 놀랐어

A: You scared me!

B: Sorry. I just felt like sitting alone in the dark.

A: 놀랐잖아! B: 미안. 어두운데 혼자 앉고 싶어서.

Isn't it amazing? 대단하지 않아?, 정말 놀랍지 않아?

A: Jill lost a lot of weight. She looks beautiful.

B: Isn't it amazing?

A: 질이 살이 많이 빠졌어. 아름다워보여. B: 멋지지 않아?

▸ That's amazing!
거 대단하다!
▸ Isn't that great?
대단하지 않니?

How do you like that? 저것 좀 봐. 황당하지 않아?. 어때?

A: My uncle won $10,000,000 in the lottery.

B: Really? Well, how do you like that!

    A: 삼촌이 1,000만 달러 복권에 당첨됐어. B: 정말? 아, 정말 놀라워!

└. 놀람/충격을 나타내거나 혹은 상대방 의견을 물어보는 표현이지만 요즘에는 예전만큼 많이 쓰이지는 않음.

How about that! 거 근사한데!. 그거 좋은데!

A: I got into the police academy!

B: Imagine that! A police officer in our family.

    A: 경찰학교에 합격했어요! B: 멋져라! 우리 집안에 경찰관이 나오다니!

▸ Imagine that!
어 정말야?, 놀라워라!

How do you do that? 어쩜 그렇게 잘하니?. 어떻게 해낸 거야?

A: How do you do that?

B: Oh, I had years of experience to learn it.

    A: 어떻게 해낸 거야? B: 그냥 수년간 배운 경험덕이지.

What a coincidence! 이런 우연이!

A: What a coincidence!

B: Right, I can't believe that we met in a foreign country.

    A: 이런 우연의 일치가! B: 맞아, 외국에서 만나다니.

What a small world! 세상 참 좁네!

A: I think I met your father once.

B: Really? What a small world!

    A: 네 아버님 한번 뵌 것 같아. B: 정말? 세상 참 좁군!

▸ It's a small world
세상 참 좁네요

You don't say! 설마!. 아무러면!. 정말!. 뻔한 거 아냐!

A: Tell the girl to go easy on him. It's his first time.

B: You don't say!

    A: 쟤보고 살살하라고 해. 걔 처음야. B: 설마!

Don't tell me! 설마!

A: Andy's got a problem.

B: Don't tell me. Did his girlfriend break up with him?

    A: 앤디에게 문제가 생겼어. B: 설마. 애인한테 차였대?

I never heard of such a thing 말도 안돼

A: They say his dog can talk.

B: I've never heard of such a thing.

A: 걔의 강아지가 말을 한다고 하던데. B: 말도 안 되는 이야기야.

What do you know! 놀랍군!, 네가 뭘 안다고!

A: What do you know! Jill arrived at work on time.

B: It's a miracle!

A: 별일야! 질이 제 시간에 출근했어. B: 기적이 일어났군!

Fancy that! 설마!, 도저히 믿지지 않는다!

A: I heard that Mary and Paula are getting married.

B: Fancy that!

A: 메리와 폴라가 결혼할거래. B: 말도 안돼!

I'm speechless 할말이 없어, 말이 안나와

A: My score on the test was perfect.

B: I'm speechless.

A: 나 시험에서 만점받았어. B: 말문이 막히는 구나.

Would you believe 주어+동사? …가 믿겨저?

A: What did your uncle do?

B: Would you believe he gave me a car?

A: 삼촌이 어떻게 했는데? B: 내게 차를 줬는데 놀랍지 않아?

▸ Would you believe it?
그게 정말이야?

A: Fran is going to England. Would you believe it?

B: That's pretty amazing.

A: 프랜이 영국에 간다는데 정말야? B: 정말 놀라워.

It was the last thing I expected 생각도 못했어

A: I heard your dad just died.

B: Yeah, it was the last thing I expected.

A: 너의 아버님이 돌아가셨다며. B: 어, 생각도 못한 일이었어.

09 이런!, 큰일났네!

Oh my God! 아이고!, 이런!, 큰일났네!

A: She's not wearing any panties!

B: Oh my God!

A: 그 여자는 팬티를 전혀 입지 않았어! B: 오 맙소사

▶ Dear me!
어머나!, 아이고!
▶ Oh, dear!
아이고!, 저런!

Good[My] heavens! 저런!, 이를 어쩌나!

A: I just found out that Ian got into an accident.

B: Good heavens!

A: 이안이 사고난 걸 방금 알았어. B: 이런 세상에나!

My goodness! 저런!, 맙소사!

A: John got caught in bed with his neighbor's wife!

B: My goodness!

A: 존이 옆집 부인과 침대에 있다 들켰대! B: 오, 맙소사!

▶ Good grief!
아이고!, 이런 어쩌나!, 야
단났네!

Holy cow! 이런!

A: Bill got fired for stealing.

B: Holy cow!

A: 빌이 횡령으로 회사에서 잘렸대. B: 저런!

▶ Great Scott!
이런! 아이고!

[Oh] Boy! 야!, 이런!, 참!

A: Oh boy! You got World Series tickets.

B: Yeah, and they cost me a pretty penny.

A: 야! 너 월드시리즈 표 구입했구나. B: 그럼, 거금을 들였다구.

Whoops! 아뿔사!, 아이구머니나!

A: The men's room is next door!

B: Whoops!

A: 남자 화장실은 옆방이에요! B: 아이구머니나!

ㄴ Oops라고 써도 된다.

Chapter 04

10 어떻게 이럴 수가 있니?

How could this[that] happen? 어떻게 이럴 수가 있니?

A: A lot of poison spilled into the river.

B: How could that happen?

> A: 많은 양의 독이 강에 퍼졌어. B: 어떻게 이런 일이 생긴거야?

▶ How can this be happening?
어떻게 이런 일이 일어나는 거지?

How could this happen to me?! 나한테 어떻게 이런 일이 생긴단 말야?!

A: I'm sorry, but you failed to get promoted.

B: How could this happen to me? I'm a hard worker.

> A: 미안하지만 너 승진에서 떨어졌어. B: 내게 어떻게 이런 일이? 열심히 일하는데.

It never happened 이런 적 한번도 없었어

A: Did Colleen throw her drink on Jim at the party?

B: No, it never happened.

> A: 컬린이 파티에서 짐에게 술을 쏟았어? B: 그런 적 없는데.

That never happened to me 이런 경험 처음이야

A: Every time I tried to use it, it wouldn't work.

B: How strange. That never happened to me.

> A: 그걸 사용할 때마다 작동이 안돼. B: 이상도하다. 난 그런 적 한번도 없는데.

That has never happened before 난생 처음 겪는 일이야

A: What do you do when this breaks?

B: That has never happened before.

> A: 이게 부러지면 어떻게 할거야? B: 한번도 그런 적이 없었어.

Can you believe this is already happening? 벌써 이렇게 됐어?

A: It's snowing, and it's only September.

B: Can you believe this is already happening?

> A: 눈이 오네, 9월인데. B: 벌써 눈이 올 때가 되었나?

▶ I guess I just can't believe any of this is happening
이런 일이 생기다니 믿을 수가 없는걸

How is that possible? 어떻게 그럴 수가 있지?

A: I lost all the money my parents gave me.

B: How is that possible?

A: 부모님이 주신 돈을 잃었어. B: 어떻게 그럴 수가 있어?

A: I'm pretty sure I'm going to be fired.

B: How is that possible? You're a good worker.

A: 나 잘릴게 확실해. B: 어떻게 그럴 수가 있어? 너 일 잘하잖아.

That can't be 뭔가 잘못된 거야. 그럴 리가 없어

A: You need to buy a new computer.

B: That can't be. This one is almost new.

A: 너 컴퓨터 새 거 하나 사야되겠다. B: 그럴 리가. 이거 거의 새거야.

A: Fred is absent today.

B: That can't be. I saw him this morning.

A: 프레드가 오늘 안나왔어. B: 그럴 리가. 오늘 아침 봤는데.

That can't be good[smart] 그럴 리 없어, 안 좋을텐데

A: His manager wants to talk to him.

B: That can't be good.

A: 부장이 걔랑 이야기하고 싶대. B: 뭔가 이상하네.

A: He put all of his money in the stock market.

B: That can't be smart.

A: 걔는 주식에 갖은 돈을 다 투자했어. B: 현명한 일이 아닐텐데.

It can't be 이럴 수가

A: Her friends say she is already married.

B: It can't be true.

A: 걔친구들이 그러는데 걔 벌써 결혼했대. B: 그럴 리가 없어.

A: We're missing $50.

B: It can't be right. Count the money again.

A: 50달러가 부족해. B: 그럴 리가. 다시 세봐.

It can't be true 그럴 리가 없어

A: I just heard that the president died.

B: It can't be true. He was very healthy.

A: 사장님이 돌아가셨대. B: 그럴 리가. 매우 건강하셨는데.

Something's wrong 뭔가 잘못된거야

A: I'm telling you, something's wrong!

B: Then we should check it out again.

A: 정말이지, 뭔가 잘못됐어! B: 그럼 다시 확인해보자.

That's weird 거 이상하네

A: That's weird. She locked the door.

B: I bet they're doing it.

A: 이상해. 걔가 문을 잠궜어. B: 그거 하겠지 뭐.

▶ That's so weird
정말 이상하네

This feels (very) weird 이상한 것 같아

A: I'm not used to having so much free time. This feels weird.

B: Just try to relax and enjoy yourself.

A: 자유시간을 많이 갖는데 익숙하지가 않아. 좀 기분이 이상해. B: 그냥 긴장 풀고 즐겨.

That's funny 거참 이상하네, 거참 신기하다

A: I'm going to Sydney this summer.

B: That's funny. So am I.

A: 이번 여름에 시드니에 갈거야. B: 거참 신기하다. 나도 갈건데.

A: My hometown is Busan.

B: That's funny. So is mine.

A: 부산이 고향야. B: 신기하네. 나도 그런대.

Chapter **05**

부탁·제안

Step 1 부탁
Step 2 허가
Step 3 제안

01 좀 도와줄래?

Can[Would] you give me a hand? 좀 도와줄래?

A: Could you give me a hand?

B: What do you need?

A: 나 좀 도와줄래? B: 뭐가 필요한데?

▶ give sb a hand
…을 도와주다

Could[Would] you do me a favor? 부탁 좀 들어줄래요?

A: Could you do me a favor?

B: Sure. What is it?

A: 부탁 좀 드려도 될까요? B: 그럼요. 도와드릴게 뭐죠?

Can[May] I ask you a favor? 좀 도와 줄래요?

A: Can I ask you a favor?

B: OK. How can I help you?

A: 좀 도와줄래? B: 그래. 뭘 도와줄까?

Can[May] I ask you something? 뭐 좀 부탁해도 돼?, 뭐 좀 물어봐도 돼?

A: Hey, can I ask you something?

B: Sure. What?

A: 야, 뭐 좀 부탁해도 돼? B: 그래. 뭔대?

▶ I'd like to ask you
something
뭐 좀 부탁할게[물어볼게]

▶ Let me ask you
something
뭐 좀 부탁할게[물어볼게]

Can you help me? 나 좀 도와줄래?

A: Can you help me?

B: Actually, I can't. I have a lot to do tonight.

A: 도와줄래? B: 실은 안돼. 오늘 밤 할 일이 많아.

▶ Would you please
help me?
좀 도와줄래요?

I need to ask for your help 네 도움이 필요해

A: I need to ask for your help again. Sorry!

B: For Pete's sake! Can't you do anything without me?

A: 다시 너한테 도움을 청해야겠어. 미안! B: 제발! 나 없인 아무 일도 못해?

▶ I need to ask you
for some help
네게 도움 좀 청해야 겠어

Would you help me + 동사[with+명사]? ···하는 걸 좀 도와줄래요?

A: Would you help me set up the computer?

B: I'll give you a hand after lunch.

A: 컴퓨터를 설치하는 거 도와줄래요? B: 점심먹고 도와줄게요.

Would you lend me your phone? 전화기 좀 빌려줄테야?

A: Would you lend me your phone?

B: I would, but I didn't bring it today.

A: 전화기 좀 빌려줄 수 있겠니? B: 물론, 근데 오늘 전화기를 놓고 왔어.

▸ Would you + 동사
~?
···해줄래요?

I'd like you to + 동사 네가 ···을 해주었으면 좋겠어

A: What do you want from me?

B: I want you to be my friend again.

A: 날더러 어쩌라고? B: 다시 나랑 친구하자.

▸ I want you to +
동사
네가 ···을 해줘

I'd appreciate it if 주어 + would + 동사~ ···해주면 고맙겠어요

A: I'd appreciate it if you could bring an appetizer.

B: Is there anything else you need?

A: 전채요리를 가져다 주면 감사하겠어요. B: 다른 것 또 필요한 게 있으세요?

I would be pleased if you + 동사 ···해주면 좋겠어요

A: I'd be pleased if you could join us for dinner.

B: I'll have to call my wife first.

A: 저녁식사를 함께 했으면 좋겠네요. B: 아내에게 먼저 전화를 해보고요.

▸ If you could + 동
사, I'd be (very)
grateful
네가 ···한다면 (정말) 고맙
겠어

Consider it done 그렇게 하지

A: I want you to contact her right away.

B: OK. Consider it done.

A: 당장 걔한테 연락해. B: 응. 그렇게 할게요.

▸ No strings
(attached)
아무런 조건없이

02 뭘 도와줄까?

What can I do for you? 뭘 도와줄까?

A: I need to ask for some help here.

B: You name it. What can I do for you?

A: 이것 좀 도와줘야겠는데. B: 말해 봐. 뭘 도와줘야 하지?

▸ Is there anything I can do for you?
뭐 도와줄 것 없어?

Do you want any help? 좀 도와줄까?

A: Do you need any help?

B: Yes I do. Thanks!

A: 뭐 좀 도와줘? B: 응, 그래. 고마워!

▸ Need any help?
도와줘?
▸ Do you need some help?
뭐 좀 도와줄까?

Can I give you a hand? 도와줄까?

A: I'm sorry, but could you hold the door?

B: Sure. Do you need a hand?

A: 미안하지만, 문 좀 잡아줄래요? B: 그럼요. 도와드릴까요?

▸ Do you need a hand?
도와줄까?

If there's anything you need, don't hesitate to ask

필요한 거 있으면 바로 말해

A: If there's anything you need, don't hesitate to ask.

B: Okay. Can you give me some advice?

A: 필요한 거 있으면 바로 말해. B: 어, 조언 좀 해줄래?

▸ Don't hesitate to+V
주저말고 …해

If you need any help, just call 뭐 도움이 필요하면 전화해

A: If you need any help, just call.

B: Thanks. I'll do that.

A: 도움이 필요하게 되면 바로 전화해. B: 고마워. 그렇게 할게.

If you need me, you know where I am 도움이 필요하면 바로 불러

A: I don't know how to thank you. I appreciate it.

B: If you need me, you know where I am.

A: 뭐라 감사해야 할 지. 감사해요. B: 내가 필요하면 바로 불러.

▸ You know where to find me
내 연락처는 알고 있지

Feel free to ask 뭐든 물어봐, 맘껏 물어봐

A: I want to get this report done before I go home.

B: Feel free to ask if you have any questions.

A: 집에 가기 전에 리포트를 끝내고 싶어. B: 질문있으면 언제라도 해.

▸ feel free to+V
편안하게 …하다

I'd be happy to help you 기꺼이 도와줄게요

A: Can you help me pick out an engagement ring?

B: I'd be happy to help you.

A: 약혼반지 고르는 거 도와줄래? B: 기꺼이 도와주지.

▸ I'd be glad to do it
기꺼이 그렇게 할게요
▸ With pleasure
기꺼이

I'll do anything for you 뭐든지 해줄게

A: I'd do anything for you, you know that.

B: That's such a nice thing to say.

A: 너라면 뭐든지 해줄게, 알잖아. B: 고맙기도 해라.

▸ Anything for you
널 위해선 뭐든지
▸ What are friends for?
친구 좋다는 게 뭐야?

Sure. What is it? 그래. 뭔대?

A: Could you do me a big favor?

B: Sure. What is it?

A: 어려운 일인데 좀 도와줄래? B: 그래. 뭔대?

Sure. How can I help? 그래. 어떻게 도와줄까?

A: Would you give me a hand over here?

B: Sure. How can I help?

A: 여기 나좀 도와줄테야? B: 알았어. 뭘 도와줄까?

▸ Sure, what can I do?
그래. 내가 어떻게 해줄까?

Have you had any problems? 뭐 문제있어?

A: Oh, is there a problem?

B: No. Everything's fine.

A: 어, 문제가 있어? B: 아니. 다 괜찮아.

▸ Is there a problem?
문제가 있는 거야?
▸ What seems to be the problem?
문제가 뭔인 것 같아?

03 들어가도 돼?

Is it okay to come in? 들어가도 돼?

A: Hey, uh, is it okay to come in?

B: Of course!

A: 야, 들어가도 돼? B: 물론!

▸ Is it okay[all right] to[if]~ ~?
…해도 괜찮아?

▸ Is it okay if I go out now?
지금 가도 돼?

Would[Do] you mind if I smoke here? 여기서 담배펴도 돼요?

A: Do you mind if I smoke?

B: Yes, I do. I'm allergic to smoke.

A: 담배 피워도 됩니까? B: 아뇨 안됩니다. 전 담배연기에 알레르기가 있어요.

▸ Would[Do] you mind if I go now?
지금 가도 될까요?

▸ Would[Do] you mind ~ing[if]~?
…해 줄래요?, …해도 돼요?

I was wondering if I could get a ride home with you

집까지 같이 타고 가도 돼?

A: I was wondering if I could get a ride home with you.

B: You can, but I'm going to the bank first.

A: 집까지 차 좀 태워줄래? B: 그럼. 그런데, 난 먼저 은행에 갈거야.

▸ I was wondering if you[I] could ~?
…할 수 있을지 모르겠네요?

I'm sorry to trouble you, but could I borrow a pen?

미안하지만, 펜 좀 빌려줄래요?

A: I'm sorry to trouble you, but could I borrow a pen?

B: I only have a pencil, but you're welcome to use it.

A: 미안하지만, 펜 좀 빌려줄래요? B: 연필 밖에 없지만 쓰도록 해요.

▸ I hate to bother you, but can I[you] ~?
미안하지만 …할 수 있을까요?

Let's leave now, if that's all right with you 네가 괜찮다면 지금 나가자

A: Let's leave now, if that's all right with you.

B: Just a moment. I'm waiting for Mike to call.

A: 네가 괜찮으면 지금 나가자. B: 잠깐만. 마이크 전화가 올거야.

▸ if you don't mind
네가 괜찮다면

▸ if it's okay with you
당신이 좋다면, 괜찮다면

04 뭐 좀 갖다 줄까?

Can I get you something? 뭐 좀 사다줄까?, 뭐 좀 갖다줄까?

A: Can I get you something?

B: No, thank you. I'm being helped now.

A: 뭐 필요한 게 있으신가요? B: 괜찮아요. 다른 사람이 봐주고 있거든요.

▸ Can I get you anything?
내가 뭐 사다줄[갖다줄] 거라도 있어?

Can I get you some coffee? 커피 좀 갖다줄까?

A: Can I get you another latte?

B: No, no, I'm still working on mine.

A: 라테 한잔 더 갖다줄까? B: 아뇨. 아직 이거 다 안마셨어.

▸ Can I get you another glass of wine?
와인 한 잔 더 갖다드릴까요?

What can I get for you? 뭘 갖다 줄까?

A: What can I get for you?

B: Could you bring me the newspaper?

A: 뭘 갖다 줄까? B: 신문 좀 갖다줄래요?

I('ve) got something for you 네게 줄 게 있어

A: I got something for you. It's a book.

B: You're so sweet.

A: 네게 줄 게 있어. 책이야. B: 정말 고마워.

▸ I got this for you
이거 너 줄거야

Here's something for you 이거 너 줄려고

A: Here's something for you. I got it on sale.

B: You're very kind.

A: 이거 너 줄려고. 세일 때 샀어. B: 정말 친절도 해라.

This is for you 널 위해 준비했어, 이건 네 거야

A: We got mail today, and this is for you.

B: Please put it on my desk. I'm busy right now.

A: 오늘 우편물이 왔는데, 이건 당신꺼에요. B: 내 책상에 둬요. 지금 바빠서.

Chapter 05

05 …해라(하자)

Why don't you + 동사? …해라

A: Ooh la la! I'd like to get a piece of that!

B: Why don't you ask for her number?

   A: 와우! 나 저 여자랑 사귀고 싶어! B: 전화번호를 물어봐.

Why don't we + 동사? …을 하자

A: Why don't we head over to the mall and do some shopping?   ▶ = Let's+V

B: That's not a bad idea.

   A: 쇼핑센터가서 쇼핑하자. B: 그래 볼까.

You should + 동사 …해라

A: You should get her a present.

B: Why should I do that?

   A: 걔한테 선물해줘라. B: 내가 왜 그래야 되는데?

Let's + 동사 …하자

A: Let's go to the coffee shop around the corner.

B: That's a good idea.

   A: 모퉁이에 있는 커피숍으로 갑시다. B: 좋은 생각이에요.

How about + ~ing[명사; 주어 + 동사]? …하는 게 어때?

A: How about we have one more beer?

B: Sounds good to me.

   A: 맥주 한 잔 더 하는 게 어때? B: 좋지.

ㄴ. How about 다음에는 동사의 ~ing형이나 명사만 오는 것이 아니라 '주어+동사'의 절의 형태로도 많이 쓰인다.

Shall we ~? …할까요?

A: Shall we say around seven?

B: That'd be great.

   A: 7시로 할까요? B: 그럼 좋죠.

Would you like[care] to + 동사 ? …할래?

A: Would you like to begin after a short break?
B: Sounds fine.

    A: 잠시 쉬었다가 시작할래? B: 좋아.

Would you like me to + 동사 ? 내가 …해줄까?

A: Would you like me to read them to everyone?
B: Please.

    A: 사람들에게 읽어줄까요? B: 그래.

Do you want to + 동사 ? …할래

A: Do you want to come over to my place tonight?
B: Sure. What time is good for you?

    A: 오늘 밤 우리 집에 올래? B: 그래. 몇 시가 좋아?

Do you want me to + 동사 ? 내가 …할까?

A: Do you want me to give you a ride to the airport?
B: Yes, I would really appreciate it.

    A: 내가 공항까지 태워다 줄까? B: 그래주면 정말 고맙지.

How would you like to + 동사 ? …하는 게 어때?

A: How would you like to get together? Say next Monday?
B: Monday is fine for me.

    A: 만나는 게 어때? 담주 월요일로? B: 나도 월요일이 좋아

If I were in your situation[shoes], I would + 동사
너의 입장이라면 …할텐데

A: I wouldn't surf the Internet during business hours if I
were you.
B: Why? How are they going to find out?

    A: 나라면 근무시간 중에는 인터넷을 하지 않겠어. B: 왜? 어떻게 알아채겠어?

▸ If I were you, I
would + 동사
내가 너라면 난 …할텐데
▸ If it were me, I
would + 동사
나라면 난 …할텐데

It would be smart to + 동사 …하는 게 좋을 걸

A: It'd be smart to work hard to get promoted.

B: You think I'm not a hard worker?

A: 승진하려면 열심히 일하는 게 현명하지. B: 내가 일 열심히 안한다는 소리야?

I have an idea 내게 생각이 있어

A: I've got an idea.

B: What is it?

A: 내게 생각이 하나 있어. B: 뭔대?

▸ I have come up with an idea
좋은 생각이 하나 떠올랐어
▸ I have a good idea
내게 좋은 생각이 있어

I suggest 주어 + 동사 …을 해봐, …을 제안할게

A: I suggest that you present a speech at the next conference.

B: What's your problem? I told you I don't want to do it.

A: 다음 회의에서 네가 발표해라. B: 왜 그래? 안한다고 했잖아.

▸ I want to make a suggestion
제안 하나 할 게

Won't you join us? 우리랑 함께 할래?

A: We're having a bachelor party for Tom. Won't you join us?

B: Sure! It sounds like fun.

A: 탐 총각파티 할거야. 너 올래? B: 물론! 재미있겠는데.

We might as well + 동사 …하는 게 나아

A: We might as well go home now.

B: You're right. It's already midnight.

A: 지금 집에 가는 게 나아. B: 맞아. 벌써 자정이네.

You do that 그렇게 해

A: I think I'm going to try snow boarding this year.

B: You do that. It should be a lot of fun.

A: 금년에 스노우보딩 해볼려고 해. B: 그렇게 해. 정말 재미있을거야.

Chapter 06

의사소통

01 잠깐 얘기 좀 할까?

Can I talk to you for a second? 잠깐 얘기 좀 할까?

A: Can I talk to you for a second?

B: Sure.

A: 잠깐 얘기 좀 할까? B: 그래.

▸ Can I talk to you for a minute?
잠깐 얘기 좀 할까?
▸ Can I tell you something?
말씀 좀 드려도 될까요?

Can we talk? 얘기 좀 할까?

A: Scott, can we talk?

B: Well, sure...just a sec, though

A: 스캇, 얘기 좀 할 수 있어? B: 어, 그래… 하지만 잠깐만.

▸ Can we have a talk?
얘기 좀 할까?

Can[May] I have a word (with you)? 잠깐 얘기 좀 할까?

A: Can I have a word with you?

B: Sure. What's going on?

A: 잠깐 얘기 좀 할까? B: 물론. 왜 그래?

▸ have a word with sb
…와 얘기나누다
▸ have words with sb
…와 언쟁하다

I want to talk to you (about that) 얘기 좀 하자고

A: Have you been thinking about my proposal?

B: I want to talk to you about that.

A: 내 제안 생각해봤어? B: 그거에 대해 이야기하고 싶어.

▸ I gotta talk to you
할 얘기가 있어

We need to talk (about that) 우리 얘기 좀 하자

A: Oh my God! What are you doing here?

B: I need to talk to you. It's pretty urgent.

A: 맙소사! 너 여기서 뭐하는 거야? B: 너랑 얘기 좀 해야 돼. 꽤 급한 일이야.

▸ We have to talk
얘기 좀 하자

Let's talk 같이 이야기해보자

A: Y'know what? Let's talk later.

B: No! No! I want to talk now! Okay?

A: 저기 말야, 나중에 이야기하자. B: 안돼! 지금 얘기하고 싶어! 알았어?

▸ We'll talk later
나중에 이야기 하죠

Let's talk about it[you] 그 문제[너]에 대해 얘기해보자

A: Shall we go on vacation together?

B: I'm not sure. Let's talk about it.

A: 함께 휴가갈까? B: 몰라. 얘기해보자.

Can I (just) ask you a question? 질문 하나 해도 될까?

A: Let me ask you a question. Which side are you on?

B: I'm with you, of course!

A: 하나 물어보자. 어느 편야? B: 물론 네 편이지!

A: Can I ask you a question?

B: Go ahead.

A: 하나 좀 물어봐도 돼? B: 해봐.

▶ Let me ask you a
question
뭐 하나 물어보자

I have a question for you 질문 있는데요

A: Got a sec? I have a question for you.

B: Sorry, how about later? I have a date.

A: 시간돼? 물어볼 게 있어. B: 미안. 나중에 하자. 나 데이트있거든.

A: I have a question for you.

B: Is it about the subject we were discussing?

A: 하나 물어볼 게 있어. B: 토론했던 거에 관한 거야?

Let me ask you something 뭐 좀 물어볼게, 뭐 좀 부탁할게

A: Let me ask you something. Was he better than me?

B: I guess so.

A: 하나 물어보자. 걔가 나보다 나아? B: 그럴 걸.

▶ Let me ask you
one thing
뭐 하나 물어보자

Let me get back to you (on that) 나중에 이야기합시다, 생각해보고 다시 말해줄게

A: Can you come to my party on Friday?

B: I'll get back to you on that. I might have other plans.

A: 금요일 날 파티에 올 수 있니? B: 나중에 말해 줄게. 다른 일이 있을지 몰라.

▶ I'll get back to
you (on that)
나중에 이야기하자고

02 이것 좀 봐

Look at this 이것 좀 봐

A: Look at this.

B: Wow, that's a beautiful painting.

A: 이거 좀 봐. B: 와, 아름다운 그림이다.

▸ Look here
이것 봐

Well 어, 저기

A: Well, I gotta go now. See you Monday!

B: Okay, have a nice weekend!

A: 저기, 나 지금 가야 돼. 월요일날 보자! B: 그래, 주말 잘 보내고!

▸ So
그래서
▸ Look
저기

Anyway 어쨌든, 좌우간

A: Anyway, how did it go with Kate?

B: Oh, it was great!

A: 어쨌든, 케이트와는 어땠어? B: 어, 멋졌어!

By the way 참, 그런데, 참고로, 덧붙여서

A: By the way, what are you doing tonight?

B: I'm headed to the library.

A: 근데, 오늘 밤에 뭐할거야? B: 도서간에 가려고.

You know 저 말야

A: You know, a lot of people don't like you.

B: I couldn't care less.

A: 저 말야, 널 좋아하지 않는 사람들이 많아. B: 알게 뭐람.

▸ As you know
너도 알다시피

Let me (just) say 말하자면, 글쎄

A: Should we get married?

B: Let me just say, I think it would be a big mistake.

A: 우리 결혼해야 돼나? B: 글쎄, 난 큰 실수하는 것 같아.

Let me see 그러니까 (내 생각엔), 저기

A: Do you have time to meet tomorrow?

B: Let me see. I'll call you.

    A: 내일 만날 시간 있어? B: 글쎄. 내가 전화할게.

ㄴ. 뒤에 명사나 절이 나오면
「...보자」, 「생각해보자」라는
의미가 된다.

A: Let me see what you've come up with.

B: It's not much, but it's a start.

    A: 네가 어떤 안을 내놓았는지 한번 보자. B: 대단하진 않아. 하지만 이건 시작이니까.

As I mentioned before 내가 전에 말했듯이

A: As I mentioned before, he's a jerk.

B: I agree with you 100%.

    A: 전에 말한 것처럼 걔는 멍청이야. B: 전적으로 동감이야.

▸ As I said before
  전에 말했다시피

How should I put it? 뭐랄까?

A: How's the new recruit doing?

B: How should I put it? He's impressing everyone.

    A: 신입사원 어때요? B: 뭐랄까? 모두 감탄하더군요.

▸ Put it another way
  달리 표현하자면
▸ put it = express

A: What is bothering you?

B: How should I put it? I think you're treating me unfairly.

    A: 왜 그래? B: 뭐랄까? 네가 날 공평하게 대하는 것 같지 않아.

How can I say this? 글쎄, 이걸 어떻게 말하죠?

A: How can I say this?

B: Just take your time.

    A: 이걸 어떻게 말하죠? B: 그냥 천천히 해.

A: I want to tell her I love her. How can I say this?

B: Just be honest with her.

    A: 걔한테 내가 사랑한다고 말하고 싶어. 이걸 어떻게 말하지? B: 그냥 솔직히 말해봐.

03 그거 알아?

You know what? 그거 알아?, 근데 말야?

A: You know what? I just got promoted.

B: Good for you! You deserve it.

A: 저 말야, 나 승진했어. B: 잘됐네. 넌 자격이 있잖아.

Guess what? 저기 말야?, 그거 알아?

A: Guess what? I aced my exam today!

B: I don't believe it! That's great, honey!

A: 있잖아요? 오늘 시험에서 A를 받았어! B: 정말이니! 잘 했다, 얘야!

I'll tell you what 이럼 어때, 이러면 어떨까, 있잖아

A: I'll tell you what. I'll buy a new notebook for you.

B: Really? That's great! You're so generous!

A: 이럼 어때. 새로운 노트북 사줄게. B: 정말? 좋아라! 정말 맘씨가 좋아.

▸ Tell you what
있지

Let me tell you something 내 생각은 말야, 내 말해두는데

A: The president says the economy is improving.

B: Let me tell you something. Don't believe it.

A: 대통령왈 경제가 나아지고 있대. B: 내 말해두는데, 그 말 믿지마.

I have to tell you (something) 말할게 있는데, (솔직히) 할 말이 있어

A: I have to tell you something. You're not pregnant.

B: What are you talking about?

A: 할 말이 있는데. 넌 임신이 아냐. B: 그게 무슨 말이야?

▸ I have to[gotta]
tell you this
이 말은 해야겠는데요

(Do) You know something? 그거 알아?

A: I've never liked you.

B: You know something? I don't care!

A: 널 좋아한 적이 없어. B: 그거 알아? 좋아하던 말던 알바아니!

▸ (Do you) (want to)
Know something?
궁금하지 않아?

I'm telling you 정말이야, 잘 들어

A: I'm telling you. I think my teacher thinks I'm cute.

B: That's not possible!

A: 정말이야. 선생님이 날 귀엽다고 생각하는 것 같아. B: 말도 안돼!

▶ I'm telling you 주어 +동사
정말이지…

A: I still plan to quit this job.

B: I'm telling you that you'll regret it.

A: 그래도 회사 그만둘거야. B: 정말이지 너 후회하게 될거야.

You won't believe this 이거 믿지 못할 걸

A: How did you do on your test?

B: Well... you're not going to believe it... I got 100%!

A: 시험 잘 봤어? B: 어, 못믿겠지만 나 만점 받았어!

▶ You're not gonna believe this
넌 못 믿을 걸, 믿기지 않을 거야

You'll never guess what I heard 내가 들은 얘기는 넌 짐작도 못할거야

A: You'll never guess what I heard.

B: Is it a secret?

A: 넌 내가 무슨 이야기를 들었는지 짐작도 못할거야. B: 비밀야?

Do you know about this? 이거 아니?

A: Do you know about this? The earth's getting warmer.

B: Yeah, I've read about it.

A: 그거 알아? 지구가 더워진대. B: 어, 들어봤어.

Have you heard? 얘기 들었어?

A: Have you heard? This factory is closing.

B: No. I'm really surprised.

A: 너 얘기 들어봤어? 공장이 문닫는데. B: 아니. 정말 놀랍군.

▶ Did you hear?
너 얘기 들었니?

Last but not least 끝으로 중요한 말씀을 더 드리자면

A: Let's introduce the final contestant.

B: OK. Last but not least, here's Jim Richards.

A: 마지막 참가자를 소개합시다. B: 예. 마지막이지만 무시할 수 없는 짐 리처드입니다.

Chapter 06

04 어떻게 말해야 할지 모르겠지만…

I'm sorry I didn't tell you this before, but~ 전에 말하지 않아 미안하지만…

A: Sorry I didn't tell you this before but I'm no longer at my job.

B: Why not?

  A: 미리 말 안해 미안하지만, 난 실직했어. B: 왜 말안했어?

I don't know how to tell you this, but~ 어떻게 이걸 말해야 할지 모르겠지만…

A: I don't know how to tell you this, but I think your wife's cheating on you.

B: What makes you think so?

  A: 뭐라 얘기해야 할지 모르겠지만 네 아내 바람피고 있어. B: 왜 그렇게 생각하는 거야?

I'm afraid to say this, but~ 이런 말 하기 좀 미안하지만…

A: I'm afraid to say this, but you're not going to get a raise.

B: What? Are you pulling my leg?

  A: 말하기 좀 그렇지만 너 임금동결야. B: 뭐라고? 날 놀리는 거야?

I've never told you this, but~ 전에 말한 적이 없지만…

A: I've never told you this, but I'm gay.

B: Really? But you're married!

  A: 전에 말한 적이 없지만 나, 게이야. B: 정말? 하지만 넌 결혼했잖아!

I don't know if I've told you this, but~ 내가 이걸 말했는지 모르겠지만…

A: I don't know if I've told you this, but I'm not rich.

B: What? I can't believe it.

  A: 이걸 말했는지 모르겠지만, 난 부자가 아니야. B: 뭐? 이럴 수가.

If (my) memory serves me correctly[right] 내 기억이 맞다면

A: What time does the game start?

B: If memory serves me correctly, it's at 7.

  A: 경기는 몇 시에 시작하니? B: 내 기억이 맞다면 7시에.

That reminds me 그러고 보니 생각나네

A: Can you lend me $20 for a few months?

B: That reminds me. You still owe me money.

A: 몇 달간 20 달러 빌려줄래? B: 그러고보니 생각나네. 나한테 빚진 것도 있잖아.

> ▸ That rings a bell
> 얼핏 기억이 나네요

Rumor has it (that) 주어+동사 …라는 소문을 들었어

A: Rumor has it that you'll be transferred to New York.

B: Right. I'm leaving next Sunday.

A: 소문듣자니 뉴욕으로 전근간다며. B: 맞아. 다음 일요일에 떠나.

> ▸ A little bird told me
> 소문으로 들었어

I heard through the grapevine that~ …라는 것을 풍문으로 들었다

A: I heard through the grapevine that you're going to get married.

B: Who told you that?

A: 결혼할거라며? B: 누가 그래?

I got wind of it 그 얘기를 들었어, 그런 얘기가 있더라

A: Is it true that Richard broke up with Jill?

B: I think so. I just got wind of it.

A: 리차드가 질과 헤어진 게 사실야? B: 그럴걸. 풍문으로 들었어.

> ▸ get wind of~
> …을 풍문으로 듣다

I'm probably out of line here 이렇게 말해도 좋을지 모르겠지만

A: I'm probably out of line here, but I think you're an alcoholic.

B: Really? You think I drink too much?

A: 지나칠지 모르지만 알코중독예요. B: 정말요? 내가 너무 많이 마시는 것 같아요?

I may be way out on a limb here 이게 맞는 말인지 모르겠지만

A: I think it's wrong. I may be way out on a limb here.

B: Please explain your feelings.

A: 그건 아냐. 내가 맞는지 모르겠지만. B: 네 느낌을 말해봐.

I have a confession to make 고백할게 하나 있어

A: I have a confession to make. I damaged your car.

B: What're you going to do next?

A: 고백할게 있어. 네 차를 망가트렸어. B: 이제 어쩔거야?

05 말 좀 해봐

Tell me something 말 좀 해봐

A: Come on Kate, tell me what you're thinking.

B: I'm thinking, I want to order a pizza.

A: 자 케이트야, 네 생각을 말해봐. B: 생각중야, 피자를 주문할려고.

▸ Tell me what
you're thinking
네 생각이 뭔지 말해봐
▸ So, tell me
자, 말해봐

Let's have it 어서 말해봐. 내게 줘

A: I'd like to tell you about my plan.

B: Let's have it.

A: 내 계획을 말해줄게. B: 어서 말해봐.

▸ Just try me
나한테 한번 (얘기)해봐, 기
회를 한번 줘봐

Like what? 예를 들면?

A: Please bring me some information on the case.

B: Like what?

A: 그 사건관련정보를 좀 가져다 줘. B: 이를 테면?

Such as? 예를 들면?

A: I think you should consider getting another job.

B: Really? Such as?

A: 다른 일 할 걸 생각해봐. B: 정말? 예를 들면?

What else is new? 뭐 더 새로운 소식은 없어?

A: The mayor was caught taking money illegally.

B: So? What else is new?

A: 시장이 불법으로 돈받다 걸렸어. B: 그래서? 뭐 더 새로운 소식은 없고?

▸ Anything else?
다른 건 없나?

You were saying? 당신 말은?. 그래서?

A: Sorry we got interrupted. You were saying?

B: I was saying I'd like to take you on a date.

A: 미안해요 얘기가 끊겼네요. 뭐라고 하셨죠? B: 당신과 데이트하고 싶다고 했어요.

▸ Please go on
계속해봐

06 깜박 잊었어

It completely slipped my mind 깜박 잊었어

A: Why didn't you call me last night?

B: It slipped my mind. Sorry.

A: 왜 어젯밤에 전화 안했어? B: 깜빡했어. 미안해.

It's on the tip of my tongue 혀 끝에서 뱅뱅 돈는데

A: Can you tell me the name of the street we're looking for?

B: Sure! Just a minute, it's on the tip of my tongue.

A: 우리가 찾는 거리명 좀 알려줄래? B: 물론! 잠깐만, 혀 끝에서 뱅뱅 도는데.

I was somewhere else 잠시 딴 생각했어요

A: How come you didn't show up at the meeting?

B: What did you say? I was somewhere else.

A: 회의에 왜 안 온 거야? B: 뭐라고? 잠시 딴 생각했어.

▸ I totally forgot
까맣게 잊어버렸어
▸ I just forgot
그냥 잊었어

Where was I? 내가 무슨 얘길 했더라?, 내가 어디까지 이야기했더라?

A: Now, where was I?

B: You were talking about your new boyfriend.

A: 근데 내가 무슨 얘기했었지? B: 새로 사귄 남자친구 얘기하고 있었어.

▸ Where were we?
우리 어디까지 얘기했지?

What was I saying? 내가 무슨 말하고 있었지?

A: What was I saying?

B: You were talking about your pets.

A: 내가 무슨 말하고 있었지? B: 네 애완동물 이야기하고 있었어.

The cat got your tongue? 왜 말이 없어?

A: Why are you so quiet? The cat got your tongue?

B: I just don't feel like talking.

A: 왜 조용해? 말을 잊었어? B: 그냥 이야기하기 싫어서.

Chapter 06

07 뭐라고?

Excuse me? 뭐라고?

A: Excuse me?

B: I said, what are you doing in here?

A: 뭐라구요? B: 제 말은, 여기서 뭐하냐구요?

▶ Excuse me, I didn't hear
미안하지만 잘 못들어서
▶ I can't hear you (well)
(잘) 못들었어

I'm sorry? 예?. 뭐라고?

A: I need you to call us again after 5 p.m. today.

B: I'm sorry?

A: 오늘 오후 5시 이후에 다시 전화줘. B: 네?

▶ Come again?
뭐라구요?

Say it again? 뭐라구요?. 다시 한번 말해줄래요?

A: I'd like to ask for your advice about something.

B: Say it once more, please.

A: 어떤 일에 대해 조언 좀 구할려고. B: 한 번 더 말해줘.

▶ Say it once more, please.
한 번 더 말해주세요

Pardon me? 죄송하지만 뭐라고 하셨어요?

A: Would you mind telling me why you're late?

B: I beg your pardon?

A: 왜 늦었는지 이유를 말해줄래요? B: 뭐라고 하셨죠?

▶ Pardon?
뭐라고요?
▶ I beg your pardon?
뭐라고 하셨죠?

What was that again? 뭐라고 했어요?

A: You have terrible body odor.

B: What was that again?

A: 너 암내가 지독해. B: 뭐라고 했어?

What did you say? 뭐라고 했는데?. 뭐라고?

A: What did you say?

B: I said I thought you were a good kisser.

A: 뭐라고 했는데? B: 네가 키스를 잘 할거라고 생각했다고 했어.

Say what? 뭐라고? 다시 말해줄래?

A: I have a date with your sister tonight.

B: Say what?

A: 나 오늘 밤에 네 여동생이랑 데이트가 있어. B: 뭐야?

▸ Says who?
누가 그래?, 누가 어쨌다
구?

Would you speak slower, please? 조금 천천히 말씀해줄래요?

A: Give me a call at 536-1362.

B: Would you speak slower, please?

A: 536-1362로 전화해주세요. B: 조금 천천히 말씀해줄래요?

Could[Would] you please repeat that? 다시 한번 말해줄래요?

A: The total sales for last month were $3,000.

B: Could you please repeat that?

A: 이번달 총매상이 3,000달러야. B: 다시 한번 말해줄래요?

Tell her what? 그녀에게 뭐라고 하라고?

A: You should tell her everything.

B: Tell her what? What does she need to know?

A: 걔한테 다 이야기해야 돼. B: 걔한테 뭘? 걔가 알아야 되는게 뭔대?

▸ You're what?
뭐하고 있다고?, 뭐라고?

You did what? 네가 뭐 어쨌다구?

A: I went to the library to get a book.

B: You went where?

A: 책 빌리러 도서관에 갔었어. B: 어디에 갔다구?

▸ You did it when?
언제 그랬다구?
▸ Who did what?
누가 무엇을 했다고?

You did? 그랬어?

A: I just got my driver's license today!

B: You did?

A: 오늘 운전면허를 땄어! B: 그랬어?

▸ You do? 아 그래?
▸ You are? 그래?
▸ You were? 그랬어?
▸ You have? 그래?

08 그게 무슨 말이야?

What do you mean? 그게 무슨 말이야?

A: You have been too friendly to the new secretary.

B: I don't know what you mean.

A: 신입비서에게 넘 다정하게 구네. B: 무슨 말씀인지 모르겠군요.

▸ What does it mean?
그게 무슨 뜻이야?

▸ I'm not sure what you mean
무슨 말인지 모르겠어

What do you mean by that? 그게 무슨 말이야?

A: I think you're not being honest.

B: What do you mean by that?

A: 네가 정직하지 않은 것 같아. B: 그게 무슨 말이야?

What do you mean 주어 + 동사? …라는 게 무슨 의미죠?

A: What do you mean you quit? You can't quit!

B: Why not?

A: 그만둔다는 게 무슨 말이야? B: 안돼! 왜 안돼?

What's your[the] point? 요점이 뭔가?, 하고 싶은 말이 뭔가?

A: What's the point?

B: The point is that we're paying too much.

A: 무슨 소리야? B: 문제는 우리가 돈을 더 내고 있다는 거지.

What are you driving at? 말하려는게 뭐야?

A: Are you not telling me a secret?

B: What are you driving at?

A: 내게 비밀을 말 안 할거야? B: 뭘 말하려는거야?

▸ What are you getting at?
뭘 말하려는 거야?

▸ I don't know what you're getting at
무슨 말 하려는건지 모르겠어

What are you talking about? 무슨 소리야?

A: Come on, you know that's not true.

B: What are you talking about?

A: 이봐, 그게 사실이 아니라는거 알잖아. B: 무슨 말 하는거야?

▸ I'm not sure what you're talking about
네가 무슨 얘기를 하는지 잘 모르겠어

What's the bottom line? 요점이 뭐야?

A: What's the bottom line?

B: We have to lay off at least ten people.

A: 핵심이 뭐야? B: 최소한 10명은 해고해야 돼.

▸ What's the catch?
속셈이 뭐야? 무슨 꿍꿍이
야?

What are you trying to say? 무슨 말을 하려는 거야?

A: Maybe you should eat better food.

B: What are you trying to say? Do I look unhealthy?

A: 음식을 좀 더 잘 들어야 될 거예요. B: 무슨 말예요? 아파 보여요?

I don't get it[that] 모르겠어, 이해가 안돼

A: What's wrong with you today?

B: I don't get it. This stuff is too hard.

A: 오늘 안 좋은 일 있니? B: 이해가 잘 안돼. 이 일은 너무 어려워

▸ I didn't quite get
that
잘 이해가 안돼
▸ I can't get it right
제대로 이해 못하겠어

I didn't catch that 그 말을 못 알아들었어요

A: I need you to come over here at 5 p.m. tomorrow.

B: I'm sorry, I didn't catch that.

A: 내일 오후 5시에 이리 와라. B: 죄송하지만, 못 알아들었어요.

▸ I didn't catch
what you just said
네 말이 무슨 뜻인지 모르
겠어

You lost me 못 알아듣겠는데

A: Could you understand my explanation?

B: No, you lost me.

A: 내 설명 이해하겠어요? B: 아뇨, 모르겠는데요.

▸ You lost me (back)
at ~
…부터는 무슨 얘긴지 모르
겠어

I can't follow you 무슨 말인지 모르겠어

A: I can't follow you. Please speak slower.

B: Sure, I'll try to make it easier to understand.

A: 이해가 안되니 좀 천천히 말해줘요. B: 좋아요, 이해하기 쉽게 말할게요.

▸ I can't see your
point
무슨 말하는지 모르겠어
▸ That's not clear
분명하지가 않아

Chapter 06

09 무슨 의미인지 알아

I know what you mean 무슨 의미인지 알아

A: I can't believe it's finally Friday!

B: I know what you mean. It's been a long week.

> A: 기다리고 기다리던 금요일이 왔구나! B: 왜 그러는지 알아. 긴 한 주였지.

▸ TGIF = Thank God It's Friday

I know what you're saying 무슨 말인지 알아

A: With this salary cut, I'll have to be frugal.

B: I know what you're saying. I lost 10 percent of my salary.

> A: 급여삭감됐으니 아껴야지. B: 맞아. 10% 깎였어.

That's what I'm saying 내 말이 그 말이야

A: We have to change our policy first.

B: That what I'm saying.

> A: 먼저 우리 정책을 바꾸어야 해. B: 내 말이 그 말이야.

I got it 알았어

A: Come on, Mandy! We're going to be late!

B: I got it. Quit yelling at me and relax.

> A: 서둘러, 맨디! 늦겠어! B: 알았어. 소리 좀 그만 지르고 마음을 느긋히 가져.

▸ I get the idea
알겠어
▸ I get the picture
알겠어
▸ I got this
내가 처리할게, 내가 계산할게

You got it 맞아, 바로 그거야, 알았어

A: Let me know if she likes me, okay?

B: You got it.

> A: 걔가 날 좋아하는 지 알려줘, 알았지? B: 알았어.

I get your point 무슨 말인지 알아들었어, 알겠어요

A: Please make it neat, short, and clear.

B: I get your point. How short should I make it?

> A: 깔끔하고 짤막하면서도 분명하게 해줘. B: 알았어, 얼마나 짧게 해야 돼죠?

▸ I (can) see your point
네 말을 알겠어

I can see that 알겠어, 알고 있어요

A: I don't like you going out with my daughter Jina.

B: Okay. I can see that.

A: 네가 내 딸 지나와 사귀는 게 싫네. B: 예, 알겠어요.

▸ I can see that ~
…임을 알겠다, …이구나

So I figured it out 그래서 (연유를) 알게 되었지

A: Did you solve the math problem?

B: Yep. I worked all night on it, so I figured it out.

A: 그 수학문제 풀었어? B: 어, 밤새 씨름해서 알아냈어.

▸ Say no more
더 말 안해도 돼, 알았어 무슨 말인지

We're talking the same language 이제 얘기가 된다

A: I'd love to eat a hamburger right now.

B: We're talking the same language. Let's go.

A: 지금 햄버거 먹고 싶어. B: 같은 생각이야. 가자.

▸ You're speaking my language
이제 얘기가 되는 구만

▸ We're not speaking the same language
말이 안 통하는군

Now you're talking 그래 바로 그거야, 그렇지!

A: Let's go down to the beach and have a bonfire.

B: Now you're talking!

A: 해변으로 가서 모닥불을 피우자. B: 야, 이제야 얘기가 돼네!

Bingo 바로 그거야

A: You mean he got fired?

B: Bingo!

A: 그 친구가 해고당했단 말이야? B: 바로 그 말이지!

▸ You took the words right out of my mouth
내가 하고 싶은 말이야

You're getting it! 이제 알아듣는 구만!

A: Do you mean he might like me?

B: You're getting it!

A: 걔가 날 좋아할 지도 모른단 말야? B: 이제 이해하네!

▸ Am I getting warm?
(정답 등에) 가까워지고 있는 거야?

▸ Not even close
어림도 없어

▸ You came close!
(퀴즈 등) 거의 다 맞췄어!

10 일리가 있어

That makes sense 일리가 있어

A: What do you think about his excuse?

B: It makes sense to me.

A: 그 사람이 한 변명에 대해 어떻게 생각해? B: 나름대로 일리가 있는 걸.

▶ That does make sense
그건 정말 일리가 있는 말이야

That figures 그럴 줄 알았어, 그럼 그렇지

A: They are getting a divorce.

B: Well, that figures. They were always getting into fights.

A: 걔네들 이혼할거래. B: 어, 그렇지. 항상 싸워잖아.

▶ figure it out
알아내다
▶ get into fights
싸우다

That explains it 그럼 설명이 되네, 아 그래서 이런 거구나

A: She was angry because her mom didn't come.

B: That explains it.

A: 걔는 엄마가 오지 않아서 화났어. B: 그래서 그랬구만.

No wonder 당연하지

A: They didn't give me a raise.

B: No wonder. You've always been late.

A: 봉급을 안 올려줬어. B: 당연하지. 넌 항상 지각했잖아.

It all adds up 앞뒤가 들어 맞아

A: They've been planning a surprise birthday party. It all adds up.

B: Yeah, you figured it out.

A: 서프라이즈 생일파티를 준비했구만. 이제 앞뒤가 맞네. B: 그래, 알아차렸구만.

I knew it 그럴 줄 알았어

A: What should I do? I got her pregnant.

B: I knew it. I told you to use a condom.

A: 어떻게 해야지? 걔를 임신시켰어. B: 그럴 줄 알았어. 콘돔쓰라고 했잖아.

It is just as I imagined 내 생각했던 대로야

A: Did you like Australia?

B: Yes. It is just as I imagined it would be.

   A: 호주 좋아해? B: 응. 내가 상상하던 대로야.

▸ It's just like I dreamed
내가 생각했던 거와 똑같아

See? I told you 거봐? 내가 뭐랬어

A: I guess she wants to be my friend.

B: See? I told you.

   A: 걔가 나랑 친구하고 싶은가봐. B: 거봐 내가 뭐랬어?

▸ See? I told you so
거봐? 내가 그랬잖아
▸ See? I'm right
거봐? 내가 맞잖아

See? Didn't I tell you so? 거봐? 내가 그러지 않았어?

A: This food is great.

B: See? Didn't I tell you so?

   A: 음식이 아주 좋아. B: 거봐? 내가 그러지 않았어?

I said that, didn't I? 내가 그랬지, 안그래?

A: Well, the new computer game is a failure.

B: I knew it would be. I said that, didn't I?

   A: 어, 새로운 컴퓨터 게임은 실패야. B: 그럴 줄 알았어. 내가 그랬지, 그렇지 않아?

You see that? 봤지?, 내 말이 맞지?

A: So the Yankees lost the baseball game.

B: You see that? I was right.

   A: 그래서 양키스가 게임에서 졌어. B: 봤지? 내가 맞았어.

That's why 주어 + 동사 그래서 …하는 거야

A: That business is really cut-throat.

B: That's why I decided to quit.

   A: 그 사업은 정말 치열해. B: 그래서 내가 그만 두려고 하는 거야.

That's because 주어 + 동사 그건 …때문이야

A: I never got an invitation to your wedding.

B: That's because I didn't want you to come!

   A: 네 결혼식 초대 못받았어. B: 네가 오길 원치 않으니까!

11 이해가 됐어?, 알았어?

You got it? 알았어?

A: All right now, memorize it. You got it?

B: Oh yes.

A: 자 이젠 메모하라고. 알았어? B: 어 알았어.

▸ You got that?
알아 들었어?
▸ You got that, right?
제대로 알아 들었어?

(Do) You know what I mean? 무슨 말인지 알겠어?

A: Do you know what I mean?!

B: Yeah! You're saying you need to get laid tonight.

A: 무슨 말인지 알겠어?! B: 어! 오늘 밤 하고 싶다는 거지.

(Do) You know what I'm saying? 무슨 얘기인지 알겠어?

A: Do you know what I'm saying?

B: Sorry, I don't understand.

A: 무슨 말인지 알겠어? B: 미안, 모르겠어.

▸ (Do) You understand what I'm saying?
내 말 이해돼요?

See what I'm saying? 무슨 말인지 알지?

A: You're just an average worker. See what I'm saying?

B: Not really.

A: 넌 평범한 직원이야. 무슨 말인지 알아? B: 정말 모르겠어.

You know what I'm talking about? 내 말이 무슨 말인지 알아?

A: You know what I'm talking about?

B: Sure. I totally agree with you.

A: 내 말이 무슨 말인지 알아? B: 물론. 전적으로 네 말에 동의해.

Are you with me? 내 말 이해 돼?, 내 편이 돼줄테야?

A: Let's sell those bonds in a hurry. Are you with me?

B: Yes, let's go for it.

A: 빨리 그 채권을 팔자. 알겠지? B: 그럽시다!

Are you following me? 알아듣고 있지?

A: Are you following me?

B: No, I don't think I agree.

    A: 알아듣고 있지? B: 아니, 난 다른 생각이야.

▸ Do you follow me?
내 말 아시겠죠?

Do I make myself clear? 내 말이 무슨 말인지 알겠어?

A: That needs to be mailed today. Do I make myself clear?

B: Yes, I'll go and mail it right now.

    A: 오늘 보내야 돼. 무슨 말인지 알지? B: 예, 지금 바로 부치도록 할게요.

▸ Am I making myself understood?
제 말이 잘 전달되었는지 모르겠어요

Am I getting through on this? 이 문제에 관해서는 내 말을 잘 알겠지?

A: Am I getting through on this?

B: Can you explain it again?

    A: 이 문제에 대해 내 말 잘 알았지? B: 다시 한번 설명해줄래?

▸ get through sth
…을 이겨내다, 해내다

(Do) You get the picture? 너 이해했어?

A: You're in trouble. You get the picture?

B: Why am I in trouble?

    A: 넌 곤란에 빠졌어. 알겠어? B: 내가 왜 곤란에 빠졌는데?

▸ Get the message?
알아들었어?

Understood? 알았어?

A: You have to improve. Understood?

B: Understood.

    A: 넌 향상되어야 해. 알았어? B: 알았어.

▸ Do you understand?
이해했어?

Is that clear? 분명히 알겠어?

A: I want you to get me a present. Is that clear?

B: Why should I do that?

    A: 선물 사다줘. 알았지? B: 왜 그래야 되는데?

▸ Do you read me?
내 말 들려?, 무슨 말인지 알겠어?
▸ (Do you) See?
알겠어?

12 내 말 좀 들어봐

(You) Listen to me! 내 말 좀 들어봐!

A: I'm not going to give up.

B: Listen to me! You are wrong!

A: 난 포기 안 할거야. B: 내 말 좀 들어봐! 네가 틀렸어!

Are you listening to me? 듣고 있어?

A: Are you listening to me? It's urgent.

B: Sorry, what did you say?

A: 듣고 있어? 급한 일이야. B: 미안, 뭐라고 했는데?

▶ You don't seem to be listening
안 듣는 것 같은데

You're just not listening 딴 짓하고 있네

A: Look, don't get so upset at me.

B: I'm angry because you're just not listening.

A: 이봐, 나한테 너무 화내지 마. B: 네가 내 말을 듣지 않으니까 화난거지.

Hear me out 내 말 끝까지 들어봐

A: Don't lie to me. I'm not stupid.

B: Please hear me out. I can explain this.

A: 거짓말 마. 내가 바보인 줄 알아. B: 끝까지 들어봐. 내가 설명할 수 있어.

I'm talking to you! 내가 하는 말 좀 잘 들어봐!

A: What're you looking at? Hey! I'm talking to you.

B: Nothing. I'm not looking at anything.

A: 어딜 보는 거야? 이봐! 내 말 잘 들으란 말야. B: 아무데도 안 보고 있었어요.

Stay with me 끝까지 들어봐

A: Stay with me on this.

B: I'm trying to understand you.

A: 이거 끝까지 들어봐. B: 이해하려고 노력하고 있어.

▶ That's not the end of the story
얘기가 끝난 게 아냐

How many times do I have to tell you? 도대체 몇번을 말해야 알겠어?

A: I forgot to lock the door to the office last night.
B: God damn it! How many times do I have to tell you?

A: 간 밤에 사무실 문 잠그는 걸 깜빡했어. B: 빌어먹을! 도대체 몇번을 말해야 알겠어?

If I've told you once, I've told you a thousand times
한 번만 더 얘기하면 천번 째다

A: You don't have to nag me about studying.
B: If I've told you once, I've told you a thousand times.
   You have to study harder.

A: 공부하라고 성가시게 하지 마요. B: 한 번만 더 얘기하면 천번 째다. 공부 더 열심히 해야지.

I'm listening 듣고 있어, 어서 말해

A: Please let me explain why I did that.
B: I'm listening. Go ahead, but make it short.

A: 내가 왜 그랬는지 설명할게요. B: 어서 말해. 어서 말하는데 짧게 해.

▸ I'm not listening to you
난 네 말 안 듣는다고

They're not listening to me 걔네들이 내 말 들으려고 하지도 않아

A: Tell those students to sit down.
B: They're not listening to me.

A: 저 학생들보고 앉으라고 해. B: 내 말을 안들어.

I am all ears 귀 쫑긋 세우고 들을게

A: Do you want to hear how we met for the first time?
B: Of course. I'm all ears.

A: 우리가 첨 어떻게 만났는 지 알고 싶어? B: 물론이지. 열심히 들을게.

▸ She was all ears
그 여자는 열심히 경청했다

Chapter 06

13 우리끼리 이야기인데

This is just between you and me 이건 우리끼리 이야기야

A: Honey, this is just between you and me.

B: Sure, I won't say a word.

A: 자기야, 이건 우리끼리 이야기야. B: 물론, 일언반구도 안 할게.

▸ It's a secret
비밀야
▸ This is for your eyes only
이건 너만 알고 있어야 돼

Keep your mouth shut(about sth or sb) …에 대해 누구한테도 말하면 안돼

A: Is this a secret?

B: Yes it is. Keep your mouth shut.

A: 이거 비밀야? B: 어 그래. 입다물고 있어.

Mum's the word 입 꼭 다물고 있어

A: There's a surprise birthday party for Cindy.

B: OK, mum's the word.

A: 신디에게 깜짝파티를 열어줄거야. B: 알았어. 입 다물고 있을게.

Don't tell anyone my secret! 아무한테도 말하지마!

A: I found out you're cheating on your husband.

B: Don't tell anyone my secret!

A: 남편몰래 바람피는 걸 알아냈어. B: 아무한테도 말하지마요!

Could you keep a secret? 비밀로 해주실래요?

A: Could you keep a secret?

B: Sure. What is it?

A: 비밀 지켜줄래? B: 그럼. 뭔대?

▸ keep a secret
비밀로 하다

Your secret's safe with me 비밀 지켜드릴게요

A: Please don't repeat this.

B: Your secret's safe with me.

A: 이건 반복하지마. B: 절대 비밀 지킬게.

A: Please don't tell anyone I'm dating my professor.

B: Your secret's safe with me.

A: 교수랑 사귄다고 얘기하면 안돼. B: 절대 비밀 지킬게.

My lips are sealed 입다물고 있을게요

A: Don't tell my wife that I cheated on her.

B: Don't worry, my lips are sealed.

A: 내가 바람폈다고 마누라한테 말하지마. B: 걱정말아, 입다물고 있을 테니.

I won't say a word 한 마디도 안 할게

A: Don't ruin the surprise party.

B: I won't say a word.

A: 깜짝파티를 망치지마. B: 한 마디도 안할게.

I'll take it to my grave 그 얘기 무덤까지 가지고 가마

A: This information is confidential.

B: I'll take it to my grave.

A: 이 정보는 비밀야. B: 무덤까지 갖고 갈게.

▶ I won't breathe a
word (of it)
입도 뻥긋 안 할게

It was a slip of the tongue 내가 실언했네

A: It was a slip of the tongue. I shouldn't have said that.

B: You better watch your mouth.

A: 내가 실언했네. 말하면 안되는 거였는데. B: 말조심해라.

I spoke out of turn 말이 잘못 나왔어, 내가 잘못 말했어

A: I didn't ask for your opinion.

B: I'm sorry. I spoke out of turn.

A: 네 의견 물어보지 않았어. B: 미안, 말이 잘못 나왔어.

▶ I let the cat out of
the bag
비밀이 들통났어

I didn't say anything 난 아무 말도 안했어

A: How did they hear about my divorce?

B: I don't know. I didn't say anything.

A: 걔들이 내가 이혼한 걸 어떻게 알았대? B: 몰라. 난 아무 말도 안했어.

▶ That's an open
secret now
지금은 다 공공연한 비밀인
데

14 고의로 그런 건 아냐

I didn't mean it 고의로 그런 건 아냐

A: Did you say I was fat and ugly?

B: I didn't mean it. I was just kidding.

A: 나보고 뚱뚱하고 못생겼다고 했어? B: 진심이 아니었어. 그냥 농담이었다구.

I didn't mean any harm 마음 상하게 할 생각은 없었어

A: You made everyone angry last night.

B: Really? I didn't mean any harm.

A: 너 때문에 어젯 밤에 다들 짜증났어. B: 정말? 맘 상하게 할 생각은 없었는데.

I really didn't mean any offense 기분상하게 할려는 건 아니었는데

A: You insulted Adam yesterday.

B: Sorry, I really didn't mean any offense.

A: 어제 넌 아담을 모욕했어. B: 미안, 기분상하게 할려고 그런게 아닌데.

I didn't mean to offend you 기분 상하게 할 의도는 아니었어

A: That was a disgusting joke.

B: I didn't mean to offend you.

A: 역겨운 조크였어. B: 기분 상하게 하려는 건 아니었는데.

That's not what I mean 실은 그런 뜻이 아냐

A: So, you think I'm a tramp?

B: That's not what I meant.

A: 그래서, 내가 헤픈 여자란 말이지. B: 내 말은 그런 뜻이 아냐.

That's not what I said 내 말은 그런 게 아냐

A: You think my new hairstyle is ugly?

B: No, that's not what I said.

A: 내 새로운 머리스타일이 추해? B: 아니, 내 말은 그런 게 아냐.

A: I heard you told Sally she wasn't pretty.

B: That's not what I said. I said she needed plastic surgery.

A: 샐리하게 예쁘지 않다고 했다며? B: 그렇게 말한게 아니고 수술해야겠다고 말했어.

I'm sorry, I meant to + 동사 미안하지만 …할 생각이었어

A: You are very ungrateful.

B: I'm sorry, I meant to say thank you.

A: 넌 감사할 줄도 전혀 모르는 구나. B: 미안하지만 네게 고맙다고 말할 생각이었어.

Don't get me wrong 오해하지마

A: Do you really hate my hairdo?

B: Don't get me wrong. I think it's OK.

A: 내 머리모양이 그렇게 마음에 안들어? B: 오해하지마. 괜찮은 것 같아.

▸ get sb wrong
…을 오해하다

You've got it all wrong 잘못 알고 있는거야

A: Tara said you were making jokes about me.

B: You've got it all wrong. I wasn't doing that.

A: 태라가 그러는데 나에 관해 조크했다며. B: 잘못 알고 있는 거야. 난 안 그랬어.

There're no hard[ill] feelings (on my part)

악의는 아냐, 기분 나쁘게 생각하지마

A: I'm sorry that we argued.

B: There are no hard feelings on my part.

A: 다투어서 미안해. B: 기분 나쁘게 생각하지마.

No offense 악의는 없었어, 기분 나빠하지마

A: I don't want to be your friend. No offense.

B: Gee, that's too bad.

A: 너랑 친구하기 싫어. 기분 나빠하지마. B: 아이고, 안타까워라.

Don't take it personally 기분 나쁘게 받아들이지마

A: What did Jesse say about me?

B: Don't take it personally, but he said you were incompetent.

A: 제시가 나에 대해서 뭐라고 그래? B: 기분 나쁘게 받아들이지마, 네가 무능하대.

▸ take it personally
기분나쁘게 받아들이다

Don't take this wrong 잘못 받아들이지마

A: Don't take this wrong, but you're not stylish.

B: Should I buy some new clothes?

A: 오해하지마, 넌 세련되지 않았어. B: 새로운 옷을 좀 사야할까?

MEMO

15 …란 말야?

Do you mean~? …란 말야?

A: I can't come to your house tonight.

B: Do you mean you won't be coming over for dinner?

A: 오늘밤에 너희 집에 못가. B: 저녁 먹으러 못 온다고?

You mean,~ 네 말은…

A: How about we go to a movie tonight?

B: You mean, you and me?

A: 오늘 밤 영화보러 가는 게 어때? B: 네 말은 너와 내가?

A: I don't think I can meet you today.

B: You mean you're not going to come over?

A: 오늘 널 못 만날 것 같아. B: 못 온다는 말이지?

Let me make sure~ 확실히 하자면 …란 말이지

A: I'm leaving my wife.

B: Let me make sure I understand. You don't love her?

A: 아내와 헤어져. B: 제대로 알아들었는지 확인해볼게. 아내를 사랑하지 않는다고?

A: Is everything ready for the presentation?

B: Let me make sure.

A: 발표회 준비 다 됐어? B: 확인해 볼게요.

Let me get this straight 이건 분명히 해두자, 얘기를 정리해보자고

A: Let me get this straight, you are not going to get married?

B: That's right!

A: 정리해보자, 결혼안하겠다는거야? B: 맞아.

▸ We need to get this straight
이건 분명히 해둬야 돼

Chapter 06

Let's just get one thing straight 이거 하나는 분명히 해두죠

A: I'm glad we could have dinner together.

B: Let's just get one thing straight. I don't want to date you.

A: 함께 식사할 수 있어 기뻐. B: 한가지 분명히 해두자고. 너랑 데이트하기 싫어.

That isn't the way I heard it 내가 들은 이야기랑 다르네

A: She stole money from me.

B: That isn't the way I heard it.

A: 걔가 내게서 돈을 훔쳐갔어. B: 내가 들은 이야기랑 다르네.

You're just saying that 그냥 해보는 소리지, 괜한 소리지

A: You look so beautiful.

B: I don't believe you. You're just saying that.

A: 너 진짜 아름다워. B: 이러지마. 그냥 해보는 소리지.

You're just saying 주어+동사 그냥 …라고 하는 거지

A: I think you're really talented.

B: You're just saying that because you're my biggest fan.

A: 난 네가 정말 재능이 있다고 생각해. B: 나의 열렬한 팬이니까 그러는거지.

Would you please be more specific? 좀 더 구체적으로 말씀해줄래요?

A: Go to the store and get me something.

B: Would you please be more specific?

A: 가게에 가서 뭐 좀 사다 줘. B: 좀더 구체적으로 얘기해줄래?

Are you saying that~? …라는 거지?

A: Are you saying that it's a bad idea?

B: That's right.

A: 그게 나쁜 생각이라고 하는 거지? B: 맞아.

Are you trying to say that~? …라고 말하려는 거야?

A: Are you trying to say that this is book is wrong?

B: Right! That's my point.

A: 이 책은 안좋다고 말하려는 거야? B: 맞아! 그게 내가 말하려는 요지야.

16 내 말이 바로 그거야

That's my point 내 말이 그거야

A: I agree with you. We need to change our plans.

B: That's my point!

A: 네 말에 동의해. 계획을 바꿔야 돼. B: 내말이 바로 그거야!

▶ That's not the point
핵심은 그게 아니라고

What I'm trying to say 주어+동사 내가 말하고자 하는 건…

A: What I'm trying to say is we're short-handed.

B: Do you want me to hire more experienced people?

A: 내 말은 일손이 부족하다는 거야. B: 경력사원을 더 뽑으라고?

What I'd like to say is that 주어+동사 내가 말하고 싶은 건…

A: What I'd like to say is that you're not qualified for this job.

B: Are you saying that you're not going to hire me?

A: 내가 말하고 싶은 건 당신은 이 일에 자격이 안 된다는 겁니다. B: 저를 채용 안하겠다는 말씀이죠?

What I'm saying is 주어+동사 내가 말하는 건…

A: What I'm saying is we have to work overtime this week.

B: Not again!

A: 내 말은 이번 주 야근해야 된다는 거야. B: 어휴 또야!

▶ What I said was 주어+동사
내가 말한 건…

I mean,~ 내 말은…

A: I mean, I don't like to be with you.

B: Why do you say that?

A: 내 말은, 너하고 함께 하고 싶지 않아. B: 왜 그렇게 말하는 거야?

I'm just saying (that) 주어+동사 내 말은 단지 …라는 거야

A: I'm just saying that we should get together more often.

B: You can say that again.

A: 그냥 우리가 자주 만나야 된다는 거야. B: 그러게나 말야.

Chapter 06

17 솔직히 말해

Be honest 솔직히 털어놔

A: Be honest! Where were you last night?

B: Honey, I swear I didn't do anything wrong.

A: 솔직히 털어놔! 어제 밤 어디있었어? B: 자기야, 맹세하건대 나쁜 짓 안했어.

▸ You have to be honest with me
너 나한테 솔직히 말해

▸ I'll be honest with you
네게 솔직히 털어놓을게

Level with me 솔직히 말해봐

A: Are you angry? Level with me.

B: Yeah, I feel pretty upset.

A: 화났어? 솔직히 말해봐. B: 어, 많이 언짢아.

▸ I'll level with you
솔직히 말할게

Tell me the truth 사실대로 말해

A: Tell me the truth. Is she hotter than me?

B: No way. You're the hottest girl that I've ever seen.

A: 사실대로 말해. 걔가 나보다 더 섹시해? B: 전혀. 너처럼 섹시한 여잔 못봤어.

You've got to come clean with me! 나한테 실토해!

A: Did you do it? You gotta come clean with me.

B: No, I swear I didn't do it.

A: 네가 그랬니? 솔직히 털어놔봐. B: 아니, 절대로 안했어.

Give it to me straight 솔직히 말해봐

A: I have some bad news for you.

B: Oh? Give it to me straight.

A: 네게 좀 안 좋은 소식이 있는데. B: 솔직히 말해봐.

Don't beat around the bush 말 돌리지 마, 핵심을 말해

A: Don't beat around the bush. What's your problem?

B: Okay, I'll come to the point.

A: 말 돌리지마. 문제가 뭐야? B: 그래, 본론을 말할게.

▸ Let's cut to the chase
단도직입적으로 물어볼게

18 정말야?

Are you serious? 정말이야?. 농담 아냐?

A: I won the lottery. They gave me a new car.

B: Are you serious? That's great!

> A: 복권 당첨됐어. 새 차 한 대 받았어. B: 진짜야? 정말 잘 됐다!

▸ Are you for real?
정말이야?

Are you sure (about that)? 정말이야?

A: We sent the wrong order.

B: Are you sure about that?

> A: 우리가 주문을 잘못했어. B: 확실해?

Is that true[right]? 정말이야?

A: I heard John was killed in a car wreck. Is it true?

B: Yes, that's what I heard.

> A: 잔이 차사고로 죽었다며. 정말야? B: 그래, 나도 그렇게 들었어.

Is that so? 확실해?. 정말 그럴까?

A: I'm going to the prom with Kathy Smith.

B: Is that so? I thought she was going with Paul.

> A: 캐시 스미스와 댄스 파티에 갈거야. B: 정말? 걔는 폴하고 가는 줄 알았는데.

You mean it? 정말야?

A: Why don't we go to Japan this summer?

B: You mean it? That would be so fun!

> A: 이번 여름에 일본에 가자. B: 정말야? 굉장히 재미있겠다!

Do you mean that? 정말야?

A: You look very pretty tonight.

B: Do you mean that?

> A: 오늘밤 너 정말 예뻐. B:정말?

Chapter 06

You're kidding! 농담하지마!, 장난하는 거지!

A: She's such a bitch!

B: You're kidding!

A: 그 계집앤 정말 못됐어. B: 정말!

▸ Are you kidding?
농담하는 거야?, 무슨 소리
야?

No kidding! 설마!, 너 농담하냐!, 진심야!

A: Wow! Everyone here looks so rich.

B: No kidding! This is Beverly Hills.

A: 와! 여기 있는 사람들은 다들 굉장한 부자인가 봐. B: 농담해! 여긴 비버리 힐스잖아.

You're not kidding 정말 그렇네

A: Chris, long time no see.

B: You're not kidding. How long has it been?

A: 크리스, 오랫만이야. B: 정말 그렇네. 이게 얼마만이지?

Is this some kind of joke? 장난하는 거지?

A: I'm going to have to fire you.

B: Is this some kind of joke?

A: 널 해고해야겠어. B: 장난하시는 거죠?

You must be joking 농담하는 거지

A: You will have to pay me $50,000.

B: No way. You must be joking.

A: 5만 달러 내셔야 됩니다. B: 말도 안돼. 농담이시겠죠.

▸ Did I hear you
right?
정말이니?, 내가 제대로 들
은 거야?

Get out of here! 농담하지마!

A: Can you believe I asked Jill out last night?

B: Get outta here! There's no way she said yes.

A: 어젯밤 질에게 데이트신청을 했다면 믿겠어? B: 그럴리가! 걔가 받아들였을 리가 없어.

Really? 정말?

A: The new secretary is a real beauty.

B: You bet!

A: 새로온 비서가 한 미모하는데. B: 정말!

▸ Oh yeah?
어, 그래?
▸ You bet!
정말!

19 진심이야

I mean it 진심이야

A: I mean it. I didn't know about that.

B: Are you sure?

A: 정말야. 난 정말 그거에 대해 몰랐어. B: 정말이지?

I mean business 진심이야

A: Are you serious?

B: Don't laugh. I mean business.

A: 정말야? B: 웃지마. 진심이야.

▸ I don't mean maybe!
장난아냐!

I'm not kidding 정말이야, 장난아냐

A: I'm not kidding. We lost the contract.

B: What are we going to tell the boss?

A: 장난아냐. 그 계약을 따내지 못했어. B: 사장한테 뭐라고 하지?

▸ I kid you not
장난삼아 하는 말 아냐

I'm telling the truth 진짜야

A: I don't believe you met Brad Pitt.

B: I'm telling the truth.

A: 네가 브래드 피트를 만났다는 건 말도 안돼. B: 정말야.

I'm not lying 정말이라니까

A: My family is very rich. I'm not lying.

B: You'll have to prove it.

A: 우리 집은 매우 부자야. 거짓말 아냐. B: 증명해봐.

I am (dead) serious (정말) 진심이야

A: I'm serious, he's in a really bad mood.

B: I'll try to avoid him.

A: 정말야. 걔 기분이 꽤나 안 좋은 것 같아. B: 피해 다녀야지.

Chapter 06

I'll bet 틀림없어, 정말이야, 확실해, 그러겠지

A: I'll be on time tomorrow.

B: I'll bet. You're always late.

A: 내일 제시간에 올게. B: 어련하시겠어. 넌 항상 늦잖아.

ㄴ, 기본적으로 I'll bet은 상대방의 말에 수긍하는 표현이지만 "그러겠지," "어련하시겠어"라는 빈정대는 뜻으로도 쓰인다.

▶ I bet (you) 맹세해
▶ I'll bet you 맹세하마

I'll say 정말이야

A: This is the best steak I've eaten in a long time.

B: I'll say.

A: 진짜 오랜만에 먹어보는 최고의 스테이크인 걸. B: 그래.

You can bet on it 그럼, 물론이지

A: Are you sure you'll be able to do it?

B: You can bet on it.

A: 정말 너 그거 할 수 있어? B: 그럼 물론이지.

You can bet 주어+동사 …인 게 틀림없어

A: You can bet she wants to go.

B: Then we'd better take her with us.

A: 걔가 가고 싶어하는 게 틀림없어. B: 그럼 걔도 함께 데려가자

Believe me 정말이야

A: How could you fail the exam?

B: Believe me, I studied hard.

A: 어떻게 시험에 떨어질 수 있는 거야? B: 정말이지, 열심히 공부했다고요.

▶ Believe you me
정말 진심이야

How true 정말 그렇다니까

A: It's not easy to find a good job.

B: How true. You have to keep trying.

A: 괜찮은 직장을 찾기가 쉽지 않아. B: 정말 그래. 계속 찾아봐.

20  **날 믿어줘**

Take my word for it 진짜야, 믿어줘

A: Take my word for it. He's a real idiot.

B: I'll keep that in mind.

A: 내 말 믿어. 걘 정말 바보야. B: 명심할게.

You have my word 내 약속하지

A: Do you promise to pay me back?

B: You have my word.

A: 돈 갚는다고 약속하는 거지? B: 내 약속할게.

I give you my word 약속할게

A: Can I trust you?

B: Yes. I give you my word.

A: 널 믿어도 돼? B: 어, 내 약속할게.

Mark my words! 내 말 잘 들어!

A: What do you think will happen to Fred?

B: He's bad and he'll end up in jail. Mark my words.

A: 프레드가 어떻게 될 것 같아? B: 못됐으니 감옥가게 될거야. 내 말 잘 들으라고.

(You can) Trust me 믿어봐

A: Please be careful with my car.

B: I will. Trust me.

A: 내 차 조심해. B: 그럴게. 날 믿어.

You'd better believe it 맞아, 정말야

A: I heard you're going to China.

B: You'd better believe it. It'll be fun.

A: 너 중국에 간다며. B: 맞아, 재미있을거야.

Chapter 06

A: Are you going to the festival?

B: You'd better believe it.

A: 축제에 갈거야? B: 맞아.

I promise (you)! 정말이야

A: I promise you, he definitely wants you back.

B: How do you know that?

A: 날 믿어, 걘 네가 돌아오길 바래. B: 네가 어떻게 알아?

∟ I promise와 I promise you 는 같은 의미이지만 I promise you의 의미가 다소 강함.

▸ Promise?
약속하는 거지?

I swear 맹세해

A: Are you sure this is real?

B: I swear it's one hundred percent real.

A: 그게 진짜라는 게 정말야? B: 맹세코 100% 정말이야.

▸ I swear to God[you]
하나님께[네게] 맹세코

I swear I told you all about it 맹세코 다 얘기한 거라니까

A: I never knew he used to be your boyfriend.

B: I swear I told you all about it.

A: 걔가 네 남친인 줄은 정말 몰랐어. B: 정말이지 네게 다 얘기했는데.

Believe what I say 내 말 믿어줘

A: That sounds ridiculous.

B: It's true. Believe what I say.

A: 그거 정말 웃긴다. B: 정말야. 내 말 믿어줘.

You can take it from me 그 점은 내 말을 믿어도 돼

A: She'll come. You can take it from me.

B: How come she's not here yet?

A: 걘 올거야. 그건 내 말을 믿어도 돼. B: 걔는 왜 아직까지 안 오는거야.

▸ Have faith in me
날 믿어줘

It may sound strange, but it's true 이상하게 들리겠지만 진짜야

A: I don't believe you can predict the future.

B: It may sound strange, but it's true.

A: 네가 미래를 예측한다는 걸 믿을 수 없어. B: 이상하게 들리겠지만 사실야.

21 어째서?

How come? 어째서?, 왜?

A: I think I deserve a raise.

B: How come?

A: 급여인상 좀 해줘요. B: 왜?

How come 주어+동사? 왜 …하는 거야?

A: How come you're late?

B: I got caught in traffic.

A: 어쩌다 이렇게 늦은 거야? B: 차가 밀려서.

▶ How is it that 주어
+동사?
왜 …하는 거야?

A: How come you never wear a suit?

B: My boss doesn't mind if I wear casual clothes to work.

A: 왜 정장을 전혀 안 입어? B: 사장이 캐주얼로 일해도 신경안써.

What makes you think so? 왜 그렇게 생각하니?, 꼭 그런건 아니잖아?

A: I think she's on drugs.

B: What makes you think so?

A: 그 여자애는 마약을 하는 것 같아. B: 왜 그렇게 생각하지?

▶ What makes you
so mad?
뭐 때문에 그렇게 화난거
야?

A: It's probably going to rain a lot tomorrow.

B: Oh yeah? What makes you think so?

A: 내일 비가 많이 올 것 같아. B: 그래? 왜 그렇게 생각해?

How did it happen? 이게 어떻게 된 거야?

A: My car broke down.

B: How did it happen?

A: 내 차가 망가졌어. B: 어떻다?

A: There was a serious accident at the factory yesterday.

B: Really? How did it happen?

A: 어제 공장에서 큰 사고가 있었어. B: 정말? 어떻게 된 건데?

What brings you here? 무슨 일로 왔어?

A: Hello, Amanda. What brings you here?

B: I came for the meeting at ten.

    A: 안녕하세요, 어맨더. 무슨 일로 오셨어요? B: 10시에 회의가 있어서 왔어요.

What for? 왜요?, 뭣 때문에?

A: Hey, can you loan me some money?

B: What for?

    A: 야, 돈 좀 빌려줄래? B: 뭣 때문에?

A: What are you going to the dentist for?

B: I'm having some false teeth put in.

    A: 치과에는 왜 가려는 거야? B: 의치 좀 해넣으려고.

▶ What ~ for?
어째서…?, 무엇 때문
에…?

For what? 왜?, 뭣 때문에?

A: I really owe you an apology.

B: For what?

    A: 정말 사과드려요. B: 뭣 때문에요?

What're you doing this for? 왜 그러는 거야?

A: I plan to cause trouble for them.

B: I don't understand. What're you doing this for?

    A: 걔네들 골탕먹힐거야. B: 모르겠구만. 왜 그러는 건대?

Why do you think that? 왜 그렇게 생각하는 거야?

A: You'd be a good lawyer.

B: Why do you think that?

    A: 넌 훌륭한 변호사가 될거야. B: 왜 그렇게 생각하는 거야?

Why do you say that? 왜 그렇게 말하는 거야?

A: I hate him! He's such a prick.

B: Why do you say that? You hardly know him.

    A: 나는 걔가 싫어. 정말이지 얼간이야. B: 그게 무슨 말이야? 걔에 대해 잘 모르면서.

A: I'm really worried about Melanie these days.

B: Why do you say that?

A: 요즘 멜라니가 정말 걱정돼. B: 왜 그러는데?

Why did you do that? 왜 그랬어?

A: Why did you do that last night?

B: I don't know. I guess I was not myself then.

A: 어젯 밤에 왜 그런거야? B: 몰라. 그때 내가 제정신이 아니었나봐.

Why would you say that? 왜 그런 말을 하는 거야?

A: Why would you say that?

B: Because I wanted to hurt you.

A: 왜 그런 말을 하는 거야? B: 그건 네게 상처를 입히고 싶어서야.

What's the reason? 이유가 뭔대?

A: The company is going to fire ten employees.

B: What's the reason?

A: 회사가 10명을 해고할거야. B: 이유가 뭔대?

Tell me why 이유를 말해봐

A: I'd like to go home early tomorrow.

B: Tell me why.

A: 내일 일찍 집에 가고 싶어. B: 이유를 말해봐.

I was just wondering 그냥 물어봤어

A: Why did you ask if Kim was married?

B: I was just wondering.

A: 왜 킴이 결혼했는지 물어본거야? B: 그냥 물어봤어.

A: Why did you ask me about my marriage?

B: I was just wondering.

A: 왜 내 결혼에 대해 물었어? B: 그냥 궁금해서.

Chapter **07**

나의 생각

Step 1 생각
Step 2 기호
Step 3 관심

01 내 생각엔 말야

The way I see it 내가 보기엔

A: My parents don't want me to study art.
B: The way I see it, it's your own choice.

A: 부모님은 내가 미술공부하는 걸 싫어하셔. B: 내가 보기엔, 네가 결정하면 되잖아.

As far as I can see 내가 보기엔

A: Does this dress look good on me?
B: As far as I can see.

A: 이 드레스가 내게 어울려? B: 내가 보기엔.

As I see it 내가 보기로는

A: What should we do?
B: As I see it, we need to save more money.

A: 우리 어떻게 하지? B: 내가 보기로는 좀 더 저축해야 돼.

The way I look at it is~ 내가 보기엔 …이야

A: The way I look at it is that we have to wait until he's back.
B: When do you think he'll get back?

A: 걔가 돌아올 때까지 기다려야 할 것 같아. B: 언제쯤 돌아올 것 같아?

The thing is (that) 주어+동사 중요한 건 …라는 거야

A: The thing is I need to find a date.
B: Well, what kind of guy are you looking for?

A: 중요한 건 데이트 상대를 찾아야 된다는 거야. B: 저기 어떤 종류의 상대를 찾는 거야?

The point is that 주어+동사 요점은 …라는 것이야

A: Could you please get to the point?
B: The point is that we are bankrupt.

A: 요지를 말씀해 주시겠어요? B: 요점은 우리가 파산했다는 겁니다.

A: Charlie needs to pay me the money he owes.

B: The point is that he won't do that.

> A: 찰리는 내게 빚진 돈을 갚아야 돼. B: 요점은 걔가 갚지 않으려고 한다는 거지.

My opinion in a nutshell is that 주어+동사 내 의견은 한마디로 …이야

A: My opinion in a nutshell is that he will win the race.

B: What makes you so sure?

> A: 내 의견은 한마디로 경주에서 걔가 이길거라는 거야. B: 뭐 때문에 그렇게 확신하는 거야?

I (will) tell you what I think 내 생각을 말하면 이래

A: How do you like my cooking?

B: I'll tell you what I think. It's fantastic.

> A: 내가 한 요리 괜찮아? B: 내 생각을 말하면 말야. 아주 끝내줘.

▶ This is what we'll do
우리 이렇게 하자

Here's my plan 내 생각은 이래

A: How can we get a day off?

B: Here's my plan. We'll pretend we're sick.

> A: 어떻게 하루를 쉴 수 있을까? B: 내 생각은 이래. 우리 아픈 척 하는 거야.

▶ Here's my idea
내 생각 들어봐

Here's the deal 이렇게 하자, 이런 거야

A: This house is a mess.

B: Here's the deal. If you clean it, I'll pay you.

> A: 이 집은 아주 엉망이군. B: 이렇게 하자. 네가 치우면 돈을 줄게.

Here's the thing 내 말인 즉은, 그게 말야, 문제가 되는 건

A: Angie lives too far from her job.

B: Here's the thing. She doesn't want to move.

> A: 앤지는 직장이 집에서 너무 멀어. B: 문제는 말야. 걘 이사를 원치 않어.

If you ask me 내 생각은, 내 생각을 말한다면

A: If you ask me, she's making a big mistake.

B: I agree with you. She should not quit her job.

> A: 내 생각에, 걔 큰 실수를 하는 것 같아. B: 내 생각도 그래. 걔는 그만두면 안돼.

Deep down 사실은 말야

A: Ted and Sue have split up.

B: Yes, but deep down, they still love each other.

A: 테드와 슈가 헤어졌어. B: 어, 실은, 걔들 서로 아직 좋아해.

MEMO

02 …인 것 같아

I think~ …것 같아

A: I think it would be better if you went to bed.

B: I'm not tired yet. I think I will watch TV.

> A: 잠자러 가는 게 좋을 것 같은데. B: 아직 피곤하지 않아요. TV볼래.

I guess~ …인 것 같아

A: I guess he got the contract.

B: I thought he was in a particularly good mood.

> A: 내 생각에는 걔가 계약을 따낸 것 같아. B: 걔가 무척 기분이 좋다고 생각했어.

It seems (like) that~ …인 것 같은데

A: What's the problem?

B: It seems that I have lost my wallet.

> A: 무슨 문제가 있으세요? B: 지갑을 잃어버린 듯해요.

▸ It seems that
I have lost my
wallet
지갑을 잃어버린 것 같아

I feel like 주어+동사 …할 것 같아

A: What's the problem?

B: I feel like my head is going to explode!

> A: 왜 그러는데? B: 머리가 폭발할 것 같아!

It looks like[as if]~ …처럼 보여

A: It looks like you don't like your meal at all.

B: No, it's just that I'm not hungry right now.

> A: 밥이 네 입맛에 전혀 맞지 않나 보구나. B: 아뇨, 그냥 별로 배가 안 고파서요.

It sounds like~ …한 것 같아

A: It sounds like you need a new mouse.

B: I probably do.

> A: 새 마우스가 필요할 것 같은데. B: 아마도 그래야겠지.

Chapter 07

A: Have you talked to Jennifer?

B: Yeah. It sounds like she's very happy.

A: 제니퍼하고 이야기해봤어. B: 어. 걔가 매우 즐거워하는 것 같아.

I'm afraid I don't know what to say 뭐라고 해야 할지 모르겠어

A: I'm afraid I don't know what to say.

B: I can't figure it out either.

A: 뭐라고 해야 할지 모르겠어. B: 나 역시 어떻게 말을 해야 할 지 모르겠어.

I doubt that they'll know what to do 걔들이 뭘 해야 하는 지 모를걸

A: I suspect that my son has been smoking.

B: You'd better talk to him before it becomes a habit.

A: 왠지 우리 아들이 담배를 피우는 것 같아. B: 습관되기 전에 아이에게 타일러야 해.

▸ I doubt~
과연 …일까 의심스러워
▸ I suspect~
아무래도 …인 것 같아

I have a feeling that they are not going to show up

개들이 안 올 것 같아

A: I have a feeling that they're not going to show up.

B: That's funny, I had the same feeling earlier today.

A: 내 느낌상 걔들이 안 올 것 같아. B: 재미있네. 나도 오늘 일찍 그랬는데.

I have a hunch that~ …라는 느낌이 들어

A: Do you believe him?

B: I have a hunch that he's lying.

A: 걔 말을 믿어? B: 걔가 거짓말하는 것 같아.

I bet 주어+동사 난 틀림없이 …라고 생각해

A: I bet you will find a new boyfriend soon.

B: I hope so, but I can't forget my ex.

A: 곧 틀림없이 새로운 남친을 만나게 될거야. B: 나도 그러길 바라는데 옛 남친를 잊을 수가 없어.

Let's just say 주어+동사 …라고 생각해

A: Fine, then let's just say she's not my type.

B: Not your type? She's gorgeous!

A: 좋아, 그럼 걔는 내 타입이 아닌 것 같아. B: 네 타입이 아니라고? 걔 끝내주잖아!

03 네 생각은 어때?

How about you? 네 생각은 어때?

A: How's it going?

B: Pretty good. How about you?

  A: 요즘 어때? B: 괜찮아. 너는?

▸ How about it?
  그거 어때?
▸ What about you?
  넌 어때?

What do you think? 네 생각은 어때?, 무슨 말이야? 그걸 말이라고 해?

A: What do you think?

B: I'm sure the store is open.

  A: 어떻게 생각해? B: 상점은 분명 열려 있을거야.

What do you think of[about] that? 넌 그걸 어떻게 생각해?

A: What do you think of the new guy?

B: He's a bit of a show-off, but he gets the job done.

  A: 새로 들어온 그 사람을 어떻게 생각해. B: 좀 잘난체 하지만 일은 해놓더라구.

What do you think~? 어떻게 …를 생각해?

A: What do you think will happen?

B: We're likely to lose everything on the hard drive.

  A: 어떻게 될 것 같아? B: 하드에 있는 게 다 날아갈 것 같아.

What is your opinion? 네 의견은 어때?

A: The doctor said I must get an operation.

B: Really? What is your opinion?

  A: 의사가 그러는데 수술받아야 한대. B: 정말? 네 생각은?

▸ What is your
  feeling about
  this?
  여기에 대해 네 생각은 어때?

What do you think is the best? 뭐가 최선인 것 같아?

A: So you can stay here or move abroad?

B: What do you think is the best option?

  A: 그럼 넌 여기 남을래 아님 해외로 이주할래? B: 어떤 게 최선의 선택인 것 같아?

Which is better, A or B? A와 B중에서 어떤 게 좋아?

A: Which is better, getting married or being single?

B: Personally, I like being single.

A: 결혼과 싱글 중 어떤 게 좋아? B: 개인적으로 싱글이 좋아.

Is it 'yes' or 'no'? 그렇다는 거야 안 그렇다는 거야?

A: I'm not sure if I want to join you.

B: You must decide. Is it yes or no?

A: 너와 함께 할는지 모르겠어. B: 결정해야지. 그럴 거야 안 그럴 거야?

▸ Yes or no?
찬성야 반대야?

Does it work for you? 네 생각은 어때?, 너도 좋아?

A: I have to do my job at night.

B: Does it work for you?

A: 밤에 일을 해야 돼. B: 괜찮겠어?

Did you like it? 좋았어?

A: We went to Disneyland last summer.

B: Did you like it?

A: 지난 여름에 디즈니랜드에 갔었어. B: 좋았어?

▸ Was it good?
좋았어?

Did you have fun? 재밌었어?

A: We went to Australia last year.

B: Did you have fun?

A: 작년에 호주에 갔었어. B: 재밌었어?

Don't you think so? 그렇게 생각되지 않아?

A: This is a nice tie. Don't you think so?

B: It's nice, but it's also expensive.

A: 이거 참 멋진 타이야. 그렇지 않아? B: 멋있어, 하지만 너무 비싸.

Like this? 이렇게 하면 돼?

A: You mean like this?

B: No! Not like that.

A: 이렇게 하라는 거야? B: 아니, 그렇게는 말고.

04 어땠어?

How was it? 어땠어?

A: So how was the honeymoon?

B: Oh, so much fun.

A: 그래 신혼여행은 어땠어? B: 어, 아주 재미있었어.

▶ How was the movie?
영화 어땠어?

How was the movie? 영화 어땠어?

A: How was the movie?

B: I thought it was kind of boring.

A: 영화 어땠어? B: 좀 지루한 것 같았어.

How did you like it? 어땠어?

A: How did you like it?

B: I liked it very much.

A: 어땠어? B: 정말 좋았어.

How'd it go? 어떻게 됐어?, 어땠어?

A: So, how'd it go?

B: I didn't get the job.

A: 그래, 어떻게 됐어? B: 취직 안됐어.

How did it go at the doctor's? 병원에 간 일은 어땠어?

A: How did it go at the doctor's?

B: He said I'm in good physical condition.

A: 병원에 간 일은 어땠어? B: 몸상태가 좋대.

How would you like +명사 ? …는 어때요?, 어떻게 (준비) 해드릴까요?

A: How would you like your meat cooked?

B: Medium rare, please...and can I have a Coke?

A: 고기는 어떻게 요리할까요? B: 약간 덜 익히고… 콜라 한 잔 주시구요.

ㄴ How would you like 다음에 'to+동사'가 오면 권유의 문장으로 「…하는 게 어때?」라는 의미이다.

How would you like it if 주어+동사 ? ···한다면 어떻겠어?

A: How would you like it if I decided to quit?

B: Well, I'd be very disappointed.

    A: 회사를 그만둔다면 어떻겠어요? B: 글쎄요, 아주 실망스러울 거예요.

A: How would you like it if we switched offices?

B: I wouldn't like it at all.

    A: 사무실을 바꾸면 어떻겠어? B: 전혀 그러고 싶지 않은데.

What do you say? 어때?

A: Let's go to Japan in May. What do you say?

B: Sounds like a good idea to me.

    A: 5월에 일본가자. 어때? B: 난 좋지.

What do you say (that) 주어+동사? ···어때요?

A: What do you say to going for a drink tonight?

B: Sounds like a good idea!

    A: 오늘 밤 한잔 하러 가는 거 어때요? B: 그거 좋죠!

▸ What do you say
to + 명사[동사~ing]?
···하는 게 어때?

A: What do you say that we eat some lunch?

B: Yes, I think that's a good idea.

    A: 점심 좀 먹는 게 어때? B: 어, 좋은 생각야.

What would you say? 어떻게 할 거야?. 넌 뭐라고 할래?

A: If your boss wanted to promote you, what would you say?

B: I'd say that it was great.

    A: 사장이 널 승진시켜주면 뭐라 할래? B: 아주 좋다고 해야지.

What would you say if 주어+동사 ? ···한다면 어떨까?

A: What would you say if I wanted to stay home?

B: I'd say that was a bad idea.

    A: 내가 집에 더 있는 건 어떨까? B: 좋은 생각같지 않아.

A: What would you say if she came to live with us?

B: I guess that would be OK.

    A: 걔가 우리와 함께 살면 어떨까? B: 괜찮을 것 같아.

05 그거 좋은데

I like that 그거 좋은데, 맘에 들어

A: Everyone thinks you look elegant tonight.

B: Good. I like that.

　　A: 네가 오늘 밤 우아해보인다고들 해. B: 좋아, 맘에 들어.

└, would를 삽입해서 I'd like that하면 "그러면 좋겠다," "그렇게 한다면 난 좋다"라는 표현으로 상대방의 제안이나 권유에 찬성을 뜻하는 표현이 된다.

I love it! 정말 좋다!, 내 맘에 꼭들어!

A: Honey, I got something for you.

B: Oh, David, this ring… it's beautiful. I love it!

　　A: 자기야, 이거 자기 꺼야. B: 어, 데이빗, 반지… 아름다워. 넘 좋아!

I like A better than B 난 B보다 A가 좋아

A: What beverage do you prefer?

B: I like tea better than coffee.

　　A: 어떤 음료를 좋아해? 차보다는 커피가 좋아.

▸ I began to like Bulgogi
불고기를 좋아하게 됐어
▸ I've started to like Pasta
파스타를 좋아하기 시작했어

I prefer A to B 난 B보다 A가 좋아

A: I think I prefer Daejon to other cities in Korea.

B: Really? Is there some special reason for that?

　　A: 한국에서 대전이 타도시보다 더 좋아. B: 그래? 뭐 특별한 이유라도 있어?

I'm fond of reading novels 소설 읽는 걸 좋아해

A: Do you have any hobbies?

B: I'm fond of reading novels.

　　A: 뭐 취미 있어요? B: 소설읽는 걸 좋아해요.

▸ be fond of~
…을 좋아하다

I want to + 동사 …하기를 원해, …해야 해

A: She's a knockout!

B: I want to get her number.

　　A: 저 여자 정말 끝내주는데! B: 전화번호를 알아내고 싶은 걸.

▸ I want + 명사
…를 원해, 필요해

Chapter 07

I'd like to + 동사 ···했으면 해

A: I'd like to go out for lunch on Friday.

B: Sounds good to me. I'll ask Greg to come along.

> A: 금요일에 같이 점심 먹으러 갔으면 하는데. B: 좋지. 그렉에게 같이 가자고 할게.

A: I'd like to meet with you this afternoon.

B: What time would be good for you?

> A: 오늘 오후에 만나고 싶은데요. B: 몇시가 좋으시겠어요?

▸ I'd like + 명사
··· 를 원해

I'd love to + 동사 ···하고 싶어

A: Are you coming to the theater with us?

B: I'd love to go, but I've got too much work to do.

> A: 너 우리하고 같이 연극 구경 갈래? B: 가고 싶지만, 할일이 많아.

▸ I'd love it if~
··· 하면 좋을텐데

I need to + 동사 ···해야 해

A: I need to take the rest of the day off.

B: For Pete's sake! You have only been here for a few hours.

> A: 오늘은 그만 쉬어야겠어요. B: 제발! 겨우 몇시간 있었잖아.

▸ I need + 명사
··· 가 필요해

I feel like ~ing ···가 하고 싶어

A: I feel like having a nice cold beer right now.

B: I have a couple in my fridge.

> A: 지금 시원한 맥주가 당기는데. B: 냉장고에 두어병 있어.

I can't wait (to+동사) 지금 당장이라고 하고 싶어

A: I can't wait to see the results of the test.

B: They should be here by Monday.

> A: 시험 성적을 알고 싶어 죽겠어. B: 월요일까지는 알게 될 거야.

I'm willing to + 동사 기꺼이 ···하고 싶어

A: I'm willing to pay as much as 2,000 dollars for it.

B: I'm not sure if he'd sell it for that.

> A: 2천달러 정도 낼 의향이 있어. B: 그 남자가 그 가격에 그걸 팔지는 모르겠네.

I'm looking forward to doing it 무척 기다려져

A: I'm looking forward to our vacation.

B: We should have a great time.

A: 방학이 무척 기다려져. B: 재미있을거야.

You up for it? 하고 싶어?

A: We're going downtown. You up for it?

B: Sure, that sounds interesting.

A: 우리 시내가는데 같이 갈래? B: 물론, 재미있겠는데.

▶ I'm just not up for it tonight
오늘 밤에는 생각없어

I'm eager to + 동사 …를 무지 하고 싶어

A: I'm eager to start my vacation.

B: Where are you going?

A: 어서 휴가를 갔으면 해. B: 어디 갈 건데?

I'm dying to + 동사 …하고 싶어 죽겠어

A: I'm itching to go travelling again.

B: When was the last time you went somewhere?

A: 다시 여행 가고 싶어서 견딜 수가 없어. B: 여행을 마지막으로 간 게 언제였는데?

▶ I'm itching to + 동사
몹시 …하고 싶어

Hopefully! 바라건대, 그랬음 좋겠다!

A: They put us on a waiting list for the flight.

B: Hopefully you'll get it.

A: 우린 비행 탑승 대기자 명단에 들어있어. B: 난 너희들이 비행기를 탈 수 있게 되기를 바래.

Good enough! 딱 좋아!

A: What do you think of this?

B: Good enough!

A: 이건 어때? B: 딱 좋아!

I'm a real fan of~ 난 …를 정말 좋아해

A: What kind of ice cream are you having?

B: Well, I'm a real fan of strawberry.

A: 어떤 아이스크림 먹을래? B: 음, 난 딸기 아이스크림이 정말 좋아.

I don't like it 싫어해

A: Oh God, I hate my job. I hate it!

B: I know honey, I'm sorry.

A: 아이고, 내 일이 싫어. 싫어한다고! B: 그래, 자기야. 안됐어.

▸ I hate it
싫어해

I'm not into it 그런 건 안해요

A: How about a glass of whiskey?

B: Sorry, I'm not into whiskey.

A: 위스키 한 잔 어때? B: 미안, 위스키는 안먹어.

I don't want to get involved 끼어들고 싶지 않아

A: I don't want to get involved in this.

B: Come on, why don't you give me a hand?

A: 끼어들고 싶지 않아. B: 이봐, 좀 도와주라.

▸ I'm not going to
be part of it
난 끼고 싶지 않아
▸ That's not for me
내 것이 아닌데, 그런 건 나
한테는 안 어울려

I don't care for it 난 싫어

A: Don't you like the food in this restaurant?

B: No, I don't care for it.

A: 이 식당 음식 좋아하지 않아? B: 응, 난 싫어.

▸ That's not my cup
of tea
내 취향이 아냐

That's not my thing 난 그런 건 질색이야

A: You must like divorcing. You've been divorced three times!

B: No, that's not my thing. I don't love getting divorced.

A: 이혼을 좋아하나 보군. 벌써 3번이나 이혼했잖아! B: 아냐, 질색이야. 이혼하는 거 싫어해.

▸ The last thing I
want to do is 주어+
동사
가장 하고 싶지 않은 건 …
이다

07 …면 좋겠어

I hope 주어+동사 …면 좋겠어

A: I hope I win so I can buy you something nice.

B: That's so sweet.

> A: 우승해서 네게 뭐 좋은 거 사주고 싶어. B: 고마워라.

I hope to + 동사 …하기를 바래

A: I hope to enroll in a course this summer.

B: Any course in particular?

> A: 올 여름에 한 과목 등록하고 싶어. B: 특별히 생각하고 있는 과목이라도 있니?

└ I wish to도 또한 「…하기를 바란다」이지만 I hope to에 비해 다분히 공식적인 경우에 쓰인다.

▶ **I wish to + 동사**
…하기를 바래

I hope so 그랬으면 좋겠어

A: Do you think the job will be finished on time?

B: I hope so. If it isn't, we'll lose a lot of money.

> A: 일이 제시간에 끝나리라고 생각해? B: 그러길 바래. 아니면 거액을 잃을거야.

└ I hope not 그러지 말았으면 좋겠다. 아니라면 좋을텐데

It would be nice if 주어+동사 …한다면 좋을 텐데

A: It would be nice if we could take a vacation.

B: Where do you want to go?

> A: 우리가 휴가를 얻는다면 좋을 텐데. B: 어디를 가고 싶은데?

▶ **I'll be pleased to + 동사**
…하면 기쁠 텐데
▶ **It is our desire to + 동사**
…하는 것이 우리가 바라는 거야

It'll be good[nice; wonderful] to + 동사 …하면 멋질 거야

A: We'll be in your hometown soon.

B: It'll be good to see my family again.

> A: 곧 네 고향에 도착할거야. B: 가족을 다시 보는 건 멋질거야.

A: It'll be good to see the school's soccer team competing.

B: Yeah, I hope they win this match.

> A: 학교 축구시합을 보면 멋질거야. B: 어, 이기기를 바래.

Chapter 07

I'd rather A than B   A하느니 차라리 B할 거야

A: I'd rather play computer games than study.

B: I absolutely agree with you.

A: 공부를 하느니 컴퓨터게임을 할거야. B: 네 말이 정말 맞아.

If only I could~   …할 수 있다면 좋을 텐데

A: If only I could remember my calling card number.

B: Why don't you just use mine?

A: 전화카드번호를 기억하면 좋겠는데. B: 그냥 내 꺼를 써.

I wish 주어+동사   …였으면 좋겠어

A: I've decided to take a holiday and go to Mexico!

B: Wild! I wish I was going!

A: 휴가받아 멕시코에 가기로 했어! B: 근사한데! 나도 갔음 좋겠다!

▶ I wish I had a little time for fun
놀 시간이 좀 있으면 좋겠어

A: I wish you would get out of my face!

B: I didn't realize you were in such a bad mood.

A: 네가 꺼져줬으면 좋겠어! B: 그렇게 기분이 안좋은줄 몰랐어.

If I + 과거, I would + 동사   …이면 …할 텐데

A: If I had his phone number, I would call him.

B: Why don't you try to get his number?

A: 걔 전화번호를 알면 전화할텐데. B: 전화번호를 알아내지 그래.

If I had + pp, I would[should; could; might] have + pp

…였다면 …했을 텐데

A: If I had never met my wife, this never would have happened.

B: Do you regret meeting her?

A: 와이프를 만나지 않았더라면 이런 일이 생기지 않았을텐데. B: 아내를 만난 걸 후회해?

Step 3 관심 >>내가 관심이 있거나 없음을 말할 때

08 그건 내게 중요한 문제야

It matters to me 그건 내게 중요한 문제야

A: Why're you always washing your car?

B: I want it to look good. It matters to me.

A: 왜 맨날 차를 세차하는 거야? B: 멋지게 보일려고. 내겐 중요한 문제야.

It doesn't matter to me 난 아무래도 상관없어요

A: Where should we go for our vacation this year?

B: It doesn't matter to me. Wherever you want.

A: 올해 우리 휴가를 어디로 갈까? B: 상관없어. 너 가고 싶은 데로.

▶ It doesn't matter
상관없어

I'm interested in~ …에 관심이 있어

A: I'm interested in the new yoga class.

B: Me too! Why don't we join together this Saturday?

A: 새로 생긴 요가교실에 관심이 있어. B: 나도! 이번 토요일에 같이 가보자.

▶ I'm not interested
in~
…에 상관없어

I'm into~ 난 …에 관심이 많아

A: How have you been? You look great!

B: Thanks! I'm really into health food now.

A: 어떻게 지냈니? 근사해 보이는데! B: 고마워! 요즘 건강식에 관심많아.

▶ I'm involved in~
…을 하고 있어

Something appeals to me …가 끌리다

A: The menu has so many choices that I'm confused!

B: I know, but nothing appeals to me today.

A: 음식종류가 넘 많아 고민야! B: 그래, 하지만 오늘은 딱 끌리는 게 없는걸.

I don't care (about it) (상대방의 부탁, 제안에 대해 승낙하며) 상관없어

A: What do you want to do tonight?

B: I don't care.

A: 오늘 밤 뭐하고 싶어? B: 별 관심없어.

Chapter 07

I don't care what they say 개들이 뭐래든 상관없어

A: We may not arrive on time.

B: I don't care if we are a little late for the party.

  A: 우리 늦을지도 몰라. B: 파티에 조금 늦는다고 해도 신경안써.

▸ I don't care if
[what; how much]
~
난 (뭐라도, 얼마나 ~해도)
상관없어

I couldn't care less 알게 뭐람

A: Rachel isn't coming to your party.

B: I couldn't care less.

  A: 레이첼이 네 파티에 안간데. B: 알게 뭐람.

A: I don't plan to see you ever again.

B: I couldn't care less.

  A: 다신 넌 보지 않을거야. B: 알게 뭐람.

▸ I couldn't care
less about + 명사
[if; what~]~
…일지라도[뭐라도] 신경안
써

It makes no difference to me 상관없어

A: What do you want to do tonight?

B: It makes no difference to me. I am flexible.

  A: 오늘 밤엔 뭐 할래? B: 뭘 해도 상관없어. 나는 다 괜찮거든.

▸ It doesn't make
any difference
상관없어

It's not going to make any difference 전혀 상관없어

A: Your cable TV service isn't working today.

B: I don't watch TV. It's not going to make any difference.

  A: 네 유선방송이 오늘 안나와. B: TV 안 봐. 전혀 상관없어.

▸ It's gonna make a
difference
차이가 있을 거야

What's the difference? 그게 무슨 상관이야?

A: You must work on Saturday or on Sunday.

B: What's the difference?

  A: 토요일 아니면 일요일 일해야 돼. B: 차이점이 뭔데요?

▸ What difference
does it make?
그게 무슨 차이야?

It doesn't mean anything to me 난 상관없어

A: The Japanese soccer team lost their last match.

B: So? It doesn't mean anything to me.

  A: 일본 축구팀이 지난번 게임을 졌어. B: 그래서? 난 상관없는데.

It's not my concern <small>난 관심없어</small>

A: The neighbors are always fighting.
B: It's not my concern.

    A: 이웃들이 항상 싸우네. B: 알게 뭐야.

▸ It's not my
  business
  <small>난 상관없어</small>
▸ It's not my
  problem
  <small>나하고 상관없어</small>

I have nothing to do with this <small>난 아무 관련이 없어</small>

A: All of you have been behaving badly.
B: I have nothing to do with this.

    A: 너희들 모두 못되게 행동하는 구나. B: 난 안그랬어요.

▸ It doesn't have
  anything to do
  with me
  <small>난 모르는 일이야</small>

Who cares? <small>누가 신경이나 쓴대?</small>

A: I don't think it's a good idea.
B: Who cares?

    A: 좋은 생각같지 않은데. B: 누가 신경이나 쓴대?

So what? <small>그래서 뭐가 어쨌다고?</small>

A: Boy, you're in a bad mood.
B: So what?

    A: 야, 기분이 안좋구나. B: 그래서 어쨌다는 거야?

▸ So shoot me
  <small>그래서 어쨌다는 거야</small>

Whatever! <small>뭐든지 간에!</small>

A: You are so cheap!
B: Yeah, whatever. I may be cheap, but at least I'm not a fool!

    A: 넌 너무 인색해! B: 그래, 뭐든. 인색할 진 몰라도 최소한 바보는 아냐!

▸ What of it?
  <small>그게 어쨌다는 거야?</small>

The hell with that <small>알게 뭐람! 맘대로 해</small>

A: The school is asking us to donate $500 each.
B: The hell with that! No way!

    A: 학교에서 각자 500달러를 기부하래. B: 빌어먹을! 말도 안돼!

▸ To hell with
  tradition
  <small>전통따위 알게 뭐람</small>
▸ The hell with
  hockey
  <small>하키고 뭐고 난 몰라</small>
▸ I don't give a
  shit[damn, fuck]
  <small>난 알바아냐</small>

Chapter **08**

동의·반대

01 그런 것 같아

I'm afraid so (안타깝게도) 그런 것 같아

A: I think now would be a good time to talk to him.

B: I guess so.

A: 지금이 걔와 얘기하기 좋은 때야. B: 그건 것 같아.

▸ I guess so
아마 그럴 걸

I think so 그래요

A: You should have a girlfriend.

B: I think so.

A: 여자친구를 사귀어봐. B: 그래요.

▸ I believe so
그럴 거라 생각해
▸ I suppose (so)
그럴 걸

It might be true 사실일 수도 있어

A: There is a rumor that Joyce is pregnant.

B: That's interesting. It might be true.

A: 조이스가 임신했다는 소문이 있어. B: 재미있군. 사실일 수도 있어.

▸ It could be
그럴 수도 있어
▸ It's possible
그럴 수 있어

Sort of 어느 정도는, 다소

A: Do you like pizza?

B: Sort of. I eat it occasionally.

A: 피자 좋아해? B: 어느 정도는. 종종 먹어.

▸ Kind of
어느 정도는

That's about it 그런 셈야

A: Do you have to buy anything else?

B: No, that's about it.

A: 뭐 다른 걸 사야 돼? B: 아니, 거의 다 끝났어.

Yes and no 글쎄 어떨지

A: Have you decided what you want for dinner?

B: Maybe yes, maybe no.

A: 저녁 뭐 먹을지 결정했어? B: 뭐라 말해야 할지.

▸ Maybe yes,
maybe no
어느 쪽이라고 말해야 할지

02 물론이지

Absolutely! 물론이지!

A: Are you coming to the show?

B: Absolutely.

A: 전시회에 올 거지? B: 그럼.

> ㄴ. 반대로 Absolutely not!
> 하면 「물론 아니지!」란 의
> 미가 되며 비슷한 표현으
> 로는 Certainly!(확실해!) –
> Certainly not!(정말 아냐!) 그
> 리고 Definitely!(틀림없어!)–
> Definitely not!(절대 아냐!)이
> 있다.

Of course 물론이지, 확실해

A: Do you really think he'll win the race?

B: Of course.

A: 정말 그 사람이 경주에서 이길 거라고 보니? B: 물론이지.

Sure 물론, 당연하지

A: How about a drink after work?

B: Sure, that sounds great!

A: 퇴근 후 한잔 어때? B: 그래, 근사한 생각야!

▶ Sure thing
물론이지, 그럼
▶ It sure is
그렇고 말고, 맞고 말고

That's for sure 확실하지, 물론이지

A: I guess we'll have to start over again.

B: That's for sure.

A: 처음부터 다시 시작해야 할까봐. B: 그럼 그래야지.

▶ (It's) For sure
물론이야

No doubt 분명해

A: She's an excellent musician.

B: No doubt. She's always playing the piano.

A: 걔는 뛰어난 음각가야. B: 물론야. 항상 피아노를 연주해.

▶ There is no doubt
about it!
틀림없어!

You bet 확실해, 물론이지

A: Did you bring me any presents?

B: You bet.

A: 나줄 선물 뭐 갖고 왔어? B: 물론이지.

Chapter 08

03 알았어

All right 알았어

A: I'll call back later.

B: All right.

　A: 나중에 다시 전화할게. B: 알았어.

▸ All right, already!
좋아 알았다구!, 이제 그만
해라!

All right then 좋아 그럼

A: I need you to copy these documents.

B: All right then. I'll be right back.

　A: 이 서류들 카피 좀 해줘. B: 좋아, 그럼. 곧 돌아올게.

▸ All right, I get it
좋아 알겠어
▸ All right, I see
좋아 알았어

Okay 좋아

A: Come over after six thirty.

B: Okay... see you there.

　A: 6시 반 이후에 와. B: 그래… 집에서 보자.

↳ Okay나 All right은 상대방
의 말에 동의하는 표현. That'
s okay나 That's all right 역시
상대방의 말에 동의하는 표
현으로도 쓰이지만 상대방의
사과에 괜찮다는 「용서의 표
현」으로도 쓰인다. 이때는 No
problem과 의미가 유사하다.

That's great 아주 좋아, 잘 됐어

A: My boss just gave me a big raise.

B: That's great.

　A: 사장님이 급여를 많이 올려줬어. B: 잘 됐어.

That's nice 좋아, 잘했어

A: I picked out a gift for Nancy.

B: That's nice. What did you get her?

　A: 낸시 줄 선물 골랐어. B: 잘했어. 뭘 줬는데?

▸ That's cool
좋아
▸ That's terrific
[wonderful]
끝내주네[훌륭해]

That's really something 거 굉장하네

A: This painting was done by Picaso.

B: That's really something.

　A: 이 그림은 피카소가 그린 거야. B: 정말 굉장하네.

I'd like that 그러면 좋겠다. 그렇게 한다면 난 좋다

A: What do you say I take you to dinner tonight?

B: Oh, I'd like that.

A: 오늘 밤 내가 나가서 저녁살게. B: 어, 그럼 좋지.

That would be great[perfect] 그럼 좋겠어

A: There's a Mets game on Sunday. You wanna go?

B: Yeah, that would be great!

A: 월요일에 메츠게임 있어. 갈래? B: 어, 그럼 좋지.

A: How about a cold beer?

B: That would be great.

A: 시원한 맥주 한 잔 어때? B: 그럼 좋지.

(That) Sounds good (to me) 좋은데

A: Let's get together again soon.

B: Sounds good. See you later.

A: 곧 다시 만나자. B: 좋아. 나중에 보자.

▸ Sounds great
아주 좋아

Sounds like a plan 좋은 생각이야

A: We can grab a bite to eat before we go.

B: Sounds like a plan.

A: 가기 전에 좀 먹자. B: 그거 좋지.

▸ Sounds like fun
재밌을 것 같은데
▸ Sounds
interesting
재미있겠는데

Sounds like a good idea 좋은 생각 같은데

A: Do you mind if I come over and watch TV with you?

B: No, that sounds like a good idea.

A: 내가 가서 너와 함께 TV를 봐도 괜찮겠니? B: 어, 좋은 생각이야.

04 맞아, 그래

That's right 맞아, 그래

A: I heard you're not going to the party.

B: That's right. I've got soccer practice.

A: 너 파티에 못 간다며. B: 그래, 축구 연습이 있어서.

You're right 네 말이 맞아

A: They need to hire more qualified people.

B: I think you're right about that.

A: 좀 더 자질있는 사람들을 뽑아야 해. B: 그 점에 있어서 네 말이 옳아.

A: We need to get together to discuss the new contract.

B: You're right. How about tomorrow morning?

A: 새로운 계약서를 토의하기 위해 만나야겠어요. B: 그래요, 내일 아침이 어때요?

▶ You're exactly right
정말 맞아

▶ I think you're right (about that)
(그 점에 있어서) 네가 옳은 것 같아

You're right on the money 네 말이 맞아

A: We can make this house nicer if we paint it.

B: You're right on the money.

A: 페인트칠하면 집이 훨 나아질거야. B: 네 말이 맞아.

A: You look like you're happy today.

B: You are right on the money.

A: 오늘 행복해 보인다. B: 바로 맞혔어.

That's a good point 좋은 지적이야, 맞는 말이야

A: If I eat less, I'll lose weight.

B: That's a good point.

A: 소식하면 살이 빠질거야. B: 좋은 지적이야.

You have a point there 네 말이 맞아

A: It's only going to make matters worse for us.

B: You've got a point there. A: 우리 상황을 더 악화시킬 뿐이야. B: 네 말에 일리가 있어.

▶ You've got a point
맞는 말이다

You got that right 네 말이 맞아

A: We finally finished and mailed those reports.

B: You got that right, but when will they get them?

A: 드디어 보고서 끝내서 우편으로 보냈네. B: 맞아, 근데 걔네들이 언제나 받게 될까?

That's correct 맞아

A: So you're saying my answer was wrong?

B: That's correct, it was.

A: 그래 내 답이 틀렸다고 말하는 거야? B: 맞아, 틀렸어.

▶ You're correct
네가 맞아

That's it 바로 그거야, 그게 다야, 그만두자

A: Is this the one?

B: That's it. Where did you find it?

A: 이거 맞어? B: 바로 그거야. 어디서 찾았어?

▶ That's it?
이걸로 끝이야?

Tell me about it! 그 얘기 좀 해봐!, 그게 맞아!, 그렇고 말고!

A: What a bitch! She always gets her own way.

B: Tell me about it!

A: 나쁜 년! 걘 항상 자기 맘대로야. B: 내 말이 그 말이야!

You're telling me! 누가 아니래!, 정말 그래!, 나도 알아!

A: I can't believe the prices at this restaurant.

B: You're telling me!

A: 이 식당 음식값이 너무하네. B: 누가 아니래!

Big time 그렇고 말고, 많이

A: I want to make a lot of money.

B: Oh yeah, big time.

A: 돈을 많이 벌고 싶어. B: 어 그래. 아주 많이.

In a word, yes 한마디로 말해서 그래

A: Are you feeling tired today?

B: In a word, yes.

A: 오늘 피곤해? B: 한마디로 말해서 그렇지.

⌐ In a sense he's right 어떤
의미에서 걔 말이 맞아

05 네 말에 동의해

I agree 그래

A: We have to get rid of that guy as soon as possible.

B: I agree with you a hundred percent.

    A: 빨리 그 작자를 잘라야겠어. B: 100퍼센트 동감이야.

▶ I agree with you 100%
전적으로 동감이야

I couldn't agree with you more 정말 네 말이 맞아

A: We need to work this weekend to get it finished.

B: I couldn't agree with you more.

    A: 이거 끝내려면 주말에도 일해야 돼. B: 네 말이 맞아.

I can't argue with that 두말하면 잔소리지, 물론이지

A: I think he's lying about the figures.

B: I can't disagree with you.

    A: 난 걔가 숫자에 대해 거짓말을 하고 있다고 봐. B: 나도 같은 생각이야.

▶ I can't disagree with you
네 말이 맞아

You can say that again 그렇고 말고, 당근이지

A: We need a holiday in the worst way.

B: You can say that again!

    A: 우리는 정말로 휴가를 얻어 쉬어야 해. B: 그렇구 말구!

▶ You could(might) say that
두말하면 잔소리지

You said it 네 말이 맞아

A: I'm really angry with that stupid Internet company.

B: You said it.

    A: 엉터리같은 인터넷회사 땜에 화나. B: 말 잘했다.

▶ Well said
그 말 한번 잘했어, 맞는 말이야

I'm with you 동감이야, 알았어

A: I think we need to get our air conditioner fixed.

B: I'm with you there.

    A: 에어컨을 고쳐야겠어. B: 그 점에 있어서 너와 같은 생각이야.

▶ I'm with you there
나도 그 말에 공감해

I feel the same way 나도 그렇게 생각해

A: This coffee should be stronger.

B: I feel the same way.

A: 이 커피는 좀 진해야 돼. B: 나도 그렇게 생각해.

I'm like you 나도 너랑 같은 생각이야

A: I'm like you. I enjoy traveling.

B: Maybe we should vacation together.

A: 나도 너랑 같아. 여행을 즐겨. B: 함께 휴가를 가야겠는 걸.

We're on the same page 우린 같은 생각이야

A: Do you know what I mean?

B: Yes I do. We're on the same page.

A: 내 말 알아들었어? B: 어 그래. 우린 같은 생각이야.

I'm on your side 난 네 편이야

A: Don't you worry. I'm on your side.

B: That makes me feel a little better.

A: 걱정하지마. 난 네 편이야. B: 그 얘기 들으니깐 기분이 좀더 나아지는데.

Same here 나도 그래

A: I can't wait to see the new play.

B: Same here. I bought tickets last night.

A: 새로 시작하는 연극을 빨리 보고 싶어. B: 나도 그래. 어젯 밤에 표를 샀어.

So am I 나도 그래

A: I like music and sports.

B: Hey, so do I.

A: 음악과 스포츠를 좋아해. B: 이봐, 나도 그래.

▸ So do I
나도 그래

Go ahead 그렇게 해

A: May I smoke here?

B: Of course. Go ahead.

A: 여기서 담배펴도 돼? B: 물론. 그렇게 해.

▸ Yes, please do
어, 그렇게 해

06 난 찬성이야

I'm for it 난 찬성이야

A: What do you think of Betty's proposal to shorten the workweek?

B: Are you kidding? I'm for it!

A: 근무시간을 줄이자는 베티의 제안에 대해 어떻게 생각해? B: 장난하니? 당연히 찬성이지!

▶ I'm for giving him another chance
개에게 기회를 한 번 더 주는데 찬성야

▶ I'm for the basic idea
기본적인 생각은 찬성야

I'm in favor of it 찬성이야

A: I'm in favor of letting the union handle our lawsuit.

B: I'm not so sure that's a good idea.

A: 노조가 고소건을 진행하는 데 찬성야. B: 과연 좋은 생각인지 잘 모르겠어.

Let's do it 자 하자, 그러자

A: I'd love to try skydiving!

B: Cool! Let's do it!

A: 스카이 다이빙 해보고 싶어! B: 근사하다! 그거 하자!

That's more like it 그게 더 낫겠어

A: I'll turn up the air conditioner.

B: That's more like it. It's too hot.

A: 에어컨 더 세게 틀게. B: 그게 더 낫겠어. 너무 더워.

I don't see why not 그래

A: Would you like to go shopping with us?

B: I don't see why not.

A: 우리랑 쇼핑갈래? B: 그래.

I'll drink to that! 옳소!, 찬성이오!

A: What do you say we take a vacation next week?

B: I'll drink to that!

A: 담주에 휴가가는 게 어때? B: 좋지!

Why not? 왜 안해?, 왜 안되는 거야?, 그러지 뭐

A: I'm sorry, but I can't come to the game tomorrow.

B: Why not?

A: 미안하지만, 내일 경기에 못가. B: 왜 못가?

A: Do you want to catch the late movie tonight?

B: Why not? I've got nothing else to do.

A: 오늘밤 심야 영화 볼래? B: 좋아, 할일도 없는데 뭐.

A deal's a deal 약속한 거야

A: I made an agreement with him, but now I regret it.

B: There's nothing you can do. A deal's a deal.

A: 걔하고 협정을 맺었는데 지금 후회 돼. B: 어쩔 수 없잖아. 맺은 건데.

[It's a] Deal! 그러기로 한 거야!, 내 약속하지!

A: I'm so tired. Let's start tomorrow morning.

B: Deal!

A: 정말 피곤해. 내일 시작하자. B: 좋아!

(It's a) Done deal 그러기로 한 거야

A: Did you purchase the house you were looking at?

B: Yes, we did. It's a done deal.

A: 네가 보던 집을 샀어? B: 어, 샀어. 그러기로 한 거야.

It's settled! 그렇게 하자!

A: I promise I'll be nicer to my sisters.

B: Good. It's settled.

A: 내 누이들에게 더 착하게 군다고 약속할게요. B: 좋아. 그럼 그렇게 하자.

I'm standing behind you 내가 뒤에 있잖아

A: Don't worry. I'm standing behind you.

B: I appreciate your support.

A: 걱정마. 내가 뒤에 있잖아. B: 네가 도와줘서 고마워.

▸ I'll stand by you
네 옆에 있어줄게

07 괜찮아

That's all right 괜찮아. 됐어

A: Thanks for being so nice to us.

B: That's all right.

A: 우리에게 잘해줘서 고마워. B: 괜찮아.

ㄴ 고맙다는 혹은 미안하다는
말에 대한 답변으로 자주 쓰
이는 표현

I'm all right with that 난 괜찮아

A: Is it OK if we eat chicken tonight?

B: Sure, I'm alright with that.

A: 오늘 저녁에 치킨 먹어도 돼? B: 물론, 난 괜찮아.

▶ They seem all
right with it
걔네들 괜찮은 거 같아

That's fine (with me) (난) 괜찮아

A: Do you want me to get you something to eat?

B: No, that's fine. I'm not really hungry.

A: 먹을 것 좀 갖다 줄까요? B: 아요, 괜찮아요. 그렇게 배고프진 않아요.

▶ That will be fine
괜찮아질 거야

That's okay (with me) 괜찮아. 난 상관없어

A: I've got no time to meet you today.

B: That's okay. How about tomorrow?

A: 오늘 널 만날 시간이 없어. B: 괜찮아. 그럼 내일은 어때?

Are you all right? 괜찮아?

A: Are you all right?

B: I'm fine! I just feel a little nervous.

A: 괜찮아? B: 좋아! 그냥 신경이 예민해서.

ㄴ All right?은 「알겠니?」라고
상대방에게 물어보는 말.

▶ Are you okay?
괜찮아?

Is it all right? 괜찮겠어? 괜찮아?

A: That's a nice blouse.

B: Is it all right? I was worried you wouldn't like it.

A: 블라우스 멋지다. B: 괜찮아? 네가 싫어할까봐 걱정했어.

I'm cool with[about] that 난 괜찮아, 상관없어

A: I'll bring a date to your party.

B: Great! I'm cool with that.

    A: 너 파티에 데이트하는 애 데려갈게. B: 좋아! 난 상관없어.

▶ Are you cool with this?
이거 괜찮아?

I can live with that 괜찮아, 참을 만해

A: We can split the profit from this deal.

B: I can live with that.

    A: 이번 거래로 생긴 수익을 나누자. B: 그래 그러자.

↳ I'm cool with that과 같은 맥락의 표현으로 의미는 It's okay with me 혹은 I will agree with that이다.

It works for me 난 괜찮아, 찬성이야

A: Your car is too old.

B: Don't complain. It works for me.

    A: 네 차 너무 고물야. B: 뭐라하지마. 난 괜찮은데

I have no problem with that 난 괜찮아요

A: Can you wait a few minutes?

B: I have no problem with that.

    A: 잠깐 기다려줄테야? B: 난 괜찮아.

It suits me (fine) 난 좋아, 내 생각엔 괜찮은 것 같아

A: How is your new apartment?

B: It suits me fine.

    A: 새로운 아파트 어때? B: 난 좋아.

I'm easy (to please) 네 결정에 따를게, 난 어느 쪽도 상관없어

A: I'm easy to please.

B: No you aren't. You complain a lot.

    A: 난 까다롭지 않아. B: 아냐, 넌 안그래. 불평 많이 하잖아.

I'm happy either way 난 아무거나 좋아

A: Would you like soda or juice?

B: I'm happy either way.

    A: 소다 먹을래 아니면 주스 먹을래? B: 아무거나 좋아.

▶ Either will do
아무거나 괜찮아

Chapter 08

08 그럼요

Be my guest 그럼요

A: Do you mind if I take a look around here?

B: Not at all, be my guest.

A: 내가 여기 좀 둘러봐도 괜찮겠니? B: 그럼, 물론이지.

Whatever you ask 뭐든 말만 해

A: Can you do me a really big favor?

B: Whatever you ask.

A: 정말로 중요한 부탁인데 좀 들어 줄래? B: 뭐든지 말만 해.

Whatever you say 말만해, 전적으로 동감이야

A: We're going to eat some Thai food.

B: Whatever you say. It sounds interesting.

A: 태국음식 좀 먹을려고. B: 뭐든지, 재미있겠다.

Whatever you want to do 네가 하고 싶은 거 뭐든 좋아

A: Do you mind if we stay home tonight?

B: Not at all. Whatever you want to do.

A: 오늘밤 집에 머물러도 돼? B: 물론, 뭐든 맘대로 해.

Whatever it takes 무슨 수를 써서라도

A: We'll need to work all night to complete this.

B: OK, whatever it takes.

A: 이거 끝내려면 밤새야 돼. B: 알았어, 무슨 수를 써서라도 해야지.

Whatever turns you on 뭐든 좋을 대로

A: I like to date several girls at once.

B: Whatever turns you on.

A: 동시에 여러 걸들과의 데이트를 좋아해. B: 꼴리는 대로 해라.

I am all yours 얼마든지, 뭐든지 다

A: Jim, can we talk for a minute?

B: I'm all yours. What's up?

A: 짐, 잠깐 시간 좀 내줄래요? B: 얼마든지요. 무슨 일이죠?

Suit yourself 마음대로 해

A: I decided that I won't accept your offer.

B: OK, suit yourself.

A: 네 제안을 받아들이지 않기로 했어. B: 좋아, 맘대로 해.

You name it 말만 해

A: I need you to do something for me.

B: You name it.

A: 날 위해 뭘 좀 해줘야 겠어. B: 뭐든지.

A: Can I choose the restaurant we eat at?

B: Of course. You name it.

A: 우리가 갈 식당 내가 골라도 돼? B: 물론. 말만해.

You are on 그래 좋았어

A: I'll bet you $5.00 that I'll win.

B: You're on.

A: 내가 이기는 데 5달러 걸겠어. B: 좋을 대로 하셔.

ㄴ 특히 내기를 받아들일 경우에 쓰는 표현.

So be it (그렇게 결정됐다면) 그렇게 해

A: We can't publish your book.

B: That's a shame. Well, so be it.

A: 네 책을 출판할 수 없어. B: 안됐네. 그래 그렇게 해.

Anything you say 말만 하셔

A: Take me to Jared's house right now.

B: Anything you say.

A: 지금 재럿의 집으로 데려다 줘. B: 뭐든 말만 해.

Anytime 언제든지

A: Can we still go out for drinks together?

B: Anytime. Just call me.

A: 함께 나가서 술 할 수 있을까? B: 언제든지. 전화만 해.

A: Thanks for helping me with my computer.

B: Sure. Anytime.

A: 내 컴퓨터 도와줘서 고마워. B: 뭘. 언제든지 말해.

MEMO

09 생각 좀 해보고

I'll think about it 그거에 대해 생각해볼게

A: I'll buy your car if you sell it for $4,000.

B: I'll think about it.

　A: 4천 달러에 팔면 네 차 살게. B: 생각 좀 해볼게.

▶ I'll think it over
검토해볼게

Let me think about it 생각 좀 해볼게

A: I want to invite the investors to see our operation.

B: Let me think about that and I'll get back to you.

　A: 투자가를 불러 회사를 둘러보게 하자. B: 생각 좀 해보고 얘기해 줄게.

Let me have time to think it over 생각할 시간 좀 줘

A: If you want, you can study in Australia for a year.

B: Let me have time to think it over.

　A: 원하면 일년간 호주가서 공부해. B: 생각할 시간을 좀 주세요.

We're having second thoughts about it 다시 생각해봐야겠어

A: Did you hire him to work for you?

B: Not yet. We're having second thoughts about it.

　A: 너 걔를 고용했니? B: 아직. 좀 생각해보는 중야.

Let me sleep on it 곰곰이 생각해봐야겠어

A: When can you give me your decision?

B: Let me sleep on it.

　A: 언제 결정을 알려줄거야. B: 곰곰히 생각 좀 해보고.

I'll see what I can do 내가 어떻게 할 수 있는지 좀 보고

A: He's going to quit unless he gets a raise.

B: I'll see what I can do.

　A: 그 친구는 급여인상없이는 그만두겠네요. B: 내가 어떻게 할 수 있는지 보고.

▶ I never looked at
it that way before
전에 그렇게 생각해 본 적
이 없는데

Chapter 08

10 그런 것 같지 않은데

I don't think so 그런 것 같지 않은데

A: I think my ex-boyfriend probably has a new girlfriend.

B: I don't think so. You just broke up last week!

A: 옛 남친이 여자를 새로 만난 듯 해. B: 아닐 걸. 니네들 지난 주에 헤어졌잖아!

▸ I don't believe so'
그런 것 같지 않은데

I guess not 아닌 것 같아

A: It's raining, so we can't go to the park.

B: I guess not.

A: 비가 오네. 그럼 공원에 못 가겠다. B: 안될 것 같아.

▸ I suppose not
아닐 걸
▸ I expect not
아닌 것 같아

I'm afraid not 아닌 것 같아

A: Have you traveled overseas?

B: I'm afraid not.

A: 해외 여행 해본 적 있어? B: 아니 없어.

I'm afraid (that) 주어+동사 …가 아닌 것 같아

A: He doesn't want to lose face.

B: I'm afraid it's too late for that now.

A: 그 친구는 자기 자존심 구겨지는 꼴 못보는데. B: 지금 자존심 내세우기에는 너무 늦었다고 봐.

I don't see that 난 그렇게 생각 안하는데, 그런 것 같지 않아

A: I think he'll cause problems.

B: I don't see that. I think he'll be fine.

A: 걔가 문제를 일으킬 것 같아. B: 그런 것 같지 않아. 걔가 괜찮을 것 같은데.

I don't see it (that way) 난 그렇게 생각하지 않아

A: Your work is not very creative.

B: I don't see it that way.

A: 너의 일은 정말이지 창의적이지 않아. B: 그렇게 생각하지 않는데요.

I don't see that happening 그렇게는 안될 걸

A: If there is an earthquake, Seoul may be destroyed.
B: I don't see that happening.

　　A: 지진이 발생하면 서울을 파괴될거야. B: 그렇지 않을 걸.

That can't happen 말도 안돼, 그렇지 않아

A: Your house may be robbed someday.
B: That can't happen. There are too many police around.

　　A: 네 집은 언젠가 도둑당할 수도 있어. B: 말도 안돼. 주변에 경찰이 아주 많아.

I can't say 주어+동사 …라곤 말 못하지

A: Is Jack guilty of the crime?
B: I can't say he is innocent.

　　A: 잭이 유죄야? B: 걔가 무죄라고는 말 못하지.

It's not what you think 그건 네 생각과 달라, 속단하지 마라

A: I saw you today kissing in the doctor's lounge.
B: It's not what you think.

　　A: 오늘 병원라운지에서 니네 키스하는 거 봤어. B: 그건 그런게 아니야.

▶ That's what you
think
그건 네 생각이고

This is a totally different situation 전혀 다른 상황야

A: Relax. You always get too angry.
B: I'm not angry. This is a totally different situation.

　　A: 진정해. 넌 항상 화를 많이 내. B: 화난 게 아냐. 전혀 다른 상황이야.

That's another[a different] story 그건 또 다른 얘기야, 그건 또 별개의 문제야

A: You can help me. I heard you helped Tracy.
B: That's a different story.

　　A: 도와줘. 트레이시도 도와줬다며. B: 그건 별개의 문제지.

I have a different opinion 내 생각은 달라

A: I think the president sucks.
B: Personally, I have a different opinion.

　　A: 대통령이 아니올시다인 것 같아. B: 개인적으로 난 생각이 달라.

Speak for yourself 그건 그쪽 얘기죠, 당신이나 그렇지

A: I'm not very hungry right now.

B: Speak for yourself. I'm starving.

A: 지금 그렇게 배고프지 않아.   B: 그건 그쪽 얘기지. 난 배고프다고.

Not me 난 아냐

A: I wish I had a lot of money.

B: Not me. I'd rather have more free time.

A: 돈이 많았으면 좋겠어.   B: 난 아냐. 시간이 더 많았으면 좋겠어.

I wouldn't do that 나라면 그렇게 안하겠어

A: I'm going to talk to Tim about our argument.

B: I wouldn't do that. Wait until you calm down.

A: 팀하고 다투었던 거 이야기해볼려고.   B: 나라면 그렇게 안해. 맘 가라앉을 때까지 기다려.

I didn't do it 내가 안 했어

A: Charlie, why did you do it?

B: I didn't do it! It was Kate!

A: 찰리, 왜 그렇게 한거야?   B: 내가 안 했어요! 케이트가 한 거예요!

▸ I didn't cause this
내가 이런 건 아냐

Me neither 나도 안그래

A: I really don't like sci-fi films.

B: Me neither.

A: 공상과학영화는 정말 싫어해.   B: 나도 그런데.

Neither did I 나도 안그랬어

A: Okay, I don't know what to do anymore.

B: Well neither do I!

A: 좋아, 더 이상 어떻게 해야할 지 모르겠어.   B: 나도 모르겠어!

▸ Neither do I
나도 안그래
▸ Neither am I
나도 안그래

Neither will I 나도 안 그럴 거야

A: I'm never going to have a baby.

B: Neither will I.

A: 절대로 얘는 안 갖을 거야.   B: 나도 안 그럴거야.

▸ Neither can I
나도 못해

11 그러고 싶지만 안되겠어

I wish I could, but I can't 그러고 싶지만 안되겠어

A: Are you coming to my party?

B: I wish I could come, but I'm busy on Saturday

A: 내 파티에 올래? B: 가고 싶지만, 토요일날 바빠.

I'd like[love] to, but~ 그러고 싶지만…

A: Do you want to go to a movie?

B: I'd like to, but I'm on call today.

A: 영화보러 갈거니? B: 그러고 싶은데, 난 오늘 대기해야 돼.

I'd have to say no 안되겠는데

A: Would you accept an invitation to my home tonight?

B: I'd have to say no.

A: 오늘 저녁 집에 초대해도 돼요? B: 안되겠는데요.

I don't feel like it 사양할래, 그러고 싶지 않아

A: Would you like some cake?

B: No, thank you. I don't feel like it.

A: 케익 좀 먹을래? B: 아니, 됐어. 먹고싶지 않아.

I'm sorry, but~ 미안하지만…

A: Could you lend me 100 dollars?

B: I'm sorry, but I don't have any money with me right now.

A: 100달러 좀 꿔줄래? B: 미안하지만 지금 수중에 돈이 하나도 없어.

No, thank you 고맙지만 사양하겠어요

A: Would you like a glass of wine before dinner?

B: No, thank you. I'd prefer a beer if you have one.

A: 저녁식사전에 와인 한잔 들래요? B: 아뇨, 됐어요. 맥주 있으면 한 잔 할게요.

▸ No, thanks
고맙지만 됐어요

▸ Nothing for me, thanks
고맙지만 난 됐어요

I'd rather not 그러고 싶지 않아

A: Let's go drinking.

B: I'd rather not.

A: 술마시러 가자. B: 그러기 싫어.

▶ I'd rather you didn't
안그랬으면 좋겠는데

Not right now, thanks 지금은 됐어요

A: Do you want go home?

B: Not right now, thanks.

A: 집에 갈래? B: 지금은 됐어. 고마워.

▶ Not now
지금은 아냐
▶ Not here
여기서는 말고

Not always 항상 그런 건 아니야

A: Mr. Jones, is this a convenient time to talk right now?

B: Not really. I'm just on my way to meet a client.

A: 존슨씨, 얘기 나눌 시간돼요? B: 좀 그런데요. 고객만나러 가는 길이거든요.

▶ Not exactly
꼭 그런 건 아니야
▶ Not really
실제로는 아니야

Not yet 아직은 아냐

A: Did you talk to him about that?

B: Not yet.

A: 그거에 대해 걔와 얘기해 봤어? B: 아직 안해봤어.

Not anymore 이젠 됐어. 지금은 아니야

A: Do you still work as a teacher?

B: No, not anymore.

A: 아직도 선생님 해? B: 아니. 지금은 아니야.

I don't think it was very good 안 좋았다고 생각해

A: What was your opinion of the film?

B: I don't think it was very good.

A: 영화에 대한 네 의견은 어때? B: 안 좋았던 것 같아.

That (all) depends 상황에 따라 다르지. 경우에 따라 달라

A: Can you provide me with all of the materials?

B: That depends. What exactly do you need?

A: 자료를 전부 제공해줄 수 있어요? B: 나름이죠. 정확히 어떤 게 필요해요?

12 네가 틀렸다고 생각해

I think you're wrong 네가 틀렸다고 생각해

A: Sometimes a nation has to go to war.

B: I think you're wrong. Nations should be peaceful.

A: 때때로 국가는 전쟁을 치뤄야 돼. B: 틀렸어. 국가들은 평화로워야 해.

▸ You're dead
  wrong
  넌 완전히 틀렸어

You got the wrong idea 틀린 생각이야

A: I think you and Bill were on a date.

B: You got the wrong idea. We were only having coffee.

A: 너와 빌이 데이트 하고 있지? B: 틀렸어. 커피마셨을 뿐야.

▸ You're on the
  wrong track
  네가 잘못 생각했어
▸ You're way off the
  mark
  네가 아주 어긋났어

That's not right 그렇지 않아

A: This is the answer I got for the math problem.

B: That's not right!

A: 그 수학문제 해답야. B: 그렇지 않아!

It doesn't work 제대로 안돼, 그렇게는 안돼

A: Why don't you use the stove?

B: It doesn't work.

A: 난로를 쓰지 그래? B: 작동이 안돼.

▸ It doesn't work
  that way
  그렇게는 안 통해

It won't work 효과가 없을거야

A: What do you think of my plan?

B: I don't like it. It won't work.

A: 내 계획이 어때? B: 맘에 안들어. 효과가 없을거야.

That's not true 그렇지 않아, 사실이 아니야

A: You two seem to be getting back together!

B: That's not true! She's still mad about me.

A: 너희들 다시 사귀는 구나! B: 그렇지 않아! 걘 나한테 아직도 화나있어.

Chapter 08

I won't 싫어, 그렇게 안할래

A: I want you to do it now

B: I won't.

A: 지금 네가 그걸 해라. B: 싫어.

▸ Let's not
그렇게 하지 말자

It's not a good idea 별로 좋은 생각이 아니야

A: Should I visit Iraq this year?

B: Absolutely not. It's not a good idea.

A: 금년에 이라크를 방문할까? B: 절대 안돼. 좋은 생각이 아니야.

I can't do anything about it 어쩔 수가 없어

A: My car is not working again.

B: I can't do anything about it. Call a mechanic.

A: 차가 또 움직이질 않아. B: 어쩔 수가 없어. 수리공을 불러.

I can't make that happen 그렇게는 안되지

A: Can you load the software onto my computer?

B: Sorry, I can't make that happen.

A: 그 소프트웨어 내 컴에 깔아줄래? B: 미안, 그렇게는 못해.

I don't buy it 못 믿어

A: I'm sorry I'm late again. The bus was delayed.

B: I don't buy it. Tell me the truth.

A: 또 늦어서 미안. 버스가 늦어서. B: 난 못 믿겠는데. 사실대로 말해봐.

▸ We aren't buying
your story
네 얘기 믿을 수 없어
▸ I can't accept that
인정 못해

That's not how it works 그렇게는 안돼

A: I'll marry you if you pay me a lot of money.

B: That's not how it works.

A: 내게 돈 많이 주면 너랑 결혼할게. B: 그렇게는 안돼.

▸ That's not how we
do things here
여기선 그렇게 하는 게 아
냐

I don't[can't] agree with that[you] 그거에[네게] 동의할 수 없어

A: Women should be allowed to serve in the military.

B: I don't agree with that.

A: 여자도 군복무해야 돼. B: 그 점엔 동의할 수 없어.

13 절대 안돼!

No way! 절대 안돼!, 말도 안돼!

A: If you work for me, I'll pay you $10 an hour.

B: No way! That's much too low.

   A: 나하고 일하면 시급 10달러를 줄게. B: 말도 안돼! 너무 적어.

Not on your life! 결사반대야, 절대 안돼!

A: Can you help me with my homework?

B: Not on your life.

   A: 내 숙제 좀 도와줄래? B: 그럴 순 없지.

▸ No, no, a thousand times no!
무슨 일이 있어도 안돼, 절대로 싫어

▸ Not by a long shot
어떠한 일이 있어도 아냐, 어림도 없지

Not a thing 전혀

A: Did Ralph tell you about his secret?

B: No, not a thing.

   A: 랄프가 자기 비밀을 말했어? B: 아니, 전혀.

▸ No, not a bit
아니, 조금도 안돼

Not that way! 그런식으론 안돼!

A: You said you'd do anything to win.

B: Not that way! I'm not going to cheat!

   A: 이기려고 뭐든지 하겠다고 했잖아. B: 그런 식으로 말한 거 아냐! 난 커닝 안 할거라고!

Not a chance! 안돼!

A: So, how about a date with me?

B: Not a chance!

   A: 그래, 나와 데이트 어때? B: 안돼!

▸ (There is) No chance!
안돼!

I said no 안 된다고 했잖아, 아니라고 했잖아

A: Did Bobby ask you to join the committee?

B: Yes he did. I said no.

   A: 바비가 네게 위원회에 참여하라고 했어? B: 어 그랬어. 난 안된다고 했고.

I'm dead set against it 난 결사 반대야

A: I heard your son wants to become an actor.

B: I'm dead set against it.

> A: 네 아들이 배우가 되려 한다며. B: 난 결사 반대야.

It's out of the question 그건 불가능해. 절대 안돼

A: Can you lend me some money, Charley?

B: It's out of the question.

> A: 찰리야. 돈 좀 빌려줄래? B: 절대 안돼.

No means no 아니라면 아닌 거지

A: Please reconsider my offer.

B: No means no. I'll never agree to it.

> A: 내 제안을 다시 한번 재고해줘. B: 아니라면 아닌 거지. 절대 동의못해.

Over my dead body 내 눈에 흙이 들어가기 전엔 안돼

A: So, are you and your wife moving to California?

B: Over my dead body! I'm staying here!

> A: 너의 부부 캘리포니아로 이사가? B: 난 절대로 안가! 여기 남을 거야!

That's impossible 그건 불가능해

A: The computer you sold me is broken.

B: That's impossible. It was working great.

> A: 네가 나한테 판 MP3가 망가졌어. B: 말도 안돼. 잘 돌아갔었는데.

It's never going to happen 그건 절대 안돼

A: This is a rocket that can fly to the moon.

B: It's never going to work.

> A: 달까지 날아갈 수 있는 로켓야. B: 절대 그렇게 되지 않을걸.

ㄴ happen 대신에 work를 써도 된다.

It's not even a possibility 절대 그런 일 없을거야

A: Someday I'll win the lottery.

B: No way. It's not even a possibility.

> A: 언젠가 복권에 당첨될거야. B: 말도 안돼. 절대로 그런 일 없을 걸.

14 알겠어

I know (that) 알아, 알고 있어

A: It's not fair that she had to die so young.

B: Yes, I know. It was a tragic death.

    A: 그렇게 젊은데 죽다니 말도 안돼. B: 그래 알아. 정말 비극적인 죽음이야.

> └ I know는 이미 알고 있다(I had that information already)라는 의미이고 I see는 상대방이 뭔가 설명하거나 보여주고 나서 이해했다(I understand)라는 의미로 쓰인다.

I know what I'm saying 나도 알고 하는 말이야. 내가 알아서 얘기한다구

A: Are you sure about this?

B: I know what I'm saying.

    A: 이거 정말 확실해? B: 나도 알고 하는 말이야.

> ▶ I know what I'm talking about
> 나도 다 알고 하는 얘기야

I know what I'm doing 나도 아니까 걱정하지마, 내가 다 알아서 해

A: I don't know if you are fixing it right.

B: Don't worry. I know what I'm doing.

    A: 네가 그걸 제대로 고치는지 모르겠어. B: 걱정마. 나도 어떻게 하는지 안다고.

> ▶ Do you know what you're doing?
> 잘 알겠지?, 어떻게 하는지 알지?

I've been there 무슨 말인지 충분히 알겠어, 정말 그 심정 이해해, 가본 적 있어

A: These days I feel quite sad and depressed.

B: I've been there.

    A: 요즘 무척 슬프고 지쳐. B: 나도 그런 적 있어.

> ▶ We have all been there
> 우리도 다 그런 적 있잖아
> ▶ Been there done that
> (전에도 해본 것이어서) 뻔할 뻔자지

I can see it in your eyes 네 눈에 그렇게 쓰여 있어

A: I really miss Bonita, my ex-girlfriend.

B: I can see it in your eyes.

    A: 옛 애인인 보니타가 정말 보고 싶어. B: 네 눈에 그렇게 쓰여있네.

> ▶ It's written all over your face
> 네 얼굴에 다 쓰여있어

Chapter 08

15 누가 알겠어?

Who knows? 누가 알겠어?

A: Is Jim supposed to be coming back this afternoon?

B: Who knows?

　　A: 짐이 오늘 오후에 돌아오는거야?　B: 누가 알겠어?

▸ Who knows
what[where] ~?
무엇이[어디서] …한지 누
가 알아?

Who can tell? 누가 알겠어?

A: Do you think she'll become a lawyer?

B: Who can tell? Maybe.

　　A: 쟤가 변호사가 될 것 같아?　B: 누가 알아? 그럴지도 모르지.

Nobody knows 아무도 몰라

A: What will the economy be like next year?

B: Nobody knows.

　　A: 내년에 경기가 어떻게 될까?　B: 아무도 몰라.

God (only) knows! 누구도 알 수 없지!

A: Is Steve coming to the party?

B: God only knows!

　　A: 스티브가 파티에 오니?　B: 누가 알겠어!

▸ Heaven[Lord;
Christ] knows!
아무도 몰라
▸ God knows what~
…가 무엇인지 아무도 모를
거야

That's anybody's guess 아무도 몰라

A: Do you think the weather will be nice tomorrow?

B: That's anybody's guess.

　　A: 내일 기상이 괜찮을 것 같아?　B: 아무도 모르지.

There's no way to tell 알 길이 없어

A: Can the Korean team win the World Cup?

B: There's no way to tell.

　　A: 한국 축구팀이 월드컵에서 이길까?　B: 알 수가 없지요.

16 잘 모르겠어

I have no idea 몰라

A: How much is this going to cost?

B: I have no idea.

A: 이게 얼마나 들까? B: 몰라.

I have no idea what you just said 네가 무슨 말 하는지 전혀 모르겠어

A: Do you know what I mean?

B: Actually, I have no idea what you are talking about.

A: 내가 말하는 것이 무언지 알겠어? B: 실은 무슨 말인지 모르겠어.

I didn't know that 모르고 있었지 뭐야

A: She lived in Norway for ten years.

B: I didn't know that.

A: 걔는 10년간 노르웨이에서 살았어. B: 몰랐네.

▶ I don't know
about that
글쎄

I don't know for sure 확실히 모르겠는데

A: Do you think we should trust him?

B: I don't know for sure.

A: 우리가 걜 믿어야 된다고 생각해? B: 잘 모르겠는데.

▶ I don't know for
certain
확실히 몰라

I'm not sure 잘 모르겠어

A: When did Jennifer say that she'd be coming home?

B: I'm not sure.

A: 제니퍼는 언제 집에 오겠대? B: 잘 모르겠어.

I'm not sure about that 그건 잘 모르겠는데

A: Do you think he understands?

B: I'm not sure if he's getting the picture.

A: 그가 이해한다고 생각하니? B: 그가 이해하고 있는지 잘 모르겠어.

▶ I'm not sure 주어+
동사
…를 잘 모르겠어

Chapter 08

I can't say (for sure) 잘 몰라, 확실히는 몰라

A: When will you be finished?

B: I can't say. Maybe I'll be done in a few hours.

A: 언제 끝낼 수 있어? B: 잘 몰라. 몇시간 후면 끝낼 거야.

You got me 난 모르겠는데, 내가 졌어

A: Where is Kathy?

B: You got me.

A: 캐시가 어디 있어? B: 몰라요.

You got me there 모르겠어, 네 말이 맞아

A: What kind of present should I buy her?

B: You got me there. I think she likes perfume.

A: 어떤 선물을 걔한테 사줘야 할까? B: 몰라. 향수를 좋아할 것 같은데.

Beats me 잘 모르겠는데, 내가 어떻게 알아

A: What is the weather forecast for tomorrow?

B: Beats me.

A: 내일 일기예보가 어때? B: 내가 알 턱이 있나.

▶ Search me
난 몰라

Not that I know of 내가 알기로는 그렇지 않아

A: Will Sofia be coming over for dinner tonight?

B: Not that I know of.

A: 소피아가 오늘밤 저녁먹으러 올까? B: 난 잘 모르겠어.

▶ Not likely
그럴 것 같지 않은데

Don't ask me 나한테 묻지마

A: Is she a good doctor?

B: Don't ask me.

A: 저 여자 의사야? B: 나도 몰라.

▶ Your guess is as
good as mine
모르긴 나도 매한가지야

I don't understand (it) 왜 그런지 모르겠어, 알 수가 없네

A: I don't understand it. It's rained every day for a month.

B: This is certainly some strange weather.

A: 모르겠어. 한달째 매일 비와. B: 기상이 이상한 게 확실해.

▶ I don't see why
이유를 몰라

17 내가 어떻게 알아?

How should I know? 내가 어떻게 알아?

A: Where is your sister?

B: How should I know? I haven't seen her.

A: 네 누이 어디있어? B: 내가 어떻게 알아? 못봤다고.

How can I tell? 내가 어떻게 알아?

A: Some wines are better quality than others.

B: How can I tell?

A: 일부 와인은 다른 와인보다 품질이 나아. B: 어떻게 알아?

What can I do? 내가 (달리) 어쩌겠어?

A: So what're you going to do?

B: What can I do?

A: 그래 어떻게 할건대? B: 내가 어쩌겠어?

▶ What more[else] can I do?
달리 방도가 있어?

What can I tell you? 뭐라고 얘기하면 되지?, 어쩌라구?

A: What type of job should I get?

B: What can I tell you? I don't know.

A: 어떤 일을 얻어야 돼? B: 뭐라고 얘기해야 하나? 나도 모르겠는데.

What can I say? 난 할 말이 없네, 나더러 어쩌라는 거야?, 뭐랄까?

A: You eat like a pig!

B: What can I say? I'm hungry!

A: 돼지처럼 많이 먹네! B: 날더러 어쩌라는거야? 배고프다고!

What do you want me to say? 무슨 말을 하라는 거야? 나보고 어쩌라고?

A: You look really unhappy.

B: What do you want me to say? I feel gloomy.

A: 너 정말 불행해보인다. B: 나보고 어쩌라고? 나 우울하다고.

Chapter 08

A: Why did you fall asleep in church?

B: What do you want me to say? I was tired.

A: 교회에서 왜 잤어? B: 어쩌라고? 피곤했다고.

(I) Can't help it 나도 어쩔 수 없어

A: You shouldn't spend so much money.

B: I can't help it. I like shopping.

A: 그렇게 돈을 많이 쓰면 안돼. B: 어쩔 수 없어. 쇼핑을 좋아한다고.

▸ It can't[couldn't]
be helped
어쩔 수 없[있]어
▸ I'm sorry, but I
couldn't help it
미안하지만 어쩔 수가 없었
어

You tell me 그거야 네가 알지

A: When is your mom's birthday?

B: You tell me. You remember things quite well.

A: 언제가 어머니 생일이니? B: 그거야 네가 알지. 너 기억 잘 하잖아.

I wouldn't know 내가 알 도리가 없지, 그걸 내가 어떻게 알아

A: Where does he plan to go to college?

B: I wouldn't know. He didn't tell me.

A: 걔는 어느 대학갈거래? B: 내가 어떻게 알아. 내게 말 안했어.

I have no other choice but to do so 그렇게 하는 거 외에는 달리 방법이 없어

A: Why are you working here? You seem to hate it.

B: I have no other choice but to do so.

A: 왜 여기서 일해? 싫어하는 것 같은데. B: 그렇게 하는 거 외에는 달리 방법이 없어.

▸ I had no choice (in
that matter)
그 문제에서 달리 방법이
없어
▸ It was my only
choice
나의 유일한 선택이었어

I don't have any idea 모르겠어

A: Has Cliff ever been to Chicago?

B: I don't have any idea.

A: 클리프가 시카코에 가본 적 있어? B: 모르겠는데.

▸ I do not have the
slightest idea
나야 전혀 모르지
▸ I don't have a clue
전혀 모르겠어

There was nothing else I could've done 달리 방법이 없어

A: I heard you had to punish your daughter.

B: She was behaving badly. There was nothing else I could have done.

A: 네 딸을 혼내야만 했다며. B: 못되게 굴어서 달리 방법이 없었어.

Start
Tray Hard
Keep Talking
Native Speaking

Section

상황영어회화

Chapter 01

교통·여행

Step 1 교통
Step 2 도로
Step 3 여행

01 차가 너무 막혀

Traffic is very heavy today 오늘 차가 너무 막혀

A: Why are you so late?

B: Traffic is very heavy today.

　　A: 왜 그렇게 늦었어?　B: 오늘 차가 너무 막혀.

▸ This is quite a traffic jam
차가 꽉 막혔네

Traffic was bumper-to-bumper 차가 엄청 막혔어

A: It was difficult to travel during the holiday.

B: Yeah, traffic was bumper to bumper.

　　A: 휴일에 여행하는 게 힘들었어.　B: 그래. 차가 엄청 막혔어.

It's a one-way street 일방 도로야

A: You should turn around.

B: I can't. It's a one way street.

　　A: 차 돌려야 돼.　B: 안돼. 여기 일방야.

▸ It's a right-turn-only lane
우회전 전용차선야
▸ This is a toll road
유료도로야

Why don't you slow down a bit? 좀 천천히 가자

A: Why don't you slow down a bit?

B: I like to drive fast.

　　A: 좀 천천히 가자.　B: 난 빨리 달리는 걸 좋아해.

▸ slow down
속도를 줄이다

I got caught speeding 속도위반으로 걸렸어

A: I got caught speeding.

B: Did you get a ticket?

　　A: 과속하다 걸렸어.　B: 딱지 끊었어?

▸ I was busted for speeding
속도위반하다 걸렸어

I just got my license 방금 면허증 땄어

A: Have you driven much?

B: No. I just got my license.

　　A: 운전 많이 해봤어?　B: 아니. 이제야 면허증 딴 걸.

Don't fall asleep at the wheel 운전 중에 졸지 마라

A: I'm going to drive to Seattle tonight.

B: Don't fall asleep at the wheel.

    A: 오늘 밤 차로 시애틀에 갈거야. B: 운전 중에 잠들지 마라.

▸ Be sure to drive carefully
운전 조심하고

Want me to take the wheel? 내가 운전할까?

A: These big highways make me nervous.

B: Want me to take the wheel?

    A: 이런 커다란 하이웨이는 긴장돼. B: 내가 운전할까?

Fill it up 기름 가득 넣어줘요

A: What can I do for you?

B: Fill it up with premium.

    A: 손님, 무엇을 도와드릴까요? B: 고급휘발유로 가득 넣어주세요.

▸ Where can we fill it up?
어디서 기름넣지?

I ran out of gas 기름이 떨어졌어

A: Did you have a problem while driving yesterday?

B: Yeah, I ran out of gas.

    A: 어제 운전하다 문제있었어? B: 어, 기름이 떨어졌었어.

▸ run[be] out of = run[be] short of

Can you give me $10 worth of gas? 10달러어치 기름 넣어줄래요?

A: How much fuel do you need?

B: Can you give me $10 worth of gas?

    A: 기름 얼마나 넣을까요? B: 10 달러어치 주세요.

Would you change the oil, please? 엔진오일 갈아줄래요?

A: What would you like done to your car?

B: Would you change the oil, please?

    A: 차 어떻게 해드려요? B: 엔진오일 좀 갈아줄래요?

The engine won't start 차가 시동이 안 걸려요

A: What's the problem with your car?

B: The engine won't start.

    A: 차가 왜그래? B: 시동이 안 걸려.

02 태워다 줄게

I'll give you a ride 태워다 줄게

A: Will you be coming to my party tonight?

B: Only if you pick me up and give me a ride.

　　A: 오늘 내 파티에 올래? B: 차로 태워다주면.

▸ Do you want a ride?
　태워다줄까?

▸ How about a ride?
　태워줄래?

Are you going my way? 혹시 같은 방향으로 가니?, 같은 방향이면 태워줄래?

A: Are you going my way?

B: Maybe. I'm headed downtown.

　　A: 나랑 같은 방향인가요? B: 아마 그럴거예요. 시내로 가거든요.

Hop in 어서 타

A: Can you drop me off at work?

B: Sure! Hop in.

　　A: 회사에 내려줄 수 있어? B: 그럼! 타.

▸ get in[out]
　차에 타다[내리다]

Where can I get a taxi? 택시 어디서 타나요?

A: Where can I get a taxi?

B: There's a taxi stand just down the street.

　　A: 어디서 택시를 타나요? B: 이 길 가다보면 택시승강장이 있어요.

▸ Where's the taxi stand?
　택시승강장이 어디예요?

Can you get me a taxi, please? 택시 좀 잡아줄래요?

A: Can you get me a taxi, please?

B: I'd be glad to.

　　A: 택시 좀 불러줄래요? B: 그럼요.

▸ Can you call a cab for me?
　택시 좀 불러줄래요?

Where to? 어디로 모실까요?

A: Where to?

B: Take me to Macy's.

　　A: 어디로 모실까요? B: 메이시백화점으로요.

▸ Where're you going?
　어디 가세요?

(Take me) To this address, please 이 주소로 가 주세요

A: Take me to this address, please.

B: I know right where that is.

　　A: 이 주소로 데려다 주세요.　B: 거기가 어딘지 알아요.

▸ I'd like to go to this address
　이 주소로 갈려고요
▸ Please take me here
　이쪽으로 가 주세요

Please take me to the airport 공항으로 갑시다

A: Please take me to the airport.

B: It's going to cost you $30.

　　A: 공항에 가 주세요.　B: 30달러 나옵니다.

Here's twenty dollars, and keep the change

여기 20달러예요, 거스름돈은 가져요

A: Here's twenty dollars, and keep the change.

B: Thanks a lot. Have a nice stay in New York.

　　A: 여기 20달러예요, 거스름돈은 가져요.　B: 감사해요. 뉴욕에서 즐겁게 보내세요.

Please stop just before that traffic light 신호등 바로 전에 세워주세요

A: Where should I drop you off?

B: Please stop just before that traffic light.

　　A: 어디에서 내려줘요?　B: 저기 신호등 못미처 세워주세요.

▸ Pull over here
　여기 세워줘요
▸ Let me out of here
　여기서 내릴게요

Where can I rent a car? 차를 어디서 렌트할 수 있어요?

A: Where can I rent a car?

B: There's a car rental desk upstairs.

　　A: 차 어디서 렌트하죠?　B: 위층에 렌탈사무소가 있어요.

▸ I'd like to rent a car, please
　차를 렌트하려고요
▸ What's the rental fee?
　렌탈비가 얼마예요?

Clear the way! 비켜주세요!

A: Clear the way! This woman is sick.

B: I hope she'll be OK.

　　A: 비켜주세요! 여자가 아파요.　B: 괜찮았으면 좋겠다.

▸ Step aside
　비켜주세요
▸ Coming through
　좀 지나갈게요

03 정거장이 어디예요?

Where's the bus stop? 버스 정거장이 어디예요?

A: Where's the bus stop?

B: It's in front of the post office.

A: 버스 정거장이 어디예요? B: 우체국 앞에 있어요.

How much is the fare? 요금이 얼마예요?

A: How much is the fare?

B: It's $16.50

A: 요금이 얼마예요? B: 16달러 50센트입니다.

Which train should I take to Kangnam? 강남가려면 어떤 전철을 타야 돼요?

A: Which train should I take to Kangnam?

B: It's marked as Line #2.

A: 어떤 전철을 타야 강남갈 수 있나요? B: 2호선 타세요.

▸ Which train goes to Kangnam?
어느 전철이 강남가요?

Does this train stop at Inchon? 이 전철이 인천에서 서나요?

A: Does this train stop at Inchon?

B: No, you'll need to transfer.

A: 이 전철이 인천에서 서나요? B: 아뇨, 갈아타셔야 돼요.

How many stops are there to Kyungbokgung?

경복궁까지 몇 정거장입니까?

A: How many stops are there to Kyungbokgung?

B: Look at this map. It's seven stops away.

A: 경복궁까지 몇 정거장입니까? B: 이 지도를 보시면 7정거장이네요.

▸ How many stops to the museum?
박물관까지 몇 정거장입니까?

Where am I supposed to change[transfer]? 어디서 갈아타야 하나요?

A: Where am I supposed to transfer?

B: Transfer to Line #2 at Shindorim Station.

A: 어디서 갈아타야 하나요? B: 신도림역에서 2호선으로 갈아타세요.

▸ You can change to Line #3 at Yaksu
약수역에서 3호선으로 갈아타세요.

Take this train 이 열차를 타세요

A: Take this train to go to Busan.

B: Thank you for your help.

A: 부산가려면 이 열차를 타세요. B: 도와줘서 고마워요.

▸ Take the orange train
오렌지 색 열차를 타세요

How often do trains come? 열차 배차시간이 어떻게 돼요?

A: How often do trains come?

B: They usually arrive about every six minutes.

A: 열차 배차시간은요? B: 보통 약 6분마다 와요.

▸ The trains come every ten minutes
열차들은 10분마다 와요

What time is the last train to Suwon? 수원행 막차는 몇 시에 있어요?

A: What time is the last train to Suwon?

B: It left around twenty minutes ago.

A: 수원행 막차는 몇 시에 있어요? B: 한 20분 전에 출발했는데요.

Could you tell me when to get off? 어디서 내려야하는지 알려줄래요?

A: How far is it to Shinsa Station?

B: It's four stops from here.

A: 신사역까지 얼마나 멀어요? B: 여기서 4정거장예요.

▸ It's four stops from here
여기서부터 4정거장에서요
▸ After the next stop
다음 정거장 후에요

What's the next stop? 다음 정거장은 어디예요?

A: What's the next stop?

B: The next stop is Anam-dong Station.

A: 다음 정거장은 어디예요? B: 다음 정거장은 안암동역이예요.

▸ The next stop is Sadang
다음 정거장은 사당이예요

 **More Expressions**

- I missed my stop 내릴 때를 지나쳤어
- The bus had just left 버스가 방금 떠났어
- Where's the ticket counter? 표 파는 데가 어디예요?
- When is the next bus to Inchon? 인천가는 다음 버스는 언제 있어요?
- I missed my train 열차를 놓쳤어
- I got on the wrong bus 버스를 잘못 탔어

04 여기가 어디죠?

Where am I? 여기가 어디죠?

A: Where am I?

B: You are in a suburb of Seoul.

A: 여기가 어디죠? B: 서울 근교에요.

Where am I on this map? 지도상에 제가 어디 있는 거죠?

A: Where am I on this map?

B: Well, this is Baker St., which is right here on the map.

A: 제가 지금 지도상 어디에 있는 겁니까? B: 어, 베이커 가(街)니까, 지도에선 바로 여기네요.

▶ I can't understand where I am on this map
지도상에 제가 어딘지 모르겠어요

▶ What's the name of this street?
이 거리명이 뭔가요?

I think I'm lost 길을 잃은 것 같아요

A: I think I'm lost.

B: Do you need some help finding your way?

A: 길을 잃은 것 같아요. B: 길찾는 데 도움이 필요한가요?

▶ Excuse me, but I'm lost
실례합니다만, 길을 잃어서요

I'm trying to go to COEX, but I think I'm lost

코엑스가려는데 길을 잃은 것 같아요

A: Where do you want to go?

B: I'm trying to go to COEX, but I think I'm lost.

A: 어디 가시려구요? B: 코엑스가려는데 길을 잃은 것 같아요.

I got lost 길을 잃었어요

A: Did you find the shopping mall?

B: No, I got lost.

A: 쇼핑몰 찾았어? B: 아니, 길을 잃었어.

▶ get lost
길을 잃다

I seem to have lost my way 제가 길을 잃은 것 같아요

A: Excuse me, I seem to have lost my way.

B: Where are you trying to go?

A: 실례합니다. 제가 길을 잃은 것 같아요. B: 어디를 가려고 하는데요?

Is this the right road to reach Wall Street?

이 길이 월스트리트로 가는 길 맞나요?

A: Is this the right road to reach Wall Street?

B: It sure is. It's five minutes from here.

A: 이 길이 월스트리트로 가는 길인가요? B: 그럼요. 여기서 5분 걸려요.

Is this the right way to go to Mapo? 이 길이 마포가는 길 맞아요?

A: Is this the right way to go to Mapo?

B: I'm not sure. You'd better ask someone else.

A: 마포가는 길 맞아요? B: 몰라요. 다른 사람에게 물어봐요.

A: You look lost. Can I help?

B: Maybe. Is this the right way to go to Cheonggyecheon?

A: 길을 잃은 것 같네요. 도와드릴까요? B: 그런 것 같아요. 이 길이 청계천으로 가는 길 맞나요?

Does this road go to the station? 이 길이 역으로 향하나요?

A: Does this road go to the station?

B: Yes. The station is about ten minutes from here.

A: 이 길이 역으로 통하나요? B: 예. 한 10분 걸어가면 돼요.

Am I on the right road for the Korean Stock Exchange?

증권거래소 가는 길 맞나요?

A: Am I on the right road for Ilsan?

B: Yes, it's a few kilometers ahead.

A: 일산 가는 길 맞나요? B: 예, 몇 킬로 미터만 가면 돼요.

Which way is it to the Blue House? 어느 길이 청와대로 가나요?

A: Which way is it to the Blue House?

B: It's just over that mountain.

A: 어느 길이 청와대로 가나요? B: 저 산 너머에 있어요.

Could you draw me a map? 약도 좀 그려줄래요?

A: It's easy to find the National Theater.

B: Could you draw me a map?

A: 국립극장은 찾기 쉬워요. B: 약도 좀 그려줄래요?

길을 잃었나요?

Are you lost? 길을 잃었나요?

A: Are you lost?

B: No, I know where I'm going.

A: 길을 잃었나요? B: 아뇨, 알고 있어요.

I think you're heading in the wrong direction

방향을 잘못 잡은 것 같은데요

A: I'm trying to find the YMCA.

B: I think you're heading in the wrong direction.

A: YMCA를 찾고 있어요. B: 방향을 잘못 잡은 것 같은데요.

Where do you want to go? 어디에 가실 건데요?

A: Could you tell me where the closest subway station is?

B: It depends. Where do you want to go?

A: 제일 가까운 지하철역 좀 알려줄래요? B: 경우에 따라 다르죠. 어디에 가실 건데요?

▶ Where is it that you are heading?
어디 가는 길인데요?

If you get lost, just give me a call 혹 길을 잃어버리면 전화주세요

A: If you get lost, just give me a call.

B: Hopefully I won't need to do that.

A: 혹 길을 잃어버리면 전화주세요. B: 그럴 일이 없었으면 좋겠네요.

I'm a stranger here myself 여기가 초행길이라서요. 여기는 처음 와봐서요

A: Can you help me with some directions?

B: Sorry, I'm a stranger here myself.

A: 길 좀 알려주시겠습니까? B: 미안하지만 저도 역시 초행길이어서요

▶ Sorry, I'm new here too
미안하지만 저도 여기가 초행길이어서요.

I'm not familiar with this area 이 지역은 잘 몰라요

A: I'm not familiar with this area.
B: Maybe we should buy a map.

A: 이 지역은 잘 몰라요. B: 지도를 사야겠구만.

Why don't you ask someone else? 다른 사람한테 물어보세요

A: Sorry, I'm new here. Why don't you ask someone else?
B: Okay. Thanks anyway.

A: 저도 초행이라 다른 사람한테 물어보세요. B: 알았어요. 어쨌든 고마워요.

I'm sorry, but I'm not from Seoul 미안합니다만 저는 서울 사람이 아니라서요

A: Could you tell me where City Hall is?
B: I'm sorry, but I'm not from Seoul.

A: 시청이 어디에 있어요? B: 미안합니다만, 저는 서울 사람이 아니라서요.

I'm not a local 이 지역 사람이 아니에요

A: Where are some tourist attractions in this town?
B: I'm not sure because I'm not a local.

A: 시내에 관광안내소가 어디에 있습니까? B: 제가 이 지역 사람이 아니어서 모르겠어요.

▶ I'm not from around here
나도 잘 몰라요

This is my first time here too 여기 나도 처음야

A: Is there a coffee shop in this mall?
B: I'm not sure. This is my first time here.

A: 여기 몰에 커피샵이 있어요? B: 잘 모르겠어요. 여기 처음이라서요.

Wait a minute, let me ask someone for you

잠깐, 다른 사람한테 물어볼게요

A: Can you tell me where the toilet is?
B: Wait a minute, let me ask someone for you.

A: 화장실이 어딘지 알려줄래요? B: 잠시만요, 다른 사람한테 물어보고요.

A: Can you tell me where Cheonggyecheon is?
B: I'm sorry, but I can't speak English very well.
Could you ask someone else?

A: 청계천이 어딘가요? B: 저기 영어를 잘 말 못해요. 다른 사람에게 물어볼래요?

ㄴ 특히 길 안내해줄 영어가 안될 때는 "I'm sorry, but I can't speak English very well" 혹은 "I'm sorry, but my English isn't very good"이라 먼저 한 다음 "Could you ask someone else?"나 "You'd better check with someone else"라고 하면 된다.

06 쇼핑몰로 가는 지름길 아니?

Do you know the shortest way to the mall?
쇼핑몰로 가는 지름길 아세요?

A: Do you know the shortest way to the mall?

B: I usually take the subway, but it might not be the fastest way.

> A: 쇼핑몰가는 빠른 길 알어? B: 보통 전철타는데 가장 빠른 방법이 아닐 수도 있어.

Can you tell me the way to Maxim's? 맥심사(社)로 가는 길을 좀 가르쳐 줄래요?

A: Can you tell me the way to Maxim's?

B: Just go three blocks and turn left.

> A: 맥심사 가는 길 좀 알려주세요? B: 세 블럭 내려가서 왼쪽으로 돌기만 하면 돼요.

▸ Can you tell me
how to get to the
nearest subway
station?
가장 가까운 지하철역 좀
알려줄래요?

I'm looking for the convention center 컨벤션 센터를 찾고 있는데요

A: I'm looking for the Museum of Modern Art.

B: Catch a cab, as it's quite far from here.

> A: 현대 미술관을 찾고 있는데요. B: 택시타세요. 미술관은 여기서 꽤 멀거든요.

▸ I'm trying to find
the National Art
Gallery
국제 미술관에 가려구요

Do you know any good outlet malls in Buffalo?
버팔로에 좋은 아웃렛몰 좀 알아?

A: Do you know any good outlet malls in Buffalo?

B: Nope. I've never been there.

> A: 버팔로에 좋은 아웃렛몰 있는 거 좀 알아? B: 아니. 가본 적이 없어.

Where is the nearest post office? 가장 가까운 우체국이 어디예요?

A: Where is the nearest post office?

B: It's over there, three streets from here.

> A: 가장 가까운 우체국이 어디예요? B: 여기에서 도로 세 개를 지나 저쪽에 있어요.

How long does it take to get to the stadium?

경기장까지 시간이 얼마나 걸리죠?

A: How long does it take to get to the stadium?

B: Probably about an hour or so.

A: 경기장까지 시간이 얼마나 걸려요? B: 아마 한 시간 정도 걸릴거예요.

How do(can) I get there? 거기에 어떻게 가죠?

A: How do I get there?

B: Just walk down the street and take a right.

A: 거기 어떻게 가요? B: 이 길따라 내려가다 오른쪽 길로 가면 돼요.

▶ Is it within walking distance?
걸어서 가도 돼나요?

▶ Can I get there by bus?
버스로 갈 수 있나요?

How far is it to Busan? 부산까지 얼마나 걸려요?

A: How far is it from the subway station to the museum?

B: Well, I've walked from there before. Maybe ten minutes.

A: 전철에서 박물관까지 얼마나 먼가요? B: 어, 전에 걸어가봤는데 한 10분쯤요.

▶ How far is it from the subway to the museum?
전철역에서 박물관까지 얼마나 걸려요?

How far is it from here? 여기서 얼마나 먼가요?

A: There's a beautiful palace you should visit.

B: How far is it from here?

A: 네가 들러야 하는 멋진 왕궁이 있어. B: 여기서 얼마나 먼대?

▶ Is it far (from here)?
(여기서) 멀어요?

▶ Is Busan far?
부산이 멀리 있나요?

Is it close[near] to Kungbu Highway? 경부고속도로까지 가까워?

A: I can find a cheap hotel for you.

B: Is it close to Kungbu Highway?

A: 네가 묵을 호텔로 싼 거 찾아줄게. B: 경부고속도로에서 가까워?

▶ Am I near[close to] Busan?
부산에 가까이 왔나요?

What's the fastest way to get there? 거기까지 가는데 뭐가 가장 빠른 길이야?

A: You'll find some good restaurants downtown.

B: What's the fastest way to get there?

A: 시내에 좋은 식당 몇 개 있어. B: 거기까지 가는 가장 빠른 길은?

▶ What's the best way to get there?
거기가는데 가장 좋은 방법은 뭐야?

▶ Which way is shorter?
어느 길이 더 빨라?

07 라블록 더 곧장 가요

Go straight for two blocks   2블록 더 곧장 가요

A: Excuse me, can you tell me where Chamsil Stadium is?

B: Go straight for two blocks. You can't miss it.

A: 잠실운동장이 어딘가요? B: 2블록 곧장 가요. 쉽게 찾을 거예요.

Go down this street and turn to the left   이 길로 내려가서 왼쪽으로 도세요

A: Can you tell me the way to the Lotte Department Store?

B: Go down this street and turn to the left. It's left.

A: 롯데백화점 가는 길 좀 알려줄래요? B: 이 길따라 가서 좌회전해요. 왼편에 있어요.

Go straight on the highway for ten kilometers

고속도로를 타서 10킬로 곧장 가요

A: How can get downtown from here?

B: Go straight on the highway for ten kilometers.

A: 여기서 시내에 어떻게 가죠? B: 고속도로로 10킬로 곧장 가요.

Go east for two blocks and then turn right

동쪽으로 2블록 간 다음 우회전해요

A: Where is your main office located?

B: Go west for three blocks and turn left.

A: 당신네 본사는 어디에 있습니까? B: 서쪽으로 3블록 간 다음 좌회전해요.

Keep going straight until you reach the church

교회가 나올 때까지 곧장 가요

A: Can you tell me where the bookstore is?

B: Keep going straight until you reach a church. It's next to the church.

A: 서점이 어디에 있나요? B: 교회가 나올 때까지 곧장 가세요. 교회 옆에 있어요.

▸ keep ~ing
계속해서 …하다

Take this road for about five minutes and it's on your left

이 길로 5분가면 왼편에 있어요

A: Excuse me, where is the Four Season's Hotel?
B: Take this road for about five minutes and it's on your left.

A: 실례지만, 포시즌호텔이 어딘가요? B: 이 길따라 한 5분가면 왼편에 있어요.

Take[Follow] this road 이 길을 따라가요

A: I'm looking for Central Park.
B: Take this road until the you reach the traffic lights. It's right there.

A: 센트럴 파크를 찾는데요. B: 신호등까지 이 길 따라 가세요. 바로 거기에 있어요.

▶ Take this road until it ends and then turn right
이 길을 끝에서 우회전해요.

Take Line #3 and get off at Shinsa Station 3호선을 타서 신사역에서 내려요

A: What's the fastest way to get to Insadong?
B: Take the red line and get off at Jokgak Station.

A: 뭐가 인사동 가는 가장 빠른 길이죠? B: 적색선을 타고 종각역에서 내려요.

▶ Take the subway for one stop and get off at Yoksam Station
지하철로 한 정거장 가서 역삼역에서 내려요

Take bus number 65 and get off at the third stop

65번 타고 3번째 정거장에서 내려요

A: I need to get to COEX. How can I get there?
B: Take bus number 65 and get off at the third stop.

A: 코엑스 가야하는데 어떻게 가죠? B: 65번 버스타고 3번째 정거장에서 내려요.

Turn right at the first traffic light 첫번째 신호등에서 우회전해요

A: Could you tell me where the taxi stand is?
B: Turn right at the first traffic light. You'll see it.

A: 택시 승강장이 어딘지 알려줄래요? B: 첫번째 신호등에서 우회전해요. 바로 보일거예요.

▶ Turn left[right] at the first intersection
첫번째 교차로에서 좌[우]회전해요

Turn to the left when you come to a post office 우체국에서 좌회전해요

A: Excuse me, where is a grocery store?
B: Turn to the left when you come to a post office. The store is there.

A: 실례지만 식료품점이 어딘가요? B: 우체국에 다다르면 좌회전하세요. 바로 거기에 있어요.

08 걸어서 10분거리예요

It's a ten minute walk from here 여기서 걸어서 10분 거리에 있어요

A: How far is it from here to the station?

B: It's a ten minute walk.

A: 여기서 역까지 얼마나 걸려요? B: 걸어서 10분 거리예요.

> ┗ 걸어서 5분 거리는 'five minutes' walk로 minutes 다음에 '(apostrophe)를 붙여야 하지만 현대의 바쁜 영어에서는 생략되기도 한다

It's about 10 minutes on foot 걸어서 10분 정도 걸려요

A: How long does it take to get to work from the station?

B: It's about 15 minutes on foot.

A: 역에서 회사까지 얼마걸려요? B: 걸어서 한 15분 걸려요.

▶ Even on foot, it's no more than 10 minutes
걸어서라도 10분 이상 안 걸려요
▶ It should take 20 minutes by car
차로 20분 정도 걸릴 거예요

The museum is ten kilometers west of City Hall

박물관은 시청 서쪽 10킬로 지점에 있어

A: Could you tell me where the Modern Museum is?

B: The museum is ten kilometers west of City Hall.

A: 현대박물관이 어딘지 알려줄래요? B: 박물관은 시청 서쪽 10킬로 지점에 있어.

> ┗ 'A' is + 거리 + west[east] of~ 'A'가 …의 서[동]쪽 거리만큼에 있어

The hospital is a five minute walk from the bus stop

병원은 정거장에서 걸어서 5분걸려

A: Excuse me, I need to go to Sungsu Hospital.

B: The hospital is a five minute walk from here.

A: 저기, 성수병원가야 되는데요. B: 병원은 여기서 걸어서 5분거리예요.

> ┗ 'A' is + 시간 walk[ride] from~ 'A'는 …에서 걸어서[차타고] ~분[시간] 거리야

It's not far from here 여기서 멀지 않아요

A: Do you know where I can find a pharmacy?

B: Absolutely. It's not far from here.

A: 약국이 어딘지 알려줄래요? B: 물론요. 여기서 멀지 않아요.

▶ It's not (that) far
(그렇게) 멀지 않아요

It's on the right 오른편에 있어요

A: How do I get to Kyobo Bookstore?

B: Go south two blocks and it's on the left.

   A: 교보문고가 어딥니까? B: 남쪽으로 2 블럭을 가면 왼편에 있어요.

▸ It's on this street,
  at the corner of
  Madison and 5th.
  메디슨가와 5번가가 만나
  는 모퉁이에 있어요.

It's around the corner, to your left 왼편 모퉁이를 돌면 있습니다

A: Could you tell me where the courtesy phone is?

B: It's around the corner to your left.

   A: 무료전화기가 어디에 있습니까? B: 왼편 모퉁이를 돌면 있습니다.

▸ It's just down the
  hall to your left
  복도를 내려가다 보면 왼편
  에 있어요

▸ You'll see it on
  your right side
  당신 오른편에 있을거에요

You can't miss it 쉽게 찾을 수 있을 거예요

A: Is it difficult to find the airport road?

B: No, you can't miss it.

   A: 공항로를 찾기 어려운가요? B: 아뇨, 쉽게 찾을 수 있을 거예요.

I'm going in that direction 저도 그 쪽으로 가는 중이에요

A: Can I get a ride with you? I'm going to the museum.

B: Sure, I'm going in that direction.

   A: 같이 타도 될까요? 박물관에 가는데. B: 그럼요, 저도 그 쪽으로 가는 중이에요.

▸ I'm going there
  myself
  저도 그리로 가는 중이에요

I'll show you the way myself 제가 직접 안내할게요

A: I'll show you the way myself.

B: Thanks. That would be great.

   A: 제가 직접 안내할게요. B: 고마워요. 그럼 좋지요.

▸ Let me show you
  the way
  제가 길을 알려드릴게요

▸ Do you want me
  to take you there?
  제가 거기까지 모셔다 드릴
  까요?

More Expressions

- It's next to the coffee shop 커피샵 옆이야
- It's across from City Hall 시청 건너편이야
- It's between the bookstore and the drugstore 서점과 약국사이에 있어
- You can use the subway 지하철을 타세요.
- The easiest way is to take a taxi 택시타는게 가장 빨라
- I'd recommend taking a subway 전철을 타는게 나요

09 5월 25일로 예약하고 싶은데요

I'd like to make a reservation for May 25th 5월 25일로 예약하고 싶은데요

A: When do you want to leave?

B: I'd like to make a reservation for May 25th.

A: 언제 떠나실려고요? B: 5월 25일로 예약하고 싶은데요.

Smoking or non-smoking? 흡연석으로 하시겠어요, 비 흡연석으로 하시겠어요?

A: Smoking or non-smoking?

B: I would prefer non-smoking.

A: 흡연석으로 드릴까요, 비흡연석으로 드릴까요? B: 비흡연석으로 주세요.

Are there any seats left on the 10 o'clock flight to LA?

10시 LA행 좌석 남았나요?

A: Are there any seats left on the 10 o'clock flight to LA?

B: I'm sorry, but the flight is all booked.

A: 10시 LA행 좌석 있어요? B: 미안하지만 항공편이 다 예약되었습니다.

▸ I'm on the waiting list
난 대기자 명단에 있어요

I'd like a round-trip ticket to Chicago 시카고행 왕복 항공권을 사고 싶은데요

A: I'd like a round-trip ticket to Chicago.

B: When would you like to depart and return?

A: 시카고행 왕복 항공권을 사고 싶은데요. B: 출발일과 돌아오는 날은 요?

▸ Round trip or one-way?
왕복권요 아니면 편도요?

All of the flights are full 모든 항공편이 예약만료되었어요

A: Can I get a ticket for Saturday?

B: I'm sorry, all of the flights are full.

A: 토요일날 표있습니까? B: 미안하지만 모든 편이 다 꽉 찼어요.

▸ All of the other flights were booked solid
다른 항공편이 모두 다 예약되었어요

Do you know when the next flight leaves? 다음 비행기는 언제죠?

A: Do you know when the next flight leaves?

B: Just a moment. Let me check.

A: 다음 비행기는 언제죠? B: 잠깐만요. 확인해볼게요.

How much is business class? 비즈니스 클래스 요금이 얼마죠?

A: Do you want first class, business or coach class?

B: Business class, please.

A: 일등석, 비즈니스, 아니면 보통석요? B: 비즈니스 클래스로 주세요.

▸ Do you want first class, business or coach class?
일등석, 비즈니스 아니면 보통석으로 드릴까요?

I'm booked on AA Flight 567 to NY 뉴욕행 AA 567편을 예약했는데요

A: I'm booked on AA Flight 567 to NY.

B: Your flight leaves from gate 69.

A: 뉴욕행 AA 567편을 예약했는데요. B: 69번 게이트에서 출발합니다.

I'd like to change my flight 비행편을 바꾸고 싶습니다

A: How may I help you?

B: I'd like to change my flight.

A: 어떻게 도와드릴까요? B: 비행편 티켓을 바꾸려구요.

May I change my return date to May 7th? 돌아오는 날짜를 5/7일로 변경해줄래요?

A: May I change my return date to May 7th?

B: Unfortunately, there are no seats available right now.

A: 돌아오는 날을 5/7일로 변경해 줄래요? B: 안됐지만 현재 좌석이 없네요.

What is your flight number? 비행편 번호가 어떻게 되시죠?

A: What is your flight number?

B: It is 492, to Washington.

A: 비행편 번호가 어떻게 되시죠? B: 492번, 워싱턴행입니다.

I'd like to reconfirm my flight 예약을 확인하려구요

A: I want to reconfirm my reservation.

B: What is your flight number?

A: 예약을 확인하려구요. B: 비행편 번호가 어떻게 되시죠?

▸ I want to reconfirm my reservation
예약을 확인하려구요

10 탑승수속 카운더로 어떻게 가죠?

How can I get to the check-in counter? 탑승수속 카운터로 어떻게 가죠?

A: How can I get to the check-in counter for Delta Airlines?

B: You need to go up 1 level and it's on the south side of the building.

   A: 델타항공의 탑승수속 카운터는 어디죠? B: 윗층의 건물 남쪽편에 있습니다.

▸ check-in counter
탑승수속 카운터

How many pieces of luggage are you checking in?
부치실 짐이 몇 개죠?

A: How many pieces of luggage are you checking in?

B: I would like to check three pieces.

   A: 부치실 짐이 몇 개죠? B: 세 개를 부치려고 하는데요.

▸ check in
(짐을) 부치다

Your luggage is over the maximum weight
짐이 수화물 제한한도를 초과했습니다

A: Your luggage is over the maximum weight.

B: How much over is it?

   A: 수화물 제한한도를 초과했어요. B: 얼마나 넘었죠?

I'm just taking my carry-on 비행기에 들고 탈 짐밖에 없습니다

A: Do you have any luggage to check?

B: No, I'm just taking my carry-on.

   A: 부치실 짐이 있으십니까? B: 아뇨, 들고 탈 짐밖에 없습니다.

I need to catch my connecting flight 연결 비행편을 타려고 하는데요

A: I need to catch my connecting flight. Could you tell me where Gate K is?

B: That gate is not in this terminal, it's in Terminal Two.

   A: 환승하려는데. K탑승구가 어디죠? B: 여기가 아니라 제2 터미널에 있어요.

▸ I missed my connecting flight to NY
뉴욕행 연결 비행편을 놓쳤어요

Your plane is now boarding 손님 비행기가 지금 탑승중입니다

A: I'm booked on Flight 709 to Chicago.

B: You'd better go to your gate. Your plane's now boarding.

A: 시카고행 709편에 예약했는데요. B: 게이트로 가요. 탑승중예요.

Could you tell me how to get to Gate 3? 3번 게이트로 어떻게 가죠?

A: Excuse me, could you tell me how to get to Gate 3?

B: I think if you follow those signs you'll get there.

A: 저기, 3번 게이트로 가는 길 좀 알려주세요. B: 저 표시들을 따라가면 돼요.

Where's the boarding gate? 탑승구가 어딥니까?

A: Where's the boarding gate?

B: It's just ahead and to your left.

A: 탑승구가 어딘가요? B: 앞으로 가다 왼편에 있어요.

▶ What time do you start boarding?
탑승은 언제 하나요?
▶ Has this flight begun boarding?
항공편 탑승 시작했나요?

Please place all metal objects in the tray 금속물건은 전부 받침대에 꺼내 놓으세요

A: Please place all metal objects in the tray.

B: Do I need to take off my belt because of its metal buckle?

A: 금속물건은 다 접시에 꺼내 놓으세요. B: 금속버클이 달린 혁대도요?

Do you have any prohibited items with you? 금지품목을 갖고 계십니까?

A: Do you have any prohibited items with you?

B: Not that I know of.

A: 금지품목을 갖고 계신 게 있습니까? B: 제가 알기로는 없습니다.

▶ Did anyone ask you to bring anything into the country for them?
누군가 손님에게 뭔가 가져다 달라고 부탁한게 있나요?

You can't bring your pet with you 애완동물은 데리고 탈 수 없어요

A: You can't bring your pet with you.

B: OK, I'll come back without him later.

A: 애완동물은 데리고 탈 수 없어요. B: 예, 데려다 놓고 나중에 오죠.

Would you mind letting me check your bag?
손님 가방 속을 확인해 봐도 될까요?

A: Would you mind letting me check your bag?

B: Not at all, go right ahead. A: 손님 가방 속을 확인해 봐도 될까요? B: 그럼요, 살펴 보시죠.

11 아침 식사용 메뉴가 어떤게 있죠?

What are my choices for breakfast? 아침 식사용 메뉴가 어떤 게 있죠?

A: What are my choices for breakfast?

B: We have a vegetarian omelet or ham and eggs.

A: 아침 식사용 메뉴가 어떤 게 있죠? B: 야채 오믈렛 아니면 햄과 계란이 있어요.

▸ What would you like for dinner, beef or fish?
저녁으로 고기와 생선 중 어느 걸로 하실래요?

What would you like to drink? 뭘 드실래요?

A: What would you like to drink?

B: I'll take some orange juice, please.

A: 뭘 드실래요? B: 오렌지 주스 먹을게요.

▸ Coffee, please
커피 주세요
▸ With sugar and cream?
설탕과 프림 넣고요?

Can I have some water? 물 좀 줄래요?

A: Would you like anything else?

B: Can I have some water?

A: 뭐 다른 필요한 거 있으세요? B: 물 좀 줄래요?

▸ Can I have some medicine?
약 좀 줄래요?

Could you tell me how to fill out this form?

이 서식 어떻게 쓰는지 알려줄래요?

A: Give this paper to the immigration authorities.

B: Could you tell me how to fill out this form?

A: 이민당국에 이 서류를 주세요. B: 이 서식 어떻게 쓰는지 알려줄래요?

▸ Can you help me with this form?
이 서식 쓰는 것 좀 도와줄래요?

Could I please get a blanket? 담요 한 장 갖다주시겠어요?

A: Could I please get a blanket?

B: Certainly. Would you like me to close the shutter as well?

A: 담요 한 장 갖다주시겠어요? B: 예. 창문가리개도 내릴까요?

▸ Could I get a copy of the Wall Street Journal?
월스트리트 한 부 좀 줄래요?

자주 듣게 되는 기내방송모음

We're about to leave the boarding gate to take off
이제 곧 탑승구를 떠나 이륙하겠습니다

- Attention, this is the head flight assistant.
  알려드립니다. 저는 객실장입니다.

- We're about to leave the boarding gate to take off and you must put your chair into the upright position.
  이제 곧 탑승구를 떠나서 이륙할 예정이오니 좌석 등받이를 곧바로 세워주십시오.

- Kindly ensure that your seat belts are fastened.
  안전벨트를 매시기 바랍니다.

- Our flight attendants will now go over the safety features of this aircraft.
  저희 승무원들이 이제 비행기의 안전 사항들을 점검하도록 하겠습니다.

Welcome on board Flight 323 to Seattle
시애틀 행 323 비행편에 탑승하신 것을 환영합니다

- Good evening and welcome on board Flight 323 to Seattle.
  안녕하십니까, 시애틀 행 323 비행편에 탑승하신 것을 환영합니다.

- Please ensure that your carry-on luggage is stored in the overhead bins.
  개인 수하물은 머리 위쪽 보관함에 넣어주시기 바랍니다.

- Once we have reached our cruising altitude, we will be serving refreshments.
  운항 고도에 도달하고 나면 간단한 음식을 제공해 드리겠습니다.

We have reached our cruising altitude
비행편이 운항 고도에 도달하였습니다

- Once again, welcome aboard Flight 564 to L.A. We have reached our cruising altitude of 30,000 feet.
  로스앤젤레스 행 564 비행편에 탑승하신 것을 거듭 환영합니다. 비행기는 지금 운항 고도인 3만 피트에 도달해 있습니다.

- Our current speed is about 700 km/h and we have a strong tailwind which should allow us to arrive ahead of schedule.
  현재 속도는 약 시속 700킬로미터이며 강한 뒷바람을 받고 있어서 예정보다 일찍 목적지에 도착할 것입니다.

We're about to make our descent into New York's JFK
이제 곧 뉴욕 JFK 공항에 착륙하겠습니다

- Passengers are reminded to give their blankets, pillows and headsets to the flight attendants.
  승객들께서는 잊지 마시고 담요와 베개, 그리고 헤드폰을 승무원에게 반납하시기 바랍니다.

- The captain has put on the fasten-seat-belt sign and passengers should put their chairs into the upright position.
  안전벨트를 매라는 신호에 불을 들어왔으므로 승객들께서는 좌석 등받이를 곧게 세우시기 바랍니다.

12 여권 좀 보여주세요

May I see your passport, please? 여권 좀 보여주시겠습니까?

A: May I see your passport, please?

B: Here it is.

A: 여권 좀 보여주시겠습니까? B: 여기 있어요.

How long are you planning to stay in the US?

미국엔 얼마나 머물 계획이세요?

A: How long are you planning to stay in the US?

B: I'm planning to stay for three weeks.

A: 미국엔 얼마나 머물 계획이세요? B: 3주간 요.

▸ I plan to stay for a week
일주일간 머물겁니다
▸ I'm going to stay for a couple of months
몇 달간 머물려구요

What's the purpose of your visit? 방문 목적이 뭡니까?

A: What's the nature of your visit to the US?

B: I'm here to see some of my relatives.

A: 미국엔 무슨 일로 오셨나요? B: 친척들을 좀 만나려고 왔어요.

A: What's the purpose of your visit?

B: I'm here for language study.

A: 방문 목적은 무언가요? B: 어학연수하러 왔어요.

▸ What brought you here?
여기 오신 이유는 요?

I'm visiting on business 사업차 왔어요

A: What's the purpose of your visit?

B: I'm visiting on business.

A: 이곳엔 무슨 일로 오셨죠? B: 사업차 왔어요.

▸ Business
사업차요
▸ I'm here on business
사업차 왔어요

I'm here on vacation 휴가차 왔어요

A: What is the purpose of your visit?

B: I'm here on vacation.

A: 방문 목적이 뭡니까? B: 휴가차 왔어요.

▸ Sightseeing
관광요

Can you tell me where you're going to stay?

여행 기간 동안 어디에 계실 건가요?

A: Can you tell me where you're going to stay?

B: I'll be staying with my cousin.

  A: 어디 머물건지 알려줄래요? B: 사촌 집에 머물겁니다.

Where are you staying? 어디 머무실거예요?

A: Where are you staying?

B: At the Washington Hotel.

  A: 어디 머무실거예요? B: 워싱톤 호텔예요.

I'm staying at the Intercontinental Hotel 인터콘티넨탈 호텔에 머물거예요

A: Do you have hotel reservations?

B: I'm staying at the Intercontinental Hotel.

  A: 호텔 예약이 되어 있습니까? B: 인터콘티넨탈 호텔에 머물겁니다.

(Do you have) Anything to declare? 신고할 물건이 있습니까?

A: Do you have anything to declare?

B: I am bringing some traditional Korean food with me.

  A: 신고할 물건이 있습니까? B: 한국 전통 음식을 좀 가지고 들어오는데요.

▶ Anything to declare?
  신고할 물건은 요?
▶ How much money do you have?
  돈은 얼마나 소지하고 있습니까?

I can't find my baggage 내 가방을 못찾겠어요

A: Do you have a problem, sir?

B: Yeah, I can't find my baggage.

  A: 왜 그러시죠? B: 예, 가방을 못 찾겠어요.

You need to go to the lost luggage counter 수화물 분실 신고대로 가보세요

A: I can't find my baggage.

B: You need to go to the lost luggage counter

  A: 제 짐을 찾을 수가 없어요. B: 수화물 분실 신고대로 가보세요.

I'm still suffering from jet lag 아직 시차가 적응이 안되었어요

A: You look sleepy today.

B: I'm still suffering from jet lag. A: 오늘 피곤해 보여. B: 아직 시차가 적응이 안되어서.

13 방 있어요?

Is there a room available for tonight? 오늘 밤 방 있나요?

A: Is there a room available for tonight?

B: We have a single for $79.95.

A: 오늘 밤 방 있나요? B: 싱글 룸이 있는데 79달러 95센트입니다.

Do you have a room for tonight? 오늘 밤 방 있어요?

A: Do you have a room for tonight?

B: No, I'm afraid there are no vacancies.

A: 오늘 밤 방 있어요? B: 아뇨, 빈 방이 없는 것 같아요.

I need to get to the Delta Inn 델타 인으로 가려고 하는데요

A: I need to get to the Delta Inn.

B: Ok. Do you need to put anything in the trunk?

A: 델타 인으로 가려고 하는데요. B: 알았어요. 짐을 트렁트에 넣어야죠?

▸ Can you tell me
how to get to the
Ford Hotel?
포드호텔에 어떻게 가는지
알려줄래요?

I have a reservation 예약을 했는데요

A: I have a reservation. I'm Jinsu Lee.

B: OK. I have your reservation.

A: 예약을 했는데요. 저는 이진수라고 합니다. B: 네, 예약되어 있네요.

▸ I reserved a room
for tonight
오늘 밤 예약했는데요

Check in, please 체인 요

A: Check in, please.

B: OK, I'll go over to the front desk.

A: 체인 요. B: 예, 프론데스크로 갈게요.

▸ I'd like to check in
체인 할게요

Your room won't be ready until 1 o'clock 한 시에 입실가능합니다

A: Hi, my name is Ho-jin Jung and I'm here to check in.

B: Unfortunately, your room won't be ready until one o'clock.

A: 정호진인데요. 체인하려구요. B: 하지만 1시 돼야 입실가능합니다.

Take my baggage, please 가방 좀 들어줘요

A: May I help you, ma'am?

B: Take my baggage upstairs, please.

A: 도와드릴까요, 부인. B: 가방 좀 윗층으로 가져다 줘요.

Can you keep my valuables? 귀중품을 맡길 수 있어요?

A: Can you keep my valuables?

B: We provide a safe for all of our guests.

A: 귀중품을 맡길 수 있어요? B: 모든 고객들을 위해 금고를 제공하고 있어요.

I'd like the key to room 1024, please 1024호 열쇠 좀 주세요

A: Can I help you, sir?

B: I'd like the key to room 1024, please.

A: 도와드릴까요? B: 1024호 열쇠 좀 주세요.

I'd like to leave my room key, please 키를 맡겨놓을려구요

A: Can I help you, sir?

B: I'd like to leave my room key with you, please.

A: 뭘 도와드릴까요? B: 룸키를 맡길려고요.

Where is the dining room? 식당이 어디예요?

A: Where is the dining room?

B: It's on the 23rd floor. It opens at 6 o'clock.

A: 식당이 어디예요? B: 23층에 있고요 6시에 문엽니다.

▸ Where can I get some beer?
맥주는 어디서 살 수 있어요?

What time do you serve breakfast? 아침은 몇 시에 먹을 수 있습니까?

A: What time do you serve breakfast?

B: The restaurant opens at 5 a.m.

A: 아침은 몇 시에 먹을 수 있습니까? B: 식당은 아침 5시에 열어요.

▸ What time does the dining room open?
식당은 언제 문 열어요?

14 모닝콜 부탁할게요

I'd like a wake-up call, please 모닝콜 좀 부탁해요

A: I'd like to request a wake-up call.

B: What time do you want the call?

A: 모닝콜을 부탁하고 싶습니다. B: 몇시에 전화해드릴까요?

▸ A wake-up call,
please
모닝콜요.

Room service, please 룸서비스 좀 부탁해요

A: Room service, please.

B: Wait a moment and I'll connect you.

A: 룸서비스 좀 부탁해요 B: 잠시만요 연결시켜드릴게요.

▸ Please bring me a
pot of coffee
커피포트 좀 갖다줘요

▸ Laundry service,
please
세탁서비스 좀 부탁해요

This is room 501. There is no hot water 501호인데요, 온수가 안 나와요

A: I'm calling from room 567 and there's no hot water.

B: We'll send someone up to fix it right away.

A: 567호인데 온수가 안 나와요. B: 지금 당장 사람을 보내서 고쳐드리겠습니다.

▸ The TV doesn't
work in my room
TV가 작동 안돼요

▸ The air
conditioner won't
shut off
에어컨이 안꺼져요

Could you send someone up? 사람 좀 보내줄래요?

A: The TV isn't working. Can you send someone up?

B: I'll send a repairman to your room.

A: TV가 안 나와요. 사람 좀 올려줘요. B: 방으로 수리공을 보내드리죠.

▸ Could you send
someone to fix it?
사람 좀 보내 고쳐줄래요?

I locked myself out 문이 잠겨서 못 들어가요

A: What's the problem here?

B: I locked myself out.

A: 왜 그러시죠? B: 문이 잠겨서 못 들어가요.

▸ I'm locked out
문이 잠겨서 못들어가요

▸ I left[forgot] my
key inside my
room
방에 열쇠를 두고 나왔어요

How much do you think we should tip the cleaning lady?
청소부 팁 얼마 줘야돼?

A: How much do you think we should tip the cleaning lady?
B: Just put a dollar under the pillow when you leave.

A: 청소부에게 팁 얼마 줘야 하지? B: 나올 때 베개 밑에 1달러 넣놔.

Are there any messages for me? 혹 메시지 온 거 있습니까?

A: Are there any messages for me?
B: No there aren't. No one called.

A: 저한테 혹 메시지 온 거 있어요? B: 아뇨, 없습니다. 전화한 사람 없었어요.

I need to stay another day 하루 더 묵으려고 하는데요

A: It's Mr. Lee in room 607, I need to stay another day.
B: Let me just check to see if a room is available for you.

A: 607호의 '이'인데, 하루 더 묵으려구요. B: 가능한지 금방 확인해보겠습니다.

▸ Unfortunately, I need to leave today instead of tomorrow
유감스럽게도 내일이 아니라 오늘 떠나게 되었습니다

I'd like to check out now 체크아웃을 하고 싶은데요

A: I'd like to check out now.
B: Could you tell me your room number, please?

A: 체크아웃을 하고 싶은데요. B: 방번호를 말씀해 주시겠습니까?

A: What time is your check-out?
B: Guests need to check out by 11:00 am.

A: 이 호텔은 몇시까지 나가야 하나요? B: 11시까지 체크아웃해야 합니다.

▸ Check out, please
체크아웃 요
▸ Here's your bill
청구서 여기 있습니다

What time does the limo leave? 리무진 버스는 몇시에 출발하나요?

A: What time does the limo leave?
B: In about ten minutes.

A: 리무진 버스는 몇시에 출발하나요? B: 한 10분쯤 후에요.

15 안내센터가 어디예요?

Where's the tourist information center? 관광 안내센터가 어디에 있어요?

A: Where's the tourist information center?

B: It's located in our lobby.

A: 관광 안내센터가 어디에 있어요? B: 로비에 있어요.

▸ May I have a city map?
시내 지도를 얻을 수 있어요?

Where is the gift shop? 기념품점이 어디에 있어요?

A: Where is the gift shop?

B: It's to the right of our restaurant.

A: 기념품점이 어디에 있어요? B: 우리 식당 오른 쪽에 있어요.

Please tell me about some interesting places in this town

시내에 볼만한 곳 좀 알려줘요

A: Can I help you with something?

B: Please tell me about some interesting places in this town.

A: 뭐 좀 도와드릴까요? B: 시내에 볼만한 곳 좀 알려줘요.

▸ What are your interests?
어디가 관심있어요?

Are there any sightseeing buses? 관광버스가 있어요?

A: Are there any sightseeing buses?

B: Yes. Would you like to take a tour?

A: 관광버스가 있어요? B: 예, 한번 돌아보실래요?

▸ Is there a sightseeing bus tour?
관광버스투어가 있어요?

I'd like a tour by a taxi 택시타고 둘러볼려고요

A: I'd like a tour by a taxi.

B: I can arrange that for you.

A: 택시타고 둘러볼려고요. B: 그럼 그렇게 짜드릴게요.

I'd like a guide 가이드가 필요해요

A: Did you enjoy walking around today?

B: Yes, but I'd like a guide tomorrow.

A: 오늘 둘러보는 거 좋았어? B: 어, 하지만 내일은 가이드가 필요해.

▶ I want a Korean-speaking guide
한국말하는 가이드가 필요해요

What a beautiful view! 참 멋진 광경아!

A: You can see the ocean from our window.

B: What a beautiful view!

A: 창문을 통해 바다를 보실 수 있어요. B: 참 멋진 광경아!

When does the museum open? 박물관은 언제 문 열어요?

A: When does the museum open?

B: It opens at 9:30, Monday through Friday.

A: 박물관은 언제 문 열어요? B: 월요일부터 금요일까지 9시 30분에 열어요.

Are they open on Saturdays? 토요일 날에도 문 여나요?

A: Let's visit the English gardens.

B: Are they open on Saturdays?

A: 영국정원을 방문하죠. B: 토요일 날에도 문 여나요?

I want to stay longer 더 머물려고요

A: I want to stay longer.

B: Please, let's leave now. My feet are killing me.

A: 좀 더 있고 싶어. B: 지금 나가죠. 발아파 죽겠어.

▶ Let's leave now
지금 나가자

May I take a picture? 사진 찍어도 돼요?

A: I want to remember this trip.

B: Me too. May I take a picture?

A: 이번 여행을 기억하고 싶어. B: 나도, 사진 찍어도 돼요?

▶ Would you mind posing with me?
저와 사진 찍어도 될까요?

I'd like two tickets for today's game 오늘 게임 표 2장 주세요

A: I'd like two tickets for today's game.

B: That will be $34, please.

A: 오늘 게임 표 2장 주세요. B: 34달러 예요.

▶ Two tickets, please
2장 요.
▶ Are there any seats available?
좌석 남아 있나요?

16 영어가 달려서요

My English isn't good enough 영어가 달려서요

A: Why are you so quiet?

B: I'm embarrassed. My English isn't good enough.

A: 왜 이리 조용해? B: 당황했어요. 영어가 달려서요.

I don't know how to say it in English 그걸 영어로 어떻게 말하는지 모르겠어요

A: What is this? I don't know how to say it in English.

B: That is a lamp.

A: 이게 뭐야? 영어로 모르겠는데. B: 램프야.

How do you say 'chobop' in English? 초밥을 영어로 뭐라고 하지요?

A: How do you say 'chobop' in English?

B: I'm not sure. What is it?

A: 초밥을 영어로 뭐라고 해? B: 잘 모르겠어. 뭔데?

▸ What's 'chobop' in English?
초밥이 영어로 뭐야?

▸ What's the English word for 'chobop?'
초밥을 영어로 하면 어떻게 돼?

What do you call this in English? 이걸 영어로 뭐라고 해요?

A: What do you call this in English?

B: We call that a steamroller.

A: 이걸 영어로 뭐라고 해요? B: 스팀롤러라고 해.

Where is the lost and found? 분실물보관소가 어디예요?

A: Where is the lost and found?

B: I think it's at the police station.

A: 분실물보관소가 어디예요? B: 경찰서에 있을 걸.

▸ the lost and found
분실물보관소

Call the police! My bag was stolen! 경찰을 불러요! 가방을 도난당했어요!

A: You look upset. What's the matter?

B: Call the police! My bag was stolen!

A: 너 당황해 보여. 왜 그래? B: 경찰불러! 가방을 도난당했어!

Who should I report it to? 어디에 신고해야 하죠?

A: I lost my passport. Who should I report it to?

B: Better call your embassy.

A: 여권을 잃어버렸는데 어디에 신고해야죠? B: 자국 대사관에 전화하세요.

I'd like to have a Korean interpreter 한국말 통역하는 사람이 필요해요

A: Do you understand what I'm saying?

B: I'd like to have a Korean interpreter.

A: 내 말을 알아듣겠습니까? B: 한국말 통역하는 사람이 필요해요.

Please cancel my credit card 신용카드를 정지시켜주세요

A: Citibank Visa, may I help you?

B: Yes. Please cancel my credit card.

A: 시티뱅크비자입니다. 뭘 도와드릴까요? B: 예, 제 신용카드를 정지시켜주세요.

Where is the Korean Embassy? 한국 대사관이 어디 있어요?

A: Where is the Korean Embassy?

B: I don't know, but we can find it on a map.

A: 한국 대사관이 어디 있어요? B: 몰라요, 하지만 지도에서 찾을 수 있을 거예요.

Does anyone here speak Korean? 여기 누구 한국말 하는 사람있어요?

A: Does anyone here speak Korean?

B: I think that old woman does.

A: 여기 누구 한국말 하는 사람있어요? B: 저 나이든 아주머니가 할 걸요.

I lost my passport 여권을 잃어버렸어요

A: What is the problem you're having?

B: I lost my passport.

A: 무슨 문제이신가요? B: 여권을 잃어버렸어요.

▸ I can't find my passport
여권을 못찾겠어요

17 원화를 달러로 바꿔주세요

I'd like to change won to dollars, please 원화를 달러로 바꿔주세요

A: I'd like to change my won to dollars, please.

B: Let me find the conversion rate.

A: 원화를 달러로 바꿔주세요. B: 환율 좀 보고요.

Yen to dollars, please 엔화를 달러로 바꿔줘요

A: What type of money do you need to change?

B: Yen to dollars, please.

A: 어떤 돈을 바꾸시려구요? B: 엔화를 달러로요.

Could you cash this traveler's check for me?

이 여행자 수표를 현금으로 바꿔줄래요?

A: Could you cash this traveler's check for me?

B: Do you have ID with you?

A: 이 여행자 수표를 현금으로 바꿔줄래요? B: 신분증 갖고 계신가요?

▸ I'd like to cash
this check
이 수표를 현금으로 주세요

I'd like cash my traveler's check 여행자 수표를 현금으로 바꿀려고요

A: I'd like to cash my traveler's check.

B: Would you like large or small bills?

A: 여행자 수표를 현금으로 바꿀려고요. B: 큰 지폐로요 아니면 작은 지폐로 바꿔드려요?

Do you have any identification? 신분 증명할 거 뭐 있어요?

A: Do you have any identification?

B: Here is my passport and driver's license.

A: 신분 증명할 거 뭐 있어요? B: 여기 여권과 운전면허증 있습니다.

Please fill this out 이걸 작성하세요

A: Can I open a checking account here?

B: Yes ma'am. Please fill this out.

당좌계좌를 여기서 개설할 수 있어요? 예, 여기에 작성해주세요.

I'd like to deposit $200 200달러 예금하려고요

A: What can I do for you?

B: I'd like to deposit $200.

A: 뭘 도와드릴까요? B: 200달러 예금하려고요.

▸ deposit
예금하다

I'd like to withdraw $100 100달러 인출하려고요

A: I'd like to withdraw $100.

B: What is your account number?

A: 100달러 인출하려고요. B: 계좌번호가 어떻게 돼요?

▸ withdraw
인출하다

I'd like to open an account at your bank 여기 은행에 계좌 하나 만들려고요

A: I'd like to open an account at your bank.

B: Are you a resident of this country?

A: 여기 은행에 계좌 하나 만들려고요. B: 여기 거주하고 계십니까?

▸ I'd like to open a
savings account
저축계좌 만들려고요

I'd like to close my account and withdraw my money
계좌 끝내고 돈 인출해주세요

A: I'd like to close my account and withdraw my money.

B: You need to fill out these forms.

A: 계좌 끝내고 돈 인출해주세요 B: 이 서류들 작성해주셔야 돼요.

Please endorse it 이서하세요

A: Can I cash this check here?

B: Yes, but please endorse it.

A: 이 수표를 현금으로 바꿀 수 있나요? B: 예, 하지만 이서하세요.

Would you please break this 100 dollar bill for me?

백달러 지폐를 작은 것으로 바꿔줄래요?

A: Would you please break this hundred dollar bill for me?

B: Sorry, I haven't got enough small bills.

    A: 100달러를 작은 걸로 바꿔줄래요? B: 미안하지만 작은 지폐가 충분하지 않네요.

▸ I'd like this fifty broken into tens
이 50달러를 10달러지폐로 바꿔줘요

Do you have an account with us? 저희 은행 계좌 갖고 계신가요?

A: Do you have an account with us?

B: Yes, I have a checking account here.

    A: 저희 은행 계좌가 있으신가요? B: 예, 여기 당좌계좌를 갖고 있어요.

I lost my ATM card and need a replacement 카드분실로 재발행해주세요

A: I lost my ATM card and need a replacement.

B: You'll need to complete these forms and show me two forms of ID.

    A: ATM카드 분실했는데 재발행해주세요. B: 이 양식서들을 완성하고 신분증 2개를 보여주세요.

The ATM in your lobby isn't working 로비에 있는 ATM기가 작동안돼요

A: The ATM in your lobby isn't working.

B: I'll call someone to look at it.

    A: 로비에 있는 ATM기가 작동안돼요. B: 사람불러서 보라고 할게요.

What's the interest rate on my savings account?

저축계좌 이자율은 요?

A: What is the interest rate on my savings account?

B: It is currently two percent.

    A: 저축계좌의 이자율이 어떻게 돼요? B: 현재 2프로입니다.

What time does your bank open? 은행은 언제 여나요?

A: What time does your bank open?

B: Banking hours go from nine to three on weekdays.

    A: 은행 언제 열어요? B: 영업시간은 9시부터 3시까지입니다.

Chapter 02

전화영어

01 밀러 씨 좀 바꿔주세요?

Can[May] I speak to Mr. Miller? 밀러 씨 좀 바꿔줄래요?

A: May I speak to Mr. Miller?

B: I'm sorry he's on the other line right now.

A: 밀러씨 좀 바꿔 줄래요? B: 지금 통화중이신데요.

I'd like to speak to the branch manager, please

지사장님과 통화하고 싶은데요

A: This is Janet. May I help you?

B: I'd like to speak with the branch manager, please.

A: 쟈넷입니다. 무엇을 도와드릴까요? B: 지사장님과 통화하고 싶어요.

I'm calling to talk to Mr. Kim in the marketing department

마케팅부 김씨와 통화하려고요

A: I'm calling to talk to Mr. Kim in the marketing department.

B: I'm sorry, but he is out of the office right now.

A: 마케팅부 김 씨와 통화하려고요. B: 죄송하지만 사무실을 비우셨는데요.

Is Mr. Jones there? 존스 씨 계세요?, 존스 씨와 통화하고 싶은데요?

A: Hello, is Mr. Jones in the office?

B: No, he's away on vacation.

A: 여보세요, 존스 씨 계십니까? B: 아니오, 휴가 가셨는데요.

▶ Is Mr. Jones in?
존스 씨 계세요?
▶ Is Mr. Jones in the office?
존스 씨 사무실에 계세요?

Mr. Levine, please 레빈 씨 좀 부탁해요

A: Mr. Levine, please.

B: I'm sorry, but he's not in right now.

A: 레빈 씨 좀 부탁해요 B: 미안하지만 지금 안계신데요.

▶ Let me talk to Mr. Levine, please
레빈 씨와 통화할게요
▶ Get[Give] me sb
…을 바꿔주세요

Is this the Astron Insurance Company? 애스트론 보험사인가요?

A: Is this the Astron Insurance Company?

B: No, it's the Astron Building Company.

    A: 거기 애스트론 보험회사인가요? B: 아뇨, 애스트론 건설회사입니다.

Chapter 02

Is Mr. Kim available? 김 선생님 계세요?

A: Is David free right now?

B: I'm sorry, he hasn't come back from lunch yet.

    A: 지금 데이빗과 통화할 수 있을까요? B: 점심 식사가셔서 아직 안오셨는데요.

▸ Is Mr. Kim free right now?
김 선생님 지금 통화 돼나요?

Is this Mr. Dennis Smith? 데니스 스미스 씨입니까?

A: Is this Miss Evans?

B: Yes, it is.

    A: 에반스 양이세요? B: 네, 그런데요.

▸ Is this the billing department?
경리부인가요?

Would you put me through to the billing department?

경리부 연결해주세요

A: Would you put me through to the manager, please?

B: Sure. Can I say who's calling?

    A: 매니저 좀 바꿔줄래요? B: 네, 실례지만 누구시죠?

Would you transfer this call to extension 104? 104번으로 돌려줄래요?

A: How can I assist you?

B: Would you transfer this call to extension 104?

    A: 어떻게 도와드릴까요? B: 이 전화 104번으로 돌려줄래요?

▸ Extension 104, please
104번 부탁해요
▸ May I have extension 104?
104번 좀 바꿔줄래요?

I'd like to get through to Mr. Berkman 버크만 씨 좀 통화려고요

A: Who would you like to speak to?

B: I'd like to get through to Mr. Berkman.

    A: 누구 바꿔드릴까요? B: 버크만 씨 좀 통화려고요.

I need to talk to Mr. Harris immediately 해리스 씨와 급히 통화해야 해요

A: I need to talk to Mr. Harris immediately.

B: Let me see if he is in. A: 해리스 씨와 급히 통화해야 해요. B: 계신지 보고요.

02 누구세요?

Who's calling please? 누구세요?

A: Could I please ask who is calling?

B: This is John Smith from the accounting department.

A: 누구신지 여쭤봐도 될까요? B: 경리부의 존 스미스라고 합니다.

▸ May I ask who's calling?
누구십니까?

Who is this, please? 누구시죠?

A: Who is this, please?

B: My name is Jim Tomson. I need to talk to Mr. Smith.

A: 누구시죠? B: 짐 톰슨예요. 스미스 씨 좀 바꿔줘요?

NTB Company, may I help you? NTB 회사입니다. 뭘 도와드릴까요?

A: Marketing department.

B: I'd like to talk to Steven, please.

A: 마케팅 부입니다. B: 스티븐 씨 좀 부탁드립니다.

▸ Marketing department
마케팅 부입니다

This is James Young 제임스 영이에요

A: Who am I speaking to?

B: This is James Young.

A: 누구시죠? B: 제임스 영이에요.

This is he 전데요

A: Could I speak to Chris, please?

B: This is Chris.

A: 크리스 좀 바꿔주세요. B: 전데요.

▸ This is Chris
제가 크리스인데요
▸ This is
전데요

Speaking 전데요

A: Is Greg Henderson available?

B: Speaking.

A: 그렉 헨더슨 씨 계세요? B: 전데요.

It's me, Jane 나야, 제인

A: It's me, Jane.

B: Sorry, Jane, I didn't recognize your voice.

   A: 나야, 제인. B: 미안, 제인. 목소리를 못 알아봤네.

▸ You got Jane.
  제인이야.

A: Bill Richard's office.

B: Hi, it's Tom from the advertising agency.

   A: 빌 리처드 사무소입니다. B: 안녕하세요, 광고국의 탐입니다.

How may I direct your call? 어디 연결해드릴까요?

A: How may I direct your call?

B: I want to talk to someone in your sales division.

   A: 어디로 연결해드릴까요? B: 영업부 사람과 통화하고 싶어요.

Who do you want to speak to? 어느 분을 바꿔줄까요?

A: Who do you want to speak to?

B: I'd like to speak with Mark, if he is available.

   A: 어느 분을 바꿔드릴까요? B: 마크씨 계시면 통화하고 싶은데요.

▸ Who would you like to talk to?
  어느 분을 바꿔드릴까요?
▸ Who are you trying to reach?
  어느 분과 통화하실려구요?

I'll put you through (right away) (바로) 바꿔드리죠.

A: May I speak to Tom?

B: I'll put you through right away.

   A: 탐과 통화할 수 있을까요? B: 바로 바꿔드리죠.

▸ I'll transfer your call
  전화 바꿔드릴게요
▸ I'll connect you
  연결해 드릴게요

I'll get him for you 바꿔드리죠

A: I'd like to speak with Chris, please.

B: I'll get him for you.

   A: 크리스와 통화하고 싶은데요. B: 바꿔드리죠.

Which Mr. Kim do you want to talk to? 어느 미스터 김과 통화하시겠어요?

A: I'm trying to reach Mr. Kim.

B: Which Mr. Kim do you want to talk to?

   A: 미스터 김과 연결해주세요. B: 어느 미스터 김과 통화하시겠어요?

▸ There are four Kims here
  여기에 미스터 김이 4명 있거든요

03 잠시만요

Hold on 잠깐만요, 끊지말고 기다려요

A: I'd like to speak with a manager.

B: Hold on.

A: 매니저 바꿔주세요. B: 잠시만요.

▶ Hang on
잠시만요

Hold the line, please 잠시만요

A: Could you just hold the line for a second?

B: Sure.

A: 잠깐 기다리시겠어요? B: 그러죠.

▶ Can you hold the
line, please?
잠시만 기다려줄래요?

Could you hold? 잠시 기다리실래요?

A: I need to speak to Ryan Brinn.

B: Could you hold? I'll try to find him.

A: 라이언 브린과 통화해야 되는데요. B: 잠시 기다리실래요? 찾아볼게요.

Wait a minute[second] 잠깐만요

A: Just a moment, please.

B: Sure, I'll wait.

A: 잠시만 기다려 주십시오. B: 네, 그러죠.

▶ Just a
moment[minute;
second], please
잠시만요

One moment, please 잠시만요

A: This is the regional manager. Is your boss available?

B: One moment, please. He's on the other line.

A: 지점장인데, 대표님 계신가요? B: 잠시만요, 다른 통화중이신데요.

Would you like to hold (on)? 기다리시겠어요?

A: Would you like to hold?

B: No, I'll call back later. Thanks.

A: 기다리시겠어요? B: 아뇨, 나중에 제가 하죠. 고마워요.

Sorry to keep you waiting 기다리게 해서 미안해요

A: Mr. Lee is still in a meeting. Sorry to keep you waiting.
B: I'll call back later today.

A: 이선생이 아직 회의중예요. 기다리게 해서 미안해요. B: 오늘중으로 다시 전화할게요.

I shouldn't have tied you up so long 너무 기다리게 하는게 아닌데

A: We've been on the phone for thirty minutes.
B: Sorry, I shouldn't have tied you up so long.

A: 30분 동안이나 전화기 잡고 기다렸는데요. B: 죄송해요, 너무 기다리는게 하는게 아닌데.

I've been on hold for a couple of minutes already

벌써 몇 분 동안 기다렸어요

A: Have you been able to speak to the customer service department?
B: I've been on hold for a couple of minutes already.

A: 고객담당부서와 연결되셨나요? B: 벌써 몇분간 기다리고 있는데요.

MEMO

04 너한테 전화왔어

(There's a) Phone call for you 너한테 전화왔어

A: Phone call for you. Are you available?

B: Sure, put it through to my office.

A: 전화왔는데 받을 수 있어요? B: 그럼요, 내 사무실로 돌려줘요.

You are wanted on the telephone 너한테 전화왔어

A: Jill, you are wanted on the telephone.

B: Really? Do you know who it is?

A: 질, 너한테 전화왔어. B: 정말, 누군지 알아?

Some guy just called for you 방금 어떤 사람한테서 전화왔었어

A: Some guy just called for you.

B: Who was it?

A: 방금 어떤 사람한테서 전화왔었어. B: 누구였는데?

▶ I have a call for you
전화왔어

You have a phone call 전화왔어요

A: Ms. Grant, you have a phone call.

B: Transfer it to my office.

A: 그랜트 씨, 전화왔어요. B: 내 사무실로 돌려줘요.

You've got a call from a friend 한 친구가 전화했어요

A: You've got a call from a friend.

B: All right. I'll take the call in my office.

A: 한 친구분이 전화했어요. B: 그래요, 사무실에서 받죠.

You have[There's] a call from Mr. Smith of Software Solutions Company 소프트웨어 솔루션 회사의 스미스 씨 전화왔어요

A: Thelma, is there someone waiting to speak to me?

B: You have a call from Mr. Smith of Software Solutions Company.

    A: 셀마, 내게 전화온 사람 있어요? B: 소프트웨어 솔루션 회사의 스미스 씨 전화와있어요.

It's your girlfriend on the line 여자 친구 전화 와 있어요

A: It's your girlfriend on the line.

B: Great! I've been waiting to hear from her.

    A: 여자 친구 전화 와 있어요. B: 아주 좋아! 소식 듣고 싶었는데.

▶ Mr. Carter for you
카터 씨예요

Excuse me, there's a call on another line

실례지만 다른 라인에 전화 와 있어요

A: Excuse me, there's a call on another line.

B: See who it is.

    A: 실례지만 다른 라인에 전화 와 있어요 B: 누구인지 보고.

MEMO

05 지금 통화중이신데요

Her line is busy now 지금 통화중이신데요

A: May I speak with the manager, please?

B: He is on another line right now.

A: 과장님 좀 바꿔주시겠어요? B: 지금 통화 중이신데요.

▸ (I'm afraid) she's on the other line now
미안하지만 지금 다른 전화 받고 계세요

Mr. Green is talking to someone else now

그린 씨는 지금 다른 분과 얘기중이세요

A: Hello, I'd like to speak to Ms. Lee, please.

B: I'm sorry, but she's talking to someone else.

A: 안녕하세요, 이선생과 통화하고 싶은데요. B: 죄송합니다만 다른 분과 얘기중인데요.

▸ I'm sorry, but he has someone with him right now
미안하지만 지금 손님이 와 계신데요

I'm sorry, he's not in right now 미안하지만 지금 안에 안 계세요

A: Could I speak to Mike, please?

B: He's not in yet.

A: 마이크와 통화할 수 있을까요? B: 아직 안계신데요.

▸ He's in, but he's not at his desk right now
안에 계시는데 지금 자리엔 없네요

▸ He's is not here now
지금 여기 안 계세요

He's out to lunch now 지금 점심 식사하러 나가셨어요

A: May I speak to Bill, please?

B: He just stepped out for lunch.

A: 빌 좀 바꿔 주시겠어요? B: 점심식사하러 방금 나가셨는데요.

▸ He hasn't come back from his lunch yet
아직 점심식사에서 안 돌아 오셨어요

He's out now 지금 외출중 이에요

A: May I speak to Carl, please?

B: I'm sorry, Carl just stepped out of the office.

A: 칼 좀 부탁드립니다. B: 어쩌죠. 칼이 방금 사무실에서 나갔는데.

▸ He's out of the office right now
지금 외출 중이에요

He's out on business 출장이에요

A: Can I speak to Jennifer?

B: I'm sorry. She's out on business.

    A: 제니퍼 있어요?　B: 미안하지만 출장중이에요.

▸ I'm afraid he's on a business trip
미안하지만 출장중이신데요

▸ He's away on business for a week
일주일 간 출장가셨어요

He's in a meeting right now 지금 회의중이세요

A: Is Jessy in the office today?

B: He is, but he is in a meeting right now.

    A: 제시 오늘 사무실에 있나요?　B: 네, 근데 지금은 회의중이신데요.

▸ The advertising department is meeting now
광고부는 지금 회의중이에요

He's off today 오늘 쉬어요

A: Can I speak to Sam, please?

B: I'm sorry, but he's off today.

    A: 샘 좀 바꿔줄래요?　B: 미안하지만 오늘 휴가예요.

▸ I'm afraid he's left for the day
오늘 퇴근했어요

▸ He won't be back in the office today
오늘 안 돌아오실거예요

When do you expect him back? 언제 돌아오실까요?

A: How soon do you expect him back?

B: He should be back in about 15 minutes.

    A: 언제쯤 돌아올까요?　B: 15분쯤 후엔 돌아오실거예요.

▸ How soon do you expect him back?
언제쯤 돌아오실까요?

▸ When is he coming back?
언제 돌아와요?

He should be back in ten minutes 10분내로 돌아올거예요

A: When do you expect him back?

B: He should be back in ten minutes.

    A: 언제 돌아올까요?　B: 10분내로 돌아올거예요.

▸ He'll be back in the afternoon
오후에 돌아올거예요

Would you like to talk to someone else? 다른 분하고 통화하실래요?

A: Would you like to talk to someone else?

B: That's okay. I'll call back later.

    A: 다른 분하고 통화하실래요?　B: 괜찮아요. 나중에 전화할게요.

06 메모 좀 전해주세요

Could[May] I leave a message? 메모 좀 전해줄래요?

A: May I leave a message?

B: Yes. Could I have your name and phone number first?

A: 메시지를 남겨도 될까요? B: 예. 성함과 전화번호부터 말씀해줄래요?

▶ I'd like to leave a message
메모 좀 남길게요

▶ Please take a message
메모 좀 남겨주세요

Could[May] I take a message? 메시지를 전해드릴까요?

A: Would you like to leave a message?

B: No, thank you.

A: 메시지를 남기시겠어요? B: 아뇨. 고맙습니다.

▶ Would you like to leave a message?
메시지를 남기시겠어요?

Would you tell him that Jim Davis called?

짐 데이비스가 전화했다고 전해줄래요?

A: Could you tell him Jim Davis called?

B: I'll give him the message.

A: 짐 데이비스가 전화했다고 전해주시겠어요? B: 그렇게 전해드리죠.

Do you want him to call you back? 전화하라고 할까요?

A: I can't talk to Mr. Gibson right now.

B: Do you want him to call you back?

A: 지금 깁슨 씨와 통화할 수가 없어요. B: 다시 전화하라고 할까요?

▶ Would you like him to call you back?
전화드리라고 할까요?

Just have him call me (back) 그냥 전화 좀 해달라고 해주세요

A: She's not home. Can I take a message?

B: Just have her call me back.

A: 걘 집에 없어. 메시지 남겨줄까? B: 그냥 전화 좀 해달라고 해주세요.

▶ Please tell[ask] him to call me
내게 전화해달라고 하세요

Please tell him that I'll call him back 내가 전화 다시 할거라고 전해주세요

A: He's not here. Would you like to leave a message?

B: Please tell him that I'll call him back.

　A: 걔 여기 없어요. 메시지 남길래요? B: 제가 전화 다시 한다고 말해주세요.

I'll tell him that you called 전화하셨다고 말할게요

A: I can talk to your boss another time.

B: OK. I'll tell him that you called.

　A: 다음에 사장님과 통화할게요. B: 좋아요. 전화하셨다고 말할게요.

▸ I'll have him call you back
전화드리도록 할게요

▸ I'll tell[ask] him to call you back
전화드리도록 말할게요

How can I get in touch with him? 그 사람 연락처가 어떻게 됩니까?

A: How can I get in touch with him?

B: You can leave your name, and I'll tell him you called.

　A: 연락할 수 있는 방법이 없을까요? B: 성함을 주시면 전화왔다고 할게요.

▸ How can he get in contact with you?
어떻게 당신께 연락드리죠?

Are there any messages? 메시지 뭐 온 거 있어요?

A: Are there any messages?

B: No one called while you were at lunch.

　A: 메시지 뭐 온 거 있어? B: 점심 식사하실 때 아무 전화도 없었어요.

▸ Do you have any messages?
메시지 뭐 있어요?

▸ Any messages or phone calls?
메시지나 전화없어요?

Mr. Miller called you during the meeting 밀러 씨가 회의중에 전화하셨어요

A: Mr. James called you during the meeting.

B: Did he say what he wanted?

　A: 제임스 씨가 회의중에 전화하셨어요 B: 전화한 이유는 말했고?

May I have your number? 번호 좀 알려줄래요?

A: May I have his cell phone number?

B: Sure. Just hold on for a second and I'll find it.

　A: 그 사람 핸드폰번호 좀 알 수 있을까요? B: 예. 잠깐만 기다리면 찾아드릴게요.

▸ Your number, please?
번호 좀 요?

▸ What's your number?
번호 어떻게 돼요?

May I have your name again, please? 성함 좀 다시 말해줄래요?

A: Tell her that Kimberly Simmons called.

B: May I have your name again, please?

　A: 킴벌리 시몬즈가 전화했다고 전해줘요. B: 성함 좀 다시 말씀해주실래요?

▸ How do you spell your name?
성함 철자 어떻게 쓰나요?

전화 잘못 거셨어요

(I'm afraid) You have the wrong number 전화 잘못 거셨어요

A: I'd like to talk to Ms. Jackson, please.

B: I'm afraid you have the wrong number.

> A: 잭슨 씨를 부탁합니다. B: 전화를 잘 못 거신 것 같은데요.

▸ You must have the wrong number
전화 잘못 하셨어요

▸ I'm sorry, you've got the wrong number
미안하지만 전화 잘 못 하셨어요

What number are you calling? 어디로 전화하셨어요?

A: Can I please speak to Howard Grossman?

B: What number are you calling?

> A: 하워드 그로스맨 좀 바꿔줄래요? B: 어디로 전화하셨어요?

▸ What number are you dialing?
어느 번호로 돌리셨어요?

▸ What number are you trying to reach?
어느 번호로 전화하신 거예요?

There's no one here by that name 그런 분 여기 안 계세요

A: May I speak to John Smith, please?

B: There is no one by the name of John here.

> A: 존 스미스씨 부탁합니다. B: 여기엔 존이란 분은 안 계신데요.

There's no Anderson in this office 사무실에 앤더슨이란 사람 없어요

A: There's no Anderson in this office.

B: Sorry, I must have the wrong number.

> A: 사무실에 앤더슨이란 사람 없어요.   B: 미안해요, 전화 잘 못 걸었나봐요.

▸ There's nobody named Anderson here
여기 앤더슨이란 이름의 사람은 없어요

I'm sorry, I must have misdialed 죄송해요 전화 잘 못 돌렸네요

A: We don't have any employees here named Cho.

B: I'm sorry, I must have misdialed.

> A: 여기 조라는 직원은 없어요.   B: 미안하지만 전화 잘 못 돌렸네요.

08 죄송하지만 잘 안들려요

I'm sorry, I can't hear you (very well) 죄송하지만 (잘) 안 들려요

A: Sorry I can't hear you. Could you repeat that?

B: I said that the Visa card number is incorrect.

> ▸ I'm having trouble
>   hearing you
>   잘 들리지 않아요

A: 잘 안 들려요. 다시 말씀해줘요. B: 비자카드 번호가 잘못됐다고 했어요.

I dialed your number by mistake 실수로 네 전화번호를 눌렀네

A: Why are you calling at 3 am?

B: Sorry, I dialed your number by mistake.

A: 왜 새벽 3시에 전화하는거야? B: 미안. 실수로 네 전화번호를 눌렀어.

I'm having trouble hearing you 네 소리가 잘 안들려

A: You keep asking me to repeat things.

B: I'm having trouble hearing you.

A: 나보고 계속 똑 같은 말을 반복하라고 하네. B: 네 소리가 잘 안들려서.

Would you speak more slowly, please? 좀 천천히 말씀해주실래요?

A: Would you speak more slowly, please?

B: I said that I need to talk to your boss.

A: 좀 천천히 말씀해주실래요? B: 네 사장에게 말해야겠다고 했어.

Could you speak a little louder, please? 좀 크게 말씀해줄래요?

A: Could you speak a little louder, please?

B: Sure. Can you hear me better now?

A: 좀 크게 말해줄래? B: 그래. 이제 좀 더 잘 들려?

Could you repeat that? 다시 한번 말해줄래요?

A: My flight will be arriving tomorrow morning.

B: Could you repeat that? It's noisy here.

A: 내일 아침 비행기편으로 도착할거야. B: 다시 말해줄래? 여기가 시끄러워서.

We have a bad connection 혼선이야

A: I think we have a bad connection.

B: Would you like to call me back to see if it is any better?

A: 전화 연결상태가 나쁜 것 같아요. B: 다시 전화하셔서 괜찮은지 알아볼래요?

▸ There's noise on
  my line
  내 전화선에 소음이 있어

You sound very far away 감이 아주 멀어

A: You sound far away.

B: My cell phone's reception sucks.

A: 감이 아주 멀어. B: 내 핸드폰 수신상태가 엉망야.

Let me call you from another line 다른 선으로 전화할게

A: I think we have a bad connection.

B: Let me call you from another line.

A: 연결상태가 안 좋은 것 같아요. B: 다른 전화로 걸어볼게요.

▸ Could you dial
  again?
  다시 걸래요?

The phone went dead 전화가 죽었어

A: Is Tara still on the line?

B: No, the phone went dead.

A: 태라가 아직 전화하고 있어? B: 아니, 전화가 죽었어.

I was cut off 전화가 끊겼어

A: I thought you were going to call Jill.

B: I tried, but I was cut off.

A: 난 네가 질에게 전화걸거라 생각했는데. B: 그랬는데, 전화가 끊겼어.

09 그만 끊어야겠어

I have to go now 전화 그만 끊어야 겠어

A: My girlfriend is calling me… gotta go!

B: Okay, I'll talk to you later.

A: 내 여자친구 전화가 오네… 전화끊을게! B: 알았어, 나중에 얘기하자.

▸ I'll have to say good bye
그만 끊어야 겠어
▸ I've got to go
그만 끊을게

It's been good talking to you 통화해서 좋았어요

A: I really must end this conversation.

B: It's been good talking to you.

A: 얘기 여기서 그만 끝내야 겠어요. B: 통화해서 좋았어요.

I'm sorry, I can't talk long 미안하지만 길게 얘긴 못해

A: I'm sorry, I can't talk long.

B: I'll give you a call later when you have more time.

A: 미안하지만 길게 얘긴 못해. B: 후에 너 시간될 때 다시 걸게.

(I'll) Talk to you soon 또 걸게, 다음에 통화하자

A: I've got to go now.

B: OK, I'll talk to you soon.

A: 그만 끊어야 돼. B: 알았어, 다음에 통화하자.

▸ Talk to you tomorrow
내일 통화하자

Could you call back later? 나중에 전화할래?

A: Could you call back later?

B: Yeah, I'll be in touch later tonight.

A: 나중에 전화할래? B: 어, 오늘 밤에 통화할게.

▸ Would you mind calling back later?
나중에 전화해도 돼?
▸ Would you call again later?
나중에 전화할래요?

Please call me back in ten minutes 10분 후에 전화 줘

A: I'm busy, but please call me back in ten minutes.

B: Sure, I can do that.

A: 바쁘지만 10분 후에 전화 줘. B: 그래, 그렇게 할게.

▸ Please call again anytime
아무때나 전화 다시 해

I'll call back later 나중에 전화할게

A: I have to leave right away for the meeting.
B: I'll catch up with you later.

▸ I'll call you again
다시 전화할게
▸ I'll catch up with you later
나중에 연락할게

A: 회의가 있어서 지금 당장 가봐야겠는데. B: 나중에 다시 전화하지 뭐.

Get back to me 나중에 연락해

A: I need a decision from you. Get back to me.
B: I'll call you tomorrow morning.

A: 너의 결정이 필요해. 나중에 연락해. B: 내일 아침 연락할게.

I'll get back to you when you're not so busy
네가 안 바쁠 때 다시 전화할게

A: I'll get back to you when you're not so busy.
B: That would be great. Talk to you soon.

▸ get back to sb
나중에 전화[통화]하다

A: 네가 안 바쁠 때 다시 연락할게. B: 그러는 게 좋겠다. 다음에 통화하자.

Could I call you? 나중에 전화해도 될까요?

A: I'd like to see you again. Could I call you?
B: I don't think that's a very good idea.

A: 다시 뵙고 싶어요. 나중에 전화해도 될까요? B: 안 그러는게 낫겠어요.

Would you please get off the phone? 전화 좀 끊을테야?

A: Would you please get off the phone?
B: Why? I can use it if I want to.

▸ get off the phone
전화를 끊다

A: 전화 좀 끊을테야? B: 왜? 내가 필요하면 써도 되는 거 아냐?

Give me a call[ring; buzz] 전화해

A: Let's have lunch sometime.
B: OK. Give me a call.

A: 언제 한번 점심먹자. B: 알았어. 전화해.

Thank you[Thanks] for calling 전화줘서 고마워

A: I'll talk to you later.
B: Sounds good. Thanks for calling.

    A: 나중에 통화하자. B: 좋아. 전화줘서 고마워.

▸ Thank you for
  your call
  전화줘서 고마워
▸ Thank you for
  returning my call
  전화걸어줘서 고마워

MEMO

10 왜 핸드폰 안 받았어?

Why didn't you answer your cell phone? 왜 핸드폰 안 받았어?

A: Why didn't you answer your cell phone?

B: I couldn't because I was in class.

A: 왜 내 핸드폰 안 받았어? B: 수업중이어서 받을 수 없었어.

I forgot it at home today 오늘 집에 놔두고 왔어

A: Where did you leave your cell phone?

B: I forgot it at home today.

A: 핸드폰 어디에 둔거야? B: 깜빡하고 집에 두고 왔어.

I turned my cell phone off 핸드폰 꺼놨어

A: I wasn't able to reach you when I called.

B: I turned my cell phone off.

A: 전화했는데 연결이 안되더라. B: 핸드폰 꺼놨어.

▸ turn off
(전원 등을) 끄다

I always have my phone on vibrate 난 핸드폰 항상 진동으로 해놔

A: What kind of ring tone do you have?

B: I always have my phone on vibrate.

A: 네 핸드폰 벨소리는 뭐야? B: 난 항상 진동으로 해놔.

My cell phone is on silent mode 내 휴대폰은 진동으로 해놨어

A: You've got to turn off your phone in the theater.

B: My cell phone is on silent mode.

A:극장에서는 핸드폰을 꺼야 돼. B:진동모드로 해놨어.

▸ be on silent mode
진동모드로 해놓다

Did you see that I sent you a text message? 내가 보낸 문자 받았어?

A: Did you see that I sent you a text message?

B: No, I haven't been able to check my texts.

A: 내가 보낸 문자 받았어? B: 아니, 문자를 확인할 수 없었어.

I'll send it to you in a text message 문자메시지로 보내줄게

A: What's the address of the hospital?

B: I'll send it to you in a text message.

A: 병원주소가 어떻게 돼? B: 문자로 보내줄게.

▶ send sth in a text message
문자메세지로 보내다

The first name on my speed dial is you 스피드 단축번호의 첫 번째 이름은 너야

A: The first name on my speed dial is you.

B: Yeah, I guess we talk on the phone a lot.

A: 스피드 단축번호의 첫번째는 너야. B: 어, 우리 전화로 얘기 많이 할 것 같네.

Call me on your cell phone 핸드폰으로 전화해

A: How should we arrange the place to meet?

B: Call me on your cell phone.

A: 만날 장소를 어떻게 정하지? B: 핸드폰으로 전화해.

She's on a cell phone 핸드폰으로 통화중이야

A: Why didn't Anne call you tonight?

B: She's on a cell phone, her reception isn't good.

A: 오늘 저녁 앤은 왜 네게 전화를 안한거야? B: 전화했는데 수신상태가 안좋대.

▶ be on a cell phone
핸드폰 통화중이다

You're breaking up 소리가 끊겨

A: Can you hear what I'm saying?

B: No, I can't. You're breaking up.

A: 내 말 들려? B: 아니 안들려. 소리가 끊겨.

▶ break up
전화소리가 끊기다

My cell phone isn't getting good reception 내 핸드폰 수신상태가 안 좋아

A: My cell phone isn't getting good reception.

B: Wait until we get out of the mountains.

A: 내핸드폰 수신상태가 안 좋아. B: 산에서 벗어날 때까지 기다려.

I've been calling your cell phone 네 핸드폰으로 계속 전화했어

A: I've been calling your cell phone.

B: Sorry, I was watching a movie and had it turned off.

A: 핸드폰으로 계속 전화했어. B: 미안. 영화보느라 껐났거든.

▶ call one's cell phone
…의 핸드폰으로 전화걸다

My battery went dead and it stopped working

배터리가 죽어서 작동이 안됐어

A: No one was able to call you yesterday.

B: My battery went dead and my phone stopped working.

A: 어제 너 전혀 연락이 안되더라. B: 밧데리가 나가서 작동이 안됐어.

My battery is dying 배터리가 다해서 끊어지려고 해

A: My battery is dying. I have to hang up.

B: Why didn't you charge your phone last night?

A: 밧데리가 다 되어가네. 끊어야 돼. B: 왜 지난밤에 충전시키지 않았어?

▸ charge one's phone
…의 폰을 충전시키다

You'd better keep your cell phone charged 핸드폰 충전해놓고 다녀

A: I'll be on the bus for at least 5 hours.

B: You'd better keep your cell phone charged.

A: 적어도 5시간 버스를 탈거야. B: 핸드폰 충전시켜라.

▸ keep ~ charged
…을 충전시키다

Is your cell phone not working? 핸드폰 안돼?

A: Is your cell phone not working?

B: No, I dropped it and it broke.

A: 네 핸드폰 안돼? B: 어, 떨어뜨려서 망가졌어.

Your cell phone is ringing 너 핸드폰 온다

A: Your cell phone is ringing. Pick it up.

B: It's just my boyfriend checking up on me.

A: 너 핸드폰 온다. 받아. B: 남친 확인전화야.

I like your ring tone 벨소리 좋네

A: I like your ring tone. What is it?

B: It's a song from the Romeo and Juliet movie.

A: 벨소리 좋네. 뭐야? B: 영화 로미오와 줄리엣에 나오는 노래야.

▸ ring tone
핸드폰 벨소리

Do you mind if I answer this call? 이 전화 받아도 돼요?

A: Do you mind if I answer this call?

B: Go ahead. I'll go get some coffee.

    A: 이 전화 받아도 돼? B: 어서 받아. 난 가서 커피 좀 가져올게.

▸ Do you mind if
S+V?
…해도 괜찮을까?

I got a new smartphone 스마트폰을 새로 샀어

A: I thought you had an old cell phone.

B: Not any more. I got a new smartphone.

    A: 네 핸드폰 구형인줄 알았는데. B: 이제 아냐. 신형을 샀어.

Download the Mentors app 멘토스 어플을 다운받아

A: How can I get the study sheets?

B: Download the Mentors app. It's new.

    그 학습자료 어떻게 구해? 멘토스 어플을 다운받아. 새로 나왔어.

I deleted the app 난 그 어플을 삭제했어

A: Didn't you have an app for meeting new people?

B: I deleted that app. It was slowing down my phone.

    A: 새로운 사람 만나는 어플 있지 않았어? B: 삭제했어. 폰이 느려져서.

Please save my phone number 내 전번을 저장해놔

A: I'd like to see you again next week.

B: Please save my phone number.

    A: 담주에 다시 보자. B: 내 전번 저장해.

I gotta take this call 이 전화 받아야 돼

A: I think someone is calling your cell.

B: It's my dad. I gotta take this call.

    A: 누가 네 핸드폰으로 전화하는 것 같아. B: 아버지야. 이 전화 받아야 돼.

▸ take this call
걸려오는 전화를 받다

I have one call to make 나 전화할 데가 하나 있어

A: I have one call to make.

B: OK, but try to make it a short one.

    A: 나 전화할 데가 하나 있어. B: 좋아, 하지만 짧게 해.

▸ make the call
전화하다, 전화걸다

11 너무 늦게 전화해서 미안해

I'm sorry for calling you this late   너무 늦게 전화해서 미안해

A: Hi, am I calling too late?

B: No, I usually go to bed late.

A: 안녕, 내가 너무 늦게 전화했니? B: 아냐. 난 보통 늦게 잠자리에 들잖아.

▸ Am I calling too late?
내가 너무 늦게 전화했니?

I hope I didn't wake you up   잠을 깨운 게 아니었으면 해

A: I hope I didn't wake you up this morning.

B: No, I was outside when I heard the phone.

A: 아침 잠을 깨운 게 아니었으면 해. B: 아냐, 전화왔을 때 밖에 있었어.

▸ I hope I'm not disturbing you
방해한 게 아니었으면 해

I'm calling to ask you for a favor   도움 좀 청할려고 전화했어

A: Chris, I'm calling to ask you for a favor.

B: I'll do my best. What would you like?

A: 크리스, 너한테 부탁할 게 있어서 전화했어. B: 힘 닿는대로 해볼게. 부탁이 뭔데?

▸ I'm calling about tomorrow's meeting
내일 회의 문제로 전화한거야

Excuse me, is there someone there who can speak Korean?

실례지만, 한국어하는 사람 있어요?

A: Excuse me, is there someone there who can speak Korean?

B: Hold on and I'll get Miss Kim.

A: 실례지만, 한국어 하는 사람 있어요? B: 잠시만요, 미스 킴을 바꿔줄게요.

Are you (still) there?   듣고 있는 거니?, 여보세요?

A: Are you still there?

B: Yes, I'm waiting for your reply.

A: 듣고 있는 거니? B: 어, 난 네가 대답하길 기다렸어.

I called, but your line was busy 전화했는데 통화중이더라

A: Why didn't you telephone my office?

B: I called, but your line was busy.

A: 내 사무실로 전화 안했어? B: 전화했는데 통화중이더라.

I was expecting your call 네 전화 기다리고 있었어

A: Mr. Carter, please. It's Bill from New York.

B: He's expecting your call. I'll connect you.

A: 카터씨 부탁해요. 뉴욕의 빌예요. B: 전화 기다리고 계셨어요. 돌려드릴게요.

▸ He's expecting
  your call
  당신 전화를 기다리고 있었
  어요

Where can I reach him? 어떻게 그 사람에게 연락하죠?

A: Where can I reach him?

B: Try his office.

A: 어떻게 그 사람에게 연락하죠? B: 사무실로 해봐요.

You can reach me at 010-3794-5450 until six o'clock

6시까진 010-3794-5450으로 하세요

A: How can I get in touch with you?

B: You can reach me at 010-3794-5450 until six o'clock.

A: 어디로 통화할까요? B: 6시까진 010-3794-5450으로 하세요.

Hello, I got your message on my answering machine

여보세요. 응답기에 메시지가 있어서

A: Hello, I got your message on my answering machine.

B: Hi, I was calling about the job you had advertised.

A: 응답기에 메시지가 있어서요. B: 안녕하세요. 광고하신 자리 때문에 전화드렸어요.

I heard you called this morning 오늘 아침 전화했다고 들었어요

A: I heard you called this morning.

B: That's right. I need to schedule a meeting with you.

A: 오늘 아침 전화했다고 들었어요. B: 맞아요. 당신과의 회의일정을 짜야 돼요.

You called? 전화하셨어요?

A: I've been trying to reach you all day.

B: You called? No one told me.

A: 하루종일 통화하려고 했어요. B: 전화하셨어요? 아무도 말 안해주던데.

I'm sorry I wasn't in when you called 전화했을 때 자리 비워서 미안해요

A: I'm sorry I wasn't in when you called.

B: That's okay. I got the answer I needed from Jerry.

A: 전화했을 때 자리 비워서 미안해. B: 괜찮아. 제리한테 물어서 알아냈어.

I'm returning your call 전화했다고 해서 하는거야

A: Hi, this is Steve Johnston.

B: Hi Steve, it's Tom. I'm returning your call.

A: 안녕, 스티븐 존스톤입니다. B: 안녕, 스티브, 탐야. 전화했다고 해서 하는거야.

▶ return one's call = call back[again]

I'm sorry I didn't get back to you sooner 더 빨리 연락 못 줘서 미안해

A: I'm sorry I didn't get back to you sooner.

B: That's all right, I have been pretty busy as well.

A: 더 빨리 연락 못 줘서 미안해. B: 괜찮아. 나도 그간 꽤 바빴어.

Hello, this is Mr. Fick and I'm returning Mr. Kim's call
픽예요 김선생이 전화했다고 해서요

A: Hello, this is Mr. Fick and I'm returning Mr. Kim's call.

B: He was waiting for your call. Hold on.

A: 저, 픽인데요 김 선생이 전화했다고 해서요 B: 전화기다리고 계세요. 잠시만요.

I'm sorry I've taken so much of your time 너무 오래 붙잡고 있었네요

A: I shouldn't have tied you up so long.

B: No problem, it was great talking to you.

A: 너무 오래 붙잡고 있었네요. B: 아뇨. 당신과 얘기나누는 게 즐거웠던 걸요.

I'm sorry, but my phone was set to vibrate

미안해요, 전화를 진동으로 했났거든요

A: Why didn't you answer your phone when I called you yesterday?

B: I'm sorry, but my phone was set to vibrate.

    A: 어제 전화했는데 왜 안 받는 거야? B: 미안, 휴대폰을 진동으로 해놨거든.

Did you see that I sent you a text message?

제가 보낸 문자 메시지 받았어요?

A: Did you see that I sent you a text message?

B: No, I haven't had time to check my phone in the last hour.

    A: 내가 보낸 문자 메시지 봤어? B: 아니, 한 시간 전부터 확인할 시간이 없었어.

I'm calling you because I saw that you called me

부재중 전화가 와서 전화드렸어요

A: I'm calling because I saw that you called me.

B: Oh yes. Do you have some time to talk now?

    A: 부재중 전화가 와 있어 전화하는 거야. B: 어 그래. 지금 더 이야기 할 수 있어?

MEMO

12 이메일 주소 좀 알려줘

Please give me your e-mail address 이메일 주소 좀 알려줘

A: Please give me your e-mail address.

B: Sure. It's Marysinclair@google.com.

> A: 네 이멜 주소 좀 알려줘. B: 그럼. Marysinclair@google.com이야.

Can you give me her e-mail address? 걔 이메일 주소 좀 알려줄래?

A: My sister wants to send you some photos.

B: Can you give me her e-mail address?

> A: 내 누이가 네게 사진 좀 보내려고 해. B: 누이 이멜주소 내게 알려줄래?

My e-mail address is sleeper5001@gmail.com

내 이메일 주소는 sleeper5001@gmail.com이야

A: How can I forward these documents to you?

B: My e-mail address is sleeper5001@gmail.com.

> A: 내가 어떻게 이 서류를 네게 전하지? B: 내 이멜 주소는 sleeper5001@gmail.com야.

You can e-mail me at sleeper5001@gmail.com

sleeper5001@gmail.com으로 메일 보내

A: Let's keep in touch when we're far apart.

B: You can e-mail me at sleeper5001@gmail.com.

> A: 우리가 멀리 떨어져 있어도 연락을 서로 하자. B: sleeper5001@gmail.com으로 메일을 보내.

I'll let you know my new e-mail address as soon as I get it

내가 이메일 만들면 바로 새 이메일주소 알려줄게

A: When I send you e-mail, it keeps getting returned.

B: I'll let you know my new e-mail address as soon as I get it.

> A: 네게 멜을 보내는데 자꾸 반송돼. B: 이멜 만들면 바로 새 이멜 주소 알려줄게.

My e-mail address has been changed to sleeper5001@gmail.com
바뀐 내 이메일 주소는 sleeper5001@gmail.com이야

A: Have you got a new e-mail address?

B: My e-mail address has been changed to sleeper5001@gmail.com.

A: 이멜 계정 새로 만들었어? B: 바뀐 내 이메일 주소는 sleeper5001@gmail.com이야.

Please change my address from ABC@gmail.com to ENC@gmail.com
내 이메일 주소를 ABC@gmail.com에서 ENC@gmail.com으로 바꾸라고

A: What do you want me to change on these forms?

B: Please change my address from ABC@gmail.com to ENC@gmail.com.

A: 이 양식서류에서 뭐를 바꿀까요? B: 내 이메일 주소를 ABC@gmail.com에서 ENC@gmail.com으로 바꿔요.

I'm afraid I sent that e-mail to the wrong address
다른 주소로 이메일을 보낸 것 같아

A: Why haven't you forwarded the contracts?

B: I'm afraid I sent that e-mail to the wrong address.

A: 왜 계약서를 보내지 않았나요? B: 다른 주소로 보낸 것 같아요.

Please delete my name from your mailing list
귀사의 발송자 명단에서 절 빼주세요

A: Please delete my name from your mailing list.

B: I can't do that without a written request.

A: 귀사의 발송자 명단에서 절 빼주세요. B: 서류제출없이는 그렇게 할 수가 없어요.

Please forward my e-mail to my new address
내 이메일을 새로운 주소로 전송해줘

A: I have several photos I'd like to e-mail to you.

B: Please forward my e-mail to my new address.

A: 이멜로 네게 사진 좀 보내려고. B: 내 새로운 이멜 주소로 보내줘.

13 시간 되면 이메일 보내

Do e-mail me when you get a chance 시간되면 이메일 보내

A: I'll be very busy over the next few days.

B: Do e-mail me when you get a chance.

　　A: 앞으로 며칠간 무척 바쁠거야. B: 시간되면 이멜보내.

▸ get a chance
　기회가 되면

Thank you for your e-mail of March 17 3월 17일자 이메일 고마워

A: Hopefully you got the e-mail we sent you.

B: I received your e-mail of June 21.

　　A: 우리가 보낸 이멜 받았길 바랍니다. B: 6월 21일자 이멜을 받았습니다.

▸ I received your
　e-mail of June 21
　6월 21일 보낸 이메일 받았
　어

I'll e-mail you later 나중에 이메일 보낼게

A: I need to have your response as soon as possible.

B: I understand. I'll e-mail you later.

　　A: 가능한 빨리 이멜답장을 받아야 돼. B: 알았어. 나중에 이멜 보낼게.

I will e-mail you again 다시 이메일 다시 보낼게

A: I never got the message that you sent.

B: I will e-mail you again.

　　A: 네가 보낸 메시지 받지 못했어. B: 이멜 다시 보낼게.

I still haven't received any e-mail from you

네게서 아직 아무런 이메일도 못 받았어

A: I still haven't received a response from you.

B: Sorry, I've been busy. I'll respond to you soon.

　　A: 너한테서 답장을 아직 못받았어. B: 미안, 바빴어. 곧 보낼게.

▸ I still haven't
　received a
　response from
　you
　아직 너로부터 답장을 못
　받았어

I just wanted to drop you an e-mail to say 'hi'

그냥 인사나 하려고 이메일보냈어

A: You sent something to my e-mail account?

B: I just wanted to drop you an e-mail to say 'hi.'

A: 내 이멜 계정으로 뭐 보냈어? B: 그냥 인사나 하려고 이메일보냈어.

I would like to take this opportunity to thank you for your kindness and hospitality 이 기회를 빌어 당신의 친절과 호의에 감사드립니다

A: I'd like to take this opportunity to thank you for your kindness and hospitality.

B: You are very welcome. I try to help when I can.

A: 이 기회를 빌어 당신의 친절과 호의에 감사드려요. B: 무슨 말씀을요. 가능하면 도와야죠.

▸ take this opportunity to+V
이 기회를 빌어 …하다

I'm sending a quick e-mail to let you know that I'll be arriving this Sunday 이번 일요일날 도착한다고 알려주려고 짧게 이메일 보내는거야

A: I'm sending a quick e-mail to let you know that I'll be arriving this Sunday.

B: Great. Do you know what time your flight will arrive?

A: 이번 일요일날 도착한다고 알려주려고 짧게 이메일 보내는거야. B: 좋아. 몇시 도착 비행기인지 알고 있어?

I'll be waiting to hear from you 연락기다리고 있을게

A: We will let you know when the work is finished.

B: I'll be waiting to hear from you.

A: 일이 끝나면 알려줄게. B: 연락기다리고 있을게.

Please write me whenever you can 언제든 시간되면 연락해

A: I don't know when I'll have time to e-mail.

B: Write back when you can.

A: 언제 시간내서 이멜 보낼지 모르겠어. B: 가능할 때 답장보내.

▸ Write back when you can
시간되면 연락해

I'm looking forward to your early reply 빨리 답장 주기를 기다릴게요

A: As soon as a decision is made, I'll let you know.

B: I'm looking forward to hearing from you soon.

A: 결정이 되는대로, 알려줄게. B: 학수고대하고 있을게.

▸ I'm looking forward to hearing from you soon
소식 주기를 학수고대하고 있겠습니다

We look forward to your prompt response 빠른 답신을 기다립니다

A: We look forward to your prompt response.

B: Sounds good. Let me review the documents first.

A: 빠른 답신을 기다립니다. B: 좋아요. 먼저 서류들을 검토할게요.

Thank you for your quick response 빨리 답장줘서 고마워

A: I decided to accept your job offer.

B: Thank you for your quick response.

A: 귀사의 취업제의를 받아들이기로 했습니다. B: 빨리 답장줘서 고마워.

Thank you for your response to my e-mail of October 25

내 10월 25일자 이메일에 답장을 해줘서 고마워요

A: Thank you for your response to my e-mail of October 25.

B: No problem. I wanted to keep you informed.

A: 내 10월 25일자 이메일에 답장을 해줘서 고마워. B: 무슨. 네가 소식을 알려주고 싶었어.

Thank you so much for your prompt reply to my e-mail of January 11 내 1월 11일자 이메일에 바로 답을 줘서 무척 고마워요

A: I responded as soon as it was possible to do so.

B: Thank you so much for your prompt reply to my e-mail of January 11.

A: 가능한 한 빠르게 답장을 보냈어요. B: 1월 11일자 이메일에 바로 답을 줘서 무척 고마워요.

I sent a reply to you 답장 보냈어

A: Did you see the e-mail from my office?

B: Yes, I did. I sent a reply to you.

A: 내 사무실에서 보낸 이멜 봤어? B: 어, 봤고 답장 보냈어.

I'm sorry I didn't reply to you sooner 빨리 답신을 못해서 미안해요

A: You took a full week to send a response.

B: I'm sorry for not answering sooner.

A: 답장 보내는데 일주일이나 걸렸네. B: 더 빨리 답장 보내지 못해 미안.

▶ I'm sorry for not
answering sooner.
더 빨리 답 못해 미안.

I'm sorry I haven't had time to write earlier, but I've been so busy.
좀 더 일찍 소식 못 전해 미안하지만 정말 바빴어

A: It was good to get an e-mail from you.

B: I'm sorry I haven't had time to write earlier, but I've been so busy.

A: 네 이멜을 받아서 좋았어. B: 좀 더 일찍 소식 못 전해 미안하지만 정말 바빴어.

▸ have time to+V
…할 시간을 갖다

It has taken me so long to respond to you.
답장 쓰는데 시간이 너무 걸렸네

A: It has taken me so long to respond to you.

B: That's right. You've kept me waiting.

A: 답장 쓰는데 시간이 너무 걸렸네. B: 맞아. 날 너무 기다리게 했어.

MEMO

14 첨부파일이 열리지 않아

I'm attaching a file to this e-mail 이 이메일에 파일을 첨부했어

A: Aren't you supposed to send them a report?

B: I'm attaching a file to this e-mail.

▸ attach a file to~
…에 파일을 첨부하다

A: 보고서 보내야 되지 않아? B: 이 이멜에 파일을 첨부했어.

I can't read the attached file 첨부파일이 열리지 않아

A: I can't read the attached file.

B: Sorry about that. I'll send it again.

A: 첨부파일이 열리지 않아. B: 미안해. 다시 보낼게.

I couldn't get this file to open. It reads 'error reading file'

파일이 열리지가 않아. "파일읽기에러"라고 적혀있어

A: Why haven't you printed the contracts?

B: I couldn't get this file to open. It reads 'error reading file.'

A: 왜 계약서를 프린팅하지 않았어? B: 파일이 열리지가 않아. "파일읽기에러"라고 적혀있어.

I downloaded it several times, but the result was the same

여러 번 다운로드했는데 마찬가지야

A: You weren't able to read the file?

B: I downloaded it several times, but the result was the same.

A: 그 파일을 읽을 수가 없었다고? B: 여러 번 다운로드했는데 마찬가지야.

I got both of your e-mails and tried to download both files, but neither would download. 네가 보내준 메일 2개를 받았는데 다운로드가 안돼.

A: I got both of your e-mails and tried to download both files, but neither would download.

B: Maybe the files have been corrupted. I'll send them again.

A: 네가 보내준 메일 2개를 받았는데 다운로드가 안돼. B: 파일들이 감염되었나보네. 다시 보낼게.

Let's try sending it to my naver e-mail: ENC@naver.com

내 네이버 이메일인 ENC@naver.com으로 보내봐

A: The attachment never arrived in my inbox.

B: Let's try sending it to my naver e-mail: ENC@naver.com.

A: 내 멜박스에는 첨부파일이 오지 않았어. B: 내 네이버 이메일인 ENC@yahoo.com으로 보내봐.

If that doesn't work, we can cut and paste the file again

그래도 안되면 텍스트를 잘라 붙여 보내자

A: I e-mailed her a copy of the new schedule.

B: If that doesn't work, we can cut and paste the file again.

▶ cut and paste~
…을 잘라 붙이다

A: 걔한테 새로운 스케줄 일정표 사본을 이멜로 보냈어. B: 그게 안되면 텍스트를 잘라 붙여 보내자.

For some reason the attachment wouldn't open

어떤 이유에선가 첨부파일이 열리지 않아

A: Where is the information about our holiday tour?

B: For some reason the attachment wouldn't open.

A: 휴일여행 정보가 어디 있어? B: 무슨 이유인지 모르겠지만 첨부파일이 열리지 않아.

Could you send the general contents within an e-mail?

이메일에 텍스트로 보내줄래?

A: We received a new set of instructions from Mr. Allen.

B: Could you send the general contents within an e-mail?

A: 알렌 씨로부터의 새로운 지시사항을 받았어. B: 이멜에 텍스트로 보내줄래?

Have you gotten any of my e-mails? 내가 보낸 이메일 받아봤어?

A: Have you gotten any of my e-mails?

B: No. I wasn't aware that you'd sent any.

A: 내가 보낸 이메일 받아봤어? B: 아니, 네가 뭘 보낼거라고는 생각못했어.

I sent several but they have been returned to me saying the message delivery was delayed

여러 번 보냈는데 발송이 지연되었다는 메시지와 함께 되돌아 와

A: Have you sent e-mails to them about the financial problems?

B: I sent several but they have been returned to me saying the message delivery was delayed.

A: 재정문제에 대해서 그들에게 이멜을 보냈어? B: 여러 번 보냈는데 발송이 지연되었다는 메시지와 함께 되돌아 와.

I'm not sure if any got through to you 네가 받은게 있는지 모르겠네

A: I'm not sure if any got through to you.

B: Yes, I got several of them last night.

A: 네가 받은게 있는지 모르겠네. B: 어, 지난밤에 몇 개 받았어.

▸ Please let me know if it gets to you
혹시 받았으면 알려줘

I got a notification that the e-mail I sent you had been delayed, so I'm sending it again

내가 보낸 이메일이 지연되었다고 해서 다시 보내는거야

A: I got a notification that the e-mail I sent you had been delayed, so I'm sending it again.

B: Thanks. It's very important that we receive it.

A: 내가 보낸 이메일이 지연되었다고 해서 다시 보내는거야. B: 고마워. 우리가 받아야 되는 중요한거거든.

I am traveling in Paris this week, and it has been difficult to find Internet access

이번 주에 파리 여행을 하고 있어 인터넷이 되는 곳을 찾기가 어려웠어

A: Why haven't you submitted the work files?

B: I am traveling in Paris this week, and it has been difficult to find Internet access.

A: 일한 파일들 왜 제출하지 않은거야? B: 이번 주에 파리 여행을 하고 있어 인터넷이 되는 곳을 찾기가 어려웠어요.

I read your email with my iPhone but couldn't reply to you

아이폰으로 네 이멜을 봤는데 답장을 할 수 없었어

A: Did you get my email?

B: I read your email with my iPhone but couldn't reply to you.

A: 내 이멜 받았어? B: 아이폰으로 네 이멜을 봤는데 답장을 할 수 없었어.

It went to my junk e-mail instead of my regular inbox

이메일이 받은메일함이 아니라 스팸메일박스로 갔어

A: Why didn't you respond to my email?

B: It went to my junk e-mail instead of my regular inbox.

A: 왜 내 이멜에 답을 안한거야? B: 이메일이 받은메일함이 아니라 스팸메일박스로 갔어.

It seems like your ENC@nate.com account is working OK now
네 ENC@nate.com 계정은 잘 되는 것 같아

A: It seems like your ENC@nate.com account is working OK now.

B: So we'll be able to use it to communicate.

A: 네 ENC@nate.com 계정은 잘 되는 것 같아. B: 그럼 이 이멜로 서로 연락하자.

I haven't had any messages returned from it lately

최근엔 반송되는게 없었어

A: Some people have had problems with that website.

B: I haven't had any messages returned from it lately.

A: 일부 사람들은 저 사이트에 문제가 있었어. B: 최근엔 반송되는게 없었어.

Most of the files to ENC@gmail.com seem to be getting returned
ENC@gmail.com로 보낸 대부분의 파일들은 계속 반송되는 것 같아

A: Most of the files to ENC@gmail.com seem to be getting returned.

B: Do you think they were addressed correctly?

A: ENC@gmail.com은 계속 반송되는 것 같아 B: 주소를 제대로 적었다고 생각해?

▶ keep returning to my inbox
받은 메일함으로 계속 돌아오다

I just sent you a file. Please check to see that you got it

방금 파일을 보냈는데 제대로 받았는지 확인해봐

A: I just sent you a file. Please check to see that you got it.

B: OK. I'll open my e-mail in a few minutes.

A: 방금 파일을 보냈는데 제대로 받았는지 확인해봐 B: 그래. 곧 메일 열어볼게.

I just wanted to confirm that I got your file today and will be working on it 오늘 네 파일 받아서 작업하고 있다는 걸 알려주려고

A: I just wanted to confirm that I got your file today and will be working on it.

B: Yeah, it arrived earlier this afternoon. .

A: 오늘 네 파일 받아서 작업하고 있다는 걸 알려주려고 B: 어, 오늘 오후 일찍 도착했을거야.

MEMO

15 문자는 보내봤어?

We're just waiting for her to send us a text message
우리는 걔가 우리에게 문자 보내기를 기다리고 있어

A: I haven't been able to contact Jim today.

B: Have you tried to send him a text?

    A: 오늘 짐하고 연락이 되질 않네. B: 문자는 보내봤어?

▸ send sb a text
message
…에게 문자메시지를 보내
다

Alex got a text message saying his mom is in the hospital
알렉스는 엄마가 병원에 계시다는 문자를 받았어

A: Alex got a text message saying his mom is in the hospital.

B: We'd better get a taxi for him right away.

    A: 알렉스는 엄마가 병원에 계시다는 문자를 받았어. B: 걔 타도록 택시 바로 잡아야겠다.

▸ get a text
message saying~
…라는 문자메시지를 받다

You'd better text them to say we'll be late
넌 걔네들에게 문자를 보내 우리가 늦을거라고 말해

A: The Smiths are expecting us at 6pm.

B: You'd better text them to say we'll be late.

    A: 스미스 씨네 가족이 저녁 6시에 우리가 올거라 생각하고 있어. B: 문자로 늦을거라고 하는게 낫겠어.

▸ text message sb
…에게 문자메시지를 보내
다

On our date, she kept texting her ex-boyfriend
데이트하는데 그녀는 계속해서 옛 남친에게 문자를 보냈어

A: Why do you think Andrea is rude?

B: On our date, she kept texting her ex-boyfriend.

    A: 왜 앤드리아가 무례하다고 생각하는거야? B: 데이트하는데 그녀는 계속해서 옛 남친에게 문자를 보냈어

▸ text sb
…에게 문자를 보내다

Text her and find out where she is   문자보내서 걔 어디 있는지 알아내

A: I'm really worried about my daughter.

B: Text her and find out where she is.

    A: 내 딸이 정말 걱정돼. B: 문자보내서 걔 어디 있는지 알아내

I got your texts　네 문자 받았어

A: I sent you some information about the schedule.
B: Thanks for that. I got your texts.

    A: 일정에 관한 것 좀 보냈어.　B: 고마워. 네 문자 받았어.

I got your text message saying "I got fired"

내가 잘렸다는 네 문자를 받았어

A: I got your text message saying "I got fired."
B: It's been the worst day of my life.

    A: 잘렸다는 네 문자를 받았어. B: 생애 최악의 날이었어.

I think I'll send him a text　걔한테 텍스트 문자를 남길까봐

A: Brad invited some people over to his house.
B: I think I'll send him a text.

    A: 브래드는 자기 집으로 몇몇 사람을 초대했어.　B: 걔한테 텍스트 문자를 보낼까봐.

Jenny didn't trouble herself to respond to the text

제니는 문자메시지를 보내려고 하지 않았어

A: Someone asked Jenny out on a date via a text.
B: Jenny didn't trouble herself to respond to the text.

    A: 누가 문자로 제니에게 데이트 신청을 했어.　B: 제니는 문자메시지를 보내려고 하지 않았어.

I'll send it to you in a text message　그 내용을 문자 메시지로 보내줄게

A: They need to know the address of your house.
B: I'll send it to you in a text message.

    A: 걔네들은 네 집주소를 알아야 돼.　B: 그 내용을 문자 메시지로 보내줄게.

How do I know you didn't just delete the text?

네가 문자를 삭제안했는지 내가 어떻게 알아?

A: Sorry, but I never got a text from you last night.
B: How do I know you didn't just delete the text?

    A: 미안, 지난밤에 너 문자 받지를 못했어.　B: 네가 문자를 삭제안했는지 내가 어떻게 알아?

16 커피숍에서 인터넷을 연결했어

We got connected to the Internet at the coffee shop
우린 커피숍에서 인터넷을 연결했어

A: Were you able to check your e-mail?

B: We got connected to the Internet at the coffee shop.

  A: 이멜을 확인할 수 있었어? B: 우린 커피숍에서 인터넷을 연결했어.

▸ connect[hook up] to the Internet
인터넷에 연결하다

We weren't able to get on the Internet 인터넷에 접속을 할 수가 없었어

A: Why haven't you started work on the book?

B: We weren't able to get on the Internet.

  A: 왜 그 책에 대한 작업을 시작하지 않은거야? B: 인터넷에 접속을 할 수가 없었어.

▸ get on the Internet
인터넷에 접속하다

I use my neighbor's wifi to tap into the Internet
이웃집 와이파이로 인터넷에 접속해

A: How do you get online at your new apartment?

B: I use my neighbor's wifi to tap into the Internet.

  A: 너 새 아파트에서는 어떻게 인터넷해? B: 이웃집 와이파이로 인터넷에 접속해.

▸ tap into the Internet
인터넷에 접속하다

I read about that on the Internet 그것에 관해 인터넷에서 읽었어

A: The country's leader has caused a lot of problems.

B: I read about that on the Internet.

  A: 그 나라의 지도자가 많은 문제를 야기하고 있어. B: 인터넷에서 그거 읽었어.

Let's search for it on the Internet 인터넷에서 그걸 찾아보자

A: We need to know the best place for a wedding.

B: Let's search for it on the Internet.

  A: 최상의 결혼식장을 알아야 돼. B: 인터넷에서 찾아보자.

You looked it up on the Internet? 그걸 인터넷에서 검색해봤어?

A: I found out where my ex-girlfriend lives.

B: You looked it up on the Internet?

  A: 내 옛여친이 어디에 사는지 알아냈어. B: 그걸 인터넷에서 찾아봤어?

▸ look up
찾아보다

Many of them do research on the Internet

대다수가 인터넷으로 자료 검색을 하고 있어

A: How do reporters write stories so quickly?

B: Many of them do research on the Internet.

  A: 기자들이 어떻게 그렇게 빨리 기사를 쓰는거야. B: 그들중 많은 사람들이 인터넷에서 검색을 해.

▸ do research on
the Internet
인터넷에서 검색하다

How about googling the company? 그 회사 구글검색해봐

A: I have no idea what to expect at the interview.

B: How about googling the company?

  A: 면접에서 무슨 말이 나올지 모르겠어. B: 그 회사 구글에서 검색해봐.

We visited Dave's blog and read his comments

우린 데이브의 블로그를 방문해서 그의 댓글을 읽었지

A: We visited Dave's blog and read his comments.

B: Did he have anything interesting to say?

  A: 우리는 데이브의 블로그에 방문해서 그의 댓글을 읽었어. B: 뭐 흥미로운 거 있었어?

I read about the problem on Andy's blog

앤디의 블로그에서 그 문제에 관한 것을 읽었어

A: The workmen haven't repaired the broken water line.

B: I read about the problem on Andy's blog.

  A: 근로자들이 파손된 수도관을 수리하지 않았대. B: 앤디의 블로그에서 그 문제에 관한 것을 읽었어.

She wrote about it on my blog. 걘 내 블로그에 그거에 관해 글을 썼어

A: You heard about Lizzie's engagement?

B: She wrote about it on my blog.

  A: 리지의 약혼소식 들었어? B: 걘 내 블로그에 글을 썼어.

17 남친에게 IM을 보냈어

I use instant messenger for contacting my sister
여동생과 연락하는데 인스턴트 메신저를 사용해

A: I use instant messenger for contacting my sister.

B: Is she still living in New Zealand?

A: 여동생과 연락하는데 인스턴트 메신저를 사용해. B: 아직 뉴질랜드에서 살고 있어?

▸ Students use instant messenger for discussing homework
학생들은 과제물을 토의하는데 메신저를 이용해

Sam sent an instant message to her boyfriend
샘은 자기 남친에게 IM을 보냈어

A: Sam sent an instant message to her boyfriend.

B: Was he trying to start an argument?

A: 샘은 자기 남친에게 IM을 보냈어. B: 남친이 싸움을 시작한거야?

▸ send an instant messenger to sb
…에게 IM을 보내다

My sister IMed me about a concert tomorrow night
누이는 내일밤 콘서트에 관해 내게 메신저로 소식을 보냈어

A: My sister IMed me about a concert tomorrow night.

B: Have you decided if you want to go with her?

A: 누이는 내일밤 콘서트에 관해 내게 메신저로 소식을 보냈어. B: 누이랑 함께 가기로 결정했어?

▸ S+IMed sb about~
…에 관해 …에게 IM을 보냈다

Just add your new friend to your Messenger list
네 메신저에 새로운 친구를 추가하면 돼

A: Will he be able to contact me on the Internet?

B: Just add your new friend to your Messenger list.

A: 걔가 인터넷으로 내게 연락할 수 있을까? B: 네 메신저에 새로운 친구를 추가하면 돼

▸ Sure, I'll add him to my Messenger list.
그럼, 난 걔를 메신저 리스트에 올릴거야.

I don't use social media 난 SNS를 하지 않아

A: I've never seen you on Facebook.

B: I don't use social media. I hate it.

A: 페이스북에 너 안보이더라. B: 난 SNS를 하지 않아. 아주 싫어해.

▸ What social media are you on?
무슨 SNS 해?

I'm going to post a message on the Internet

난 인터넷에 메시지를 올릴 생각이야

A: Better tell everyone tonight's meeting is cancelled.

B: I'm going to post a message on the Internet.

A: 오늘 저녁 미팅 취소됐다고 모두에게 말해. B: 인터넷에 메시지를 올릴거야.

▶ post[write] sth on the Internet
인터넷에 …을 써서 올리다

I posted my opinion about the government

난 정부에 대한 내 견해를 올렸어

A: What made everyone start arguing?

B: I posted my opinion about the government.

A: 뭐 때문에 다들 다투기 시작한거야? B: 내가 정부에 대한 내 생각을 올렸거든.

▶ I just posted my address in a chat room.
내 주소를 채팅방에 방금 올렸어.

He's just trolling on the Internet 걘 인터넷에 악성 댓글을 올리고 있어

A: Your brother is always insulting people online.

B: He's just trolling on the Internet.

A: 네 형은 온라인상에서 항상 사람들을 안좋게 말하더라. B: 인터넷에 악성댓글을 올리고 있어.

▶ Troll
온라인상에서 무례하고 악성댓글을 올리는 사람

▶ I think trolls on the Internet need to be banned.
악성댓글은 금지되어야 해.

Someone was cyber bullying her on the Internet

누군가 사이버상에서 걜 괴롭혔어

A: What led to her suicide attempt?

B: Someone was cyber bullying her on the Internet.

A: 뭐 때문에 걔가 자살 시도를 한거야? B: 인터넷에서 누가 걜 괴롭혔어.

They invited everyone to leave a comment

누구나 댓글을 달도록 초대했어

A: It was an interesting discussion forum.

B: They invited everyone to leave a comment.

A: 이건 흥미로운 토론방였어. B: 누구나 댓글을 달도록 초대했거든.

The posts were deleted because of negative comments

그 게시물은 부정적인 글로 삭제됐어

A: Why didn't anyone post an opinion here?

B: The posts were deleted because of negative comments.

A: 왜 여기에 아무도 글을 올리지 않았어? B: 게시글들이 악성으로 삭제되었어.

You clicked on her article and wrote a comment?

그녀의 글을 보고 댓글을 달았단 말야?

A: Lea is angry about the comment I left.

B: You clicked on her article and wrote a comment?

A: 리아는 내가 단 댓글로 화났어. B: 걔의 글을 보고 댓글을 달았단 말야?

▸ write a comment
댓글을 달다

Why do people take the time to write malicious comments?

왜 사람들은 시간들여 악성댓글을 다는거야?

A: Someone wrote that I look fat and really ugly.

B: Why do people take the time to write malicious comments?

A: 내가 뚱뚱하고 못생겨 보인다고 누가 썼어. B: 왜 사람들은 시간들여 악성댓글을 다는거야?

MEMO

18 인스타에서 나를 팔로워해

Do you think he'll tweet about his trip overseas?
걔가 자기 해외여행에 관해 트위터에 올릴 것 같아?

A: Scott says he'll be in France for a week.

B: Do you think he'll tweet about his trip overseas?

▸ tweet (about) sth
트위터에 (…에 관해) 올리다

A: 스캇은 일주일간 프랑스에 있을거야. B: 걔가 자기 해외여행에 관해 트위터에 올릴 것 같아?

Several people liked the tweet about our festival
몇몇 사람들이 우리 축제에 관한 트윗을 좋아한다고 표시했어

A: Several people liked the tweet about our festival.

B: I hope their friends will come down and join us.

▸ "Like" a tweet
트윗의 내용이 좋다고 표시하다

A: 몇몇 사람들이 우리 축제에 관한 트윗을 좋아한다고 표시했어. B: 걔네 친구들이 와서 함께 하면 좋겠어.

Ray is in his bedroom updating his Facebook page
레이는 침실에서 자신의 페이스북 페이지를 업데이트하고 있어

A: How come your brother isn't drinking with us?

B: Ray is in his bedroom updating his Facebook page.

▸ update one's Facebook
페이스북을 업데이트하다

A: 왜 네 형은 우리와 함께 술을 하지 않아? B: 레이는 침실에서 자신의 페이스북 페이지를 업데이트하고 있어.

An old girlfriend found me on Facebook
오래된 여친이 페이스북을 통해 날 찾았어

A: An old girlfriend found me on Facebook.

B: That's great. Is she still attractive?

▸ find sb on Facebook
페이스북에서 …을 찾다

A: 오래된 여친이 페이스북을 통해 날 찾았어. B: 잘됐네. 아직 매력적이야?

I friended all of them on Facebook 난 페이스북에 친구로 다 등록해놨어

A: Have you been in contact with my cousin?

B: I friended him on my Facebook.

▸ unfriends sb on Facebook
페이스북에서 친구 삭제하다

▸ block sb
…을 차단하다

A: 내 사촌과 연락하고 지냈어? B: 난 페이스북에 친구로 등록해놨어.

It was a great vacation, and I'm going to facebook the experience 정말 멋진 여행이었어. 경험한 것들을 페이스북에 올릴거야

A: Did you enjoy your trip to Japan and China?

B: It was a great vacation, and I'm going to facebook the experience.

A: 일본과 중국 여행 좋았어? B: 정말 멋진 여행이었어. 경험한 것들을 페이스북에 올릴거야.

▸ facebook
페이스북으로 연락하다

Chapter 02

You need to login to Facebook to check her status

걔가 어떻게 지내는지 확인하려면 페이스북에 로그인해야 돼

A: Cathy didn't say whether she was in a relationship.

B: You need to login to Facebook to check her status.

A: 캐시는 누구와 사귀고 있는지 여부를 말하지 않았어.

B: 걔가 어떻게 지내는지 확인하려면 페이스북에 로그인해야 돼.

▸ login to Facebook
페이스북에 로그인하다
└ Facebook status는 일상에 있었던 일들을 올려 놓은 상태를 말한다.

I had to delete my Facebook account 난 페이스북 계정을 삭제해야만 했어

A: There are too many creeps online.

B: I know. I had to delete my Facebook account.

A: 온라인에는 너무 많은 이상한 놈들이 있어. B: 알아. 난 페이스북 계정을 삭제해야만 했어.

▸ delete one's Facebook account
페이스북 계정을 삭제하다

Is there a way for me to link to Tracey's Facebook page?

내가 트레이시의 페이스북에 연결하는 방법이 있어?

A: Is there a way for me to link to Tracey's Facebook page?

B: Yeah, just click the button on the lower right.

A: 내가 트레이시의 페이스북에 연결하는 방법이 있어? B: 어, 오른쪽 하단의 버튼을 누르기만 하면 돼.

▸ link to a Facebook page
페이스북에 연결하다

Let's connect on Instagram 인스타그램에서 봐

A: How can we stay in contact?

B: Let's connect on Instagram.

A: 어떻게 연락을 주고 받지? B: 인스타그램에서 보자고.

How many followers do you have on Instagram?

인스타그램에서 팔로워가 몇 명이야?

A: How many followers do you have on Instagram?

B: It was over 30,000 at the beginning of the month.

A: 인스타그램에서 팔로워가 몇 명이야? B: 이달 초에 3만명이 넘었어.

▸ How many are you following on Instagram?
인스타그램에서 몇 이나 팔로워해?

Please follow me on Instagram 인스타에서 나를 팔로워해

A: You seem to lead an interesting life.

B: Please follow me on Instagram.

A: 너 흥미롭게 사는 것 같아. B: 인스타에서 나를 팔로워해.

I friended him on my Instagram 난 걔를 인스타에서 친구로 했어

A: You know a popular movie actor?

B: I friended him on my Instagram.

A: 유명한 영화배우 알아? B: 인스타그램에서 친구했거든.

I posted it on my Instagram 그걸 내 인스타그램에 올렸어

A: The news about your break-up spread quickly.

B: I posted it on my Instagram.

A: 이별 소식은 빠르게 퍼져나갔어. B: 난 내 인스타에 그걸 올렸거든.

She said they met on Instagram 걔가 그러는데 걔네들 인스타에서 만났대

A: Rachel never told me how she met her boyfriend.

B: She said they met on Instagram.

A: 레이첼은 어떻게 남친을 만났는지 말하지 않았어. B: 걔가 그러는데 걔네들 인스타에서 만났대.

People like my posts on Instagram 사람들이 인스타의 내 게시물들을 좋아해

A: What is the secret to your on-line popularity?

B: People like my posts on Instagram.

A: 온라인에서 유명해진 비결이 뭐야? B: 사람들이 인스타의 내 게시물들을 좋아해.

I liked your posts on Instagram 인스타에서 네 게시물을 좋아했어

A: I liked your posts on Instagram.

B: Thanks. I spend a lot of time selecting them.

A: 인스타에서 네 게시물을 좋아했어. B: 고마워. 선택하는데 많은 시간을 들였어.

There are 400 likes on one of my posts 내 게시물을 좋아하는 사람이 400명이 넘어

A: There are 400 likes on one of my posts.

B: Tell me what is interesting about it.

A: 내 게시물을 좋아하는 사람이 400명이 넘어. B: 네 게시물의 뭐가 재미있는지 말해줘.

Thank you for your likes 좋아요를 눌러줘서 고마워

A: I liked the videos you posted on the Internet.

B: Great, thank you for your likes.

A: 네가 인터넷에 올린 비디오 좋았어. B: 잘했어, 좋아요 눌러줘서 고마워.

Hit me up on Facebook 페이스북에서 보자

A: I'll stay in touch while I'm in Canada.

B: Hit me up on Facebook when you get a chance.

A: 캐나다에 있는 동안에도 연락을 주고 받자. B: 시간되면 페이스북으로 연락해

They are going to be live streaming the conference
그들은 회의를 실시간으로 중계할거야

A: So you don't have to attend the meeting?

B: They are going to be live streaming the conference.

A: 그럼 넌 회의에 참석할 필요가 없어? B: 그들은 회의를 실시간으로 중계할거야.

▸ be live streaming
인터넷으로 생중계하다

Look at this. I found it on YouTube 이것봐. 유튜브에서 찾은거야

A: Look at this. I found it on YouTube.

B: It looks like a video about ghost stories.

A: 이것봐. 유튜브에서 찾은거야. B: 괴담에 관한 비디오 같은데.

He plans to broadcast it on YouTube 유튜브에서 생방송할 예정이야

A: How can we watch Jim's wedding?

B: He plans to broadcast it on YouTube.

A: 우린 어떻게 짐의 결혼식을 볼 수 있어? B: 갠 유튜브로 생방송할 예정이야.

▸ broadcast the on
YouTube
유튜부에서 생방송하다

You can upload it to YouTube 유튜브에 올려

A: I have a video of my brother scoring the winning goal.

B: You can upload it to YouTube.

A: 내 형이 결승골을 넣는 비디오가 있어. B: 유튜브에 올려.

▸ download sth
from YouTube
유튜브에서 다운로드하다
▸ upload[post]
videos to YouTube
for dollars
유튜브에 비디오를 올려 돈
을 벌다

Chapter 03

음식·식당

01 가장 가까운 한국 식당이 어디예요?

Could you recommend a good restaurant near here?
근처에 좋은 식당 추천해줄래요?

A: Could you recommend a good restaurant near here?

B: Sure. Do you like Italian food?

> A: 이 근처에 좋은 식당추천해줄래요? B: 그럼요. 이태리 음식 좋아해요?

▸ Where is the
closest Korean
restaurant?
가장 가까운 한국식당이 어
디예요?

Are there any restaurants still open near here?
근처에 아직 문 연 식당 있나요?

A: Are there any restaurants still open near here?

B: Denny's is open 24 hours.

> A: 이 근처에 아직 문 연 식당 있나요? B: 데니스 식당이 24시간 영업해요.

Do I need a reservation? 예약이 필요합니까?

A: Do I need a reservation?

B: Yes, we require all of our diners to make reservations.

> A: 예약이 필요합니까? B: 예약 손님만 받아요.

I'd like to reserve a table for seven 일곱명 예약하고 싶은데요

A: I'd like to reserve a table for seven.

B: What time, sir?

> A: 일곱명 예약하려구요. B: 몇시로요. 선생님?

▸ I'd like to reserve
a table near the
window
창가에 예약하고 싶어요

What time can we make a reservation for? 몇 시에 예약할 수 있나요?

A: What time can we make a reservation for?

B: We have some openings around 6 p.m.

> A: 몇 시에 예약할 수 있나요? B: 오후 6시부터 부분적으로 영업시작합니다.

Would you like smoking or nonsmoking?

흡연석 아니면 금연석, 어디로 해드릴까요?

A: Would you like smoking or nonsmoking?

B: We'll sit in the nonsmoking section, please.

> A: 흡연석 아니면 금연석, 어디로 해드릴까요? B: 금연석으로 해주세요.

I'd like to make a reservation for four tonight

오늘 밤 4명으로 예약하려구요

A: I'd like to make a reservation for four tonight.

B: Would you like smoking or nonsmoking?

> A: 오늘 밤 4명으로 예약하려구요. B: 흡연석 아니면 비흡연석으로 할까요?

▸ I'd like to make an reservation for eight people at six o'clock tonight
오늘 밤 6시에 8명 예약하려구요

I'm sorry. We're all booked up tonight

미안하지만 오늘밤은 예약이 다 끝났어요

A: Can I make a reservation for two people?

B: I'm sorry. We're all booked up tonight.

> A: 2명으로 예약할 수 있나요? B: 미안하지만 오늘 밤은 예약이 다 끝났어요.

▸ I'm sorry. We're quite full tonight
미안하지만 오늘 밤은 다 찼습니다

How long is the wait? 얼마나 기다려야 하나요?

A: I can put your name on our waiting list.

B: How long is the wait?

> A: 대기자 명단에 올려놓을게요. B: 얼마나 기다려야 하나요?

▸ How long do we have to wait?
얼마동안 기다려야 합니까?

▸ Is the wait long?
오래 기다려야 합니까?

I'm sorry, but I have to cancel my reservation

미안하지만 예약취소해야 될 것 같아서

A: Angelo's Restaurant, may I help you?

B: I'm sorry, but I have to cancel my reservations.

> A: 앤젤로 식당입니다. 무슨 일이시죠? B: 미안하지만 예약을 취소하려고요.

I'd like to take her out for dinner on the weekend

주말에 걔 데리고 가서 저녁먹고 싶어

A: I'd like to take you to try some Japanese food.

B: That'd be great!

A: 널 데리고 식당가서 일본음식 좀 먹고 싶어. B: 그럼 아주 좋지!

▸ I'd like to take you to try some Japanese food

널 데리고 식당가서 일본음식 좀 먹고 싶어

Would you like to join us for some cocktails?

우리와 함께 칵테일 좀 마실테야?

A: Would you like to join us for some cocktails?

B: I'd be glad to. Where will we be going?

A: 우리와 함께 칵테일 좀 마실테야? B: 좋지. 어디로 갈거야?

MEMO

02 뭐 먹을래요?

What would you like (to have)? 뭘 드시겠어요?

A: What would you like?

B: Anything. I'm not hard to please.

A: 뭐 먹을래? B: 아무거나. 난 아무거나 잘 먹어.

▸ What will you have?
뭘 할래요?

Chapter 03

What would you like to have for an appetizer?

애피타이저로 뭘 할래요?

A: What would you like for an appetizer?

B: I think I'll just have a salad.

A: 애피타이저로 뭐 할래? B: 샐러드 먹을게.

▸ What would you like to have for dinner this evening?
오늘 밤 저녁식사로 뭐 할래요?

What do you want to eat for lunch today? 오늘 점심 뭐 먹을래?

A: What do you want to eat for lunch today?

B: I'm in the mood for a hamburger.

A: 오늘 점심 뭐 먹을래? B: 햄버거 먹고 싶어.

What's your favorite food? 어떤 음식을 좋아하세요?

A: What's your favorite food?

B: I like ice cream, even though it's fattening.

A: 좋아하는 음식이 뭐야? B: 살은 찌겠지만 아이스크림을 좋아해.

▸ Is there any special dish that you like?
뭐 특별히 좋아하는 음식 있어?

Which do you prefer to have, Italian or Mexican food?

이태리 아니면 멕시칸음식이 좋아?

A: Which do you prefer to have, Italian or Mexican food?

B: I could go for some Mexican tonight.

A: 이태리음식 아니면 멕시칸음식이 좋아? B: 오늘 밤은 멕시칸 음식 좀 먹어보지.

Would you like some coffee? 커피 좀 들래요?

A: Would you like some coffee?

B: No, I've got to get back to work.

A: 커피 좀 들래? B: 아뇨, 일하러 가야 돼.

▸ Would you care for some coffee?
커피 좀 들래요?

How about some coffee? 커피 어때?

A: How about a cup of coffee?

B: Sounds like a great idea.

A: 커피 한 잔 마시자? B: 좋은 생각야.

Let's have a light meal 간단한 식사로 하자

A: Let's have a light meal.

B: Why? Are you dieting?

A: 간단한 식사로 하자. B: 왜? 다이어트 중이야?

▸ I don't care for heavy foods
배불리 먹는 건 싫어

I don't have any strong likes or dislikes 특별히 좋아하거나 싫어하는 거 없어

A: What type of food do you like most?

B: I don't have any strong likes or dislikes.

A: 어떤 음식 가장 좋아해? B: 특별히 좋아하거나 싫어하는 거 없어.

Sushi is my favorite dish 스시는 내가 가장 좋아하는 음식야

A: What do you eat when you go to Japan?

B: Sushi is my favorite dish.

A: 일본에 가면 뭘 먹어? B: 스시를 가장 좋아해.

▸ Raw fish is my least favorite food
날 생선은 내가 가장 좋아하지 않은 음식야

I'm sick of hamburgers 햄버거는 싫증나

A: I thought we'd grill some burgers this afternoon.

B: Oh no! I'm sick of hamburgers.

A: 오후에 햄버거 좀 구울까 생각했어. B: 안돼! 햄버거는 보기도 싫어.

I don't have much of an appetite 식욕이 별로 없어

A: Are you hungry yet?

B: No, I don't have much of an appetite right now.

A: 배고프니? B: 아니, 지금 식욕이 별로 없어.

03 주문하시겠어요?

Chapter 03

Are you ready to order? 주문하시겠어요?

A: Are you ready to order your food?

B: No, I haven't decided yet.

A: 주문하시겠어요? B: 아뇨, 아직 못정했는데요.

▸ May I take your order?
주문 받을까요?

What's your order? 뭘 주문하시겠습니까?

A: We're ready now.

B: OK. What's your order?

A: 이제 주문할게요. B: 알았습니다. 뭘 주문하시겠습니까?

▸ What would you like to order?
뭘 주문하시겠습니까?

▸ Which dressing would you like with your salad?
샐러드에 무슨 드레싱을 해 드릴까요?

What can I get you, sir? 뭘 갖다 드릴까요, 손님?

A: What can I get you, sir?

B: I'd like a mug of draft beer, please.

A: 뭘 갖다 드릴까요, 손님? B: 생맥주 한 잔 갖다 주세요.

Would you care for dessert? 디저트 드시겠어요?

A: Would you care for dessert?

B: No, but I'd love some coffee.

A: 디저트를 드시겠어요? B: 아뇨, 그냥 커피만 좀 주세요.

▸ Have you chosen your dessert?
디저트를 고르셨나요?

How would you like your steak? 스테이크를 어떻게 해드릴까요?

A: How would you like your steak, sir?

B: I would like it well-done, please.

A: 스테이크를 어떻게 해드릴까요? B: 완전히 익혀주세요.

A: How would you like your steak cooked?

B: Cook it medium rare.

A: 스테이크를 어떻게 해드릴까요? B: 아주 조금만 익혀주세요.

▸ How would you like your steak cooked [prepared]?
스테이크를 어떻게 해드릴까요?

▸ How would you like it done?
그걸 어떻게 해드릴까요?

How do you like your coffee? 커피 어떻게 해드릴까요?

A: How do you like your coffee?

B: With cream and sugar, please

A: 커피 어떻게 해드릴까요? B: 크림과 설탕을 넣어주세요.

▶ What do you take in your coffee?
커피에 뭘 넣으시나요?

Would you care for a glass of wine with your dinner?

저녁식사에 와인 한 잔 할래요?

A: Would you care for a glass of wine with your dinner?

B: No thanks, I've given up drinking alcohol.

A: 저녁식사에 와인 한 잔 할래요? B: 아뇨, 됐어요. 술을 끊어서요.

Is that all? 그게 전부입니까?

A: Is that all?

B: Actually, no. I think I'll also have your soup of the day.

A: 그게 전부입니까? B: 음, 아뇨. 오늘의 수프도 줘요.

▶ Would you like to order something else, or will that be all?
다른 주문하실래요 아님 다 됐나요?

Is there anything else you'd like? 다른 거 뭐 더 필요한 거는 요?

A: Is there anything else?

B: Yes, could we order some more drinks, please?

A: 더 필요한 게 있으십니까? B: 네, 음료수를 좀더 주시겠어요?

▶ Anything else?
다른 건요?
▶ Anything else you want?
다른 거 더 필요한 건요?

That's all (for me) (전) 됐어요

A: How about some more potatoes?

B: I'm really full. That's all for me.

A: 감자 더 드실래요? B: 배불러요. 전 됐습니다.

▶ That's it
됐어요
▶ That will be all
그게 다예요

My order hasn't come yet 주문이 아직 안 나왔어요

A: I didn't order this!

B: I'm sorry, I'll get you your food right away.

A: 이건 제가 주문한 음식이 아니잖아요! B: 죄송합니다. 곧 주문하신 음식을 갖다드리겠습니다.

▶ This is not what I ordered
내가 주문한 게 아닌데요
▶ I didn't order this
이거 주문 안했는데요

04 메뉴 좀 부탁해요

I'd like to see a menu, please 메뉴 좀 갖다주세요

A: How can I help you, sir?

B: May I see a menu, please?

    A: 어떻게 도와드릴까요, 손님? B: 메뉴판 좀 보여주시겠어요?

▸ Could[May] I have a menu, please?
메뉴 좀 보여주세요?

Chapter 03

What do you suggest[recommend]? 당신은 뭘 권하시겠어요?

A: Do you have any recommendations?

B: Well, the T-bone steak is delicious.

    A: 추천 좀 해주시겠어요? B: 음, 티본 스테이크가 맛이 좋습니다.

▸ What would you recommend as an appetizer?
애피타이저로 뭘 추천해줄래요?

Can you tell me what's good here?

이 곳은 어떤 요리가 괜찮은 지 말씀해 주시겠어요?

A: Can you tell me what's good here?

B: People say our pies are quite delicious.

    A: 여기서 잘하는 음식이 뭐예요? B: 파이가 정말 맛있다고들 해요.

▸ What do you think I should order?
뭘 주문해야 될까요?

▸ What do you think is the best?
뭐가 가장 좋은 것 같아요?

What kind of wine do you have? 와인은 무슨 종류가 있어요?

A: What kind of wine do you have?

B: We have two European red wines and a white wine from California.

    A: 와인은 무슨 종류가 있어요? B: 유럽산 적포도주 2병과 캘리포니아산 백포도주 1병이 있습니다.

▸ May I see the wine list, please?
와인리스트 좀 볼 수 있을까요?

What kind of dressing do you have? 드레싱으론 뭐가 있어요?

A: What kind of dressing do you have?

B: You can get ranch, Italian, or blue cheese.

    A: 드레싱으론 뭐가 있어요? B: 랜치, 이태리언, 블루치즈가 있습니다.

What is the special of the day? 오늘의 스페셜은 뭔가요?

A: What's the special of the day?

B: Fried shrimp with a side of salad.

A: 오늘의 특별요리가 뭔가요? B: 샐러드를 곁들인 새우튀김 요리예요.

▸ Can you tell me
about the specials
of the day?
오늘 스페셜이 뭔지 알려줄
래요?

▸ Do you have any
local specialities?
이 지역 특산물이 있어요?

I can recommend the cheesecake. It's excellent

치즈스테이크 드세요. 훌륭해요

A: Do you have any good cakes?

B: I can recommend the cheesecake. It's excellent.

A: 맛좋은 케익 뭐 있어요? B: 치즈스테이크를 추천해요. 아주 맛나요.

▸ I'd suggest the
chicken wings to
go with your beer
맥주엔 닭날개를 드세요

What comes with that? 함께 뭐가 나오나요?

A: Would you like our special for tonight?

B: What comes with that?

A: 오늘밤 특별요리를 드시겠어요? B: 뭐가 따라나오나요?

▸ Does it come with
soup or salad and
dessert?
수프나 샐러드, 디저트가
함께 나오나요?

What is that like? 그거 어떤 거예요?

A: Our special today is roast beef and gravy.

B: What is that like?

A: 오늘의 스페셜은 로스트 비프와 그레이비입니다. B: 그게 어떤건데요?

▸ What kind of dish
is this?
이건 어떤 음식인가요?

▸ I haven't made up
my mind yet
아직 결정을 못했는데요

Does it contain any alcohol? 알코올이 들어있나요?

A: You've got to try this punch.

B: Does it contain any alcohol?

A: 이 펀치 좀 먹어봐야 돼. B: 알코올이 포함되어 있어?

▸ Do they contain
any additives?
첨가물이 뭐 들어 있나요?

05 같은 걸로 주세요

I'll have the same 같은 걸로 주세요

A: I'd like the chicken salad with ranch dressing.

B: And I'll have the same.

A: 랜치드레싱된 치킨샐러드 주세요. B: 그리고 나도 같은 걸로 줘요.

▸ Can I have the
  same as him?
  저 사람과 같은 걸로 줄래
  요?
▸ The same for me
  나도 같은 걸로요

Make it two 같은 걸로 2개 주세요

A: I'm going to have a club sandwich with fries.

B: Make it two, please.

A: 감자튀김과 샌드위치 주세요. B: 같은 걸로 2개요.

I'll have that 그걸로 주세요

A: Our soup of the day is chicken gumbo.

B: OK, I'll have that.

A: 오늘의 수프는 치킨검보입니다. B: 좋아요. 그걸로 주세요.

▸ I'll take this and
  this
  이거하고 이거 먹을게요

I'd like a steak 고기 먹을래요

A: Are you ready to order your meal yet?

B: Yes, I'd like the Mediterranean pizza.

A: 이제 식사를 주문하시겠어요? B: 네, 메디테라니안 피자로 주세요.

▸ I'd like some
  Italian food
  이태리 음식 좀 주세요
▸ I'd like a
  hamburger and
  an ice tea
  햄버거하고 아이스티 주세
  요

I'd like to try the steak 고기를 먹어보죠

A: What'll it be?

B: I'd like to try the steak.

A: 뭘로 할까요? B: 고기를 먹어보죠.

I'd like something to drink 마실 것 좀 주세요

A: I'd like something to drink.

B: Can I get you some juice?

A: 마실 것 좀 주세요. B: 주스 좀 갖다 줄까요?

I'd like some more wine 와인 좀 더 주세요

A: Can I get you folks anything else?

B: I'd like some more wine.

A: 여러분들 다른 거 뭐 더 필요하세요? B: 와인 좀 더 주세요.

▸ I'd like a cup of coffee, please
커피 한잔 주세요

▸ I'd like another cup of coffee
커피 한잔 더 주세요

I'll have a chocolate muffin 초코렛 머핀으로 주세요

A: Do you want a snack?

B: Sure. I'll have a chocolate muffin.

A: 스낵 드실래요? B: 그래요. 난 초코렛 머핀으로 주세요.

▸ I'll have the chocolate mousse and my wife will have the cheesecake
전 초콜릿 무스, 아낸 치즈 케익으로 줘요

Can I get a steak sandwich and a Coke?

고기 샌드위치랑 콜라 한잔 주실래요?

A: Can I get a steak sandwich and a Coke?

B: Coming right up.

A: 고기 샌드위치랑 콜라 한잔 주실래요? B: 바로 갖다 드릴게요.

Can you get me a glass of water, please? 물 한잔 갖다 줄래요?

A: What would you like to drink?

B: Can you get me a glass of water, please?

A: 뭘 마실래요? B: 물 한잔 갖다 줄래요?

May I have two hot dogs, please? 핫도그 두 개 주실래요?

A: May I have two hot dogs, please?

B: Yep. What do you want on them?

A: 핫도그 두 개 주실래요? B: 예. 어떻게 해드릴까요?

I'd like my steak medium 고기는 미디엄으로 해주세요

A: How do you want it cooked?

B: I'd like my steak medium.

A: 어떻게 해드릴까요? B: 고기는 미디엄으로 해주세요.

▸ Well-done, please
웰던으로 해줘요

06 마음껏 드세요

Help yourself 마음껏 드세요, 어서 갖다 드세요

A: Is this coffee for people in the office?

B: Yes, help yourself.

A: 이 커피, 사무실 사람들 마시라고 있는 겁니까? B: 예, 갖다 드세요.

▶ Help yourself to
some cheese and
crackers
치즈하고 크래커 갖다 드세요

▶ Help yourself to
whatever you like
원하는 거 아무거나 갖다
드세요

Enjoy your meal 맛있게 드세요

A: Enjoy your meal.

B: Could we get another pitcher of water?

A: 맛있게 드세요. B: 물 좀 더 갖다 주시겠어요?

What's for dinner? 저녁식사 메뉴가 뭐야?

A: What's for dinner tonight?

B: I didn't have time to cook so I bought two TV dinners.

A: 저녁식사 메뉴가 뭐지? B: 요리할 시간이 없어서 그냥 'TV dinner'를 샀어.

▶ Is dinner ready?
저녁 됐어?

▶ Today, we're
having curry
오늘은 카레라이스야

Come and get it 자 와서 먹자, 자 밥먹게 와라

A: Is it ready yet?

B: It sure is. Come and get it!

A: 아직 준비 안됐어? B: 물론 됐지. 자 와서 먹자!

Please feel free to have another 어서 더 들어요

A: This piece of cake is great.

B: Please feel free to have another.

A: 이 케익은 아주 맛있네요. B: 어서 더 갖다 드세요.

▶ Please take
anything you like
from the dessert
tray
디저트 아무거나 다 갖다
드세요

Would you like some? 좀 드실래요?

A: I'm going to get some beer. Do you want some?

B: Yeah, it's such a hot day.

A: 맥주 좀 마실건데. 너도 마실래? B: 응, 찐다 쪄.

▶ Would you like
another drink?
한 잔 더 할래요?

Do you want some more? 더 들래요?

A: That pizza was great. Want some more?

B: I'd love another piece if there is any left.

A: 피자는 정말 맛있었어. 더 좀 먹을래? B: 남은 게 있으면 한 조각 더 먹었으면 좋겠는데.

▶ Do you want some?
더 들래?

▶ Have some more
좀 더 드세요

Do you want a bite of this? 이거 좀 더 들어볼래요?

A: Do you want a bite of this?

B: No, thank you. I'm full.

A: 이거 좀 더 드셔 보실래요? B: 아뇨, 됐습니다. 배가 불러서요.

▶ Let's grab a bite to eat
뭐 좀 먹으러 가자

I've had enough 많이 먹었어요

A: Would you like another bowl of soup?

B: No, I've had enough.

A: 스프 한 그릇 더 먹을래? B: 아니, 배불러.

▶ I'm (getting) full
배가 불러요

I'm stuffed 배불러

A: How was dinner?

B: Excellent. I'm stuffed.

A: 저녁 어땠어? B: 아주 좋았어. 배불리 먹었어.

I'm on a diet 다이어트 중이야

A: You've hardly touched your breakfast.

B: I'm on a diet.

A: 아침 거의 손도 대지 않네 B: 다이어트 중이야.

More Expressions

- **I'm starving** 배가 고파 죽겠어
- **Don't eat too much** 과식하지 마
- **Don't spill it** 흘리지 마라
- **Dinner is served** 식사가 준비되었습니다(집사가 말하듯 공식적인 어투)

- **I'm very hungry** 배가 정말 고파
- **Soup's on!** 식사준비 다 됐어요
- **Do the dishes!** 설거지 해!

07 고기 맛이 어때?

How do you like the steak? 고기 맛이 어때?

A: How do you like the steak?

B: It's the juiciest steak I have ever eaten!

A: 스테이크 맛이 어때? B: 이렇게 맛있는 스테이크는 처음이야!

▶ How do you like the food?
음식이 어때?

How was the meal? 식사 어땠어요?

A: How was the meal your girlfriend cooked?

B: Honestly, it didn't taste very good.

A: 네 여친이 해준 식사 어땠어? B: 솔직히 말해, 별로였어.

▶ How's the food?
맛이 어때?

Does your soup taste all right? 스프 맛이 괜찮아?

A: Does the food taste all right?

B: It's very good, but it's a little spicy.

A: 음식 맛 괜찮아요? B: 정말 맛있어요. 근데 좀 매운 걸요.

▶ Does it taste good?
맛이 좋아?

▶ Is this delicious?
맛있어?

This looks great[good; delicious] 이거 맛있게 보인다

A: Supper is ready everyone.

B: This looks great.

A: 다들 저녁 준비됐어. B: 아주 맛있게 보여.

▶ This smells great
냄새가 좋은데

▶ This is so good
맛 좋다

▶ It's good
맛 좋아

▶ It's delicious
맛있어

That was good 맛 좋았어

A: That was good!

B: I'm glad you liked it.

A: 맛 좋았어! B: 네가 좋아했다니 좋네.

▶ It was delicious
맛있었어

This is the best steak I've eaten in a long time

이렇게 맛난 스테이크는 오랜만에 처음야

A: This is the best steak I've eaten in a long time.

B: It's worth it to pay a little more for quality.

　　A: 이렇게 맛난 스테이큰 오랜만에 처음야. B: 맛이 좋으면 돈을 더 낼만해.

It doesn't taste good　맛이 안 좋아

A: How is the chicken Susan cooked?

B: It doesn't taste good.

　　A: 수잔이 요리한 닭요리 어때? B: 맛이 안 좋아.

▸ This doesn't taste as good as it looks
보기처럼 맛있지 않아

▸ This has a strong flavor
맛이 너무 강해

It's spicy　매워

A: Have you tried Thai food?

B: Yeah. It's spicy, but I like it.

　　A: 태국 음식 먹어봤어? B: 어. 맵지만 좋아해.

▸ It's (too) salty 짜
▸ It's too greasy
기름기가 너무 많아
▸ It's sweet 달아
▸ It's too hot
너무 뜨거워

This sauce is so spicy. It's making my mouth burn

소스가 매워. 입이 탄다 타

A: This sauce is so spicy. It's making my mouth burn!

B: Whoops, maybe I used too many hot peppers.

　　A: 소스가 매워. 입이 탄다 타! B: 앗, 매운 후추를 넘 많이 넣었나 봐.

▸ My mouth is burning 입이 타
▸ My mouth is on fire 입이 불나

This tastes strange[weird]　이건 맛이 넘 이상해

A: This tastes strange.

B: Do you think it's missing some ingredients?

　　A: 이건 맛이 이상해 B: 뭔가 들어갈 게 빠진 것 같아?

▸ This yogurt tastes odd
이 요구르트는 맛이 이상해
▸ This ham must be past its due date
이 햄은 유효기간이 지났을 거야

I hope you enjoyed your meal　식사 맛있었길 바래

A: I hope you enjoyed your meal.

B: It tasted great.

　　A: 식사 맛있었길 바래. B: 아주 맛있었어.

▸ We enjoyed it very much
아주 맛있게 먹었어
▸ You're a good cook
너 참 요리 잘 한다

08 당신을 위해 건배

Here's to you! 당신을 위해 건배!. 너한테 주는 선물이야!

A: I'm so proud of your recent promotion. Here's to you!

B: Thank you so much.

A: 승진축하해. 당신을 위하여! B: 너무 고마워.

▸ Here's to your health!
당신의 건강을 위하여!

I'd like to propose a toast 축배를 듭시다

A: I propose a toast to Bill for all the hard work he's done.

B: I'll drink to that.

A: 빌의 모든 노고에 대해 건배하죠. B: 저도 동감이에요.

▸ Let me propose a toast to Mr. Kim
미스터 김을 위해 건배할게요

Let's drink to Miss Park's future! 미스 박의 미래를 위해서 건배합시다!

A: Let's drink to Miss Park's future!

B: Thank you all for your good wishes.

A: 미스 박의 미래를 위해 건배합시다! B: 좋은 말씀해주셔서 감사해요.

▸ Bottoms up!
위하여!
▸ Cheers!
건배!

Say when 됐으면 말해

A: Can you put some whiskey in my glass?

B: No problem. Say when.

A: 위스키 좀 따라줄래? B: 그래. 됐으면 말해.

ㄴ. 됐다고 말할 때는 When이라고 하면 된다.

How about a drink? 술 한잔 어때?

A: How about a drink?

B: That's a great idea.

A: 술 한잔 어때? B: 좋은 생각야.

▸ I need a drink
술 한잔 해야 겠어
▸ Would you like to have a drink after work?
퇴근 후 한잔 할테야?

How much do you usually drink? 보통 술 얼마나 마셔?

A: How much do you usually drink?

B: I'll have a few beers when I'm out with friends.

A: 보통 술 얼마나 마셔? B: 친구들과 어울리면 맥주 몇잔은 마셔.

Chapter 03

He's a heavy drinker 갠 술 잘 마셔

A: John always has a red face.

B: That's because he's a heavy drinker.

    A: 존은 언제나 얼굴이 붉어. B: 술은 엄청 마셔대니까 그래.

▸ I can drink a lot
  술 많이 마실 수 있어

I have a hangover 술이 아직 안 깼나봐

A: Boy, you look terrible today.

B: I was drinking last night and I have a hangover.

    A: 야, 오늘 무척 안 좋아 보여. B: 지난밤 술마셨는데 아직 술이 안깼어.

▸ I'm suffering from a hangover today
  오늘 아직 숙취가 있어

I get drunk easily 난 쉽게 취해

A: I'm drunk.

B: Let me drive you home.

    A: 술 취했어. B: 집까지 태워다줄게

▸ I feel a little tipsy
  아직 취기가 있어
▸ I'm loaded [drunk]
  술 취했어

Please don't drink too much 너무 과음하지마

A: I'm going to a nightclub right now.

B: Please don't drink too much.

    A: 지금 나이트클럽에 가는 중야. B: 너무 마시지마.

▸ I don't drink
  난 술 안마셔
▸ I prefer draft beer
  생맥주가 좋아

I don't smoke anymore 더 이상 담배 안펴

A: I'm dying for a cigarette. How about you?

B: I don't smoke anymore.

    A: 담배피고 싶어서 미치겠어. 넌? B: 더 이상 담배 안펴.

▸ I quit smoking
  담배 끊었어
▸ I stopped smoking
  이제 담배 안펴

How many packs a day? 하루에 몇 갑이나 펴?

A: I think I smoke too much.

B: Really? How many packs a day?

    A: 담배를 너무 피는 것 같아. B: 그래? 하루에 몇 갑 펴?

▸ I'm a chain[heavy] smoker
  난 줄담배 펴
▸ Can I bum a smoke?
  담배 한가치 줄래?

09 여기서요 아니면 포장요?

Is that for here or to go? 여기서 드실 겁니까, 가지고 가실 겁니까?

A: Is that for here or to go?

B: To go, please.

A: 여기서 드시겠어요, 아니면 가져 가시겠습니까? B: 가져갈 거예요.

▶ Will this be for here or to go?
여기서 드실거예요 아니면 포장예요?

For here or to go? 여기서요 아니면 포장요?

A: I'd like a large black coffee.

B: For here or to go?

A: 블랙커피 큰 걸로 주세요. B: 여기서요 아님 포장요?

▶ For here, please
여기서 먹을게요

(Do you want to) Eat here or take it out? 여기서 드실래요 아니면 포장요?

A: Can I get a burger and some fries?

B: Do you want to eat here or take it out?

A: 버거하고 프라이 좀 주실래요? B: 여기서 드실래요 아니면 포장요?

Will that be to go? 가져가실 건가요?

A: I'll take these three donuts.

B: Will that be to go?

A: 이 도너츠 3개 주세요. B: 가져가실 건가요?

▶ Take-out?
포장요?

Can I get it to go? 포장 되나요?

A: So you want a six piece chicken meal and a soda?

B: Right. Can I get it to go?

A: 치킨밀 6개와 소다 하나죠? B: 예, 포장되나요?

▶ I'd like it to go, please
포장으로 해줘요

Could I[we] have a doggie bag, please? 포장지 좀 줄래요?

A: Could we have a doggie bag?

B: Sure. Do you want me to wrap everything here?

A: 남은 음식 좀 싸주시겠어요? B: 그러죠, 전부 다 싸드릴까요?

▶ Could you pack the rest of the meal for take-out?
남은 음식 가져가게 싸줄래요?

It's on me 내가 낼게

A: This one is on me.

B: Thanks a lot! I'll pay for lunch tomorrow.

　　A: 이번은 내가 낼게. B: 고마워! 내일 점심은 내가 낼게.

▸ This one is on me
　이번엔 내가 낼게

It's on the house 이건 서비스입니다

A: How much do I owe you?

B: Nothing… it's on the house!

　　A: 얼마인가요? B: 무료예요… 서비스예요!

I'll pick up the tab[check] 내가 계산할게

A: Jim said that he'd pick up the tab.

B: In that case I'll have another drink.

　　A: 짐이 자기가 계산한다고 했어. B: 그러면 한잔 더 해야지.

▸ Let me pick up
　the tab
　내가 계산할게
▸ Let me take care
　of the bill
　내가 계산할게

This is my treat 내가 살게

A: Let's go to a fancy restaurant. It's my treat.

B: That sounds great.

　　A: 고급 레스토랑에 가자. 내가 쏠게. B: 그거 좋지.

▸ I'll treat you
　내가 대접하죠
▸ This is my round
　이건 내가 쏜다
▸ It's my treat this
　time
　이번은 내가 대접하는 거야

I'm buying 내가 살게

A: I could really go for a beer.

B: Let's go get one. I'm buying.

　　A: 정말이지 맥주 먹고 싶어. B: 가서 한잔하자. 내가 살게.

▸ I'll pay for dinner
　저녁은 내가 낼게

(I'd like the) Check, please 계산서 좀 주세요

A: Could I have the check, please?

B: Do you want separate checks?

　　A: 계산서 주시겠어요? B: 각각 따로 끊어드릴까요?

▸ I'd like to pay the
　bill, please
　계산을 좀 할려구요
▸ Could you bring
　me my bill?
　계산서 갖다 줄래요?

What's the damage? 얼마죠?

A: Well, what's the damage?

B: It comes to twenty seven dollars and eighty cents.

　　A: 저기, 얼마죠? B: 27달러 80센트입니다.

▸ What is this for?
　이거 얼마죠?
▸ What is this
　charge for?
　이거 얼마입니까?

May I have a receipt, please? 영수증 주실래요?

A: Here is your change, sir.

B: May I have a receipt, please?

A: 여기 잔돈 있습니다. B: 영수증 주실래요?

▸ Is tax included?
세금이 포함되나요?

Here is a little something for you 이건 얼마 안되지만 팁이에요

A: Are you all finished, sir?

B: Yes. Here is a little something for you.

A: 다 드셨습니까? B: 예. 이건 얼마 안되지만 받으세요.

▸ How much should I leave on the table?
테이블에 얼마 남겨야 돼?
▸ What kind of tip should I leave?
팁 몇 프로를 남겨둬야 돼?

We'd like to pay separately 각자 내려고요

A: How would you like your checks?

B: We'd like to pay separately.

A: 계산서 어떻게 드릴까요? B: 각자 내려고요.

▸ Let's go halves
반반 내자
▸ Let me share the bill
나도 반 낼게

Let's split the bill 나누어 내자

A: Let's split the bill.

B: That sounds like a good idea.

A: 각자 내자. B: 좋은 생각이야.

▸ Let's go Dutch
자기가 먹은 건 자기가 내자

How much is my share? 내 몫은 얼마지?

A: How much is my share?

B: It comes to $8.50.

A: 내 몫은 얼마야? B: 8달러 50센트야.

▸ How much is mine?
난 얼마야?

Chapter 04

건강

Step 1 상담

Step 2 통증

01 오늘 기분 어때?

How do you feel? 오늘 기분 어때?

A: How are you feeling these days?

B: I'm getting better every day.

A: 오늘 기분 어때? B: 매일 나아지고 있어.

▸ Are you (feeling) okay?
기분 괜찮아?

You don't look very well 오늘 안 좋아 보여

A: You don't look very well.

B: Maybe I'd better see a doctor.

A: 오늘 안 좋아 보여. B: 병원에 가봐야 할 것 같아.

▸ You look pale
창백해 보여
▸ You look like you've lost weight lately
최근 너 살 빠진 것 같아

Are you all right? 괜찮아?

A: I was sick for two weeks last month.

B: Are you all right now?

A: 지난 달 2주 동안 앓았어. B: 지금은 괜찮아?

▸ Are you well again?
다시 괜찮아졌어?
▸ Are you back to normal?
다시 좋아 진거야?

Are you in good shape? 건강 좋아?

A: Are you in good shape?

B: Well, I exercise regularly.

A: 건강 좋아? B: 어, 정기적으로 운동해.

▸ I'm in good shape[health]
건강이 좋아

My biggest problem is my pot belly 불쑥 나온 배가 나의 가장 큰 문제야

A: My biggest problem is my pot belly.

B: You need to cut back on beer drinking.

A: 불쑥 나온 배가 나의 가장 큰 문제야. B: 맥주 마시는 것 좀 줄어야 돼.

What's your secret for staying healthy? 건강을 유지하는 비결이 뭐야?

A: What's your secret for staying healthy?

B: I eat a lot of raw vegetables.

A: 건강을 유지하는 비결이 뭐야? B: 생야채를 많이 먹어.

Have you completely recovered? 완전히 회복된거야?

A: I was in the hospital because of a car accident.

B: Have you completely recovered?

A: 차사고로 병원에 있었어. B: 완전히 나은거야?

▸ I feel better
기분이 나아졌어
▸ I don't feel any better
하나도 나아진 게 없어

I always stop eating before I feel full 난 항상 배가 부르기까지 먹지 않아

A: I always stop eating before I feel full.

B: No wonder you're so thin.

A: 난 항상 배가 부르기까지 먹지 않아 B: 날씬한 이유가 있구만.

▸ I keep early hours
일찍 일어나
▸ I always get enough sleep
충분히 수면을 취해

You should quit smoking 넌 담배 끊는 게 나아

A: I've had this cough for several months.

B: You should quit smoking.

A: 몇 달째 기침이 나. B: 담배를 끊는 게 좋지.

▸ I gave up smoking for my health
건강때문에 담배 끊었어

Do you get regular physical check-ups? 정기적으로 건강검진을 받아?

A: How much does your family doctor charge for a checkup?

B: His checkup fee is about $55.

A: 주치의(醫)는 진료비가 얼마야? B: 진료비는 55달러 정도야.

▸ I get a dental check-up every six months
6개월마다 치과에서 정기 검진을 받아

Have you had your hepatitis shot yet? 아직 간염주사 안 맞았니?

A: Have you had your hepatitis shot yet?

B: No, but I want to get one.

A: 아직 간염주사 안 맞았니? B: 응, 하지만 맞고 싶어.

Nothing can take the place of good health 건강만큼 중요한 게 없어

A: I'm trying to live a healthier life these days.

B: Nothing can take the place of good health.

A: 요즘 더 건강한 삶을 살려고 노력중야. B: 건강만큼 중요한 게 없지.

02 진찰 좀 받고 싶은데요

I'd like to see the doctor 진찰 좀 받고 싶은데요

A: I'd like to see the doctor.

B: Please fill in this form about your medical history.

A: 진찰 좀 받고 싶은데요. B: 이 양식에 병력(病歷)을 기입하세요.

▶ You'd better go see a doctor
병원에 가봐야 돼

Could you send me a doctor? 의사 좀 보내줄래요?

A: Could you send me a doctor?

B: You're going to have to visit the hospital.

A: 의사 좀 보내줄래요? B: 병원으로 오세요.

▶ Do you need a doctor?
의사가 필요하세요?
▶ Please call an ambulance
앰블런스 불러줘

What's wrong? 어디가 아파요?

A: What's wrong with you?

B: I'm feeling a little sick to my stomach.

A: 어디가 아프시죠? B: 위에 통증이 약간 있어요.

▶ What's wrong with you?
어디가 아프세요?

What's your complaint? 어디가 아프세요?

A: What's your complaint?

B: I've got a splitting headache.

A: 어디가 아프세요? B: 머리가 빠개질 것 같아요.

What's the matter? 어디가 아프세요?

A: What's the matter?

B: I think I broke my arm.

A: 어디 아파요? B: 팔이 부러진 것 같아요.

▶ Is anything wrong?
어디 안 좋은데 있어요?

Where does it hurt? 어디가 아파요?

A: Where does it hurt?

B: My stomach feels terrible right now.

A: 어디가 아파요? B: 지금 배가 아주 안 좋아요.

What are your symptoms? 증상이 어때요?

A: I feel really sick today.

B: What are your symptoms?

A: 오늘 무척 아파요. B: 증상이 어떤대요?

Let me check your temperature 체온 좀 재볼게요

A: What's my blood pressure, doctor?

B: A hundred and thirty over ninety.

A: 혈압이 어때요, 선생님? B: 130에 90예요.

▸ Let me check your blood pressure
혈압 좀 재볼게요

Is there a history of heart disease in your family?

가족중 심장병 앓은 분이 있나요?

A: Is there a history of heart disease in your family?

B: Not that I know of.

A: 가족 중에 심장병을 앓은 분이 있나요? B: 제가 아는 바로는 없어요.

Do you have a high temperature? 열이 많이 나요?

A: Do you have a high temperature?

B: No, but I still feel funny.

A: 열이 많이 나요? B: 아뇨, 하지만 아직 좀 이상해요.

▸ Do you have a fever?
열이 있어요?

Where do you feel the pain most? 어느 부위가 가장 아파요?

A: Where do you feel the pain most?

B: In my abdomen.

A: 어느 부위가 가장 아파요? B: 복부요.

How's your vision? 시력이 어떠세요?

A: How's your vision?

B: Fine. I don't need glasses.

A: 시력이 어떠세요? B: 좋아요. 안경을 안써요.

Are you allergic to any kind of medication?

특정 약에 앨러지 반응이 있나요?

A: Are you allergic to any kind of medication?

B: Not that I know of.

A: 특정 약에 대해 앨러지 반응이 있나요? B: 제가 알기로는 없어요.

Does anyone in your family suffer from diabetes?

가족 중에 당뇨병 환자 있나요?

A: Does anyone in your family suffer from diabetes?

B: Yes, my father had diabetes before he died.

A: 가족 중 당뇨병 걸린 사람 있나요? B: 네, 아버님이 돌아가시기 전 당뇨병였어요.

Do you suffer from insomnia? 불면증에 시달리나요?

A: Do you suffer from back pain?

B: Only if I lift heavy objects.

A: 등 통증에 시달립니까? B: 무거운 물건을 들어올릴 때만 그래요.

▶ Do you suffer
from back pain?
등 통증에 시달립니까?

Did you eat something unusual? 좀 색다른 거 드셨나요?

A: I've been using the toilet all day.

B: Did you eat something unusual last night?

A: 오늘 종일 화장실에 들락날락했어요. B: 간밤에 좀 색다른 거 드셨나요?

When was your last bowel movement? 마지막으로 변을 본 것이 언제지요?

A: When was your last bowel movement?

B: This morning at around 11:00.

A: 마지막으로 변을 본 것이 언제지요? B: 오늘 아침 11시 쯤이요.

How long have you had a problem with indigestion?

소화불량으로 얼마나 고생했나요?

A: How long have you had a problem with indigestion?

B: Ever since I started my new job.

A: 소화불량으로 얼마나 고생했죠? B: 새 일을 시작한 후로 줄곧 그래왔어요.

Have you ever fractured your leg before? 전에 다리가 부러진 적 있습니까?

A: Have you ever fractured your leg before?

B: No, this is my first time.

> A: 전에 다리가 부러진 적 있습니까? B: 아니요, 이번이 처음이예요.

A: I keep feeling pain here.

B: Have you ever fractured your leg before?

> A: 여기가 계속 아파요. B: 전에 다리가 부러진 적 있어요?

That's a nasty bruise. How did it happen?

타박상이 심하군요. 어쩌다 그랬어요?

A: That's a nasty bruise. How did it happen?

B: I got hit while playing hockey.

> A: 타박상이 심하군요. 어떻게 하다 그랬어요? B: 하키경기를 하다 부딪혔어요.

Are you taking any medication? 치료는 받고 있나요

A: I'm having trouble focusing on moving objects.

B: Are you taking any medication?

> A: 움직이는 물체에 초점맞추기가 어려워요. B: 치료는 받고 있나요?

Have you had your wisdom teeth pulled out? 사랑니 뽑았어요?

A: Have you had your wisdom teeth pulled out?

B: No, but I'm planning to have them extracted next month.

> A: 사랑니 뽑았어요? B: 아뇨, 다음 달에 뽑을 거예요.

 병원에서

- 전문의 specialist
- 일반의 general practitioner
- 주치의 family doctor
- 수의사 veterinarian
- 약제사 pharmacist
- 외과 surgery
- 외과의 surgeon
- 내과 internal medicine
- 내과의 physician
- 정신과 psychiatry
- 정신과의 psychiatrist

- 안과의 eye doctor
- 비뇨기과 urology
- 비뇨기과의 urologist
- 청진기 stethoscope
- 체온계 thermometer
- 혈압계 blood pressure machine
- 초진 first visit
- 재진 revisit
- 진단 diagnosis
- 건강진단 check-up

- 진단서 medical certificate
- 병력 medical history
- 가족병 family history
- 주사 injection
- 치료 treatment
- 수혈 transfusion
- 외상 trauma
- 회진 doctor's rounds
- 위생 hygiene
- 정제 tablet; pill

Chapter 04

03 몸이 아주 안좋아요

I'm not feeling very well 몸이 아주 안 좋아요

A: Why are you still in bed?

B: I'm not feeling very well.

   A: 왜 여태 침대에 있는거야? B: 컨디션이 안좋아.

▸ I don't feel well
  몸이 좋지 않아요

I get tired easily 쉽게 피곤해져요

A: I get tired easily these days. Something's wrong with me.

B: Why don't you go get a check-up?

   A: 쉽게 피곤해져. 좀 이상해. B: 가서 검사 받아 봐?

I'm getting fat 살이 쪄

A: I'm getting fat.

B: Well, maybe you need to exercise.

   A: 살 쪘어 B: 그래, 너 운동해야 할 거야.

▸ I've put on[gained]
  weight
  살 쪘어
▸ I tend to put on
  weight easily
  난 살이 쉽게 찌는 스타일
  이야

I have a headache 머리가 아파

A: I've got a terrible headache.

B: Can I get you some aspirin?

   A: 머리가 아파 죽겠어. B: 아스피린 좀 줄까?

▸ My head hurts
  머리가 아파
▸ My head feels
  heavy
  머리가 무거워

I have high[low] blood pressure 고[저]혈압야

A: What did your doctor say?

B: She said I have high blood pressure.

   A: 의사가 뭐래? B: 내가 고혈압이래.

My fever has gone down 열이 내려갔어

A: How're you doing today?

B: Better. My fever has gone down.

   A: 오늘은 어때? B: 나아. 열이 내려갔어.

I'm running a fever 열이 나

A: Do you feel OK?

B: Not really. I'm running a fever.

    A: 몸 괜찮아? B: 실은 안그래. 열이 나.

▸ I think I have a fever
열이 있는 것 같아

▸ I have a bit of a fever
열이 좀 있어

I have a stomachache 복통야

A: Are you suffering from diarrhea?

B: No, but I have a stomachache.

    A: 설사가 있으신가요? B: 아니요, 위통예요.

▸ My stomach's upset
배탈났어

I have food poisoning 식중독야

A: What caused you to have a stomachache?

B: I have food poisoning.

    A: 왜 복통이 일어난거야? B: 식중독야.

I feel like throwing up 토할 것 같아

A: I feel like throwing up.

B: I'd better stop the car.

    A: 토할 것 같아. B: 차를 세워야겠어.

▸ I feel nauseated
토할 것 같아

I feel dizzy 어지러워

A: It's too hot here. I feel dizzy.

B: Let's go inside for a while.

    A: 여기 너무 더워. 어지러워. B: 잠시 들어가있자.

▸ I feel sluggish
피곤해

▸ I feel chilly
으실으실 추워

I've got the runs 설사했어요

A: I've got the runs.

B: We'd better pick up some medicine at the drugstore.

    A: 설사했어요. B: 약국에서 약 좀 사야되겠어.

▸ I have diarrhea
설사했어요

I don't have any appetite 식욕이 없어

A: You are very thin, Liz.

B: I know. I don't have any appetite.

    A: 리즈야 무척 말랐구나. B: 그래. 식욕이 없어.

▸ I have only a small appetite
식욕이 별로 없어

I have a toothache 치통이 있어

A: I have a toothache.

B: Do you want to go to a dentist?

  A: 치통이 있어. B: 치과에 갈래?

▸ My tooth hurts
  이가 아파
▸ My tooth is killing me
  이아파 죽겠어

I caught a cold 감기 걸렸어

A: What's wrong with you?

B: I caught a cold yesterday.

  A: 어디 아파요? B: 어제 감기에 걸렸어요.

▸ I've got the flu
  유행성 감기에 걸렸어
▸ I caught a cold from you
  감기 너한테 옮았나봐
▸ There's a bad cold going around
  독감이 유행야

I have a runny nose 코가 흘러

A: The kid has a runny nose and is coughing a lot.

B: Does he have a fever?

  A: 애가 콧물나고 기침을 많이 해요. B: 열도 나나요?

▸ My nose is running
  코가 흘러
▸ My nose won't stop running
  코가 멈추지 않고 계속 흘러

I'm a diabetic 당뇨예요

A: So you want a diet soda to drink?

B: Right. I'm a diabetic.

  A: 다이어트 소다를 드신다고요? B: 맞아요. 당뇨예요.

I've got a really stiff neck 목이 너무 뻣뻣해서요

A: What brings you here today?

B: I've got a really stiff neck.

  A: 오늘은 무슨 일로 오셨지요? B: 목이 너무 뻣뻣해서요.

Doctor, my chest is killing me 의사 선생님, 가슴이 너무 아파요

A: Doctor, my chest is killing me.

B: Let's have a look at it.

  A: 의사 선생님, 가슴이 너무 아파요. B: 검사 좀 해보죠.

I have stiff shoulders 어깨가 뻣뻣해요

A: What's wrong?

B: My shoulders are stiff and my back hurts.

  A: 어디가 아픈가요? B: 어깨가 뻐근하고 등이 아파요.

▸ My shoulders are stiff
  어깨가 뻣뻣해요

My throat's sore 목이 아파요

A: My throat's sore. Let's leave.

B: Yeah, there are too many smokers here.

A: 목이 아파. 나가자. B: 그래, 여기 담배피는 사람이 넘 많네.

▶ I've got a really sore throat
목이 정말 아파요
▶ My throat is swollen
목이 부었어요

I burned my hand 손이 데였어

A: Why are you wearing a bandage?

B: I burned my hand cooking.

A: 반창고는 왜 붙였어? B: 요리하다 손이 데였어.

▶ I've got a cut here
여기 칼로 베었어

I'm a little nearsighted 약간 근시(近視)예요

A: How's your vision?

B: I'm a little nearsighted.

A: 시력이 어떠세요? B: 약간 근시(近視)예요.

I've got a pain in my side 옆구리에 통증이 있어

A: I've got a pain in my side.

B: When did you first feel it?

A: 옆구리에 통증이 있어. B: 통증을 처음 느꼈을 때가 언제니?

My legs have been cramping up 다리에 쥐가 났어요

A: My legs have been cramping up.

B: Since when?

A: 다리에 쥐가 났어요. B: 언제부터요?

▶ I have a cramp in my thigh
허벅지에 쥐가 났어

I sprained my ankle 발목이 삐었어요

A: What happened to your leg?

B: I sprained my ankle while playing basketball.

A: 다리는 왜 그래? B: 농구하다가 발목을 삐었어.

▶ I sprained my finger
손이 삐었어요
▶ I twisted my ankle
발목이 겹질러졌어요

I broke my leg 다리가 부러졌어

A: How did you break your leg?

B: I fell off my bicycle.

A: 어쩌다가 다리가 부러진거야? B: 자전거 타다가 넘어졌어.

It's itchy 가려워요

A: I'm not sure why, but my legs sure are itchy.

B: You'd better go to the doctor and get his opinion.

A: 웬지 모르겠지만, 다리가 가려워요. B: 의사 선생님께 가서 상담하세요.

▸ It's bleeding
피가 나요

It hurts 아파요

A: It looked like you injured your leg.

B: I'm pretty sure I did. It hurts!

A: 다리가 다친 것 같네요. B: 그랬어요. 아파요!

▸ Ouch!
아!
▸ Is somebody hurt?
누가 다쳤어요?

I'm not taking any medicine 먹는 약 없어요

A: Can you drink alcohol?

B: Yes, I'm not taking any medicine.

A: 술 마실 수 있어? B: 어, 약 먹는 거 없어.

Do I need an operation? 수술해야 하나요?

A: This x-ray shows us your broken leg.

B: It looks bad. Do I need an operation?

A: 이 x—ray로 부러진 다리가 보여요. B: 안 좋군요. 수술해야 하나요?

▸ Should I be hospitalized?
입원해야 하나요?

How long will you be in the hospital for?

얼마나 오래 입원해 있어야 하는 거야?

A: How long will you be in the hospital for?

B: About three weeks.

A: 얼마나 오래 입원해 있어야 하는 거야? B: 한 3주간.

Chapter 05

쇼핑

Step 1 구매
Step 2 결재/배송

01 뭘 도와드릴까요?

How may I help you? 어떻게 도와드릴까요?

A: May I help you?

B: Yes, I'm looking for running shoes.

   A: 도와드릴까요? B: 네, 운동화를 찾고 있는데요.

▸ How can I help[serve] you?
어떻게 도와드릴까요?
▸ What can I do for you?
뭘 도와드릴까요?

(No thanks,) I'm already being helped 이미 다른 분이 봐주고 계세요

A: Can I get you anything?

B: Actually, I'm being helped now. Thanks anyway.

   A: 뭐라도 좀 가져다 드릴까요? B: 실은, 이미 부탁했어요. 어쨌든 고마워요.

I'm just looking (around) 그냥 구경하고 있는 거예요

A: Can I help you with anything?

B: No, thank you, I'm just looking around.

   A: 도와드릴까요? B: 고맙지만 괜찮아요. 그냥 구경만 하는 거예요.

▸ (I'm) Just browsing
그냥 구경하는 거예요

When do you open? 언제 열어요?

A: When do you open?

B: We'll be open at 10 o'clock, tomorrow morning.

   A: 언제 열어요? B: 내일 아침 10시에 열어요.

▸ When is closing time?
언제 닫아요?

Eighth, please 8층 부탁해요

A: What floor do you want?

B: Eighth, please.

   A: 몇 층 가세요? B: 8층 부탁해요.

▸ The eighth floor, please
8층 부탁해요
▸ Going down? Going up?
내려가세요? 올라가세요?

Where can I find ladies' wear? 여성복은 어디 있어요?

A: Where can I find ladies' wear?

B: You need to go to our second floor.

   A: 여성복은 어디 있어요? B: 2층으로 가셔야 돼요.

What're you looking for? 뭘 찾으세요?

A: What are you looking for?

B: I need to find an umbrella.

    A: 뭘 찾고 계시는데요? B: 우산을 사려구요.

▸ Are you looking for anything in particular?
특별히 뭐 찾는 게 있습니까?

I'm looking for a jazz CD 재즈 CD를 찾는데요

A: I'm looking for a jazz CD.

B: We have many in the back room.

    A: 재즈 CD를 찾고 있는데요. B: 안쪽 매장에 많이 있습니다.

▸ I'm looking for a bag
가방을 찾는데요
▸ I'd like a suit
옷을 사려고요

I want to buy a snowboard 스노보드를 사려고요

A: I want to buy a fashionable winter hat.

B: I'll show you a few that seem to be popular.

    A: 요즘 유행하는 겨울 모자를 사고 싶어요. B: 인기있는 걸로 몇 개 보여드리죠.

Do you have a shirt with a plainer pattern? 더 평범한 무늬 셔츠 있어요?

A: This is a very fashionable style this year.

B: Do you have a shirt with a plainer pattern?

    A: 금년에 유행하는 거예요. B: 평범한 무늬의 셔츠 있어요?

Do you carry watch batteries? 시계 배터리 파세요?

A: Do you carry watch batteries?

B: Yes, we do.

    A: 시계 건전지 파나요? B: 네, 팔아요.

I'm sorry, we don't carry that brand 미안해요, 그 브랜드는 취급안해요

A: Do you have any Swatch watches?

B: I'm sorry, we don't carry that brand.

    A: 스와치 시계 있나요? B: 죄송하지만 저희 가게에선 팔지 않습니다.

We're having a big sale this week 이번주에 큰 세일해요

A: We're having a big sale this week.

B: When does the sale start? How long will it last?

    A: 이번 주에 대 바겐 세일이 있습니다. B: 세일 언제 시작해요? 얼마동안요?

▸ This is a hot sale item nowadays
요즘 잘 나가는 품목이예요

02 입어봐도 돼요?

May I try it on? 입어봐도 돼요?

A: May I try on a pair of shoes?

B: Sure. What size do you need?

A: 신발 좀 신어봐도 될까요? B: 물론이죠. 사이즈가 어떻게 되시는데요?

▶ I'd like to try this on
이거 입어보고 싶어요

▶ Would you like to try it on?
입어보실래요?

Where is the fitting[dressing] room? 탈의실이 어디예요?

A: Where is the fitting room?

B: It's in the center aisle, on the left.

A: 탈의실이 어디예요? B: 중앙복도 왼편에 있어요.

It's too small[big] for me 내게 너무 작[크]네요

A: How does that shirt fit?

B: It's too small for me.

A: 이 셔츠 맞으세요? B: 내게 너무 작아요.

▶ It's a little bit tight
너무 쪼이네요

Could you please show me another jacket? 다른 자켓 보여줄래요?

A: We just got a shipment of those sweaters.

B: Do you have them in any other colors?

A: 이 스웨터 방금 들어온 겁니다. B: 이거 다른 색상으로 있나요

▶ Do you have them in any other colors?
이거 다른 색상들 있나요?

What size do you wear? 사이즈가 어떻게 돼요?

A: What size do you wear?

B: I think I wear a size eight.

A: 사이즈가 어떻게 되세요? B: 8사이즈 정도 입어요.

▶ Would you have one in a smaller size?
좀 더 작은 사이즈 있어요?

▶ Do you have this shirt in a smaller size?
이 셔츠 작은 사이즈 있어요?

How's this? 이건 어때요?

A: I'd like a fashionable t-shirt.

B: How's this? I think you'd look good in it.

A: 유행하는 티셔츠 주세요. B: 이거 어때요? 입으시면 잘 어울릴 것 같아요.

This is nice 이거 좋은데요

A: Do you like the blue or green better?

B: I like the green better.

A: 파란색하고 초록색 중에 어떤게 더 낫죠? B: 초록색이 더 좋은데요.

▸ This is better
이게 더 나아요
▸ I like this better
이게 더 좋아요

It looks good on you 잘 어울리네요

A: What do you think?

B: It looks good on you.

A: 어때요? B: 잘 어울리세요.

The skirt matches this blouse, doesn't it?

이 치마가 이 블라우스랑 어울리죠 그렇죠?

A: The pants go well with the shirt.

B: What do you think about the vest?

A: 바지가 셔츠랑 잘 어울려요. B: 조끼는 어떤 것 같아요?

▸ This skirt and this blouse go together well
이 치마와 이 블라우스가 잘 어울려요

I'll take[get] this one 이것으로 할게요

A: I'll take this one.

B: Do you want me to wrap it up for you?

A: 이걸로 사겠어요. B: 포장해 드릴까요?

▸ I'd like this one
이걸로 주세요
▸ I'd like to buy this one
이거 살게요

Will that be all? 달리 더 필요한 것은 없으십니까?

A: Will that be all?

B: Yes, I'm ready to pay for these items.

A: 다 되셨나요? B: 예, 지불할게요.

▸ Is that everything?
다 되셨습니까?
▸ Will there be anything else?
더 필요한 건 없습니까?

Please wrap it 포장해주세요

A: How would you like this necklace packaged?

B: Please wrap it. It's a gift.

A: 이 목걸이 어떻게 담아드릴까요? B: 포장해주세요. 선물이거든요.

03 얼마예요?

How much do I owe you? 내가 얼마를 내면 되지?, 얼마죠?

A: How much do I owe you?

B: That will be fifty-five dollars.

A: 얼마 내면 되죠? B: 55달러입니다.

▶ What do I owe
you?
얼마인가요?
▶ What's the
damage?
얼마예요?

How much? 얼마예요?

A: How much does it cost?

B: It costs $99.99.

A: 이건 얼마죠? B: 99달러 99센트예요.

▶ What's the price
of this?
이거 가격이 어떻게 돼요?
▶ How much is
this?
이거 얼마예요?

What's that in dollars? 달러로는 얼마예요?

A: The tax will be seven euros.

B: What's that in dollars?

A: 세금은 7유로입니다. B: 달러로는 얼마죠?

▶ It's twenty dollars,
including tax
세금포함해서 20달러예요

How much can you afford to spend? 예산은 얼마쯤 잡고 계시는데요?

A: I really want to get a set of new golf clubs.

B: How much can you afford to spend?

A: 새 골프세트를 꼭 하나 구입하고 싶어. B: 예산은 얼마쯤 잡고 있는데?

▶ What's your
budget?
예산은 얼마로 잡고 계신데
요?
▶ I can't afford to
buy it
그걸 살 여유가 없어

That's expensive! 무척 비싸구만!

A: I think it's too expensive.

B: There are cheaper ones in the store.

A: 너무 비싼 것 같은데요. B: 가게에 더 싼 것들도 있어요.

▶ How expensive!
엄청 비싸네!
▶ That's too much!
너무 비싸다!

It's a bargain 싸다, 싸잖아

A: Do you think I should buy that car for $5,000?

B: Absolutely. It's a bargain.

A: 5천 달러 주고 저 차를 사야 할까? B: 당연하지. 싸잖아.

▶ That's cheap!
야 싸다!
▶ How cheap!
정말 싸다!

It's a real good buy at that price 그 가격이면 진짜 잘 사는 거야

A: I really like the sofa in your display.

B: It's a real good buy at that price.

A: 전시돼 있는 저 소파가 정말 맘에 들어요. B: 저 가격이면 정말 잘 사시는 겁니다.

▸ Wow, that's a steal!
와, 거저네!
▸ At 40 percent below market, this is a good buy
40%할인가면 잘 산거지

Can[Would] you give me a discount? 좀 깍아 주실래요?

A: Can you give me a better price?

B: I can only give you a discount if you buy more than 10.

A: 할인해 주실 수는 없나요? B: 10개이상 구입시 할인가능해요.

▸ Can you give me a discount for paying cash?
현금내면 할인해줘요?
▸ Can you make it cheaper?
좀 더 싸게 안돼요?

I'm sorry, I can't take a penny off 한 푼도 못 깍아드려요

A: Don't I get a discount?

B: I'm sorry, I can't take a penny off.

A: 할인은 안 되나요? B: 죄송하지만 한 푼도 깎아 드릴 수 없습니다.

▸ Take it or leave it
사시던지 아님 그냥 가세요
▸ That's my final offer
내가 하는 마지막 제안예요

I got it at a bargain price 싼 가격에 그걸 샀어

A: I see you bought a new sofa.

B: I got it at a bargain price.

A: 소파 새로 샀구나. B: 싸게 샀어.

▸ I picked it up at a flea market for $5
벼룩시장에서 5달러에 샀어
▸ I bought this on impulse
이거 충동구매했어

I got it for next to nothing 거의 거저에 샀어

A: Are you sure that painting is valuable?

B: Who cares? I got it for next to nothing.

A: 저 그림이 값어치 있는게 확실해? B: 알게 뭐람? 거의 거저에 샀는 걸.

▸ I bought this for almost nothing
거의 거저에 산거야

04 현금으로요 아니면 신용카드로요?

(Will that be) Cash or charge? 현금으로요 아니면 신용카드로요?

A: I'd like to buy this coat.

B: Will that be cash or charge?

A: 이 코트를 사고 싶은데요. B: 현금으로요 아니면 신용카드로요?

▸ Would you like to pay by cash or charge?
현금으로 낼래요 아님 신용
카드로 낼래요?

How would you like to pay for this? 어떻게 계산하실래요?

A: How would you like to pay for this?

B: With my credit card, if it's all right.

A: 어떻게 계산하시겠습니까? B: 괜찮다면 신용카드로 낼게요.

Do you take checks? 수표 받나요?

A: Do you take checks?

B: Yes, as long as you have proof of identification.

A: 수표 받나요? B: 네, 신분증을 제시하시면요.

▸ Do you accept traveler's checks?
여행자수표 받아요?

Do you accept[take] Visa? 비자카드 받아요?

A: Do you accept Visa?

B: We accept all major credit cards.

A: 비자카드 받아요? B: 주요 신용카드는 다 받아요.

▸ Can I use VISA?
비자카드 돼나요?

Can I pay in Korean won? 한국 원화로 낼 수 있어요?

A: Can I pay in Korean won?

B: No, I'm sorry, we accept only dollars here.

A: 한국 원화로 낼 수 있어요? B: 아뇨, 미안하지만 여긴 달러만 받아요.

Cash, please 현금으로요

A: How would you like to pay for this?

B: Cash, please.

A: 어떻게 지불하실래요? B: 현금으로요.

▸ I'll charge it, please
현금으로요

I'll pay by check 수표로 낼게요

A: How would you like to pay for this?

B: I'll pay by check.

A: 이거 어떻게 지불할래요? B: 수표로 할게요.

I'd like to buy it on credit 신용카드로 낼게요

A: I'd like to buy it on credit.

B: Our store doesn't accept credit cards.

A: 신용카드로 낼게요. B: 우린 신용카드 받지 않아요.

I think there's something wrong with the amount
계산이 잘못된 것 같은데요

A: That will be $256, please.

B: I think there's something wrong with the amount you're charging.

A: 다 합쳐서 256달러 되겠습니다. B: 청구하신 계산이 뭔가 좀 잘못 된 것 같아요.

Can I have a receipt, please? 영수증을 받을 수 있을까요?

A: Here is your change, sir.

B: Thank you. May I have a receipt, please?

A: 여기 잔돈 있습니다, 손님. B: 고마워요. 영수증을 받을 수 있을까요?

▶ Here is your change and receipt
여기 잔돈과 영수증요

Can I have these delivered to this address? 이 주소로 배달돼요?

A: How can I help you?

B: Can I have these delivered to this address?

A: 어떻게 도와드릴까요? B: 이 주소로 배달돼요?

▶ Please deliver it to my home
이거 집으로 배달해줘요

Would you like these items delivered? 이 물건들을 배달해 드릴까요?

A: Would you like these items delivered?

B: Do I have to pay extra for delivery?

A: 이 물건들을 배달해 드릴까요? B: 배달하는 데 추가요금을 내야 하나요?

Do you send packages overseas? 해외로 배송하나요?

A: Does your store send packages overseas?

B: Yes, we have a shipping service.

A: 여기 상점은 해외배송 하나요? B: 예, 배송서비스 합니다.

I still haven't received the merchandise I ordered

주문한 거 아직 못받았어요

A: I still haven't received the merchandise I ordered.

B: I can check on your order for you.

A: 주문한 거 아직 못받았어요. B: 주문서 확인해볼게요.

I didn't receive the same merchandise I ordered

주문한 거랑 다른 게 왔어요

A: I didn't receive the same merchandise I ordered.

B: I see. Maybe there was a mix-up.

A: 주문한 거랑 다른 게 왔어요. B: 알겠습니다. 아마 물건들이 섞였나본데요.

The merchandise I received was damaged 주문한 물품이 손상이 됐어요

A: How were the items you ordered from the Internet?

B: The merchandise I received was damaged.

A: 인터넷에서 주문한 상품 어때? B: 주문한 물품이 손상됐어.

Would you exchange it for me? 교환해줍니까?

A: How can I help you?

B: I'd like to exchange this for something else.

A: 어떻게 도와드릴까요? B: 이걸 다른 걸로 교환하고 싶은데요.

▸ I'd like to exchange this for something else.
다른 걸로 교환해주세요

▸ Please exchange it for a clean one
깨끗한 걸로 바꿔주세요

I'd like to return this 이거 반품할게요

A: I'd like to return this.

B: Do you have your receipt with you?

A: 이거 반품하려고요. B: 영수증 갖고 계세요?

Can I have a refund? 환불되나요?

A: Can I have a refund for this?

B: Yes. Here you go.

A: 이거 환불되나요? B: 예 됩니다. 여기 있습니다.

▸ I'd like to get a refund, please.
환불받고 싶어요

▸ I'd like a refund, please
환불해 주세요

I'd like my money back, please 돈을 환불해주세요

A: I'd like my money back, please.

B: Was there a problem with this item?

A: 돈을 환불해주세요. B: 이 물품에 문제가 있었나요?

Can you accept Samsung Pay? 삼성페이 되나요?

A: Our store sells exclusively online.

B: Can you accept Samsung Pay?

A:우리 가게는 온라인으로만 판매합니다. B: 삼성페이 되나요?

I'd like to pay using Payco 페이코로 결제할려구요

A: How will you pay for the shoes you bought?

B: I'd like to pay using Payco.

A: 구매하신 구두결제는 어떻게 하시겠어요? B: 페이코로 할게요.

I paid for those things using Paypal 페이팔로 결제한거야

A: You buy a ton of stuff from e-bay.

B: I paid for those things using Paypal.

A: 너 이베이에서 많은 물건을 사는구나. B: 페이팔로 결제한거야.

Chapter 06

비즈니스

Step 1 회사
Step 2 업무
Step 3 회의

01 직업이 뭐예요?

What do you do for a living? 직업이 뭐예요?

A: What do you do for a living?

B: I'm a stockbroker.

A: 무슨 일을 하세요? B: 주식 중개인입니다.

▸ What do you do?
무슨 일 하세요?

Who do you work for? 어디서 일해?

A: Who do you work for?

B: I work for a government agency.

A: 어디에서 일하니? B: 정부기관에서 일해.

A: Excuse me, who do you work for?

B: I'm trainer here at the gym.

A: 실례지만 어디서 일하세요? B: 여기 체육관에서 트레이너로 있어요.

I work for Mr. Anderson 앤더슨 씨 회사에서 일해

A: What's the name of your boss?

B: I work for Mr. Anderson.

A: 사장님 성함이 어떻게 돼? B: 앤더스 씨 회사에서 일해.

▸ I work at[in]~
…에서 일해

I have been working here for 3 years 여기서 일한지 3년 됐어

A: Have you been working here long?

B: Not really… about three months.

A:여기서 일한지 오래됐어? B: 아니, 한 3개월 정도.

He got fired 걘 해고됐어

A: Did he get the sack at the office?

B: Yes, the boss fired him.

A: 그는 잘렸나요? B: 네, 사장님께서 그를 해고시켰어요.

I'm being transferred 나 전근 가

A: I'm being transferred.
B: Where are they sending you?

A: 나 전근 가. B: 어디로 가?

I hear you've been promoted 승진했다며

A: I heard you've been promoted.
B: Yeah, my job is a lot more stressful now.

A: 승진했다고 들었어. B: 어, 이제 훨씬 <u>스트레스가 많은 일이야.</u>

You changed jobs? 직업을 바꿨어?

A: So, what do you do for a living?
B: Right now I'm between jobs.

A: 그럼, 직업이 뭐야? B: 지금은 백수야.

▶ I recently changed jobs
최근에 직업을 바꿨어
▶ I'm between jobs
백수야

I'm thinking of retiring soon 퇴직할까 생각중야

A: I'm thinking of retiring soon.
B: What will you do if you retire?

A: 퇴직할 까 생각중야 B: 퇴직하면 뭐 할거야?

▶ I opted for early retirement last year
작년에 명예퇴직 신청했어

Chapter 06

What are the (working) hours? 근무시간은?

A: I enjoy working in a hospital.
B: What are the working hours?

A: 병원에서 일하는 게 즐거워. B: 근무시간은?

Let's call it a day 퇴근합시다

A: I am bushed. Let's call it a day.
B: But we have a lot of work to do.

A: 난 지쳤어요. 집에 갑시다. B: 하지만 할 일이 많아.

A: Boy, I sure am tired.
B: Me too. Let's call it a day.

A: 야, 정말 피곤해. B: 나도 그래. 퇴근하자고.

▶ Why don't we call it a day now?
오늘은 이제 그만 퇴근하자

Let's call it quits 퇴근합시다

A: I can't stay up any longer.

B: Let's call it quits.

A: 더 이상 밤샘은 못하겠어. B: 그럼 오늘은 이만하자.

▸ Let's quit for today
오늘 그만 퇴근하죠

He's gone for the day 그 분은 퇴근했습니다

A: Is he in his office right now?

B: I'm sorry, but he's gone for the day.

A: 지금 사무실에 계시나요? B: 죄송합니다만 퇴근하셨습니다.

▸ We're done for the day
그만 가자, 그만 하자

Are you working overtime tonight? 오늘 밤 야근해?

A: Are you working overtime tonight?

B: Yeah, I have to finish this report.

A: 오늘 밤 야근해? B: 어, 이 보고서를 끝내야 돼.

I'm working nights 난 밤근무야

A: I'm working nights right now.

B: Do you find it hard to sleep well?

A: 지금 밤근무야. B: 숙면하기 힘들지?

▸ I have the night shift this week
이번주 밤근무야

I'll be out of town all next week 다음 주 내내 출장갈거야

A: Can I call you on Wednesday?

B: No, I'll be out of town all next week.

A: 수요일날 전화해도 돼? B: 아니, 다음 주 내내 출장갈거야.

▸ I'll be on the road most of next month
다음 달 대부분 출장중일거야

Can you take care of my work while I'm away?
나 없을 때 내 일 좀 맡아줄래?

A: Can you take care of my work while I'm away?

B: How long is your vacation?

A: 나 없을 때 내 일 좀 맡아줄테야? B: 휴가가 얼마동안인데?

I have to call in sick 아파서 결근한다고 전화해야겠어

A: I have to call in sick.

B: What kind of illness do you have?

A: 아파서 결근한다고 전화해야겠어. B: 어디가 아픈데?

A: I have to call in sick today.

B: Really? What's the matter?

A: 오늘 아파서 결근한다고 전화해야겠어 B: 정말? 왜 그러는데?

 사무기기에 관한 표현들

- Please copy these papers 이 서류 좀 카피해요
- Would you copy these papers? 이 서류들 좀 카피해줄래요?

- This copy machine isn't working 복사기가 작동이 안돼요
- This copy machine doesn't work 복사기가 작동안돼요
- This copier is broken 복사기가 망가졌어요

- I think it ran out of paper 종이가 떨어졌어요
- I think it's out of paper 종이가 떨어졌어요
- We're out of paper 종이가 부족해요

- My computer is down again 컴퓨터가 다시 다운됐어
- We're sick and tired of these breakdowns 컴퓨터 다운이 지긋지긋해

- I think the paper's jammed 종이가 물린 것 같아
- The printout is all screwed up 프린터나온 게 엉망이네
- We're out of toner 토너가 떨어졌어
- When does the lease on this PC expire? 컴퓨터 임대가 언제끝나?
- Who's going to cover the cost of repairs? 누가 컴퓨터 수리비를 대는 거지?

- It's still under warranty 아직 보증기간예요
- It must be about time to change it 이제 바꿀 때가 되었나보군
- Show me how it works 어떻게 작동하는 지 알려줘요
- It's working fine 기계가 잘 돌아간다

A: The copy machine isn't working. 복사기가 작동안해요.
B: You'd better call the repair center. 수리센터에 전화해라.

A: Why aren't you working? 왜 일을 안하는 거야?
B: My computer is down again. 컴퓨터가 또 다운됐어요.

A: What does this light on the copier machine mean? 복사기 이 불빛은 왜 그러는 거야?
B: It means it's out of order. 고장났다는 표시야.

A: Have you seen this new software program? 이 새로운 소프트웨어 본 적있어?
B: Nope. Show me how it works. 아니. 어떻게 하는 건지 알려줘.

02 내일까지 마무리 해

Please get it done by tomorrow morning 내일 아침까지 마무리해

A: Please get it done right away.

B: Don't worry, you can count on me.

A: 지금 당장 이것 좀 해줘. B: 걱정마. 나만 믿어.

▸ Can you have the report done by 6 o'clock?
6시까지 보고서 끝낼 수 있어?

Finish this report today! 오늘 이 보고서 끝내!

A: I want you to have the report finished by noon.

B: Get real!

A: 정오까지 이 보고서 끝내도록 해. B: 제 정신이야!

Do this right away 이거 지금 바로 해

A: Is it urgent that I finish this?

B: It is. Do it right away.

A: 이거 급히 끝내야 하는 거예요? B: 어. 지금 바로 해.

▸ Please do this
이거 해요
▸ Would you please do this for me?
이것 좀 해줄래요?
▸ Do this when you can
시간 될 때 해요

Please take care of this 이것 좀 처리하도록

A: Please take care of this.

B: What is it?

A: 이것 좀 처리하도록. B: 뭔데요?

Would you take a look at this paper? 이 서류 좀 한번 봐주실래요?

A: Would you take a look at this paper?

B: It looks like a letter to the president.

A: 이 서류 좀 한번 봐주실래요? B: 사장한테 보내는 편지같아 보이는데요.

This is top priority 이게 최우선야

A: I'll check that after lunch.

B: Do it now. This is top priority.

A: 점심 후에 확인해볼게요. B: 지금 바로 해. 최우선사항야.

▸ I want you to give this top priority
이거에 최우선을 두게

Please submit the document to me 이 문서를 내게 제출해요

A: Who should I give the report to?

B: Please give the document to me.

A: 이 보고서를 누구에게 제출해야 하죠? B: 그 문서는 내게 제출해요.

▸ Please hand the
  document in to
  me
  이 문서를 내게 제출해요

This has to go out today 이건 오늘 나가야 돼

A: Those contracts absolutely had to go out today!

B: I'm sorry, but you didn't give me any contracts.

A: 계약서 오늘 발송되어야 했다구! B: 죄송하지만 계약서 주신 게 없어요.

Who is handling this account? 이 건은 누가 맡고 있어?

A: Who is handling this account?

B: I think that Jim is.

A: 이 건은 누가 맡고 있어? B: 짐이 맡고 있을걸요.

▸ Who's going
  to handle the
  paperwork?
  이 서류작업은 누가 맡을
  건가?

That can't wait 이건 급해

A: Is it important to fix this computer?

B: That can't wait. Fix it as quickly as you can.

A: 이 컴퓨터를 고치는 게 중요해? B: 급해. 가능한 한 빨리 고치도록 해.

▸ This can wait
  그건 나중에 해도 돼
▸ Can't that wait?
  미루면 안돼?, 급한 거야?

You'd better work harder 더 열심히 일해라

A: Why are you angry at me?

B: I think you're lazy. You'd better work harder.

A: 왜 내게 화내는 거야? B: 넌 게을러. 더 열심히 해야 돼.

▸ Do your best!
  최선을 다해!

Make sure they all know about it 걔들이 모두 알고 있도록 해

A: There is a picnic for the students on Friday.

B: Make sure they all know about it.

A: 금요일날 학생들 피크닉 있어. B: 걔네들에게 모두 확실히 알려주도록 해.

03 일 시작합시다

LET'S GET STARTED

Let's get down to business 자 일을 시작합시다

A: Let's get down to business.

B: Great, let's start.

A: 자 일을 시작합시다. B: 좋아. 시작하자구.

Let's get started 자 시작하자

A: Our whole crew has arrived.

B: Great. Let's get started.

A: 우리 모든 직원이 도착했어. B: 좋아. 출발하자고

▸ Let's get started
  on the wedding
  plans
  결혼식 계획을 실행하자
▸ I gotta get started
  on my speech
  연설을 시작하겠습니다

Let's roll 자 시작합시다

A: It's time to drive to the beach.

B: Let's roll.

A: 차타고 해변갈 시간야. B: 자 시작하자.

▸ Let's get on with
  it
  시작합시다

Get set[ready]! 준비해라!

A: Get ready! It's going to rain soon.

B: I'll fetch my umbrella.

A: 준비해! 곧 비가 올거야. B: 우산 좀 가져올게.

▸ Get ready for
  Christmas
  크리스마스를 준비해
▸ Get ready to run
  뛸 준비해

All right, are you ready? 좋아. 준비됐어?

A: Our plan is to leave in ten minutes.

B: All right, are you ready?

A: 우리 계획은 10분 안에 떠나는거야. B: 알았어, 넌 준비됐어?

▸ Ready?
  좋아, 준비됐어?
▸ You guys ready?
  너네들 준비됐어?

I'll go 내가 할게

A: Who's going to take the first shot?

B: I'll go.

A: 누가 먼저 할래? B: 내가 할게.

All set 준비 다 됐어요

A: How is the copier working?

B: It's all set. It was fixed this morning.

A: 복사기가 어떻게 돌아가는 거야? B: 다 됐어. 오늘 아침에 수리했어요.

▸ I'm[We're] all set
난[우린] 준비 다 됐어
▸ We're ready
준비됐어요

I'll get to work on it right now 지금 바로 시작할게요

A: You've got to finish this today.

B: I'll get to work on it right now.

A: 오늘 이거 끝내야 돼. B: 지금 바로 시작할게요.

▸ Just get to work
바로 일 시작해

I'll get right on it 당장 그렇게 하겠습니다

A: Mr. Burns has called you several times.

B: I'll get right on it.

A: 미스터 번즈가 여러 차례 전화했어요. B: 바로 내가 전화할게요.

First things first 중요한 것부터 먼저 하자

A: Can we get started?

B: First things first. Get me some coffee.

A: 시작할 수 있어요? B: 중요한 것부터 먼저 하자. 커피 좀 갖다 줘.

▸ Work comes first
일이 우선이야

I'm working on it 지금 하고 있어

A: I'm going to work on this stuff at home tonight.

B: If you have any problems give me a call.

A: 오늘 밤 집에서 이 일을 할거야. B: 문제가 생기면 나한테 전화해.

▸ I'm on it
내가 처리 중이야

I'll look it over first thing in the morning 내일 아침 일찍 바로 검토할게

A: I'm sending you a copy of the agreement.

B: I'll look it over first thing in the morning.

A: 동의서 사본을 보낼게. B: 내일 아침 일찍 바로 검토할게.

▸ I'll do it
immediately
당장 할게

04 언제까지 해야 하는거야?

When is this due? 마감일이 언제야?

A: When is the final report due?

B: The deadline is tomorrow.

A: 최종 보고서 마감일이 언제인가요? B: 내일이 마감일이야.

A: When is this due?

B: On April 15th.

A: 마감이 언제야? B: 4월 15일.

▸ When is the paper due?
이 서류 언제 마감야?
▸ What's the due date?
마감일이 언제야?
▸ It's due on the thirtieth
13일이 마감야

What's the deadline for this job? 이 일 마감이 언제야?

A: What's the deadline for this job?

B: It has to be completed in six months.

A: 이 일 마감이 언제예요? B: 6개월 내에 마쳐야 돼.

▸ How much time do I have?
시간이 얼마나 있어?

The deadline is coming up 마감일이 다가오고 있어

A: The deadline is coming up.

B: We'd better start working faster.

A: 마감일이 다가오고 있어 B: 일을 더 빨리 처리하도록 해야 돼.

▸ The deadline's just a week away
마감일이 일주일 앞이야

We're behind schedule 일정보다 늦었어

A: Why do I have to stay late tonight?

B: Because we're behind schedule.

A: 왜 오늘밤 늦게까지 있어야 하는 거죠? B: 일정보다 늦어졌기 때문에.

▸ The project is running a week behind schedule
그 프로젝트가 예정보다 일주일 늦고 있어

The schedule is just too demanding 일정이 너무 빡빡해

A: Why aren't you finished yet?

B: The schedule is just too demanding.

A: 왜 아직 못 끝낸거야? B: 일정이 너무 빡빡해서요.

▸ This is a tight schedule
일정이 빡빡하네

We're about two days ahead of schedule 일정보다 한 이틀 앞서가고 있어

A: How is your timetable working?

B: We're about two days ahead of schedule.

A: 업무일정이 어때? B: 일정보다 한 이틀 앞서가고 있어.

When will it be ready? 언제 준비될까?

A: The problem with your car isn't serious.

B: When will it be ready?

A: 차는 심각한 문제가 없어요. B: 언제 준비돼요?

▶ When does this have to be finished by?
이거 언제까지 끝내야 돼?

Is the report ready? 보고서 준비됐어?

A: Is the report ready?

B: I put it on your desk.

A: 보고서 준비됐어? B: 책상에 올려놨어요.

▶ Are the papers ready?
서류들 준비됐어?

Have you finished the report? 보고서 끝냈어?

A: How is the report coming? Have you finished it yet?

B: Not yet, sir. I'll get it done by Friday.

A: 보고선 어떻게 돼가? 끝냈어? B: 아직요. 금요일까지는 끝내겠습니다.

What happened to the project? 그 프로젝트는 어떻게 됐어?

A: What happened to the project?

B: It's been cancelled.

A: 그 프로젝트는 어떻게 됐어? B: 취소됐어.

▶ What happened to the documents I left here?
내가 여기 둔 문서는 어떻게 됐어?

We're still at it 아직도 하고 있어

A: Did you finish that report?

B: We're still at it.

A: 보고서 끝냈어요? B: 아직도 하고 있어요.

There are no problems so far 지금까지는 아무 문제없어

A: How is your new job?

B: There are no problems so far.

A: 새로운 일 어때? B: 지금까지는 아무 문제도 없어.

▶ Right now, things look pretty good
지금 상황은 꽤 좋아보여

It's moving right along · 잘 되어 가고 있어

A: Did you overcome the problems with your project?

B: Yes, it's moving right along.

A: 네 프로젝트의 문제점들 극복했어? B: 예, 잘 되어 가고 있어.

It's still in the planning stage · 아직 기획단계예요

A: I thought you were going to build a factory.

B: It's still in the planning stage.

A: 공장을 신축하는 걸로 생각했는데. B: 아직 기획단계예요.

Nothing has been done about that project · 그 프로젝트는 아직 된 게 없어

A: Nothing has been done about the project.

B: Do you think they'll postpone it?

A: 그 프로젝트는 아직 된 게 하나도 없어. B: 연기될 것 같아?

It's challenging work · 만만치 않은 일이야

A: Do you like working in construction?

B: It's challenging work.

A: 건설업에서 일하는 게 좋아? B: 만만치 않은 일야.

▶ This paperwork is really a pain
이 서류작업은 정말 골칫거리야

We're finally getting somewhere · 마침내 좀 진전했네요

A: I'll agree to your proposal.

B: We're finally getting somewhere.

A: 당신의 제안에 동의합니다. B: 마침내 진전이 이루어졌네요.

We should start pushing them · 걔들을 다그치기 시작해야겠어

A: Our employees are not very productive.

B: We should start pushing them.

A: 우리 직원들이 매우 비생산적이야. B: 그사람들을 다그치기 시작해야 겠어.

That can't be done overnight · 밤새 그렇게 한다는 건 불가능해요

A: I need you to finish this by tomorrow.

B: What? That can't be done overnight.

A: 당신은 내일까지 이걸 끝내야 해. B: 뭐라구요? 밤새 그렇게 한다는 건 불가능해요.

05 최선을 다 했어요

I did all I could do 난 할 수 있는 최선을 다 했어요

A: How come you take longer than anyone else to finish your job?

B: I don't know, but I did all I could.

A: 자넨 왜 딴 사람보다 더뎌? B: 모르겠어요. 하지만 항상 최선을 다했어요.

▸ That's all I can do
이게 내가 할 수 있는 최선
야

We're putting every effort into it 모든 노력을 기울이고 있어요

A: Just try to get it done sometime soon.

B: Sure. We're putting every effort into it.

A: 조만간에 꼭 끝내놓도록 해. B: 예. 모든 노력을 기울이고 있어요.

I have to work late today 오늘 야근해야 돼

A: Let's have a drink after work tonight.

B: I can't. I have to work late today.

A: 오늘 밤 퇴근 후에 술 한잔 하자. B: 안돼. 오늘 야근해야 돼.

▸ I have to work
overtime today
오늘 야근해야 돼

He's a hard worker 걘 일 열심히 하는 사람야

A: How is your new employee?

B: I like him. He's a hard worker.

A: 새로 고용한 직원 어때? B: 좋아. 일을 열심히 하는 친구야.

▸ I'm a workaholic
난 일밖에 모르는 사람야

Let's see what happens 어떻게 되나 보자고

A: They may decide to sell this store.

B: Let's see what happens.

A: 그 사람들이 이 가게를 팔지 몰라. B: 어떻게 되나 보자고.

I'll be sure to double-check everything from now on

지금부터 철저히 확인할게요

A: You shouldn't have made this mistake.

B: I'll be sure to double-check everything from now on.

A: 이런 실수는 하면 안되지. B: 지금부터 철저히 확인할게요.

▸ I'll try not to let
you down
실망하지 않도록 할게요

06 다했어?

You done? 다했어?

A: You done?

B: No. Give me another five minutes.

A: 다했어? B: 아뇨. 5분만 더 시간줘요.

Are you done with this? 이거 끝냈니?

A: Are you done with the proposal?

B: I'm having trouble getting it finished on time.

A: 그 건의안 다 끝냈나? B: 제시간에 끝내기가 어려워.

▶ Are you done with
your meal?
밥 다 먹었니?

When will you be done with your work? 언제까지면 일이 끝날 것 같아?

A: When will you be done with your project?

B: I don't expect to be finished until next week.

A: 언제까지면 일이 끝날 것 같아? B: 담주까지 끝마치지 못할 것 같아.

I'm done with this 이거 다 끝냈다

A: I'm done with this.

B: Let's grab some dinner.

A: 이거 다 끝냈어. B: 저녁 좀 먹자.

▶ I'm (all) done with
my work
이 일 (거의) 다 끝냈어

I'm finished working 일 끝냈어

A: I'm finished working.

B: Good. Let's go home now.

A: 일 끝냈어. B: 좋아. 이제 집에 가자.

All done! 다 끝냈어!

A: How are you doing there?

B: All done.

A: 거기 어떻게 하고 있어? B: 다 끝냈어!

▶ It's done
끝냈어

I'm not done 못 끝냈어

A: Where is the report I asked you to do?

B: I'm sorry, but I'm not done yet. I'm still working on it.

　　A: 내가 부탁한 보고서 어디 있어? B: 미안하지만 아직 못 끝냈어요. 하고 있어요.

It's 90 percent finished 90% 정도 끝냈어

A: Are you almost done?

B: Just give me a second. It's 90 percent finished.

　　A: 거의 다 끝냈나? B: 조금만 있어보세요. 거의 다 끝냈어요.

We're almost there 거의 다 됐어, 거의 끝났어

A: Has the new computer network been activated?

B: We're almost there.

　　A: 새로운 컴퓨터 네트워크가 작동되고 있어? B: 거의 다 됐어.

▶ We're almost
finished
거의 다 마쳤어

We'd like to wrap this up today 이거 오늘 끝내자고

A: We'd like to wrap this up today.

B: I'll tell everyone to hurry.

　　A: 이거 오늘 끝내자고. B: 다들 서두르라고 말할게요.

Let's get it over with 이거 끝내자, 해치우자

A: Are you ready for your examination?

B: Let's get it over with.

　　A: 조사 준비됐어요? B: 후딱 해치우자고.

ㄴ 원하지 않은 것을 해야 될
경우 빨리 해치워버리자(Let'
s do it quickly and finish as
soon as possible)라는 의미.

Let's finish it up 이거 끝내자

A: We're almost finished with this design.

B: Let's finish it up.

　　A: 이 디자인 거의 끝내가고 있어. B: 끝내버리자고.

07 생각 좀 해보고요

I'd like to think it over 생각 좀 해볼게요

A: Let me have some time to think it over.
B: Okay, I'll give you until the end of the week.
A: 좀 생각해볼 시간을 주십시오. B: 좋아요. 이번 금요일까지 시간을 드리죠.

- Let me think it over a little longer 좀 더 생각 좀 해볼게요
- It's under review 검토중이야

I'll give you an answer after giving it some thought
생각 좀 해보고 답줄게

A: What do you think about the new contract we offered you?
B: I'll give you an answer after giving it some thought.
A: 우리가 제안한 새로운 계약서 어때? B: 생각해 본 후 답줄게.

- I'll give you an answer after I've talked with my manager 상사와 논의후 답줄게

I don't have the authority to do that 그렇게 할 권한이 없어요

A: You have to shut down these machines!
B: I don't have the authority to do that.
A: 이 기계들의 작동을 멈추어야 해! B: 내겐 그럴 권한이 없어요.

- I don't have the authority to decide on this matter 이 건에 대한 결정권이 없어요

I have to talk it over with the boss 사장과 그 문제를 이야기해봐야 돼

A: Can you discount these items?
B: I have to talk it over with the boss.
A: 이 물품을 할인해줄래요? B: 상사와 이야기해봐야 돼요.

- Let me check with my superiors 상사분들과 확인해볼게요

You'd better check with the boss 사장에게 확인해봐요

A: Do you think we should give Ted the project?
B: I'm not sure. You'd better check with the boss.
A: 그 프로젝트를 테드에게 맡길까? B: 몰라. 사장과 상의해봐.

- You'd better run it by the boss 사장과 상의해봐요

We're waiting for a decision from the people upstairs
윗분들 결정 기다리고 있어

A: Why haven't you given me an answer?

B: We're waiting for a decision from the people upstairs.

  A: 왜 답을 안 주는 거죠? B: 윗사람들 결정 기다리고 있어요.

▸ The boss refuses to give it his OK
사장이 승낙하지 않고 있어

I can't say for sure right now 지금 당장 확실히 말씀 못 드려요

A: Will you be here tomorrow afternoon?

B: I can't say for sure right now.

  A: 내일 오후에 여기 올거야? B: 지금 당장은 확실치 않아요.

▸ It requires a detailed analysis
세부적인 분석이 필요해요

Do you need an answer right now? 지금 당장 답변이 필요해요?

A: Do you need an answer right now?

B: We can wait until tomorrow morning.

  A: 지금 당장 답변이 필요해요? B: 내일 아침까지 기다릴 수 있어요.

I'll give you a firm answer by Friday 금요일까지 확실한 대답을 줄게요

A: Are you willing to accept the promotion?

B: I'll give you a firm answer by Friday.

  A: 승진을 받아들일거예요? B: 금요일까지 확실한 답을 드리죠.

▸ Thank you for your quick decision
빠른 결정을 해줘 감사해요

I'm going with it 난 그것으로 할게요

A: Do you trust this economic forecast?

B: I think so. I'm going with it.

  A: 이 경제전망을 신뢰해? B: 그럴 것 같아. 난 신뢰해.

▸ go with = choose

It's now or never 지금 아니면 안돼

A: Should I go to college?

B: Yeah, it's now or never.

  A: 대학에 가야 돼? B: 어, 지금 아니면 안돼.

▸ The sooner, the better
빠를수록 좋아

It's all or nothing 모 아니면 도야

A: We're betting all of our money.

B: Yeah, it's all or nothing. A: 가진 돈 모두를 걸자. B: 그래, 모 아니면 도지.

08 누가 책임자야?

Who is in charge? 누가 책임자야?

A: Who should I ask about extending my vacation?

B: Me, I'm the one in charge.

A: 휴가연장을 누구에게 요청해야죠? B: 제게 하세요. 저도 담당자 중 한사람이니까요.

▶ I'm in charge of
the project
내가 이 일의 책임자입니다

Who calls the shots? 누가 결정권자야?

A: Who calls the shots?

B: You'll have to talk to my boss.

A: 누가 결정권자야? B: 사장님과 얘기하셔야 돼요.

▶ I'm calling the
shots
내가 결정해

That's(It's) your call 네가 결정할 문제야. 네 뜻에 따를게

A: Should I agree to a salary decrease?

B: That's your call.

A: 임금삭감에 동의해야 되나? B: 네가 알아서 해.

You decide 네가 결정해

A: Do you want to go out or stay home?

B: You decide.

A: 나갈래 집에 있을래? B: 네가 결정해.

▶ You must decide
네가 결정해야 해

It's up to you 네가 결정할 일이야

A: What should I wear to the party tonight?

B: It's up to you. I can't decide for you.

A: 오늘 밤 파티에 뭘 입고 가는 게 좋을까? B: 그거야 네 맘이지. 내가 대신 정해줄 순 없다구.

▶ It's your choice
네가 선택하는 거야
▶ The choice is up
to you
선택은 너한테 달렸어

You're the boss 분부만 내리십시오. 맘대로 하세요

A: We're going to have to fire Tim and Ray.

B: You're the boss.

A: 팀과 레이를 해고해야 될거야. B: 그렇게 하세요.

▶ You're the doctor
네 조언에 따를게

09 좀 쉬자

Let's take a break 좀 쉽시다

A: Man, I'm really tired.

B: Let's take a break.

    A: 야, 정말 피곤해. B: 좀 쉬자.

▸ Let's break for coffee
쉬면서 커피 한잔 합시다

I need some rest 좀 쉬어야겠어

A: Why don't you get some rest?

B: That's a good idea.

    A: 좀 쉬지 그래? B: 좋은 생각야.

I need a day off 하루 쉬어야 되겠어

A: I would like to take tomorrow off.

B: Just leave your cell phone on in case we need to get in touch.

    A: 전 내일 쉬고 싶은데요. B: 연락할지 모르니 핸드폰 켜놔.

▸ He has a day off
그 사람은 오늘 하루 쉬어요

I need to take a day off 하루 좀 쉬어야겠어

A: I need to take a day off.

B: Why? Are you feeling sick?

    A: 하루 좀 쉬어야 겠어. B: 왜? 몸이 안 좋아?

How about going out for a drink tonight? 오늘 밤 한잔하러 나가자?

A: How about going out for a drink tonight?

B: Yes, let's do that.

    A: 오늘 밤 한잔하러 나가자? B: 좋아, 그렇게 하자.

▸ Let's go have a drink together tonight
오늘 밤 함께 한잔 하자

Let's have a drink 한잔 하자

A: I'm so happy it's Friday night.

B: Absolutely. Let's have a drink.

    A: 금요일 밤이어서 너무 좋아. B: 물론이지. 한잔 하자.

Chapter 06

10 할 일이 너무 많아

I've got so much to do 할 일이 많아

A: I've got so much to do.

B: Don't worry. You can manage it.

    A: 할 일이 많아. B: 걱정마. 넌 할 수 있어.

▶ I have so much to do
  할 일이 많아
▶ I have many things to do
  할 일이 많아

I have a lot to do 할 일이 많아

A: Want to come with us for a drink tonight?

B: I'd love to, but I have a lot to do.

    A: 오늘 밤 우리랑 술 한잔 하러 갈래? B: 가고야 싶지만 할 일이 많아.

▶ There's a lot of work piled up on my desk
  내 책상에 할 일이 쌓여있어

I'm tied up all day 하루 온종일 꼼짝달싹 못하고 있다

A: Will you have any time for lunch this afternoon?

B: I can't because I'm all tied up in meetings.

    A: 오늘 오후에 점심시간 낼 수 있어? B: 아니, 회의 때문에 꼼짝도 못해.

▶ I'm tied up with something urgent
  급한 일로 꼼짝달싹 못해
▶ I'm tied up at the moment
  지금 바빠서 꼼짝도 못해

I'm not available 바빠, 시간이 안돼

A: If they ask where you are, what should I tell them?

B: Just tell them that I'm not available at the moment.

    A: 너 어디갔냐고 물으면 뭐라 하지? B: 그냥 지금 바쁘다고 해.

I'm swamped (with work) 나 (일이) 엄청 바빠

A: Do you think you can give me a hand today?

B: I'm swamped with work.

    A: 오늘 저 좀 도와주실 수 있으세요? B: 일로 엄청 바쁜데요.

I had a pretty hectic day 정신없이 바빴어

A: What's up? You look so exhausted.

B: Right. I had a pretty hectic day.

    A: 왜 그래? 너 무척 지쳐보인다. B: 맞아. 오늘 정신없이 바빴어.

I'm busy with with a client 손님 때문에 바빠요

A: Are you able to take a phone call right now?

B: No, I'm busy with a client at the moment.

A: 지금 당장 전화를 받을 수 있어요? B: 아니요, 지금은 손님 때문에 바빠요.

▸ I kept myself busy
그동안 바빴어

I don't have time to breathe 숨쉴 시간도 없어

A: Is it busy at your job?

B: Yeah. I don't have time to breathe.

A: 일이 바빠? B: 어. 숨쉴 시간도 없어.

▸ I don't (even) have time to catch my breath
숨쉴 겨를이 없어

My hands are full right now 지금 무척 바빠

A: Could you come over here for an hour or two?

B: Sorry, my hands are full right now.

A: 이리와서 한두 시간 지낼 수 있어? B: 미안, 지금 무척 바빠.

▸ I've got my hands full with the work I'm doing now
지금 하는 일로 무척 바빠

I'm totally burned out 완전히 뻗었어

A: I'm stressed out. I've got so much to do.

B: Let me help you.

A: 할 일이 넘 많아. 스트레스에 지쳤어. B: 내가 도와줄게.

▸ I'm tired[worn] out
녹초가 됐어
▸ I'm stressed out
스트레스로 피곤해

I'm exhausted 지쳤어

A: Well, it looks like you haven't had much sleep lately.

B: As a matter of fact, I'm exhausted.

A: 저, 요즘 잠 못잔 것처럼 보여. B: 실은 정말 너무 피곤해.

▸ I'm so beat
지쳤다

I'm burned out 난 완전히 기운이 소진됐어

A: Why'd you quit? I thought you were making a lot of money.

B: I'm burned out.

A: 왜 그만뒀어? 돈 많이 벌었잖아. B: 너무 지쳐 녹초가 되었어.

▸ I'm wiped out
완전히 뻗었어

11 나 이건 못해

I can't do this 나 이건 못해

A: I can't do this.

B: Why not? I thought you were good at math.

A: 나 이건 못해 B: 왜 못해? 너 수학 잘하는 줄로 알고 있는데.

I'm not very good at promoting myself 나 자신을 홍보하는데 서툴러

A: I'm not very good at promoting myself.

B: You have to do that on a resume.

A: 나 자신을 홍보하는데 서툴러. B: 이력서에는 그렇게 해야 돼.

▸ I'm bad at
accounting
회계에 약해
▸ I'm hopeless with
machines
난 기계치야

I'm allergic to things like computers 컴퓨터 같은 거에 앨러지가 있어

A: I'm allergic to things like computers.

B: I bet you don't want to work in an office.

A: 컴퓨터 같은 거에 앨러지가 있어. B: 사무실에 일하면 안되겠구만.

I don't know the first thing about computers 컴퓨터의 컴자도 몰라

A: I don't know the first thing about computers.

B: I'll teach you some programming tricks.

A: 컴퓨터의 컴자도 몰라. B: 프로그래밍 요령 좀 알려줄게.

It's far beyond my ability 내 능력 밖이야

A: Why didn't you complete your assignment?

B: It's far beyond my ability.

A: 왜 과제를 다 안 한거야? B: 내 능력 밖이에요.

I'll never get through this 난 절대 못해낼거야

A: I'll never get through this.

B: You have to try harder.

A: 난 절대 못해낼거야. B: 더 열심히 해야 돼.

I don't feel up to it 내 능력으론 안돼

A: Can you help me out, Jeff?

B: I don't feel up to it.

A: 제프야 도와줄 수 있어? B: 내 능력으론 안돼.

▸ It's not up to that yet
아직 그정도는 안돼요

I can't handle all this work on my own 나 혼자 이 일을 다 처리할 수 없어

A: I can't handle all this work on my own.

B: You should hire a bookkeeper.

A: 나 혼자서 이 일을 다 처리할 수 없어. B: 경리직원을 고용해야겠네.

▸ I'm afraid it's more than I can manage
내가 할 수 있는 것 이상인 것 같아

I don't stand a chance 난 가능성이 없어

A: I heard you applied for a promotion.

B: I did, but I don't stand a chance.

A: 승진신청했다며. B: 했는데, 가능성이 없어.

▸ It was a long shot
안될걸

He doesn't have what it takes, does he? 걔는 자질이 없어. 그지?

A: Brian has been very disappointing.

B: He doesn't have what it takes, does he?

A: 브라이언에 엄청 실망했어. B: 걔는 자질이 없어. 그지?

I got cold feet 나 자신없어

A: Why did you call off your project?

B: I'm not sure. I got cold feet.

A: 왜 그 프로젝트를 취소한거야? B: 모르겠어. 자신이 없어서.

That's easy for you to say 그렇게 말하긴 쉽지

A: We expect you to follow Jeff's example.

B: That's easy for you to say.

A: 네가 제프의 전례를 따랐으면 해. B: 너희야 그렇게 말하는 게 쉽겠지.

▸ That's easier said than done
행동보단 말이 쉽지

12 내가 할 수 있어

I can do that[it, this] 내가 할 수 있어

A: We'll have to put together a proposal by the end of the week.

B: I think that we can do that.

A: 금요일까지 제안서 짜야돼. B: 난 우리가 할 수 있다는 생각이 들어.

I can do it better 내가 더 잘 할 수 있어

A: He cooks Italian food pretty well.

B: I can do it better.

A: 걘 이태리 음식을 잘 요리해. B: 내가 더 잘 할 수 있어.

Let me take care of it 나한테 맡겨

A: This guy keeps bothering me.

B: Let me take care of it.

A: 이 친구가 날 계속 괴롭히네. B: 나한테 맡겨.

▶ take care of~
처리하다, 돌보다

I'll take over now 이제 내가 책임지고 할게요

A: I'll take over now.

B: Good. I'm ready to go home.

A: 이제 내가 책임지고 할게요. B: 좋아. 나 집에 가야지.

You can count on me 나한테 맡겨

A: Can I trust you to keep a secret?

B: Sure, you can count on me.

A: 비밀 지킬거라고 믿어도 돼나요? B: 물론, 날 믿어.

▶ I'm counting on
you
난 널 믿고 있어

Leave it to me 나한테 맡겨, 내가 할게

A: Can you fix my DVD player?

B: Sure. Leave it to me.

A: DVD 플레이어 고칠 수 있어? B: 물론. 내게 맡겨.

He's very good at arithmetic 걘 계산에 능해

A: What do you think of the new computer technician?

B: He's as good at fixing problems as anyone I've ever seen.

    A: 신임 컴퓨터기술자는 어때? B: 문제 해결하는데 최고야.

▸ He's good with numbers
  걘 숫자에 강해
▸ He's familiar with all phases of this business
  걘 이 사업의 모든 단계를 잘 알아

Let me handle it[this] 내가 처리하죠

A: I'm not sure how to input these numbers.

B: Let me handle it.

    A: 이 숫자들을 어떻게 넣는지 모르겠어. B: 내가 처리하죠.

All in all, I feel he's the best choice 종합해 볼 때 걔가 최고의 선택인 것 같아

A: So you think Simon Reese should get the job?

B: All in all, I feel he's the best choice.

    A: 넌 시몬 리스가 일을 맡아야 한다고 생각해? B: 종합해볼 때, 걔가 최선인 것 같아.

▸ He's the man you want
  쟤는 네가 찾던 사람야

She's cut out for this job 쟨 이 일에 타고 났어

A: Andrea is wonderful.

B: She's cut out for this job.

    A: 앤드리어는 정말 훌륭해. B: 쟨 이 일에 타고 났어.

▸ be cut out for+N[to be~]
  …가 되기에 적합하다

Can you manage? 할 수 있겠어?

A: I've got to leave early. Can you manage?

B: Don't worry about a thing.

    A: 난 일찍 나가야 하는데, 할 수 있겠어? B: 걱정하지 마세요.

It's much easier than you think 네가 생각하는 거보다 훨씬 쉬워

A: That looks really difficult.

B: It's much easier than you think.

    A: 정말 어려워 보여. B: 네가 생각하는 거보다 훨씬 쉬워.

▸ There's nothing to it
  별거 아냐
▸ It's a cinch
  거저 먹기야(= It's a piece of cake)

13 해냈어

I made it! 해냈어!

A: I made it!

B: I'm surprised you finished the race.

A: 해냈어! B: 네가 완주하다니 놀라워.

▸ He made it big
개는 크게 해냈어
▸ You made it!
너 해냈구나!

I did it! 해냈어!

A: I did it!

B: Very nice job!

A: 해냈어! B: 아주 잘했어!

▸ You did it!
해냈구나!

You win 내가 졌어

A: I want to spend more time with my family.

B: You win. We'll visit your parents on Saturday.

A: 가족과 함께 시간을 보내고 싶어. B: 졌어. 토요일날 네 부모님 방문하자.

▸ I won
내가 이겼어
▸ You're a loser
넌 패자야, 멍청이야

You got me beat 나보다 낫네

A: Do you like the plans I created?

B: You got me beat.

A: 내가 착안한 계획 좋아? B: 나보다 낫네.

You've got me 나도 몰라.

A: Who did it?

B: You've got me.

A: 누가 그랬어? B: 나도 몰라.

She is on a roll 그 여자 한창 잘나가고 있어

A: Stephanie has been winning all night.

B: She is on a roll.

A: 스테파니가 밤새 이기고 있어. B: 한창 잘나가고 있구만.

▸ I'm on fire
잘 풀리고 있어

Now there you have me 그건 정확한 지적이야, 내가 졌어, 모르겠어

A: What will he do next?

B: Now there you have me. I don't know.

A: 걔가 다음에 뭘 할거야? B: 잘 지적해주었는데 나도 모르겠어.

▸ I've got to hand it to you!
너 정말 대단하구나, 나 너한테 두손 들었다

It works! 제대로 되네!, 효과가 있네!

A: Let's see if our cable box has been fixed.

B: It works! The repairman must have come.

A: 케이블박스가 수리되었는지 보자고. B: 된다! 수리공이 왔었구나.

▸ It worked!
된다!

I'm making (some) money 돈을 좀 벌고 있어

A: How do you like being a stockbroker?

B: I'm making some money.

A: 주식중개인은 어때? B: 돈 좀 벌고 있어.

▸ I'm making money hand over fist
돈을 왕창 벌고 있어
▸ I made a killing
떼돈 벌었어

Show me the money 돈을 벌어다 줘

A: I can offer you $169,000 for your house.

B: Yeah? Show me the money.

A: 16만 9천 달러에 너 집 살게. B: 그래? 돈 갖고와 봐.

▸ Money talks
돈으로 안되는 일 없지

I'm broke 빈털터리야

A: I'm broke.

B: It's time you got a job.

A: 돈이 다 떨어졌어. B: 직장을 가질 때도 됐지.

▸ I have no money
돈이 없어
▸ I don't have much money on me now
지금 수중에 돈이 많이 없어

I'm out of money[cash] 현금이 없어

A: Why are we going to the ATM?

B: I'm out of money.

A: 현금지급기에는 왜 가는 거야? B: 돈이 없어서.

▸ I'm a little short of money now
지금 현금이 좀 부족해

Chapter 06

14 회의 일정이 변경됐어요

- 회의 일정이 변경됐어요.

There's been a change in the meeting schedule.

> Everyone must attend the morning meeting tomorrow at 5:00 a.m.
> 모두 내일 아침 5시의 오전 회의에 참석하도록 하세요.

- 오늘 오후에 있을 회의에 참석해주세요.

I need you to attend my meeting this afternoon

> It looks like it's going to be a long meeting, doesn't it?
> 회의가 길어질 것 같네요. 그렇지 않아요?

- 회의는 차후 통보시까지 연기되었습니다.

The meeting has been put off until further notice.

> Is the conference room available?
> 회의실 쓸 수 있어요?

- 회의를 다음달까지 연기해도 되겠습니까?

Do you mind if we postpone our meeting until next month?

> There's been a change in the meeting schedule. It was postponed.
> 회의일정이 변경되었어요. 연기되었습니다.

- 전부 다 준비됐나요?

Is everything all set up?

> Can I please have a copy of the schedule?
> 일정표를 한 부 얻을 수 있을까요?

- 오늘 오후에 있을 회의시간 좀 확인해 주세요. 시간 변경은 없겠죠, 그렇죠?

I need you to double-check the time of the meeting this afternoon. There hasn't been any change in the time, has there?

- 회의는 어땠어요?

How was the meting?

▶ The meeting went well
  회의는 잘 되었습니다

MEETING

Check It Out!

Jane: I can't wait any longer.

Mark: If they're not here by now, they're probably not coming.

Jane: Let's get this show on the road.

Mark: *(to the people in the board room)* We are going to start now.

제인: 더이상 기다릴 수 없어요.
마크: 그들이 지금까지도 오지 않는 걸로 봐서 아마도 안올 모양이예요.
제인: 이제 그만 시작합시다.
마크: (회의실 안의 사람들을 향해) 이제 회의를 시작하겠습니다.

15 여러분 주목해 주십시오

- 여러분 주목해 주십시오.

May I have your attention, please?

▶ Please take your seat, as we are about to begin the meeting
모두 자리에 앉아 주십시오, 곧 회의를 시작하겠습니다

▶ Now that everyone is finally here, let's get this meeting started
이제 모두 모였으니, 회의를 시작하겠습니다

- 우선, 갑작스런 소집에도 불구하고 오늘 이렇게 참석해 주셔서 감사합니다.

First of all, I would like to thank you for coming today on such short notice.

- 회장님의 개회사로 회의를 시작하겠습니다.

We would like to begin with some opening remarks from our CEO.

- 회의를 시작하기 전에, 오하이오의 자매사(社)에서 오신 맥케이씨를 소개하겠습니다.

Before we get started, I'd like to introduce Mr. Mackay from our sister company in Ohio.

- 오늘 회의에는 영업을 담당하는 스미스 씨와 품질 관리 전문가인 클라크 씨가 함께 하겠습니다.

At our meeting today, we have Mr. Smith, who is in charge of sales. Also, we have Ms. Clark, who is a quality control specialist.

● 카터씨, 지난번 회의록을 낭독해 주시겠습니까?

Mr. Carter, would you please read the minutes from the last meeting?

▶ Before we start, let's briefly review the last meeting's notes
시작하기 전에 간단히 지난번 회의록을 검토해 봅시다

● 잠깐 통화를 할 동안 여러분끼리 자기소개를 하시지 그래요?

Why don't you introduce yourselves while I take this short phone call?

▶ Let's speak(talk) in English
영어로 말합시다

Check It Out!

Susan: Everyone, this is Jim, our new marketing expert.

Paul: Welcome aboard, Jim.

Susan: Paul, would you mind reading the minutes from the last meeting?

Paul: Not at all, just let me get my glasses.

수잔: 여러분, 이 분은 새 마케팅 전문가로 오신 짐입니다.
폴: 반가워요, 짐.
수잔: 폴, 지난 번 회의록을 낭독해 주시겠어요?
폴: 그러죠, 잠깐 안경 좀 끼구요.

16 이번 회의의 목적은…

- 이번 회의의 목적은 첫째 3사분기의 이윤을 검토하기 위함이며, 둘째로 4사분기의 새 전략에 관해 의논하기 위해서입니다.

Our goal for this meeting is, first, to go over our third quarter's profit, and secondly, to discuss new strategies for the fourth quarter.

▶ The goal for this meeting is to~
이번 회의의 목적은…

- 이미 알고 계시겠지만, 우리의 주식이 이번 분기 말까지 한 번 더 분할될 것입니다.

As you probably know, our stock is going to split once again before the end of the quarter.

▶ As you (probably) know,~
아시다시피,…

- 현재, 상황이 위급합니다. 따라서 우리는 앞으로 48시간 이내에 결정을 내려야 합니다.

The situation is now critical, so we will need to make a decision in the next 48 hours.

▶ The situation is now~
현재상황은…

- 이번 회의는 첫째 우리 경영진에 대해 떠도는 소문에 관해 얘기하고, 둘째로 회사 재정상태가 어렵다는 소문을 종식시키기 위해 소집되었습니다.

I've called this meeting first, to discuss the rumors about our manager, and secondly, to put an end to the speculation that the company is in financial trouble.

▶ I've called this meeting to~
이번 회의를 소집한 것은….

- 아시다시피, 우리가 이번 회의를 갖는 것은 내년도 우리 회사의 비즈니스 전략을 토의하기 위함입니다.

As you probably know, we are holding this meeting to discuss our company's business strategy for next year.

▶ We're holding this meeting to discuss~
이번 회의는 …을 논의하기 위해서입니다

Check It Out!

Speaker: Good afternoon ladies and gentle-men. As you may have read in the agenda for today's meeting, the main objective here today is to educate you on the dangers of not using a water filter for your tap water. Mr. Jones... a local environmental scientist... will join us later to talk about his findings. Please hold all of your questions until the end of the presentation... at which time either myself or Mr. Jones will be happy to try to answer them.

사회자: 신사숙녀 여러분 안녕하십니까. 오늘 회의에 대한 의사 일정에서 읽으셨다시피, 오늘의 주요 의제는 수도에 필터를 이용하지 않을 시의 위험성에 대한 교육입니다. 지역 환경 연구가이신 존스 씨께서 잠시 후 자신의 연구 결과에 대해 얘기해 주시겠습니다. 발표가 끝날 때까지 질문을 삼가해 주십시오. 존슨씨의 발표가 끝나면 저나 존슨씨가 기꺼이 질문에 대답해 드리겠습니다.

17 안건을 시작하죠

● 오늘 우리가 집중적으로 다뤄야 할 본 안건으로 들어갑시다.

Let's get started on the main issues that we're going to focus on today.

▶ Let's get started on the main issues (that)~
…한 본 안건을 시작합시다

● 본론으로 들어가 이제 토론하죠.

Let's get down to the business that we are all here to discuss.

▶ Let's get down to the business (that)~
…한 본론으로 들어가죠

● 첫번째 안건은 채용절차 개선 문제입니다.

The first thing on the agenda is revising our hiring procedures.

▶ The first thing on the agenda is the issue involving a reorganization of our staff.
첫번째 안건은 사원 재편성에 관한 문제입니다.

▶ The first thing on the agenda is~
첫번째 안건은…

● 이 문제는 이제 그만 마무리하고 다음 주제로 넘어가죠.

I think it's time to close up this argument and go on to our next topic.

▶ Shall we go on to the next item on the agenda?
다음 안건으로 넘어갈까요?

● 블랙 씨께서 먼저 시작해 주시겠어요?

Mr. Black, would you like to begin?

▶ A, would you like to begin?
A씨, 시작해주시겠어요?

• 그린 씨께서 사내 안전에 관한 토론을 먼저 시작해 주시겠어요?

Mr. Green, would you like to begin the discussion on safety in the workplace?

▶ A, would you like to open[begin] the discussion on~ A씨, …관한 토론을 시작해주시겠어요?

▶ Who would like to begin the discussion today? 누가 오늘 토론을 시작하시겠어요?

▶ Whose turn is it next? 다음은 누구 차례죠?

▶ Who's next? 누가 할 차례죠?

Check It Out!

Black: The first thing on the agenda is the matter concerning the decrease in numbers here at our location.

Jax: What do you mean?

Black: Well, we have 144 employees, but we are going to have to downsize.

Jax: How many people do you expect to have to let go?

Black: Well, we worked out a scenario that would leave us with 134 workers.

Jax: So only ten staff would have to leave?

Black: Yes, but ten is a lot, and we will have to figure out where to take them from.

Jax: Why don't we think about combining some job responsibilities?

Black: Actually, that is next on our agenda! Shall we go on to the next item already since it has come up?

Jax: Sure. Who's next?

블랙: 첫번째 안건은 이곳에 있는 인원을 줄이는 것에 관한 문제입니다.
잭스: 무슨 말씀이시죠?
블랙: 음, 현재 우리는 144명의 직원이 있는데, 감원을 해야 하겠습니다.
잭스: 몇 명이나 해고해야 할까요?
블랙: 글쎄요, 134명의 직원을 남겨둔다는 계획을 세웠습니다.
잭스: 그럼 고작 10명만 그만두게 되겠군요?
블랙: 그래요, 하지만 10명은 많은 인원입니다. 그리고 어느 부서의 인원을 줄여야할 지도 생각해야 하구요.
잭스: 직무를 통합하는 건 어떨까요?
블랙: 사실, 다음 안건이 바로 그거예요! 이미 말이 나온 김에 다음 안건으로 넘어갈까요?
잭스: 그러죠. 다음 차례가 누구죠?

MEETING
Board of Directors

 …에 대해 어떻게 생각하십니까?

● 쓰레기 매립지에 대한 새 제안에 대해 어떻게 생각하십니까?

What do you think about the new proposal for the landfill site?

▶ What do you think about~ ?
…에 관해 어떻게 생각하십니까?

● 우리의 뮤츄얼펀드에 투자액이 증가하고 있는 현상에 대해 어떻게 생각하세요?

What are your views on the increasing amount of money being invested in our mutual fund?

▶ What are your views on~ ?
…대해 어떻게 생각하시나요?

● 모금행사 운동을 통해 지역사회를 후원하는 문제에 대해 어떻게 생각하세요?

What's your opinion about supporting the local community through their fundraising efforts?

▶ What's your opinion about~ ?
…관해 어떤 의견을 갖고 계신가요?

● 지난 달 매출 감소에 대해 어떤 의견이라도 있으십니까?

Do you have any concerns about the decrease in sales that has been occurring this past month?

▶ Do you have any concerns about~ ?
…에 대해 어떤 의견이라도 있습니까?

● 최종표결에 들어가기 전에 이 상황에 대해 의견을 제시하실 분 계십니까?

Has anybody any comments to make before we take a final vote on the situation?

▶ Has anybody any comments to make~ ?
의견을 제시할 분 계십니까?

▸ Does anyone have any comments or considerations ~ ?
　…할 문제나 의견이 있는 사람 있나요?

● 내일 아침에 있을 인수건에 대해 어떻게 생각하십니까?

What are your feelings about the takeover that is scheduled to occur tomorrow morning?

▸ What are your feelings about~?
　…에 관해 어떻게 생각하십니까?

Check It Out!

Janet: What are your feelings about the new project?

Stanley: I have mixed feelings and would like more time to reflect on the issue.

Janet: What are your views on the layout of the building?

Stanley: I like the proposed building, but I'm just unsure of the project location.

Janet: How about another idea?

Stanley: Well, give me some time and I may be able to think of an alternative.

Janet: Okay. How about if I give everyone until Monday to decide?

Stanley: That sounds all right, but don't we have to send off a response today?

Janet: Yes, but I think I can stall them.

Stanley: Well, I think that would be the best idea.

자넷: 새 프로젝트에 대해 어떻게 생각하십니까?
스탠리: 혼란스럽습니다. 좀더 생각할 시간이 있다면 좋겠군요.
자넷: 건물설계에 대한 의견은 어떠세요?
스탠리: 제안된 건물은 마음에 듭니다만,부지 선정 계획에 대해선 확신할 수가 없습니다.
자넷: 다른 아이디어가 있나요?
스탠리: 글쎄요, 시간을 좀 주시면 대안을 생각해낼 수 있을 것 같은데요.
자넷: 알겠습니다. 모두에게 월요일까지 생각할 시간을 드리면 되겠습니까?
스탠리: 물론 그러면 좋지만, 오늘 회답을 보내야 하지 않나요?
자넷: 네, 하지만 제가 시간을 좀 벌어 볼게요.
스탠리: 음, 그러면 최고죠.

19 개인적으로 …하다고 생각합니다

● 개인적으로 매우 힘든 프로젝트라고 생각됩니다.

Personally, I believe that it would be a very difficult project.

▶ (Personally), I think[believe] that~
(개인적으로) …라고 생각합니다

● 계속 밀고 나가면, 매출이 증가하리라고 확신합니다.

I really believe that if we persist, there will be an increase in sales.

▶ I really believe that~
…을 확신합니다

● 제 의견으로는 그밖의 다른 문제가 발생하기 전에 즉시 공장 가동을 중단해야 한 다고 생각합니다.

In my opinion, we should close the plant immediately, before there are any other problems.

▶ In my opinion,~
제 의견으로는

▶ As I see it,~
제가 보기에

● 그 보고서는 무작위 표본 조사는 아닌 것 같습니다만.

It seems to me that the report is not a random sample study.

▶ It seems to me that~
…인 것 같습니다

▶ It seems to me that we might be making the right decision
올바른 결정을 내리는 것 같아요

● 이 일에 보다 적합한 사람을 찾을 수 없다고 확신합니다.

I'm sure that you won't be able to find a better person for the job.

▶ I'm sure that~
…을 확신합니다

● 몇 달 새 시장경기가 반전되리라 확신합니다.

I'm convinced that the market will turn around in a few months.

▶ I'm convinced that~

…을 확신합니다

● 틀림없이 그가 우리의 요구에 응하여 거래를 맺게 될 것입니다.

I feel quite sure that he will return our calls and sign a deal with us.

▶ I feel quite sure that~

틀림없이 …라고 생각합니다

Check It Out!

Bill: What do you think of the decision to merge companies?

Anna: It seems to me that a merger will mean that we have to restructure internally.

Tom: Well, in my opinion we are in need of some restructuring amongst the employees anyway.

Bill: That may be the case, but let's remain focused on the issue at hand.

Anna: The way I see it is that it would be in our best interest financially, but it will be quite chaotic.

Tom: In the short term it would be messy, but in the long term, we would be much better off.

빌: 회사를 합병하자는 결정에 대해 어떻게 생각하십니까?
안나: 합병을 하게 되면 내부 구조조정이 필요할 것 같은데요.
톰: 글쎄요, 제 생각으론, 어찌됐건 종업원 구조조정은 필요하다고 봅니다.
빌: 그럴 수도 있겠죠. 하지만 지금은 당면한 문제에 초점을 맞춰 얘기를 해나갑시다.
안나: 제가 보기엔 재정적으로는 최상의 이득을 볼 수도 있겠지만, 큰 혼란이 있을 것으로 예상됩니다.
톰: 단기적으로는 혼란이 따르겠지만, 장기적으로는 훨씬 나은 일이 될 겁니다.

20 …을 강력히 제안하는 바입니다

- 시제품(試製品)은 좀더 테스트를 거쳐야 한다고 강력히 제안하는 바입니다.

We strongly recommend that the prototype undergo more testing.

▶ We strongly recommend that~

…을 강력히 제안합니다

- 비록 그게 일시적인 해고라는 대가를 치르더라도 우린 계획대로 밀고 나가야 합니다.

We must stick to our plan, which may mean some temporary layoffs.

▶ We must~

…을 해야 합니다

- 시장이 달아있을 때 부동산을 매각하자고 건의하는 바입니다.

My recommendation is that we sell the property while the market is hot.

▶ My suggestion [recommendation] is that~

…을 제안합니다

- 지난 주 제 동료 한사람이 알려준 건의사항이 하나 있습니다.

I have a suggestion that was given to me by a colleague last week.

▶ I have a suggestion that ~

…을 제안합니다

- 유일한 해결책은 논쟁을 멈추고 그들에게 5% 급여인상을 해주는 것입니다.

The only solution is to give in and give them the five-percent raise.

▶ The only solution is to~

유일한 해결책은…

- 가능한 한 빨리 대안을 제시하는 수밖에 다른 방도가 없습니다.

The only other alternative is to submit a counteroffer as soon as possible.

▶ The only other alternative is to~
유일한 대안은….

- 몇 명이나 건의된 계획을 마음에 들어하는지 알아봅시다.

Let's get an idea of how many people like the proposed plan.

▶ How about~ ? …은 어떨까요?
▶ Why don't we~? …을 합시다

Check It Out!

Michael: We strongly recommend that you take the offer.

Louise: I think we should think it over.

Michael: If I were you I wouldn't wait too long.

Louise: It might be a good idea to take this offer before they change their mind.

Michael: Is there an expiry date on the offer?

Louise: Yes. It can be rescinded at the end of the week.

Michael: That gives you a few days to think about it.

Louise: You're right.

Michael: Are we likely to get such an offer from another company?

Louise: You might, but it is really hard to say for sure.

마이클: 그 제의를 받아들여야 한다고 강력히 주장하는 바입니다.
루이스: 제 생각엔 꼼꼼하게 검토를 해봐야 할 것 같은데요.
마이클: 저라면 그리 오래 두고보지는 않겠습니다.
루이스: 그 사람들이 마음을 바꾸기 전에 제의를 받아들이는 것도 괜찮을 것 같군요.
마이클: 그 제의에 기한이 있습니까?
루이스: 네. 이번 금요일에 무효가 됩니다.
마이클: 그러면 생각할 시간이 며칠은 남아있는 거로군요.
루이스: 그런 셈이죠.
마이클: 다른 회사에서도 이런 제의가 들어올 가능성이 있을까요?
루이스: 그럴 수도 있겠지만, 자신은 못하겠습니다.

21 ···하자는데 찬성입니다

MEETING

● 월요일 아침 일찍 그 계약에 관해 총투표를 하자는 데 찬성입니다.

I'm for having a general vote on the contract first thing Monday morning.

▶ I'm for~
···에 찬성합니다

● 네, 그건 사실입니다만, 지금으로부터 2년 후면 이 상황이 어떻게 될까요?

Yes, that may be true, but what will the situation be like two years from now?

▶ That may be true, but~
그건 사실이지만···

▶ Well, you have a point there, but~
음, 당신 말에도 일리는 있습니다만···

● 무슨 말씀인지 잘 알겠습니다만, 다른 사람들도 그렇게 생각하지는 않을 겁니다.

I can see your point, but I don't think the others feel the same way about it.

▶ I can see your point, but~
무슨 말씀인지 알겠지만···

● 말도 안됩니다. 현재 우리에겐 재정지원이 없잖습니까.

That's out of the question, we don't have the financial backing.

▶ That's out of the question,
말도 안됩니다···

● 우리에게 협력사가 없다면 그 의견에 전적으로 반대입니다.

I'm absolutely against the idea, unless we have a partner.

▶ I'm (absolutely) against~
전적으로 ···반대합니다

- 그 제안에 반대합니다. 왜냐하면, 첫째 시행착오를 거칠 여유가 없고, 둘째 그것은 성장을 고려하지 않았습니다.

I'm against the proposal, because firstly, there is no room for error, and secondly, it doesn't allow for growth.

▶ I'm against~ , because firstly, 주어+동사~ and secondly, 주어+동사~
첫째는 … 둘째는 …라는 이유로 반대합니다

Check It Out!

Sean: I'm in favor of the new contract.

Beth: I wouldn't say that I'm in favor, but it's better than nothing.

Sean: What does the union think of the proposal?

Jimmy: We just gave it to them a few hours ago, but they seem to be happy.

Sean: Do we have an idea when they will vote on it?

Jimmy: I think they're hoping to vote on it next week.

Beth: Can we extend the contract for another year?

Jimmy: I think if we offer them an additional two percent in year three they would.

Sean: Let's open the floor for discussion on extending the contract.

Beth: I think it's a good idea and it would make the union happy.

손: 저는 새로운 계약에 찬성입니다.
베스: 찬성한다고 하긴 좀 그렇지만, 아무일도 않는 것보단 낫겠지요.
손: 노조에서는 이 제안에 대해 어떻게 생각하고 있습니까?
지미: 몇 시간 전에 그들에게 막 얘기를 했는데, 만족스러운 듯이 보였습니다.
손: 그들이 이 문제로 언제 투표를 할 거라고 보십니까?
지미: 제 생각으론 다음 주쯤에 투표를 하고싶어 하는 것 같습니다만.
베스: 계약을 한 해 더 연장할 수 있을까요?
지미: 우리측에서 3년째 되는 해에 추가 2퍼센트를 그들에게 제공한다면 가능할 겁니다.
손: 그럼, 계약 연장 문제에 관해 토론해 봅시다.
베스: 훌륭한 아이디어라고 생각합니다. 노조에서도 좋아할 거라고 봐요.

22 …하는데 동의하십니까?

● 협상을 계속해야 한다는데 동의하십니까?

Do we agree that we should proceed with the negotiations?

▶ Do we agree that~ ?
…에 동의하십니까?

● 더 이상의 반대의견이 없으시면 투표에 들어가겠습니다.

If there are no more objections then we should vote on the matter.

▶ If there are no more objections (then) we should~
더이상 반대의견이 없으면, …을 하겠습니다

● 모든 분들이 다 찬성하신다면 이제 이 문제를 처리할 위원회를 조직해야겠습니다.

If everyone's in favor, we should create a committee to deal with the issue.

▶ If everyone's in favor[agreement] (then) we should~
모두 찬성한다면 …을 하겠습니다

● 지금까지 우리가 토론한 것을 정리해 봅시다.

Let's summarize what we have done up until now.

▶ Let's summarize~
…을 정리해보죠

● 이로써 우리는 사람들에게 정보를 제공하기 위한 일련의 모임을 개최해야 한다는데 동의했습니다.

To summarize, we agreed that we should hold a series of meetings to inform the public.

▶ To summarize[conclude], we agreed[decided] that~
요약하자면, …에 동의했습니다

- 최종결론엔 이르지 못했지만 내일이면 협상을 마무리할 수 있을 것입니다.

We haven't made a final decision, but we expect to finish negotiations tomorrow.

▶ We haven't made a final decision, but~
최종결론엔 이르지 못했지만, …

Check It Out!

Jude: Does anyone have an objection to the proposal, or the dates surrounding the implementation?

Steve: No.

Jude: Good, then we can move on. Are there any questions regarding who's in charge of what?

Bacon: I wasn't clear of who was in charge of the on-site construction.

Jude: Mr. Green will be looking after everything on-site.

Steve: Let's summarize the project, shall we?

Jude: Sure. The construction is running on time. So far we have decided that we will meet every Wednesday to discuss how the project is progressing.

쥬드: 이 제안에 대해서나 완공일자에 대해 반대의견 있으신 분 계십니까?
스티브: 없습니다.
쥬드: 좋습니다. 그럼 다음으로 넘어가서, 각 업무의 담당자에 관해 의문점은 없습니까?
베이컨: 건설 현장 담당자가 누구인지 잘 모르겠습니다.
쥬드: 그린 씨께서 현장의 모든 일을 처리하실 겁니다.
스티브: 이만 프로젝트를 요약해볼까요?
쥬드: 그럽시다. 공사는 예정대로 진행되고 있습니다. 지금까지 우리는 이 프로젝트가 어떻게 진척되고 있는지를 토론하기 위해 매주 수요일마다 모이기로 결정했습니다.

Chapter 07

숫자영어

01 87.5점을 받았어

I got a score of 87.5(eighty-seven point five) percent

87.5점 받았어

A: How did you do on your exam?

B: I got a score of 87.5(eighty-seven point five) percent.

A: 시험 어떻게 봤어? B: 87.5점 받았어.

I usually wear size 9 1/2(nine and a half) 보통 9와 2분의 1사이즈를 신어

A: What size shoes do you wear?

B: I usually wear size 9 1/2(nine and a half).

A: 신발사이즈가 어떻게 돼? B: 보통 9와 2분의 1사이즈를 신어.

I saved five times as much as I did last year 작년보다 5배나 저축했어

A: How much money did you save this summer?

B: I saved five times as much as I did last year.

A: 이번 여름에 얼마나 저축했어? B: 작년보다 5배나 더했어.

I think it's about 4.5[four point five] meters long 4.5 미터쯤 될 거예요

A: How long is the rope?

B: I think it's about 4.5[four point five] meters long.

A: 로프 길이가 어떻게 돼? B: 4.5 미터쯤 될 거예요.

 분수 소수 말하는 법

1. **분수** 기수/서수, 기수/서수s(분자가 복수일 때)

   ex. 1/5 = one fifth   2/3 = two thirds   6 3/4 = six and three quarters

2. **소수** 기수 + .(point) + 기수

   ex. 3.3 = three point three   15.57 = fifteen point five seven   0.2 = (zero) point two

3. **수식**

   ex. 3 + 7 = 10 : Three plus seven equals ten, Three plus seven makes ten.

   ex. 6 - 4 = 2 : Six minus four equals two, Six minus four is two.

   ex. 5 x 9 = 45 : Five times nine equals forty-five, Five nines are forty-five.

   ex. 6÷3 = 2 : Six divided by three equals two. Six divided by three is two

02 1978년에 태어났어

He was born in 1978 1978년에 태어났어

A: How old is your father?

B: He was born in 1978.

A: 아버님 연세가 어떻게 돼? B: 1978년에 태어나셨어.

In the early '90s(nineties) 90년대 초반에요

A: When did you graduate from university?

B: In the early '90s(nineties).

A: 대학교 언제 졸업했어요? B: 90년대 초반에요.

What're you planning to do on the 31st of December? 12/31일에 뭐해?

A: What're you planning to do on the 31st of December?

B: I'll get together with my friends.

A: 12월 31일에 뭐 할거야? B: 친구들이랑 놀거야.

She's in her early twenties 그녀는 20대 초반야.

A: Tell me about your new girlfriend.

B: Well, she's in her early twenties.

A: 새로 사귄 애인에 대해 얘기해봐. B: 그래, 그녀는 20대 초반야.

 연월일/나이 말하는 법

1. 월일(month, date) 말하기

   「month+ date의 서수」 ex. November 25th

   「the + date의 서수 + of + month」 ex. the 25th of November

   ex. September 15th = September fifteenth 혹은 the fifteenth of September.

2. 년도 말하기 | 4자리를 두개씩 끊어읽는 것이 일반적이다

   ex. 1999 nineteen ninety-nine ex. 2000 two thousand

   ex. 2005 two thousand five ex. 2012 two thousand twelve

3. 나이말하기 20대: in one's twenties 30대: in one's thirties

   ex. 20대 초(중,후)반 : in one's early(mid, late) twenties

Chapter 07

03 4달러 50센트입니다

Here we are, sir. That'll be $4.50 다 왔습니다. 손님. 4달러 50센트입니다

A: Here we are, sir. That'll be $4.50.

B: Keep the change.

A: 다 왔습니다. 손님. 4달러 50센트입니다. B:거스름돈은 가져요.

It's area code four, one, six, two, two, five, double oh, four, one 지역번호 416에 225-0041야

A: What's his office telephone number in Toronto?

B: It's area code four, one, six, seven, six, eight, double oh, four, one (416 768-0041). A: 그의 토론토 사무실 번호가 어떻게 돼지? B: 지역번호 416에 778-0041야.

It's 010-3794-5450 010-3794-5450입니다

A: Do you have an office telephone number?

B: Yes, but my cell phone is easier to reach. It's 010-3794-5450.

A: 사무실에 전화 있죠? B: 네, 근데 휴대폰으로 하시는 게 더 편할 거예요. 010-3794-5450입니다.

It's Jero_[underline or underbar]t@aol.com

제로 언더라인 티 앳 에이오엘 닷컴야

A: What's your e-mail address?

B: It's Jero_t@aol.com A: 이메일 주소가 어떻게 돼? B: 제로 언더라인 티 앳 에이오엘 닷컴야.

 카드(전화)번호/돈 말하는 법

1. 카드번호 말하기 숫자를 하나하나 따로 기수로 읽어주면 된다

2. 돈말하기
   ex. $9.23: nine twenty-three / nine dollars and twenty-three cents
   ex. $11.03: eleven oh three / eleven dollars and three cents
   ex. $3,000: three thousand dollars / three grand

3. 전화번호 카드번호 읽듯이 숫자 하나하나를 각각 기수로 읽어주면 된다
   ex. 867-0023 : eight, six, seven, double oh, two, three
   ex. 010-9876-5100 oh, one, oh, nine, eight, seven, six, five, one hundred

04 5시 24분이야

What time is it now? 지금 몇시야?

A: Do you have the time?

B: It's twelve o'clock.

A: 시간 좀 알려줄래요? B: 12시네요.

▶ Do you have the time?
몇시야?
▶ What time have you got?
몇시야?

It's five twenty-four 5시 24분야

A: What time do you have?

B: It's five twenty-four.

A: 지금 몇시야? B: 5시 24분.

▶ It's ten to two
10시 2분야
▶ It's five after[past] one
1시 5분야

The clock is five minutes slow[behind] 시계가 5분 늦어

A: Is that the right time?

B: No. The clock is five minutes slow.

A: 맞는 시간야? B: 아니, 5분 늦게가.

▶ The clock is five minutes fast
시계가 5분 빨리가

It's 37°(thirty-seven degrees) celsius and sunny 37도이고 화창해

A: How's the weather in Florida?

B: It's 37°(thirty-seven degrees) celsius and sunny.

A: 플로리다의 날씨는 어때? B: 37도이고 화창해.

 시간/기온 말하는 법

1. **시간/기온말하기** 시간과 분을 구분해서 각각 기수로 읽으면 된다

ex.11: 34 : (It's) eleven thirty-four   ex. 9시 14분 : nine fourteen

ex. 7:04 : seven oh[ou] four   ex. 4:00 : It's exactly four o'clock

ex. 9:05 : It's five past nine   ex. 8시 56분 : It's four to nine

Chapter 07

05 맨체스터가 3대 1로 이겼어

Manchester United won three to one 맨체스터 유나이티드가 3대 1로 이겼어

A: Who won the game last night?

B: Manchester United won three to one.

    A: 지난밤에 누가 이겼어? B: 맨체스터 유나이티드가 3대 1로 이겼어.

Can you believe Chicago White Sox crushed the Yankees by a score of five to zero?

시카고 화이트삭스가 양키스를 5대 0으로 묵사발냈다는 것이 믿기지 않아

A: Can you believe Chicago White Sox crushed the Yankees by a score of five to zero?

B: No, way!!

    A: 시카고 화이트삭스가 양키스를 5대 0으로 묵사발냈다는 것이 믿기지 않아. B: 그럴리가!!

We're winning by two goals 우리가 두 골차로 이기고 있어

A: Who's winning the game?

B: We're winning by two goals.

    A: 누가 이기고 있어? B: 우리가 두 골차로 이기고 있어.

Colorado is leading by two points 콜로라도가 2점차로 이기고 있어

A: What's the score?

B: Colorado is leading by two points.

    A: 점수는? B: 콜로라도가 2점차로 이기고 있어.

The Red Sox lost five to four 보스톤이 5대 4로 졌어

A: The Red Sox lost five to four.

B: It's because of David Wells. He's lost his pitching ability.

    A: 보스톤 레드삭스가 5:4로 졌어. B: 데이빗 웰스가 제대로 던지질 못해서 그랬어.

They won by four points 4점차로 이겼어

A: What was the score of Korea's soccer match against Iran?

B: It wasn't even close. They won by two points.

A: 한국과 이란과의 축구 결과가 어떻게 됐어? B: 차이가 많이 났어. 2점차로 이겼어.

The Jets beat the Flames seven to five 젯츠가 플레임즈를 7:5로 이겼어

A: Who won the game?

▶ Giants by five
자이언츠가 5점차로 이겼어

B: The Jets beat the Flames seven to five.

A: 누가 이겼어? B: 젯츠가 플레임즈를 7대 5로 이겼어.

They were ahead at halftime 그들이 전반전에 이기고 있었어

A: Do you know the results of the Cowboy's football game?

B: No, but they were ahead at halftime.

A: 카우보이팀 미식축구 결과 알아? B: 아니, 하지만 전반전에는 앞서고 있었어.

3-2[three two] with 15 minutes to go 15분 남겨놓고 3대 2로 이기고 있어

A: What's the score?

B: 3-2[three two] with 15 minutes to go.

A: 점수는? B: 15분 남겨놓고 3대 2로 이기고 있어.

It ended in a one-one draw 1:1로 끝났어

A: France played Italy in yesterday's soccer match.

B: Yep. It ended in a one-one draw.

A: 어제 프랑스와 이태리가 축구했어. B: 그래. 일대일로 무승부됐어.

Their players didn't try hard enough, and they lost

열심히 안뛰더니 지더라고

A: Why do you think Real Madrid only had one goal?

B: Their players didn't try hard enough, and they lost.

A: 레알마드리드가 왜 겨우 한 점을 얻은거야? B: 선수들이 열심히 뛰지 않더라고, 그러더니 졌어.

She just couldn't turn it around 다시 뒤집지를 못했어

A: Why wasn't Shrarapova able to win her tennis match?

B: She started losing by two sets and she just couldn't turn it around.

A: 사라포바가 왜 게임을 졌어? B: 2세트를 지고나서는 다시 뒤집지를 못했어.

Sung-Hyun Park is five strokes behind the leader

박성현은 선두와 5타 뒤져

A: Sung-Hyun Park is five strokes behind the leader.

B: I don't think she'll be able to win this tournament.

A: 박성현은 선두와 5타 뒤지고 있어. B: 이번 토너멘드는 이기지 못할 것 같아.

Michelle had an impressive round of golf today

미셸이 오늘 골프를 인상적으로 쳤어

A: Michelle had an impressive round of gold today.

B: She was able to score less than seventy on the course.

A: 미셸이 오늘 골프를 아주 인상적으로 쳤어. B: 70타도 안되게 쳤어.

스포츠 경기 결과 말하는 법

1. 몇 대 몇으로 이겼다고 할 때는
    - ex. The Boston Red Sox beat the New York Yankees by a score of 10 to 3 (ten to three)
    - ex. The Bears defeated the Raiders (by a score of) 42 to 7
    - ex. The Blue Jays won 5 to 3

2. 졌다고 말하는 경우는
    - ex. The Mariners were defeated by the Yankees in overtime by a score of 1 to 0 (one to zero, one to nothing)
    - ex. The Giants lost the game by a score of 3 to 2
        Montreal lost to Denver by two goals last night

3. 비겼을 경우에는
        The game ended in a tie

4. 기타로는
    - ex. We're winning by three goals ex. We are down 2 to 3
    - ex. The Bulls are leading by eight points

Chapter 08

연애영어

Step 1 데이트
Step 2 사랑
Step 3 결혼/이혼

01 그 사람 내 타입이네

He's really my type 그 사람 내 타입이네

A: What do you think about her?

B: Oh, she's not really my type.

    A: 걔 어떻게 생각해? B: 어, 걔 정말 내 타입 아냐.

▶ You're my type
년 내 타입야

He is Mr. Right 걘 내 이상형이야

A: Why did you decide to get married to Glenn?

B: He is Mr. Right. I know it.

    A: 왜 글렌과 결혼하기로 결심한거야? B: 걘 내 이상형야. 난 알아.

▶ The right woman
is just waiting for
you
네 연분이 널 기다리고 있
다구

What type of man[woman] do you like? 어떤 남자[여자]를 좋아해?

A: What type of man do you like?

B: I like guys who are smart and a little cute.

    A: 어떤 남자형을 좋아해? B: 똑똑하고 좀 귀여운 남자를 좋아해.

May I ask you out? 데이트 신청해도 돼요?

A: May I ask you out?

B: Sorry, I have a boyfriend.

    A: 데이트 신청해도 되나요? B: 미안, 남자친구가 있어요.

▶ Would you go on
a date with me?
나와 데이트 할래요?

Are you asking me out? 데이트 신청하는거야?

A: I was wondering if I could maybe buy you a cup of coffee.

B: Are you asking me out?

    A: 커피 사줘도 될까요? B: 데이트 신청하는거예요?

▶ Are you asking
me for a date?
데이트 하자고 하는 거야?

▶ Are you asking
me out on a date?
데이트 신청하는 거야?

He's going out with Jane 그 사람은 제인하고 사귀는 중이야

A: I wish Frank would ask me out.

B: Impossible. He's going out with Jane.

    A: 프랭크가 내게 데이트 신청하면 좋을 텐데. B: 불가능해. 걘 제인하고 사귀잖아.

Are you seeing someone? 누구 사귀는 사람 있어?

A: Are you seeing someone these days?

B: Yeah, I'm going out with Eric again.

   A: 요즘 만나는 사람 있어? B: 어, 에릭과 다시 사귀고 있어.

▸ Are you dating anyone now?
지금 사귀는 사람 있어?
▸ Are you going steady with someone?
애인 있어?

I'm seeing her 난 그녀하고 사귀고 있어

A: How is your relationship with Jinny?

B: I'm seeing her, but not seriously.

   A: 지니와의 관계는 어때? B: 만나고는 있지만 심각한 사이는 아냐.

▸ I'm not seeing anybody
난 지금 사귀는 사람 없어

I'm just flirting 좀 추근거린 것뿐이야, 작업 좀 들어간 것뿐인데

A: Are you interested in Tina?

B: I'm just flirting.

   A: 티나에게 관심있어? B: 좀 작업들어간 것뿐인데.

Are you coming on to me? 지금 날 유혹하는 거예요?

A: Are you coming on to me?

B: I find you really attractive.

   A: 날 유혹하는 거예요? B: 당신 정말 매력적이야.

▸ Are you trying to seduce me?
날 유혹하는 거야?

Are you hitting on me? 지금 날 꼬시는거야?

A: I think your sister was hitting on me.

B: What are you talking about?

   A: 네 누이가 날 꼬시는 것 같아. B: 그게 무슨 말야?

He made a move on me 그 사람 내게 추근대던데

A: Why don't you like my husband?

B: He made a move on me.

   A: 왜 내 남편을 싫어하는 거야? B: 내게 수작 걸었어.

▸ He made a pass at me
그 남자가 나한테 수작을 걸었어

02 난 너한테 빠져있어

I'm crazy about you 난 너한테 빠져있어

A: I'm crazy about her.

B: And she feels the same way?

A: 난 걔한테 푹 빠졌어. B: 걔도 그래?

▸ I'm nuts[mad]
about you
널 미친듯이 좋아해

I've got a crush on you 난 네가 맘에 들어

A: I've got a crush on you.

B: Gosh, this is a little embarrassing.

A: 난 네가 맘에 들어. B: 맙소사. 좀 당황스럽구만.

▸ I had a crush on a
teacher once and
it was so hard
선생님을 좋아한 적이 있는
데 무척 힘들었어

I'm so into you 나 너한테 푹 빠져 있어

A: Do you really like me?

B: Absolutely. I'm so into you.

A: 정말 날 좋아해? B: 당연하지. 난 너한테 푹 빠져 있어.

I have (strong) feelings for her 나 쟤한테 마음있어

A: Melissa still has feelings for you!

B: She does?

A: 멜리사는 아직도 네게 감정이 있어! B: 걔가 그래?

▸ You've had
feelings for me?
너 나한테 마음있지?

He has[got] a thing for her 걘 그 여자를 맘에 두고 있어

A: Why is Ryan always with Lisa?

B: He has a thing for her.

A: 라이언은 왜 항상 리사와 함께 있어! B: 걔를 좋아해.

What do you see in her? 그 여자 뭐가 좋아?, 어디가 좋은 거야?

A: What do you see in her?

B: She's smart, and she likes stylish clothes.

A: 그 여자 뭐가 좋아? B: 똑똑하지 그리고 멋진 옷을 좋아한다고.

▸ What do you see
in this guy?
이 사람 어디가 좋은 거야?

They really hit it off 쟤네들은 바로 좋아하더라고

A: I'm looking forward to meeting your sister.

B: I just know that you'll hit it off.

A: 네 여동생과 만나길 손꼽아 기다리고 있어. B: 넌 내 동생하고 잘 맞을거야.

▸ I (really) hit it off with her[him]
난 걔랑 정말 금세 좋아졌어

We have chemistry 우린 잘 통해

A: Are you going to see her again?

B: I hope so, there was a lot of good chemistry between us.

A: 그 여자를 다시 만날거야? B: 그래, 우린 잘 통해.

You turn me on 넌 내 맘에 쏘옥 들어. 넌 날 흥분시켜

A: Do you think I'm sexy?

B: Yes I do. You turn me on.

A: 내가 섹시한 것 같아? B: 그럼. 널 보면 흥분돼.

I fell in love with Dick 딕하고 사랑에 빠졌어

A: I fell in love with Dick.

B: Don't you know he's a heartbreaker?

A: 딕하고 사랑에 빠졌어. B: 걔가 바람둥이인지 몰랐어?

▸ I'm deeply in love with Jessica
제시카와 깊은 사랑에 빠졌어

I can't live without you 너 없이는 못살아

A: I've got to break up with you.

B: Don't do that! I can't live without you.

A: 너랑 헤어져야 겠어. B: 그러지마! 너없인 못살아.

▸ I don't want to live without you
너없이 살고 싶지 않아

Life isn't worth living without you 너없는 삶은 살가치가 없어

A: Life isn't worth living without you.

B: Do you really mean that?

A: 너없는 삶은 살가치가 없어. B: 정말 진심야?

▸ You mean everything to me
난 너밖에 없어

I can't stop myself from loving you 널 사랑하지 않고는 못베겨

A: Why do you always follow me?

B: I can't stop myself from loving you.

A: 왜 날 항상 따라다니는 거야? B: 널 사랑하지 않을 수 없어.

I'm happy to have been part of your life 네 삶의 일부가 되어서 기뻐

A: We've had a long marriage.

B: I'm happy to have been part of your life.

   A: 우리 결혼생활 오래됐지. B: 네 삶의 일부가 되어와서 기뻐.

You make me happy 네가 있어 행복해

A: Why are you attracted to me?

B: You make me happy.

   A: 왜 나한테 끌린 거야? B: 네가 있어 행복하잖아.

You belong to me 넌 내 소유야

A: You belong to me.

B: No! I don't belong to anyone!

   A: 넌 내꺼야. B: 아냐! 나 누구의 소유도 아니야!

▸ You're mine
  넌 내꺼야

I'm [all] yours 난 네꺼야

A: Will you be my girlfriend?

B: I'm yours!

   A: 내 여친이 되어줄래? B: 난 네꺼야!

It was meant to be 운명이었어. 하늘이 정해준거야

A: Rich and Simone fell in love the first time they met.

B: It was meant to be.

   A: 리치와 사이몬이 처음 만나 사랑에 빠졌어. B: 하늘이 정해준거구만.

▸ You're the one for
  me
  넌 내 짝이야

I'm dying to see her 걔 보고 싶어 죽겠어

A: So, your girlfriend's coming back from Hawaii today?

B: Yep. I'm dying to see her.

   A: 그래, 여친이 오늘 하와이에서 돌아와? B: 그래, 보고 싶어 죽겠어.

I've never felt like this before 이런 기분 처음이야

A: I've never felt like this before.

B: Me either. It must be love.

   A: 이런 기분 처음이야. B: 나도 처음야. 사랑인가봐.

03 그 사람과 사랑을 나누었어

He made love to me 그 사람과 사랑을 나눴어

A: What is your biggest wish?

B: I want to make love to you in your house.

A: 너의 가장 큰 바람은 뭐야? B: 너희 집에서 너랑 사랑을 나누고 싶어.

It was just a one night thing 하룻밤 잔 것뿐이야

A: Do you plan to see him again?

B: No. It was just a one night thing.

A: 걔 다시 만날거야? B: 아니. 그냥 하룻밤 잔 것뿐인데.

▸ I want to have a fling
번개 좀 해야겠어
▸ How about a quickie?
가볍게 한번 어때?

I want to make out with my girlfriend 애인하고 애무하고 싶어

A: Aren't you going to the party?

B: I wanna stay here and make out with my girlfriend!

A: 파티 안 갈거야? B: 여기 남아 여친과 애무할래!

I want to have sex with you 너하고 섹스하고 싶어

A: She really wants to have sex with me.

B: Crazy bitch.

A: 걘 나하고 정말 섹스를 하고 싶어해. B: 미친년.

▸ I want to get laid
섹스하고파
▸ Your place or mine?
너희 집 아니면 우리 집에서 할래?

They're doing it 쟤네들 그거 한다

A: We saw them doing it through the window.

B: What?! He's such a lucky guy. I envy him.

A: 창문으로 걔네들이 그거 하는 것 봤어. B: 뭐라고?! 걘 운도 좋아. 부러워.

▸ He got lucky with Julie
걔가 줄리랑 잤대

(Did you) Get(ting) any? 요즘 (섹스) 좀 했어?

A: I took Pam on a date last night.

B: Did you get any?

A: 어제 밤에 팜과 데이트했어? B: 좀 했어?

Chapter 08

04 나랑 결혼해줄래?

Will you marry me? 나랑 결혼해줄래?

A: Will you marry me?

B: You know I only have eyes for you. Of course I'll marry you!

A: 나랑 결혼해 줄래? B: 너밖에 없어. 결혼하자고!

▸ Will you be my wife[husband]?
내 아내[남편]이 되어줄래요?
▸ I want to share the rest of my life with you
나의 여생을 당신과 보내고 싶어

She wants to start a family 걔는 가정을 꾸미고 싶어해

A: Why did you break up with Linda?

B: She wants to start a family. I'm not ready.

A: 왜 린다와 헤어진 거야? B: 걘 가정을 꾸미려고 하는데 난 준비가 안돼서.

She is not marriage material 그 여자는 결혼상대는 아냐

A: Kate really wants to start a family with me.

B: You know she's not marriage material.

A: 케이트는 정말 나랑 가정을 꾸미고 싶어해. B: 걘 결혼감은 아니라는 거 알잖아.

▸ He is not boyfriend material
그 사람은 애인감이 아냐

How's your married life? 결혼생활 어때?

A: How's your married life?

B: We're pretty happy together.

A: 결혼생활 어때? B: 우린 함께 무척 행복해.

We're a well-matched couple 우린 잘 어울리는 커플야

A: We're a well matched couple.

B: Does that mean you never fight?

A: 우린 잘 어울리는 커플야. B: 한번도 안싸웠다는 거야?

I'm pregnant 나 임신했어

A: What did she have?

B: It's a girl.

A: 남자야 여자야? B: 여자래.

▸ I'm going to have a baby 애를 갖을거야
▸ I'm expecting 임신중야
▸ What did she have? 남자야 여자야?

I'm going to break up with you 우리 그만 만나자

A: I'm going to break up with my boyfriend.

B: I don't blame you. He's such an asshole.

남자 친구랑 헤어질거야. 그럴만도 해. 정말이지 추잡한 녀석이야.

▸ We're on a break
잠시 떨어져 있는거야

I'm over you 너랑은 끝났어

A: Are you still sad we broke up?

B: No. I'm over you.

A: 헤어져서 아직도 슬퍼? B: 아니. 이제 괜찮아.

▸ I'm through with you
너랑 이제 끝이야
▸ I dumped him
내가 걔 찼어

We fight a lot 우린 싸움을 많이 해

A: Do you have a good relationship with David?

B: Not really. We fight a lot.

A: 데이빗과 좋은 관계 유지해? B: 그렇지 못해. 우린 많이 싸워.

My wife's cheating on me 아내가 바람을 폈어

A: Why did they get divorced?

B: Well, she caught him cheating on her with her sister.

A: 왜 이혼한거야? B: 어, 처제랑 바람피다 들켰어.

▸ My wife's a two-timer
아내가 바람둥이야
▸ I had an affair with my secretary
내가 비서와 바람을 폈어

We're living separately now 우린 현재 별거하고 있어

A: Have you split with your wife?

B: We're living separately now.

A: 부인과 헤어졌어? B: 지금 별거하고 있어.

▸ I'm separated from my wife
아내와 별거하고 있어

I wish I had never met you 널 안 만났더라면 좋았을 텐데

A: I wish I had never met you.

B: Me too. You made my life hell!

A: 널 안 만났더라면 좋았을 텐데. B: 나도 그래. 너 때문에 인생이 지옥이 되었어!

▸ I regret meeting you
널 만난 걸 후회해
▸ I wish you were never a part of my life
너를 만나지 않았더라면 좋았을 텐데

Start
Tray Hard
Keep Talking
Native Speaking

Section **3**

나와 너를 말하기

01 대부분 지현이라고 불러

● 반가워. 민지현이라고 해. 대부분 지현이라고 부르지.

Hi. I'm Ji-hyun Min. Most people just call me Ji-hyun.

● 내 이름은 이민수이야. '이'는 성이고 '민수'는 이름이지.

My name is Lee Min-soo. Lee is my family name, and Min-soo is my first name.

▶ My family name, 'Gil,' is pretty rare in Korea 성이 '길'인데 한국에선 드문 성이야

● 이달 21일이 내 24번째 생일야.

The 21st of this month is my twenty-fourth birthday.

▶ I was born in Seoul in 1974 1974년 서울에서 태어났어
▶ I was born on August 10, 1983 1983년 8월 10일에 태어났어

● 다음 주 월요일이면 나 30살 돼.

I'm going to be thirty next Monday.

▶ I turned thirty-one last month 지난 달에 31살이 되었어

● 난 캐나다에서 왔는데 토론토에서 나고 자랐지.

I'm from Canada, born and raised in Toronto.

● 난 식구들하고 옥수동에 살아. 그 동네에 관해서 들어봤을 거야, 그렇지?

I live with my family in Ok-su Dong. You've probably heard about that area, right?

● 난 고려대학교 근처의 종암동에 살아. 그 동네 알아?

I'm living over in Jong-am Dong, near Korea University. Do you know that neighborhood?

- 23살 때 고향을 떠나왔어.

I left my hometown when I was twenty-three.

▸ It's located about 30 kilometers from Daegu 대구에서 한 30킬로 미터 지점에 있어

- 자전거타고 역에 가.

I go to the station by bike.

▸ I ride my bike to the station 자전거타고 역까지 가
▸ My house is about 300 meters from the station 집은 역에서 300미터 떨어진 곳에 있어

- 아파트 건물 2층에 살아.

I live on the second floor of an apartment building.

▸ I live in an apartment 아파트에서 살아
▸ My house has five rooms 집에는 방이 5개야

- 월세로 50만원을 내고 있어.

I pay 500,000 won a month for rent.

▸ I'm going to rent a larger room 더 큰 방을 얻으려고 해
▸ How much is your rent? 월세가 얼마야?

- 거기서 5년 째 살고 있어.

I have lived there for five years.

 예상되는 질문들

- Where are you from, Kevin? 고향이 어디야?
- May I ask your name, please? 이름이 뭐예요?
- Where were you born? 어디서 태어났어?
- When's your birthday? 생일이 언제야?
- How old are you? 몇살이야?
- What's your age? 나이가 어떻게 돼?
- Where do you come from? 출신이 어디야?
- Where do you live? 어디서 살아?
- How far is it from the station to your house? 역에서 집까지 얼마나 멀어?

서른 살에 결혼했어

● 서른 살에 결혼했어.

I got married at the age of thirty.

- ▶ I got married when I was thirty-one 스물 한 살에 결혼했어
- ▶ We have been married for 10 years 우린 10년 전에 결혼했어
- ▶ I'm married 유부남(녀)야

● 오는 12월에 결혼할거야.

I'm getting married next December.

- ▶ I got to know my wife through one of my friends 아내 친구 통해서 알게 됐어

● 결혼기념일은 6월 15일이야.

Our wedding anniversary is June 15th.

- ▶ We went to Cheju Island for our honeymoon 제주도로 신혼여행 갔었어
- ▶ We're going to have a baby in July 출산예정은 7월야

● 2년 전에 이혼했고 지금은 혼자야.

I got divorced two years ago, so I'm single now.

- ▶ That was my first, and her second marriage 난 초혼이고 아내는 재혼이었어

● 식구는 3명야.

There are three in my family.

- ▶ We are a family of five 식구가 다섯이야

● 애가 둘이야.

I have two children.

- ▶ I have a son and two daughters 아들 하나고 딸이 둘야
- ▶ I have a son in middle school 중학교 다니는 아들 하나야
- ▶ I don't have any children 애가 없어
- ▶ My son is a high school student 아들은 고등학생야

● 남자형제가 셋 있고, 누이가 둘 이야.

I have three brothers and two sisters.

> ▸ I have two brothers 형이 둘이야
> ▸ I have no brothers or sisters 형제가 없어
> ▸ I'm an only child 외아들(외동녀)야

● 난 5형제 중 둘째야

I'm the second of five brothers and sisters

> ▸ I'm the oldest 장남(녀)야
> ▸ I'm the youngest of three sisters 3자매 중에서 막내야

● 아들놈이 공부를 안할려고 해서 걱정야

I'm worried about my son because he doesn't like to study.

> ▸ He doesn't like to study 공부하는 걸 싫어해
> ▸ My son won't listen to us at all 아들놈이 우리말을 전혀 듣지 않으려고 해

● 부모님은 다 건강하셔.

My parents are in good health.

> ▸ My father retired last year 아버지는 작년에 퇴직하셨어
> ▸ My parents live on their pensions 부모님은 연금으로 사셔

● 우린 맞벌이 부부예요.

We're a working couple.

> ▸ My wife is a housewife 와이프는 전업주부야

● 애완동물을 안 키워.

I don't have any pets.

> ▸ I have a dog 강아지를 키워
> ▸ It's a female named Mimi 암놈이고 이름은 미미야

 예상되는 질문들

· How long have you been married? 결혼한 지 얼마나 됐어?
· How did you get to know your wife? 어떻게 와이프를 만났어?
· When is your wedding anniversary? 결혼기념일이 언제야?
· How many people are there in your family? 식구가 몇이야?
· Any children? 애는 있고?

03 내 혈액형은 B형야

● 내 혈액형은 B형이야.

I have type B blood.

● 키는 175센티야.

I'm 175 centimeters tall.

▶ I'm about 5 feet 5 inches tall 키는 한 5피트 5인치야
▶ I weigh 74 kilograms now 지금 74킬로 나가

● 노안이 돼서 조그만 글자를 읽기가 힘들어.

My eyes are getting weak, so it's hard to for me to read small letters.

▶ I'm afraid I'm becoming forgetful 점점 깜박하는 게 걱정돼
▶ I'm losing my hair these days 요즘 머리가 빠져

● 푸시업을 30개 할 수 있어.

I can do 30 push-ups.

▶ I walk up and down the stairs instead of taking elevators
엘리베이터 대신 계단으로 오르내리고 있어

● 요즘 충분한 운동을 못하고 있어.

● I haven't been getting enough exercise recently.

건강을 유지하기 위해 일찍 일어나고 있어.

● I get up early to keep me in good health.

▶ Getting up early is the secret of my good health 일찍 일어나는게 내 건강비결야

 예상되는 질문들

• How tall are you? 키가 어떻게 돼?   • What's your weight? 몸무게는 얼마야?
• What's your blood type? 혈액형을 어떻게 돼?
• What kind of exercise do you usually do? 보통 무슨 운동을 해?

04 난 사교적이야

● 난 사교적이야.

I'm sociable.

▶ I'm optimistic 난 낙천적이야
▶ I'm pessimistic 난 부정적이야

● 내 강점중의 하나는 신중하다는 거야.

One of my strong points is that I'm cautious.

▶ I really like jokes very much 정말 조크를 아주 좋아해

● 난 너무 수동적이야.

I'm too passive.

▶ Being passive is one of my weak point 수동적인 게 내 약점중 하나야
▶ I've become quite conservative lately 최근 내가 아주 보수적으로 되었어

● 난 쉽게 화를 내는 경향이 있어.

I'm afraid I tend to lose my temper easily.

● 내가 좋아하는 속담으로는 "현재를 즐겨라!"야.

My favorite saying is "Seize the day!"

● "불굴의 의지로 끝까지 최선을 다하자"라는 슬로건으로 좋아해.

I like the slogan, "Just do it. "

▶ "Get real" is my motto "현실을 직시하라"가 내 모토야
▶ It's important to be punctual 시간을 지키는 게 중요해

 예상되는 질문들

• What kind of person do you think you are? 네가 보기에 넌 어떤 성격인 것 같아?
• What's the most important thing in your life? 네게 있어 가장 중요한 것은 뭐야?

05 2012년에 대학교를 졸업했어

● 2012년에 대학교를 졸업했어.

I graduated from college in 2012.

● 2005년에 고려대학교에 진학했어.

I started Korea University in 2005.

▶ I'm a Yonsei graduate   연세대학교 졸업했어

● 경영학을 전공했어.

I majored in business administration.

▶ My major was English literature   내 전공은 영문학이야
▶ My graduation thesis was about "The Big Bang."   졸업논문은 "빅뱅"이야
▶ I'm majoring in economics   경제학을 전공하고 있어

● 난 조선대학교에 다니고 3학년이야.

I'm a third-year student at Chosun University.

● 서울대학교에서 법학을 공부하고 있어.

I'm studying law at Seoul National University.

● 언젠가 형사 사건 전문 변호사가 되고 싶어.

I hope to be a criminal defense lawyer someday.

● 난 서강대학교에서 생물학을 공부하고 있는데, 환경과학에 굉장히 흥미가 있어.

I'm studying biology at Sogang University. I'm really interested in environmental science.

- 매주 월요일과 수요일에 영어회화 수업을 듣고 있는데, 강사가 굉장히 잘 가르쳐서 학생들을 항상 웃게 만들지.

I'm taking an English conversation class on Mondays and Wednesdays. My teacher is really great and always makes us laugh.

- 약사증을 따고 싶어.

I want to get a pharmacist's license.

I want to qualify as a lawyer 변호사 자격을 따고 싶어

- 금년도에 졸업하기를 바래.

I'm hoping to graduate this year.

- 공부를 해서 석사학위를 받으려고 해.

I'm planning to study for a master's degree.

- 졸업해서 직장 구하기를 바라고 있어.

I'm looking forward to graduating and getting a job.

- 이번주 우리 대학은 중간고사 기간야.

Our university is having mid-term exams this week.

- 고려대학교는 법대쪽이 유명해.

Korea University is well known for its law program.

- 전공을 바꿔서 다른 흥미로운 전공을 택했으면 해.

I wish I could change my major to a more interesting subject.

예상되는 질문들

- What was your major in college? 대학 때 전공이 뭐야?
- Where did you go to college? 어느 대학교 갔어?
- What school do you go to? 어느 학교에 다녀?
- What year are you in? 몇 학년야?

06 사무직일 해요

● 사무직일 해.

I'm an office worker.

> ▸ I'm a cashier 출납하는 일 해
> ▸ I'm secretary to the president 사장비서야

● 파트타임으로 일 해.

I'm a part-timer.

> ▸ I'm a freelance writer 프리랜서 작가야
> ▸ I work freelance as a designer 프리랜서로 디자이너일을 해

● 공무원이야.

I'm a government employee.

> ▸ I work for a trading company 무역회사다녀
> ▸ The company I work for is a travel agency 내가 다니는 회사는 여행사야

● 내 직책은 영업차장야.

My title is assistant sales manager.

● 우린 여성화장품을 수입해서 판매해.

We import and sell cosmetics for women.

> ▸ We make computer parts 컴퓨터 부품을 제조해

● 우리 사무실은 중앙빌딩 3층에 있어.

Our office is on the third floor of the Jungang Building.

> ▸ Do you see the Lotteria? Our office is behind it 롯데리아 보여? 사무실은 그 뒤에 있어
> ▸ Our office is in a white five-story building 우리 사무실은 하얀 5층 건물에 있어
> ▸ There're parking space next to our office building 회사건물 옆에 주차장이 있어

- 사무실가는 데 한 50분 걸려.

It takes about 50 minutes to get to the office.

▸ I drive to work   차로 출근해

- 사당역에서 2호선으로 갈아타.

I change to the green line at Sadang Station.

▸ Every commuter train is overcrowded during rush hour
러시아워에 모든 전철은 다 만원야

▸ I always have to stand on the train   난 항상 전철에서 서 있어

- 수입회사를 운영해.

I have my own importing company.

▸ I'm self-employed   사업해   ▸ I run a boutique   미용실을 하고 있어

▸ I have about 20 people working for me   종업원이 한 20여 명야

- 지금 실직상태야.

I'm out of work now.

▸ I don't have a job now   현재 직업이 없어   ▸I'm not working right now   현재 놀고 있어

- 전직하고 있는 중야.

I'm changing jobs.

▸ I'm job hunting now   현재 직장을 알아보고 있어 ▸ I'm retiring next year   내년에 퇴직해

- 여기 내 명함야.

Let me give you my card.

예상되는 질문들

- What do you do? 직업이 뭐예요?
- Which company do you work for? 어느 회사 다녀?
- How long is your commute? 출퇴근하는데 얼마나 걸려?
- What do you usually do on the train? 전철에서 보통 뭐해?
- Which department do you work for? 어느 부서에서 일해?
- How long have you been doing that job? 그 일을 한 지 얼마나 돼?

07 근무시간은 7시부터 5시까지야

● 근무시간은 7시부터 5시까지야.

Our working hours are from seven to five.

● 주 5일제 근무하고 있어.

We're on a five-day week.

▶ Our company is on five-day week. 우리회사는 주 5일제 근무하고 있어.

● 토요일마다 쉬어.

We're off on Saturdays.

▶ We're off on every other Saturday 격주 토요일은 쉬어

● 거의 매일 야근야.

I work overtime almost every day.

● 휴일에도 난 고객들과 가끔 골프를 쳐.

Even on holidays, I sometimes go play golf with clients.

● 일년에 수차례 해외출장을 가

I go abroad on business several times a year.

● 이번 달에 일정이 아주 바빠.

I have a heavy schedule this month.

▶ We're busy as bees during the fiscal term 결산기간동안엔 엄청 바빠

- 급여로 세금떼고 월 3백만원 정도 받아.

I'm paid about 3,000,000won a month, after taxes.

- ▸ My work is paid by the hour 시급으로 일해
- ▸ I'm paid on an hourly basis 시급으로 돈을 받아
- ▸ I get 3,000 won an hour 시급 3천원받아

- 능력급으로 받고 있어.

We're paid according to ability.

- 7월과 12월에 보너스를 받아.

We receive a bonus in July and December.

- 보통 패스트푸드 식당에서 점심을 먹어.

I usually have lunch at a fastfood restaurant.

- ▸ I like to have noodles for lunch 점심으로 국수먹는 걸 좋아해
- ▸ I bring my own lunch every day 매일 점심을 가져와

- 우린 12시부터 1시까지 점심식사 시간야.

We have an hour's lunch break, from twelve to one.

- 퇴근 후 종종 동료들과 술한잔 하러 가.

I often go for a drink with my co-workers after work.

 예상되는 질문들

- Are you off on Saturdays? 토요일날 쉬니?
- Do you often work overtime? 가끔 야근해?
- What time does your office start? 출근시간이 몇시야?

08 여행하는 걸 좋아해

● 여행을 무척 좋아해.

I like traveling very much.

▶ Traveling is one of my favorite hobbies 여행은 내가 가장 좋아하는 취미생활야

● 뉴욕에 한번 간 적 있어.

I've been to New York once.

▶ I took a trip to Canada in 1999 1999년에 캐나다에 여행갔었어

▶ Chicago is a really nice place to visit 시카고는 정말 가보기 좋은 곳이야

▶ I've never been abroad 해외에 나가 본 적이 없어

● 한달에 다섯번 요리강의를 들어.

I go to cooking class five times a month.

▶ I enjoy baking cakes during my holidays 휴일마다 케익 굽는 걸 좋아해

● 일년에 4권 이상의 책을 읽어.

I read more than 4 books a year.

▶ I usually read a book each month, depending on how busy I am
얼마나 바쁘냐에 따라 다르지만, 나는 대체로 매달 한 권 정도의 책을 읽어

● 위성 TV 그리고 케이블 TV 보는 걸 좋아해.

I enjoy satellite TV and cable TV, too.

▶ I like watching good movies on TV TV에서 좋은 영화 보는 걸 좋아해

● 음악을 무척 좋아해.

I'm a fan of music.

● 한달에 4, 5섯 번은 영화관에 가.

I go to the movies four or five times a month.

▶ My favorite actress is Angelina Jolie 내가 제일 좋아하는 여배우는 안젤리나 졸리야
▶ I was deeply moved by "Alexander" 알렉산더를 보고 감동받았어

● 기타를 쳐.

I play the guitar.

▶ I can play the clarinet a little 클라리넷을 조금 불 수 있어

● 가끔 락 콘서트를 보러 가.

I sometimes go to rock concerts.

▶ Queen's "We Are the Champion" is a song I enjoy singing
  퀸의 챔피언은 내가 즐겨 부르는 노래야
▶ I'm not good at singing 노래를 잘 못 불러

● 쉬는 날에는 박물관에 가는 걸 좋아해.

I like to go to museums on my days off.

● 그림을 그리진 않지만 그림감상을 무척 좋아해.

I don't draw pictures, but I like to look at artwork very much.

● 고전음악 감상을 좋아해.

I like listening to classical music.

▶ I often buy folk music CDs these days 요즘 종종 포크음악시디를 사
▶ I listen to CDs whenever I have free time 시 간날 때마다 CD를 들어

 예상되는 질문들

· Do you have any hobbies? 취미가 있어?
· What are your hobbies? 취미가 뭐야?
· What do you do during your free time? 시간나면 뭐해?
· How do you spend your days off? 쉬는 날에는 뭐해?
· How many films do you see a month? 한 달에 영화 몇 편을 봐?
· What kind of music do you like? 어떤 음악을 좋아해?

09 난 야구를 좋아해

● 난 야구를 좋아해.

My favorite sport is baseball.

● 축구를 무척 좋아해.

I'm a huge soccer fan.

▶ I support FC Seoul FC서울을 응원해

● 실외운동보다는 실내운동을 좋아해.

I prefer indoor sports to outdoor sports.

● 스포츠를 보는 것도 좋아하고 하는 것도 좋아해.

I like both watching and playing sports.

● TV로 K-1 경기 보는 걸 좋아해.

I like to watch K-1 on TV.

● 건강을 위해 매일 조깅해.

I jog every day for my health.

▶ I started jogging 조깅을 시작했어
▶ I jog every morning 매일 아침 조깅해

● 일주일에 두 번 헬스클럽에 가.

I go to the sports[fitness] club twice a week.

● 다음 달에 에어로빅을 시작할거야.

I'm going to start doing aerobics next month.

▶ I belong to a tennis club 테니스 클럽에 들었어

- 퇴근 후에 보통 운동을 해.

I usually work out after work.

▶ I usually go to the gym after work 보통 퇴근 후에 체육관에 가

- 골프를 친 지가 1년 밖에 안됐어.

It's only been a year since I started playing golf.

▶ My golf handicap is 20 핸디캡이 20야
▶ My score was 3-under-par 69 3언더파로 69타야
▶ I took up golf two months ago 골프를 두달 전에 시작했어

- 골프를 잘 쳐.

I'm good at playing golf.

▶ I finished the round at 2 under par 2언더파로 라운드를 마쳤어
▶ I'm into golf 골프를 쳐

- 매 겨울마다 스키를 타.

I enjoy skiing every winter.

▶ I can't wait to go skiing 스키타고 싶어 죽겠어

- 수영강습을 들어.

I'm taking swimming lessons.

▶ I'd like to go rafting 래프팅하는 걸 좋아해

- 요즘 충분한 운동을 못하고 있어.

I haven't been getting enough exercise lately.

▶ You need exercise 넌 운동 좀 해야 돼

 예상되는 질문들

- What sport do you like best? 무슨 운동을 가장 좋아해?
- Do you exercise? 운동 좀 하는 거 있어?
- Have you played golf lately? 최근에 골프쳤어?
- Do you work out? 운동해?

10 음력 새해를 설날이라고 해

● 한국에서는 음력 새해를 「설날」이라고 하죠.

In Korean, the word for the Lunar New Year is Sul-nal.

● 한국에는 새해가 두번 있어요. 하나는 양력 1월 1일, 또 하나는 음력 1월 1일입니다.

There are two New Year's days in Korea. One is January 1st on the solar calendar, and the other is on the lunar calendar.

● 「설날」은 한국에서 가장 큰 전통 명절입니다.

Of the many traditional holidays in Korea, Sul-nal is one of the biggest.

● 설날에 한국 사람들은 고향집을 찾아가기 때문에 전국의 교통이 상당히 혼잡합니다.

Koreans travel home during Sul-nal, which causes heavy traffic throughout Korea.

● 설날에는 집안 어른들이 자녀나 손주들에게 새해를 기념하는 특별한 절을 받는데, 이를 「세배」라고 해요.

On Sul-nal, parents and grandparents expect their offspring to perform a special New Year's bow, called sae-bae in Korean.

● 한국 사람들은 설날에 쫀득쫀득한 쌀떡으로 만든 「떡국」을 먹습니다.

On New Year's day, Koreans eat tok-guk, a soup made with slices of rice paste.

● 설날에는 장남의 집에 온 가족이 모입니다.

The eldest son hosts a party on New Year's.

● 한복은 예를 들어 설날이나 추석 같은 명절과 전통의식용으로 입어.

The hanbok is worn for traditional ceremonies and festivals, like Sulnal or Chusok, for example.

Winnie: I've heard that the Lunar New Year is a special holiday in Korea.

Jung-min: Yes, it is. It's one of the biggest traditional Korean holidays.

Winnie: How do you usually celebrate it?

Jung-min: Well, most Koreans travel home in order to bow to our elders.

Winnie: There must be a lot of traffic with all those people going home on the new year.

위니: 음력 설날은 한국에서 특별한 명절이라고 들었어.

정민: 맞아. 그날은 한국의 제일 큰 전통 명절이지.

위니: 그날은 대개 어떻게 지내?

정민: 그러니까, 어른들께 세배하러 고향집에 가는 한국 사람들이 대부분이야.

위니: 정초엔 사람들이 전부 집에 가느라고 길이 많이 막히겠네.

11 미래를 보려고 점을 봐

● 새해가 시작되면 점을 보는 한국 사람들이 많습니다.

At the start of the year, many Koreans visit a fortune-teller.

● 한국에서는 자신들의 미래를 알아보려고 점장이에게 찾아가는 사람들이 많아.

A lot of people in Korea visit fortunetellers to have their future predicted.

● 한국 사람들은 옛부터 중대사를 앞두고 점을 봤습니다.

Koreans have traditionally sought divination before important events.

● 무료로, 혹은 요금을 받고 운세를 알려주는 인터넷 사이트도 많아졌습니다.

It has become common for Internet sites to offer both predictions for a fee and predictions which are free of charge to Internet users.

● 점술을 연구하는 사람들을 고용하여 손님들의 점을 봐주는 사주까페도 많아요.

There are a lot of coffee shops specializing in telling fortune. They hire students who're studying fortune telling for customers to consult.

● 한국사람들 사이에는 시험과 관련해서 미신이 많습니다.

Koreans have a lot of superstitions associated with the exams.

- 시험이 다가오면, 수험생들은 보통, 행운을 기원하는 여러 종류의 선물을 받지요.

As an examination draws near, students who are preparing for it are usually given presents for good luck.

- 한국말로 찐득찐득하게 「붙는다」는 말과 시험에 「붙는다」는 말이 똑같이 「붙다」거든요. 그래서 찐득찐득한 엿을 선물하는 거랍니다. 엿은 한국 고유의 사탕이에요.

The word for both "stick" and "pass" in Korean is but-da, which is why sticky yot candy is given. Yot is a traditional Korean taffy.

Check It Out!

Jin-a: Have you ever consulted a fortune-teller?

Ralph: Actually, no. But sometimes I read my horoscope.

Jin-a: I recently asked a fortune-teller for my year's prediction, using To-jong-bi-gyul, the traditional Korean fortune telling system.

Ralph: Interesting. Do many Koreans do that?

Jin-a: Yeah. To-jong-bi-gyul is popular in the beginning of the new year.

진아: 점을 본 적 있어?

랠프: 아니, 없는데. 하지만 별자리 운세는 가끔 봐.

진아: 난 요전에 토정비결로 올해 운세를 봤어. 토정비결은 한국에서 전통적으로 전해내려오는 점(占)이야.

랠프: 재미있네. 한국사람들은 그 점을 많이 보니?

진아: 응. 토정비결은 정초에 많이 보지.

12 서울은 차가 너무 막혀

● 서울의 교통상황이 이렇게 나쁜 줄 미처 몰랐어요.

I had no idea that traffic was this bad in Seoul.

● 차들이 몰리는 출퇴근 시간은 교통정체 때문에 정말 골칫거리입니다!

Rush hour is a real headache with these traffic jams!

● 고급차를 선호하는 사람들이 많아서 고급차들이 불티나게 팔립니다.

Many people prefer luxurious cars, and they are selling like hot cakes.

● 한국의 교통사고 사망률은 다른 나라들과 비교해서 아주 높은 편입니다.

The death rate from traffic accidents in Korea is very high compared to other nations.

● 주차공간이 부족해서, 주차하는 게 마치 전쟁을 치르는 것 같아요.

Parking is a nightmare, as there are not enough spaces for cars.

● 도로에서 다른 차에 길을 내주게 되면 손해본다고 생각하는 운전자들이 많아요.

Many drivers feel like they are being victimized when they give other drivers a break.

● 이 푸른색 차선은 정해진 시간동안에는 버스만이 이용할 수 있습니다.

Blue lanes are for buses only during specific hours.

▶ Only buses are permitted to use the blue lanes during specific hours.
일정시간동안 버스만이 푸른색 차선을 통행할 수 있어

● 목적지까지 더 편하고 느긋하게 갈 수 있기 때문에 저는 자주 지하철을 탑니다.

I often take the subway because I find that I arrive at my destination feeling more relaxed.

 Check It Out!

Sam: Wow, do you drive to work everyday?

Ji-sun: I do, but some days I just can't take the traffic.

Sam: I couldn't do it. It seems like if the driving didn't make you crazy, the parking situation would.

Ji-sun: I should just take the subway, but I like my own car.

Sam: I would too if I drove a BMW!

샘: 이야, 너 매일 차를 몰고 출근하니?
지선: 응, 하지만 어떤 날은 차가 많아서 견딜 수가 없어.
샘: 나라도 그럴 거야. 운전하다가 열받는 일이 없으면 주차문제가 속을 썩이는 것 같아.
지선: 지하철을 타야 되겠는데, 난 내 차를 모는 게 좋아.
샘: BMW를 몬다면야 나도 직접 운전하는 게 좋을 거야.

13 대부분 7, 8월에 휴가 가

- 6월과 7월에 적어도 연 강수량의 반이 내려요.

We get at least half of our annual rainfall in June and July.

▶ More than half of our rainfall comes in June and July
강수량의 반이상이 6,7월에 내려요

▶ We receive more than fifty percent of the year's rainfall in June and July
연강수량의 50%이상이 6월과 7월에 내려요

- 8월은 여름 중에서도 날씨가 가장 좋은 달이죠.

August is the nicest of the summer months.

Of all the summer months, August is the nicest
여름중에서 8월이 가장 좋아요

- 대부분 7월에서 8월 사이에 휴가를 갖지요.

Most Koreans take their vacations between the months of July and August.

- 한국사람들은 여름에 보통 일주일 정도 휴가를 갖습니다.

Koreans usually have around a week off in the summer.

- 보통 가족이나 친구들과 함께 휴가를 보내요.

Koreans usually spend their vacations with family and friends.

- 여름휴가 때는 휴가여행을 계획하는 사람들이 아주 많은데, 해외로 나가려고 하는 사람들이 점점 많아지고 있습니다.

A large number of people plan getaway trips for their summer holidays, and more and more Koreans want to use this time to go abroad.

- 꽉 막힌 도로와 혼잡한 휴양지를 피하려고 성수기 전후로 휴가를 계획하는 사람들도 있습니다.

In order to avoid sitting in traffic and experiencing crowded resorts, some people plan their vacations after the peak season.

Denis: What are your plans this summer?

Hye-min: I'm going to the beach in Naksan with my family. I have my summer vacation at the end of July.

Denis: That sounds great!

Hye-min: Yeah. Since most Koreans take their vacation then, the resorts might be crowded.

Denis: That sounds like the US. A lot of Americans hit the beach with their families in midsummer.

데니스: 올 여름에 뭐 할 거니?

혜민: 가족들하고 낙산 해수욕장에 갈 거야. 7월말에 여름휴가가 있거든.

데니스: 재밌겠다!

혜민: 그럼. 하지만 그때쯤엔 한국 사람들 대부분이 휴가라서, 피서지가 붐빌 거야.

데니스: 미국하고 같구나. 한여름엔 가족들하고 해변을 찾는 사람들이 많지.

14 여자들이 결혼을 늦게 해

● 한국의 젊은 세대들, 특히 여자들은 부모세대들보다 결혼하는 시기가 더 늦습니다.

A lot of the younger generation in Korea, especially women, are waiting longer than their parents to get married.

● 과거에는 여자들이 서른 살이 넘으면 결혼하기에는 늦은 나이라고 여겼지만, 요즘에는 서른 살이 되야 비로소 결혼하는 여자들이 많습니다.

It used to be that a woman over thirty was considered too old to marry. But these days, many women don't marry until they're thirty years old.

● 백년가약을 맺기 전에 동거를 해봐야 한다고 생각하는 젊은이들도 꽤 있어.

There are a lot of young people that think couples should definitely live together before they tie the knot.

▶ Our parents just can't get why our generation thinks unmarried couples should live together 부모님 세대는 왜 우리 세대가 동거를 해야하는지 이해 못하서

● 혼전동거는 연인들이 서로 잘 맞는지 알 수 있는 좋은 방법인 것 같아.

I think living together before marriage is a great way for couples to know for sure if they are compatible.

● 난 종교적인 이유로, 결혼 전에 동거하는 건 정말 옳지 않다고 생각해.

I really think it is wrong to live together before marriage because of my religious beliefs.

● 동거하는 게 옳지 않은 일이라고는 생각하지 않지만, 나의 경우라면, 그렇게 안할거야.

I don't think it's wrong to live together, but personally, I wouldn't do it.

- 과거와는 달리 직업을 갖고 있는 한국 여성들이 많으며, 이들은 결혼을 미루는 경향이 있습니다.

Many Korean women have a job, unlike in the past, and they tend to put marriage on a back burner.

- 결혼을 한다해도, 일하는 여자들은 아이 갖는 일을 미루려는 경향이 있습니다.

Once they're married, working women tend to put off starting a family.

- 또한 젊은이들 중에는 아예 결혼은 반드시 해야 하는 것은 아니라고 생각하는 이도 많죠.

Many young Koreans think marriage isn't necessary in the first place.

- 심지어는 결혼을 완전히 포기하고 독신 생활을 즐기기로 결심한 여자들도 있습니다.

Some Korean women have even decided not to get married at all, and to simply enjoy being single for life.

- 한국의 이혼율이 최근 상승하고 있습니다.

Korea's divorce rate has grown in recent years.

- 통계에 의하면 이혼의 가장 큰 이유는 배우자의 부정(不貞)이었다고 합니다.

According to the statistics, the number one reason for divorce was unfaithfulness.

- 요즘에는 아내측의 부정이 이혼 사유로 꼽히고 있는데, 반면 과거에는 남편측에서 대부분 부정을 저질렀죠.

Nowadays, adultery on the part of wives has become a major reason for divorce, while in the past, it was done by husbands.

- 심지어는 사오십년 동안 결혼 생활을 해온 나이든 부부들도 이혼을 하고 있습니다.

Even older couples are divorcing after 40 or 50 years of marriage.

Check It Out!

Jun-hee: The divorce rate is rising these days in Korea.

Tim: Really?

Jun-hee: Yeah. I heard that adultery is mostly responsible for the increased divorce rate.

Tim: I guess both husbands and wives are finding it hard to stay faithful.

Jun-hee: Yeah, what a sad story!

준희: 요즘 우리나라에선 이혼률이 증가하고 있어.

팀: 정말?

준희: 응. 늘어나는 이혼률의 가장 주된 이유는 배우자의 부정(不貞)이래.

팀: 남편들이나 아내들이나 한사람에게 충실한다는 것에 어려움을 느끼고 있는 것 같구나.

준희: 그래, 참 슬픈 얘기지!

15 미국의 추수감사절과 비슷해

● 추석은 음력 8월 15일인데, 일년 중 가장 풍요로운 때야.

Chu-sok is celebrated on August 15th of the lunar calendar, around the time of the year's harvest.

● 미국의 추수감사절과 흡사해요.

Chu-sok is somewhat similar to the American Thanksgiving.

● 다른 점 중의 하나는 조상에게 경의를 표한다는 점인데 이걸 「차례」라고 하지요.

Chusok and Thanksgiving are a little different because during Chusok, we honor our ancestors.

● 추석은 가족과 친구들을 만나러가는 시기로, 이 때의 교통상황은 정말 악몽같죠.

Chu-sok is a time to visit families and friends. Traffic at this time of year is an absolute nightmare.

● 서울에 사는 사람들은 대개 서울을 떠나 부모를 찾아뵙지만 요즘엔 아들딸을 보러 서울로 올라오는 부모들도 많습니다.

Usually people in Seoul go to visit their parents, but many parents now make a trip to Seoul to see their sons or daughters.

● 추석에는 조상의 묘소에 가 차례를 드리고 묘지를 보살피죠. 이것을 「성묘」라 해요.

On Chu-sok, people visit their ancestors' graves to attend a worship service and to care for the grave. This is called sung-myo.

● 추석에 한국 사람들은 「송편」을 먹는데, 「송편」은 솔잎 위에 얹어서 찐 쌀떡입니다.

On Chu-sok, Koreans eat song-pyun, a cake made of rice and cooked on top of pine needles.

Check It Out!

Tina: It sounds like Chu-sok is a very busy time of year.

Jun-young: You're right, but it also gives us a chance to meet old friends and relatives.

Tina: What's the traffic like during this time of year?

Jun-young: It's very busy.

Tina: Are you going away for Chu-sok?

티나: 추석은 일년 중에서 굉장히 바쁜 시기인 것 같구나.
준영: 맞아, 하지만 그날은 정든 친구들과 가족들을 만나는 기회가 되기도 해.
티나: 이 시기 교통상황은 어떠니?
준영: 아주 번잡하지.
티나: 넌 추석때 어딘가 갈 거니?

16 건강에 관심이 많아

● 최근에 한국 사람들은 자신의 몸매와 건강에 관심을 아주 많이 갖게 되었어요.

It has become really popular lately for Koreans to pay a lot of attention to their bodies and their health.

● 요즘 한국에서는 남자든 여자든 건강미가 풍기는 몸매를 원해요.

What both men and women want is a healthy, good looking body.

● 다이어트를 하는 여자들이 많은데, 다른 계절에 비해 노출이 심해지는 여름에 특히 많아요.

A lot of women go on diets, especially in the summer, when their bodies are more exposed than in other seasons.

● 빨리 날씬해지려고 지방흡입 수술을 받는 사람들도 있어요.

Some people have liposuction, in order to become slender quickly.

● 한국 사람들 중에는 담배를 피우는 사람들이 많습니다. 성인 남성 중에는 담배를 피우는 사람이 절반을 넘고, 여성과 청소년 흡연자의 숫자도 점점 늘고 있어요.

Many people smoke in Korea. Over half of male adults smoke, and the number of female and teenage smokers is increasing.

● 보약은 일종의 전통적인 한국 강장제(强壯劑)라고 할 수 있지요.

Boyak is a kind of traditional Korean medicine for improving health.

- 인삼이 노화를 방지하고 질병치료와 면역체계에 도움이 돼요.

Ginseng is said to slow aging, cure illnesses and boost immune systems.

Brad: You are really looking buff these days. Are you working out?

Jin-ho: Yeah, I started to go to the gym every day after work.

Brad: Well, it's working. You have really shaped up.

Jin-ho: And not only that! I have met so many single women there!

Brad: I heard that fitness was becoming popular in Korea now. Can I join you?

브랫: 너 요즘 몸이 굉장히 탄탄해 보인다. 운동하니?
진호: 응, 매일 퇴근 후에 헬스클럽에 다녀.
브랫: 이야, 효과가 있네. 너 몸이 굉장히 보기 좋게 다듬어졌다구.
진호: 근데 그뿐이 아냐! 거기서 결혼 안한 여자들도 되게 많이 만났다구!
브랫: 요즘 한국에서 건강관리가 보편화되고 있다는 얘길 들었어. 나, 너랑 같이 헬스클럽에 다녀도 돼?

17 인터넷이 너무 편리해

● 대금을 지불하거나 편지를 쓰고 정보를 찾아내는 것이라면 인터넷이 정말 너무 편리해요.

The Internet is so convenient when it comes to paying bills, writing letters, and finding information.

● 좋아하는 사이트에 가서 농담거리와 음악, 게임 같은 재밌는 것들을 다운받아요.

I go to my favorite sites and download lots of neat things, like jokes, music, and games.

● 내 컴퓨터는 더 이상 문서 작성용만으로 쓰는 것이 아니라 이제는 오락센터예요

My computer is no longer just used for word processing. It is also an entertainment center.

● 인터넷을 많이 사용하면서 생기는 문제들 중의 하나는 가끔씩 시간을 잊어버린다는 건데, 시간이 얼마나 지났는지도 모르고 접속한 채 시간을 보내죠.

One of the problems with using the Internet so much is that I often lose track of time and I spend hours on-line without noticing how much time has passed.

● 인터넷에는 포르노 사이트, 도박 사이트, 자살 사이트 등, 문제있는 사이트들이 굉장히 많아요.

There are many controversial sites on the Net, such as porn sites, gambling sites, suicide sites, etc.

- 이런 유해한 사이트들은 심지어 아이들도 아주 쉽게 접속할 수 있는데, 특히 스팸 메일이나 블로그를 통해 쉽게 접할 수 있어요.

It's easy for young children to access these sites, usually through spam emails or blogs.

- 한국인들은 인터넷을 잘 활용하고 있다고 스스로 자랑스럽게 생각하고 있어요.

We are proud of ourselves as Koreans for using the Net well.

Check It Out!

Jamie: Tae-soo, did you know that Korea ranks second in its number of harmful Internet sites?

Tae-soo: Yes. It is second only to English language sites. It's a huge problem.

Jamie: What is being done about this?

Tae-soo: It is very hard to stop people operating sites out of Korea.

Jamie: Wow. I hope something changes soon.

제이미: 태수야, 한국의 유해 사이트 숫자가 세계 2위라는 거 알고 있었니?
태수: 응. 영어로 된 유해 사이트에 이어 두번째라면서. 그거 문제가 큰걸.
제이미: 이런 일에 대해서 어떻게 조치를 취하고 있어?
태수: 다른 나라에서 그런 사이트를 운영하는 걸 막기란 어려운 일이잖아.
제이미: 이야 그렇구나. 어서 뭔가 변했으면 좋겠다.

18 스마트폰 없는 사람이 없어

● 한국의 핸드폰 산업은 고도로 발달했어요.

The cellphone industry in Korea has reached a high level of sophistication.

● 한국은 핸드폰이 다른 어느 나라보다도 더 많이 보편화되어 있습니다. 한국 사람들 대부분이 핸드폰을 갖고 있지요.

Cellphones are more popular in Korea than any other country. Most Koreans own a cellphone.

● 핸드폰이 통화기능 뿐만 아니라, 여러가지 다른 일도 하는데 사용돼요.

Cellphones are a used for making phone calls and many other tasks.

● 핸드폰으로 문자 메시지를 주고받는 것은 보편화되어 있어요.

It's popular for people to exchange text messages with their cellphones.

● 인터넷 기능을 갖춘 핸드폰으로는 인터넷 검색도 할 수 있고, 게임을 즐길 수도 있으며 심지어 인터넷 채팅방에 접속하는 것도 가능해요.

Cellphones with an Internet option allow us to surf the Net, play games, and even enter chat rooms.

● 핸드폰은 성능이 향상되어 은행업무를 볼 수 있는 기능도 추가되었어요.

Cellphones have been upgraded to include the option of banking.

- 핸드폰을 무절제하게 사용하여 어마어마한 액수의 고지서를 받아들게 되는 사람들도 있습니다. 특히 미성년자들 중에 많죠.

Some people - especially minors - use cell phones recklessly, and end up with high bills.

Check It Out!

Gale: It's incredible how advanced the cellphones have gotten.

Tae-su: I know. My girlfriend has a top-of-the-line model.

Gale: What all can she do with it?

Tae-su: All kinds of stuff. She even chats online during her commute.

Gale: Wow. Technology certainly is incredible, isn't it?

게일: 휴대폰 기능이 얼마나 발달했는지 놀라울 따름이야.
태수: 맞아. 내 여자친구는 최신기종을 갖고 있지.
게일: 그걸로 뭘 할 수 있는 거니?
태수: 뭐든 다 하지. 심지어는 출퇴근길에 채팅도 한다니까.
게일: 이야. 기술이란 건 정말 놀랍구나, 안그래?

19 인사동에 가봤어?

● 인사동은 한국 문화의 거리로 한국의 전통 골동품을 살 수 있는 곳이예요.

Insa-dong is a street where visitors can see Korean culture and buy traditional Korean antiques.

● 만약 고국에 있는 가족이나 친구에게 줄 특별한 선물을 찾고 있다면 이곳이 가장 적당한 장소일 거예요.

If you are looking for a special gift for someone back home, Insa-dong would be the best place to get it.

● 판문점은 서울에서 자동차로 한 시간 반 거린데, 군사분계선에 걸쳐 있어요. 판문점을 방문하는 사람은 왜 이곳이 평화를 유지해야 하는 것이 얼마나 중요한 지를 실감하게 될 거예요.

Panmunjom is about an hour and a half outside of Seoul by car, straddling the Military Demarcation Line. Visitors can see why it is important that the area should remain peaceful.

● 제주도는 우리나라에서 가장 큰 섬으로 여자, 돌, 바람이 많아 「삼다도」로 알려져 있어요.

Cheju Island is the largest of Korea's islands, and it is known as the island of three "many's"; many women, many rocks, and much wind.

● 이건 돌하르방[石祖]이에요. 이 지역의 구멍이 숭숭 뚫려 있는 화산암을 크고 작은 형태로 조각한 것이죠.

The dolharubang(stone grandfather) is sculptured in large and small sizes from the porous lava stone of the area.

- 민속촌은 수세기 전 생활양식을 재현해 놓은 한국의 민속 마을이예요.

Minsokch'on is a Korean folk village that recreates the lifestyles of several centuries ago.

- 민속촌에는 공예품 제작을 통해 전통문화를 보존하고 있는 장인(匠人)들이 있어요.

In the Minsokch'on, there are artisans and craftsmen who preserve the traditional culture through their artwork.

- 남대문 시장은 값싼 물건들과 사람들로 가득한 상가들이 아주 많이 있어요.

The Namdaemun Market has tons of stores. There are great bargains and lots of people there.

- 동대문 시장은 요즘에 남대문 시장보다 더 인기가 많아지고 있는 또 다른 시장이죠.

The Tongdaemun Market is another market that's becoming more popular than the Namdaemun Market these days.

- 우리나라 동해안에 설악산이라는 곳이 있어요.

There is mountain on the east coast of Korea called Mt. Sorak.

- 설악산은 높이 솟은 화강암 봉우리들과 수풀이 우거진 푸른 계곡들, 울창한 숲과 폭포, 개울이 있는 멋진 곳이지요.

Mt. Sorak is a lovely area, with granite peaks, lush green valleys, dense forests, waterfalls and streams.

- 사물은 네 개의 전통적인 타악기인 꽹과리와 징, 장구와 북을 가리켜요.

Samul refers to 4 traditional percussion instruments: the small and large gong, the hourglass drum, and the barrel drum.

- 사물놀이는 농악과 무속 음악의 민속 가락에 뿌리를 두고 있어요.

Samul-nori has its roots in both the folk rhythms of farmers' music and Shamanistic music.

- 탈을 쓰고 하는 무용극인데, 거드름을 피우는 양반들과 승려들을 비웃는 사회 풍자극이예요.

A talchum is a mask dance-drama which began as a social satire that made fun of snobby aristocrats and monks.

- 씨름은 전에는 명절때마다 경기를 열면서 인기가 많았어. 하지만 지금은 인기를 많이 잃었지.

Ssireum used to be more popular. This sport was used to open games on festival days. But it has lost a lot of popularity.

Check It Out!

Mi-kyung: I'm going to the Minsokch'on this weekend, would you like to join me?

Glen: What is that?

Mi-kyung: It's a Korean folk village that recreates the lifestyles of several centuries ago.

Glen: Wow! How do they do that?

Mi-kyung: Well, they have artisans and craftsmen who live there, and they preserve the traditional culture through their artwork.

Glen: What goes on in the village?

Mi-kyung: There are traditional potters, weavers, blacksmiths, and other craftsmen working, and there are folk dances, musical performances and ceremonies in the amphitheater. And maybe we will even get to see a traditional wedding.

Glen: It sounds fantastic! I'm definitely going to join you!

미경: 이번 주말에 민속촌에 갈 건데, 너도 같이 갈래?
글렌: 뭐하는 곳인데?
미경: 수세기 전 생활양식을 재현해 놓은 한국의 민속 마을이야.
글렌: 왜 어떤 식으로 재현하는데?
미경: 음, 민속촌에는 거기에 거주하는 장인(匠人)들이 있는데, 그들이 공예품 제작을 통해 전통문화를 보존하고 있어.
글렌: 민속촌에서는 어떤 행사가 열리니?
미경: 전통 도공(陶工)이나 직공(織工), 대장장이 같은 장인들이 작업을 하고 있고 야외 공연장에서는 전통춤과 음악공연, 그리고 갖가지 의식이 열려. 전통 혼례도 볼 수 있을 거야.
글렌: 굉장하구나! 꼭 같이 가야겠어!

20 한국음식 먹어봤어요?

● 지금까지 한국식당에서 식사할 기회가 많았나요?

Have you had much of a chance to eat out at Korean restaurants?

▶ Have you had an opportunity to eat at a Korean restaurant?
한국식당에서 식사해보신 적 있어요?

● 김치는 한국 전통음식인데, 대개 반찬으로 내놔요. 김치는 소금물에 절인 채소같은 건데, 배추와 무, 파와 마늘을 한데 버무린 거구요.

Kimchi is a traditional Korean food. We usually serve it as a side dish. It is made from a variety of pickled vegetables; cabbages, turnips, green onions and garlic, all mixed together.

● 불고기는 여러시간 동안 양념에 재워 두기 때문에 고기가 굉장히 연해. 마늘과 간장, 설탕, 참기름, 후춧가루와 양파, 생강, 술로 만든 양념예요.

Bulgogi is incredibly tender because it has been marinating in a sauce for hours. The marinade is made from garlic, soy sauce, sugar, sesame seed oil, black pepper, onions, ginger and wine.

● 떡은 일종의 쌀로 만든 케이크로 보통 설날이나 추석, 결혼식날 같은 특별한 경우에 먹어요.

T'tok is a kind of rice cake, and Koreans generally eat t'tok on special occasions, such as New Year's Day, the Harvest Moon Festival, and on wedding days.

● 비빔밥은 한국에서 대중적인 음식으로 여러 야채들과 밥 그리고 매운 고추장을 비벼서 만들어요.

A bibimbop is a popular Korean dish that is made from a mix of vegetables, rice, and spicy pepper sauce.

- 설렁탕은 조선시대부터 유래한 음식으로 주 성분은 소의 내장, 그리고 소의 뼈 등 이예요.

Sulrungtang is a dish that originated in the Chosun period and its ingredients consist tripe, and certain beef bones.

- 김치찌게는 우리나라에서 유명한 찌게로 김치와 여러 야채들 그리고 밥반찬들을 섞어서 만들어요.

Kimchi chigae is well known stew that blends kimchi, certain vegetables and a side dish of rice.

- 삼겹살은 고기이고 사람들이 바로 앞에서 그릴로 구워서 상추에 싸서 먹는 음식이 예요.

Samgyeopsal is composed of meat that is cooked on a grill in front of diners before being wrapped in lettuce and consumed.

- 김밥은 단순하고 원형모양의 음식으로 바같은 김이 싸고 있고 안쪽에는 밥 그리고 가운데에는 야채, 계란, 그리고 고기나 생선들을 넣어 만들어요.

Kimbop is a simple, round shaped snack that consists of an outer layer of seaweed, an inner layer of rice, and a center of various ingredients including vegetables, eggs, and possibly meat or fish.

- 라면은 요리하기 쉬운 음식으로 세계적으로 알려졌으며 독특하고 매운 한국적인 맛으로도 먹을 수 있어요.

Ramyen noodles are known worldwide for being easy to prepare, and are available here with a distinctive, spicy Korean flavor.

- 자장면은 중국에서 유래된 국수요리로 한국에선 특히 점심식사때 많이들 먹어요.

Jajangmyun is a noodle dish which originated in China and which is very popular in Korea, especially when eaten during lunch.

- 된장 bean paste
- 간장 soy sauce
- 고추장 hot pepper paste (음식에서 hot은 「매운」 (spicy)이라는 뜻으로 자주 쓰인다)
- 밥 boiled rice (「숭늉」은 rice water)
- 비빔밥 rice and assorted vegetables
- 김밥 rolled rice with dried seaweed
- 김치찌개 kimchi stew
- 죽 porridge

- 국 boiled soup
- 떡국 rice cake soup
- 냉면 buckwheat noodles in a chilled broth
- 삼계탕 chicken and ginseng soup
- 보신탕 dog meat soup
- 막걸리 rice wine
- 송편 stuffed rice cakes steamed with pine needles
- 식혜 fermented rice punch

Check It Out!

Yun-Young: Do you like spicy foods?

Bill: I'm from Louisiana, I love hot food.

Yun-Young: Then, I'm sure you're going to like kimchi.

Bill: What's kimchi?

Yun-Young: It's a traditional Korean food. We usually serve it as a side dish.

Bill: What is it made out of?

Yun-Young: It is a kind of like pickled vegetables; cabbage, turnip, green onions and garlic all mixed together.

Bill: It sounds very good. How do I eat it?

Yun-Young: You can eat on its own, but it's very hot.

Bill: I'm going to try it.

Yun-Young: Are you all right?

Bill: Yeah. I just need some water.

윤영: 너 매운 음식 좋아하니?

빌: 난 루이지애나 주 출신이라구. 매운 음식을 무척 좋아해.

윤영: 그럼, 김치를 좋아하겠구나.

빌: 김치가 뭔데?

윤영: 한국 전통음식인데, 대개 반찬으로 내놔.

빌: 뭘로 만드는데?

윤영: 소금물에 절인 채소같은 건데, 배추와 무, 파와 마늘을 한데 버무린 거야.

빌: 정말 맛있겠는데. 어떻게 먹는 거야?

윤영: 그것만 먹을 수도 있지만, 굉장히 매워.

빌: 먹어볼게.　　윤영: 괜찮아?　　빌: 응. 물이나 좀 마셔야겠어.

21 판문점 가봤어?

● 판문점을 2018년에 역사적인 정상회담이 열린 곳이야.

Panmunjom was the sight of a historic summit in 2018.

● 수십년간, 판문점은 한국 분단선의 중심에 있었어.

For seven decades, Panmunjom has been at the center of the line dividing Korea.

● 세계 지도자들은 판문점에서의 평화협정이 통일로 이어지기를 바래.

World leaders hope a peace agreement at Panmunjom will lead to reunification.

● 김정은은 판문점 남측지역으로 넘어온 첫번째 북한 지도자가 되었어.

Kim Jong Un became the first North Korean leader to enter the South at Panmunjom.

● 판문점은 적대행위를 끝내기 위해 외교관들이 모이는 중심지가 될거야.

Panmunjom will continue to be the focus of diplomats seeking an end to hostilities.

● 서울에서 자동차로 한 시간 반 거린데, 군사분계선에 걸쳐 있어.

Panmunjom is about an hour and a half outside of Seoul by car, straddling the Military Demarcation Line.

● 판문점을 방문하는 사람은 누구나 세계 평화를 위해 그곳이 얼마나 중요한 지를 실감하게 될 거야.

Any visitor to Panmunjom will realize its importance for world peace.

- 그곳은 평화의 상징이자, 한국통일에 대한 염원이 집중된 곳이야.

Well, it is a symbol of peace and a focal point of hopes for the reunification of Korea.

- 회담이 개최돼. 평화적인 남북 접촉 말야. 그리고 가장 오래된 휴전협정을 감시하고 있어.

Talks are held there, peaceful North-South contacts, and it's the guardian of the longest truce.

- 유엔의 점령하에 아직도 긴장이 감도는 지역이지만, 꼭 가보는 게 좋을거야.

It's still a tense arena, occupied by the United Nations, but I would definitely recommend that you go there.

Check It Out!

A: How would you like to visit Panmunjom?

B: It sounds interesting. Why is it a tourist destination?

A: It's the village where the armistice was agreed on ending fighting in the Korean War.

B: That sounds like it's close to North Korea.

A: It is an area where you can see the border between North and South Korea.

B: So is it dangerous? Is there any danger of shooting?

A: It's quite safe. There was a summit in 2018 between the leaders of the two countries.

B: Well, let's go. I've always been interested in historical places.

A: 판문점에 한번 가보는게 어때?

B: 흥미로운데. 거기가 왜 관광지인거야?

A: 그곳은 한국전쟁을 끝내는 휴전협정이 서명된 곳이야.

B: 북한과 가까운 것 같네.

A: 남북한의 경계선을 볼 수 있는 지역이야.

B: 그럼 위험한거야? 총격이 일어날 수도 있어?

A: 꽤 안전한 곳이야. 2018년도에 양국 정상간에 정상회담이 있었어.

B: 그럼 가자. 난 항상 역사적인 장소에는 흥미를 느끼거든.

22 너 인상이 참 좋아

- 너 인상이 참 좋다.

You're fairly good-looking.

▶ He looks like Ashton Kutcher 걔는 애쉬튼 커처럼 생겼어

- 넌 나보다 어려보여.

You look younger than me.

▶ He looks old for his age 걔는 나이에 비해 늙어보여

▶ He looks older than he is 걔는 실제보다 나이가 들어보여

▶ You look young for your age 너는 나이에 비해 어려보여

- 걔는 취향이 고상해.

He has a taste for luxury.

▶ She's a smart dresser 걔는 옷을 아주 잘 입어

- 걔는 좀 섹시해.

He's sort of sexy.

▶ He's very popular with the girls 걔는 여자들한테 인기가 좋아

▶ She's wearing a lot of makeup 걔는 화장을 떡칠해.

- 너 배 나왔어.

You have a pot belly.

▶ He's bald 걔는 대머리야

- 걔는 매우 날카로워.

She's very sharp.

▶ He's a wise guy 걔는 현명한 친구야

▶ He's wise for his age 걔는 나이에 비해 현명해

● 걔는 진짜 완벽주의야.

He's a perfectionist.

▸ He has good judgement 걔는 분별력이 좋아

● 너는 아주 대담해.

You have a lot of nerve.

▸ He's got a lot of nerve 걔는 아주 대담해
▸ You're very brave 넌 매우 용감해
▸ You're bold 너는 대담해

● 쟤는 정말 말을 잘해.

She's a smooth talker.

▸ He's flexible in his thinking 걔는 생각이 유연해

● 걔는 어울리기 쉬운 친구야.

He's easy to get along with.

▸ He's very friendly 걔는 매우 우호적이야
▸ She's a good mixer 걔는 매우 잘 어울려

● 성격이 좋은 사람야.

He's an easy-going person.

▸ He knows a lot of people. 걔는 사람들을 많이 알아.
▸ He's the outgoing type 걔는 외향적이야

● 걔는 마음이 따뜻한 친구야

He's a warm-hearted guy.

▸ You're so generous 너는 정말 맘씨 좋아
▸ She's always willing to help out 걔는 항상 도와줄려고 해
▸ He just can't turn down a request 걔는 단지 거절을 못하는 거야

● 걔는 정말 수완가야.

He's a real go-getter.

- 걔는 약속을 일단하면 절대로 말을 바꾸지 않아.

Once he makes a promise, he never goes back on his word.

▶ He's not the type to break his word 약속을 깨는 타입을 아니야

- 걔는 매너가 좀 거칠지만 실은 괜찮은 녀석이야.

He has a rough manner, but deep down, he's a nice guy.

▶ He is good humored 걔는 유머감각이 좋아

▶ He's a very modest man 걔는 점잖은 사람야

Check It Out!

A: Your cousin is very handsome. 네 사촌 정말 잘 생겼다.

B: He's very popular with the girls. 여자들한테 인기 아주 좋아.

A: And Helen fixed him up with a blind date? 헬렌이 소개팅을 주선했다며?

B: She's always willing to help out. 걘 항상 도움을 주려고 해.

A: I don't like Al. He's rude. 난 알이 싫어. 무례해.

B: He has a rough manner, but deep down, he's a nice guy.
매너가 좀 없지만 사실은 좋은 친구야.

A: What about me? Don't you think I'm attractive?
난 어떻고? 난 매력적이라고 생각하지 않는거야?

B: You're fairly good-looking. 넌 인상이 아주 좋아.

A: You look young for your age. 넌 나이에 비해 젊어보여.

B: Thanks. Many people say that. 고마워. 많은 사람들이 그래.

A: But you also have a pot belly. 하지만 너 배가 나왔잖아.

B: I guess I should exercise more. 운동을 좀 더 해야겠네.

23 걔는 내성적이야

● 걔는 매우 내성적이야.

He's so reserved.

▸ He's shy 걔는 수줍어 해
▸ You're too timid 너는 너무 소극적이야

● 걔는 쉽게 화를 내.

He gets angry easily.

▸ He loses his temper quickly 걔는 쉽사리 성질을 부려
▸ He has a bad temper 성질이 못됐어
▸ He has a short temper 성질이 안좋아

● 걔는 매우 민감해.

She's so sensitive.

▸ She shows her feelings easily 걔는 쉽게 자기 감정을 노출해

● 걔한텐 뭔가 이상한 게 있어.

There's something strange about her.

▸ She's not herself today 걔는 오늘 제정신이 아니야
▸ She's not acting like herself 걔는 자기 답지 않게 행동을 하고 있어
▸ He's weird 걔는 이상해

● 걔는 냉소적이야.

He's sarcastic.

▸ He's very outspoken 걔는 말을 거침없이 해
▸ He's talkative 걔는 수다장이야

- 걔는 종종 말도 안되는 이야기를 해.

He often says absurd things.

▸ He often says ridiculous things 걔는 종종 우스운 이야기를 해

▸ He lacks common sense 걔는 상식이 부족해

- 걔는 책임감이 없어.

He has no sense of responsibility.

- 걔는 자기가 모두 다 아는 것처럼 행동해.

He acts like he knows it all.

▸ He's acting like a hot shot 걔는 자기가 대단한 사람인양 행동해

▸ He's acting big 걔는 거물처럼 행동해

- 걔는 거래하기 힘든 사람야.

He's hard to deal with.

▸ He's a difficult man to deal with 걔는 거래하기 어려운 사람야

- 그 사람은 자신이 틀렸다는 걸 절대로 인정 안 해.

He never admits he is wrong.

▸ That man never admits defeat 저 남자는 패배를 절대로 인정하지 않아

▸ He can't handle defeat 걔는 패배했을 때 어떻게 할 줄 몰라

- 걔는 이기적이야.

He's selfish.

▸ He's self-centered 걔는 자기 중심적이야

▸ He only cares about himself 걔는 오직 자기만 생각해

▸ He's stingy 걔는 인색해

- 걔는 항상 양다리를 걸쳐.

He always sits on the fence.

▸ He's very vague 걔는 분명하지가 않아

● 걔는 매우 공격적이야.

He's very offensive.

● 너는 정말 문제다.

You're really causing a problem.

▸ He's a brown noser 걔는 아첨꾼이야

Check It Out!

A: What makes you upset with your husband? 왜 남편한테 골이 난거야?

B: He never admits he is wrong. 자기 잘못을 절대로 인정하지 않아.

A: Is there anything else that bothers you? 그거 말고 다른 건 없어?

B: He loses his temper quickly. 화도 쉽사리 내.

A: He acts like he knows it all. 걘 자기가 다 아는 것처럼 행동해.

B: Right. People consider him arrogant. 맞아. 사람들은 걔가 교만하다고 생각해.

A: He's also a brown noser. 걘 또 아첨꾼이야.

B: The whole office seems to hate him. 사무실 사람들 다 걜 싫어하는 것 같구만.

A: I can't help criticizing Elliot. 엘리엇을 비난하지 않을 수가 없어.

B: You're really causing problems for him. 너 정말 걔한테 문제를 일으키겠다.

A: But I don't like him. He's very offensive. 하지만 걘 정말 싫어. 너무 공격적이야.

B: Just do your best to ignore him. 최선을 다해 무시하도록 해.

24 걘 실망시키지 않을거야

- 걔는 널 절대로 실망시키지 않을 거야.

He'll never let you down.

▸ He gets things done efficiently   걔는 효율적으로 일을 처리해
▸ He's efficient   걔는 실력있어
▸ He handles things quickly   걔는 일을 빨리 처리해

- 걔는 센스가 빨라.

He has a quick mind.

▸ He catches on quickly   걔는 빨리 알아들어

- 걔는 사무실의 자랑거리야.

He's the pride of our office.

▸ He's a real asset   걔는 정말 인재야

- 그들은 걔를 아주 높게 평가해.

They have a high opinion of her.

▸ The boss has high expectations of him   사장은 걔한테 많은 기대를 하고 있어

- 걔는 일을 무리없이 잘 처리해.

He's a smooth operator.

▸ He's a fast worker   걔는 일을 빨리해

- 걔는 일을 잘 해.

He's good at his job.

▸ She really knows her job   걔는 일을 잘 해

- 걔의 생각은 매우 독창적이야

His ideas are unique.

- 걔는 정말 일벌레야

He's a real workaholic.

- 걔는 정말 무용지물야.

He's a good for nothing.

  ▶ He isn't good for anything   걔는 할 수 있는 게 아무 것도 없어
  ▶ He's a nobody   걔는 별 볼일 없는 친구야

- 걔는 사람 다룰 줄 몰라.

He just doesn't know how to handle people.

- 걔는 일처리 능력이 없어.

He's not capable of doing the work.

- 걔는 똑똑하지가 않아.

He isn't so smart.

  ▶ He has poor judgement   걔는 분별력이 없어
  ▶ He's simpleminded   걔는 단순해
  ▶ His best days are behind him   그 사람 좋은 시절은 다 갔어

- 걔는 한물간 사람야.

He's a has-been.

  ▶ He's history   걔 한물 갔어
  ▶ He's a goner   그 사람 한물 간 사람이야

- 너는 한심한 놈이야.

You're (such) a loser.

  ▶ He's a loser   걔 골통야
  ▶ You are not so great   그렇게 잘난 것도 없으면서.

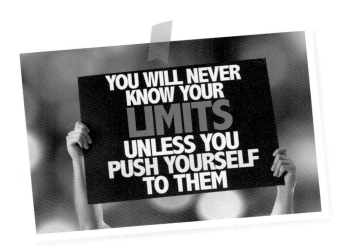

Check It Out!

A: What is your opinion of the new manager? 새로운 매니저 어때?

B: He gets things done efficiently. 일을 아주 효율적으로 해.

A: How about the guy who used to be manager? 예전 매니저는 어땠어?

B: He's a has-been. He needed to retire. 한물간 사람이야. 퇴직해야 했어.

A: You like the way Mark thinks? 너 마크의 생각이 맘에 들어?

B: Sure. His ideas are unique. 그럼. 걔 생각은 독창적이야.

A: He seems very intelligent to me. 내게도 아주 똑똑해보여.

B: That's right. He catches on quickly. 맞아. 걔는 빨리 알아들어.

A: We've been considering firing Dave. 우리는 데이브를 해고할까 생각중야.

B: He's not capable of doing the work anymore. 걘 더 이상 업무를 할 능력이 없어.

A: I think he's just too old for the job. 그 일을 하기에 너무 늙은 것 같아.

B: His best days are behind him. 그 사람 좋은 시절은 다 갔지.